DELIA WEBSTER

AND THE

UNDERGROUND RAILROAD

.

DELIA WEBSTER
AND THE
UNDERGROUND
RAILROAD

Randolph Paul Runyon

Researched in collaboration with
William Albert Davis

THE UNIVERSITY PRESS OF KENTUCKY

Copyright © 1996 by The University Press of Kentucky

Scholarly publisher for the Commonwealth,
serving Bellarmine College, Berea College, Centre College of
Kentucky, Eastern Kentucky University, The Filson Club,
Georgetown College, Kentucky Historical Society, Kentucky State
University, Morehead State University, Murray State University,
Northern Kentucky University, Transylvania University,
University of Kentucky, University of Louisville,
and Western Kentucky University.

Editorial and Sales Offices: The University Press of Kentucky
663 South Limestone Street, Lexington, KY 40508-4008

03 02 01 00 99   5 4 3 2 1

Library of Congress Cataloging-in-Publication Data

Runyon, Randolph, 1947-
    Delia Webster and the Underground Railroad / Randolph
Paul Runyon ; researched in collaboration with William Albert
Davis.
    p.   cm.
    Includes bibliographical references and index.
    ISBN 0-8131-1966-9 (cloth : alk. paper);
    ISBN 0-8131-0974-4 (paper: alk. paper)
    1. Webster, Delia Ann. 2. Women abolitionists—United
States—Biography. 3. Abolitionists—United States—
Biography. 4. Underground railroad. 5. Antislavery
movements—United States. 6. Kentucky—History—
1792-1865.   I. Title.
    E450.R86   1996
    973.5'092—dc20
    [B]   95-44094

For Elizabeth,
and for Augusta and Ezekiel
—who will one day write their own history
or maybe make it

Lake Erie

Oberlin

INDIANA

OHIO

Cincinnati

Madison
Milton
Bedford

Ripley
Aberdeen
Washington
Mayeville

Blue Licks

Louisville

Frankfort

Millersburg

Paris

Lexington

KENTUCKY

Ohio River

Kentucky River

N

0   50 miles
0   80 kilometers

jmh

Contents

List of Illustrations   viii

Acknowledgments   ix

  1. "Deceived in the distance"   1

  2. "Perhaps you can decipher its contents"   22

  3. "Partner of his guilt"   40

  4. "On account of her sex"   56

  5. "The error of a woman's heart"   70

  6. "Did . . . entice and seduce"   87

  7. "It might not appear what I shall be"   106

  8. "The sincere desire of your fond father"   125

  9. "I am afraid they will not always be
on as friendly terms"   142

10. "The very madness of the moon"   164

11. "A very bold and defiant kind of woman"   184

12. Aftermath: "This remarkable history"   199

Notes   225

Bibliography   249

Index   255

ILLUSTRATIONS

Lexington, Kentucky   2

Maysville, Kentucky   17

Megowan's Hotel   23

The Kentucky Penitentiary   55

Newton Craig   60

Benajah Webster   80

A ticket of admission to one of Delia Webster's lectures   101

Lewis Hayden   112

Dillard Craig   137

Laura Haviland   156

Street scene, Madison, Indiana   172

Madison viewed from the Kentucky side   191

Lucy Craig   197

Calvin and Mandana Fairbank   213

"The Webster Girls"   222

ACKNOWLEDGMENTS

A decade and a half ago, idly perusing the books in the library of my stepfather, Earle D. Jones, of Maysville, Kentucky, I happened upon the story of Delia Webster and Calvin Fairbank in J. Winston Coleman, Jr.'s *Slavery Times in Kentucky*. Fascination set in at once, fed by the Maysville connection, as well as a certain coincidence of names (I had labored for years over *Délie*, a 1544 book by French poet Maurice Scève).[1] Earle later caught mention in the *Lexington Herald* of an exhibition of Cindy Kelly's paintings of women in Kentucky history, which included some of Delia (of whom at that time no likeness had come to light). Cindy put me in touch with William Albert Davis, who was equally obsessed with the story. Bill and I decided to combine our resources to assemble the material for this book. His skills as a genealogist have been especially helpful, for he it was who tracked down the descendants of the characters in this drama, to whom I am enormously grateful for their willingness to share family documents. These include Mrs. Hazel Young Winter, Mrs. Isabelle Pautz, Mrs. Galey Coleman, Bard and Gina Prentiss, John Prentiss, and Philip Fairbank.

The interlibrary loan personnel of the Miami University Library have done their utmost to make materials accessible, and gratitude must be expressed as well to librarians at the Indiana State Archives; the Indiana State Historical Society; Purdue University; the University of Kentucky; Ohio State University; Oberlin College; Columbia University; the University of Cincinnati; the Cincinnati Historical Society; the Addison Public

---

[1] Not to mention a certain chain of coincidences linking such disparate elements as the numerical structure of Scève's poem, the Library of Congress cataloging system, and a crucial date in Delia Webster's life, together with some uncanny events in my own. Some of this was anticipated, before I encountered Delia Webster, in my first book, *Fowles/Irving/Barthes: Canonical Variations on an Apocryphal Theme* (Columbus: Ohio State University Press, 1981)—for example, in the penultimate endnote's allusion to Karl Jung's Good Friday/April Fool's Day's synchronicities (*F/I/B*, 116n20).

Library in Vergennes, Vermont; the Madison-Jefferson County Public Library in Madison, Indiana; and the Boston Public Library.

The comments of readers for the University Press of Kentucky have improved this book in many ways. For the energy and conscientiousness with which they performed their task I am most grateful.

Most of all, thanks to my wife Elizabeth, who created the home environment that made it all possible.

1

"DECEIVED

IN THE DISTANCE"

Shortly before five o'clock on the afternoon of Saturday, September 28, 1844, Delia Ann Webster left her lodgings at the home of Mr. and Mrs. David Glass, on West Second Street in Lexington, Kentucky, and stepped into a hackney coach that the Reverend Calvin Fairbank had rented from Parker Craig. The fall racing season was at its height, and farmers and gentry alike from all over the state had converged on the city to see the best of breed in action. Webster and Fairbank, however, were not headed for the track. For what they had in mind to do with the carriage, however, the crowds of out-of-town visitors and vehicles on the streets would provide a useful cover.[1]

Around the first of September, Fairbank had arrived in Lexington from Oberlin College, that hotbed of antislavery activity in the North. He had knocked on the door of the boarding house and asked the proprietress if a Miss Webster lived there. Her boarder had stepped out but was expected back soon, Mrs. Glass replied. Fairbank said he very much wanted to see her, that while they were not personally acquainted they did have friends in common. He would wait. While they chatted, Mrs. Glass may well have been favorably impressed by this handsome man of the cloth, a Methodist who did not overburden her with the depth of his piety, nor, indeed, reveal his abolitionist inclinations. Fairbank, well seasoned in the business of rescuing slaves, knew how to dissimulate.[2]

When Webster returned, Fairbank introduced himself, and immediately asked if they could speak alone. They retired to the parlor and remained there together and alone for some time. When they returned, Webster asked Mrs. Glass if Fairbank could stay on as a boarder. Permission was granted, and during the month of September, Mrs. Glass later recalled, they would often hold long conversations together, though they seemed to want to avoid being seen doing so.[3]

What Fairbank told Webster was that Gilson Berry, a slave who had escaped to Oberlin, had persuaded him to go into Kentucky to bring out his

1

Lexington, Kentucky, from an 1851 lithograph.

wife and children. Fairbank was counting on Miss Webster's assistance, which she was quick to promise. Twenty-six years old and a native of Vergennes, Vermont, Delia Webster had first come to Kentucky in 1842 in the company of an Oberlin clergyman and his wife by the name of Spencer. Webster herself had studied at Oberlin, though only briefly in 1842. Together Webster and the Spencers gave painting classes in various towns in north-central Kentucky (including Flemingsburg, Georgetown, and Cynthiana) before establishing themselves in Lexington in July of 1843.[4] Such was their success that they were "repeatedly and urgently solicited by clergymen and other prominent men in the city to establish a permanent school for young ladies."[5] Stricken with an illness intensified by the summer heat, the Spencers departed Lexington, leaving Webster in charge. The Lexington Academy "soon became one of the most interesting and flourishing institutions in the State," Webster wrote, "bringing me an income of about $800 per year."[6] This was significantly more than a public school teacher could make in Webster's native Vermont, where a schoolmistress could count on earning an average of but $4.80 a month above room and board.[7]

Kentucky in the 1840s was only just beginning to establish a system of public education that would not really be in place until the next decade. Hence, Lexington parents who could afford it sent their children to private academies, which were separately established for boys and for girls. Historian Thomas Clark has written that, like the rest of the Old South, "Kentucky was overrun with private 'female' academies of a literary nature, which taught young ladies the art of writing, reading, grammar, ornamental literature, poetry, painting, and fancy and practical needlework." Boys were taught the rudiments of business and practical affairs, while girls were trained to ornament the home.[8] Yet there was an intellectual component in feminine education, for among other qualities a good mind was essential to attract a good partner in marriage. Or to keep one, as one Kentucky father warned his daughter: "If you do not study now, after your marriage your mind will collapse, and you will fail to amuse your husband."[9]

The *Lexington Observer and Reporter* for August 28 and 31, 1844, lists advertisements for a number of such private institutions: Saint Catherine's Female Academy, "not surpassed by any institution in the West," offered "tuition in the ordinary branches." Others included the Lafayette Seminary, the Aspasia Female Institute ("located in the country. . . . No situation in Kentucky can be more healthy"), the Young Ladies' Institute (including "ancient and modern languages"), and the Female Collegiate High School ("Music, with the use of the piano . . . drawing and painting . . . [and] French"). As for Webster's Lexington Academy, the "school received the patronage of the highest and wealthiest in the city," she later claimed, "while the lowest and the poorest were also encouraged to come and participate in its advantages, on equal footing with the rich, without money and without price. It was difficult to obtain convenient rooms in the city of sufficient size to accommodate [the] pupils, for before this school had been in operation two years it numbered about one hundred young ladies."[10]

Webster had begun her teaching career at the age of twelve by taking charge of some classes of younger children in the school in which she was herself a pupil, the Vergennes Classical School.[11] The *Vergennes Vermonter* for February 8, 1838 (just before Webster began teaching there), surveyed the current state of public education in that city of twelve hundred souls. The public schools were found lacking: "The present system of primary education," according to the article, "seems calculated as successfully to promote any other object as that which it proposes to accomplish." Mention is made of the Vergennes Classical School, where Webster was then a student and would soon be a teacher: "We have one 'classical school.' Whether the name honors the school or the school the name, we are not prepared to state. We however unhesitatingly give it as our opinion, that, if in that institution, *good* instruction can be obtained on one half the departments of study, enumerated in a late advertisement . . . there is a manifest propriety in appropriating to it the name of 'classical school.'" While a more detailed description of that school could not be found, the March 22, 1838, *Vermonter* does feature an advertisement for the Vergennes Female Seminary, whose curriculum was no doubt similar: "Instruction will be given in the fundamental branches of an English education, [such] as spelling, reading, writing, arithmetic, grammar and geography." Other subjects included mathematics, astronomy, natural and intellectual philosophy, history, botany, Latin, French, and music. "Instruction will also be given in the new and admired styles of Chinese and mezzotinto painting." It may well have been these recently fashionable styles of painting that Webster would be teaching five years later in Kentucky.

Exactly what—besides teaching young ladies to paint—Webster and the Spencers were up to in their wanderings about the state before they settled in Lexington is unclear. Several considerations point to the likelihood that they were also spiriting away slaves: the Oberlin connection; the fact that they never stayed long in the same place; and the readiness with which Webster agreed to assist Fairbank's attempt to rescue Gilson Berry's wife and children.

Though only just graduated from the Oberlin Theological Seminary, Fairbank at age twenty-eight had already acquired extensive experience in the underground line. By the summer of 1844 at least forty-three slaves had crossed the Ohio River through his assistance. He was born November 3, 1816, in Pike County, New York, to a family of evangelical Methodists. "Often, when alone in the forest," he recalled of his childhood there, "I imagined myself with an audience before me, pointing them to the Lamb of God." When he was a child, Fairbank's parents once took him to a church meeting in a neighboring town, where they spent the night in the home of a pair of fugitive slaves. The boy sat by the fire and listened as they recounted their life stories. The woman had been sold off from her husband and family, the auctioneer's hammer breaking all ties of affection. "My heart wept," wrote Fairbank, "my anger was kindled, and antagonism to slavery was fixed upon me."[12]

The first rescue had been remarkably easy, and in fact was unpremeditated. Young Fairbank had been hired, together with Almon Carpenter, to float a raft of logs that stretched an acre down the Ohio in the spring of 1837. One April morning, as they were drifting past the Virginia (now West Virginia) shore, they saw a black man with an axe on his shoulder, humming a tune as he made his way along the river bank. Striking up a conversation, they learned that the fellow's wife and children had been sold off and that he never expected to see them again. Fairbank invited him to join them on the raft and be carried over to the other side. After a little persuasion, "he came on board. I swung my raft to the Ohio bank, and, springing ashore, and throwing down axe and hat, he shuffled a jig upon free frozen soil . . . then picking up hat and axe, and waving a good-bye, he was soon out of sight."

Years later, Fairbank ran into the man by chance on a street in Detroit, and found out that the wife and children had since escaped as well, and that all were now prospering on a farm of their own.[13]

When Carpenter and Fairbank reached Cincinnati, landing on the Kentucky side just opposite the mouth of the Little Miami River, they were called upon to perform another rescue. A tall black woman some eighty years of age approached them and asked if they would transport her children to safety. Fairbank recounts that the next slave he helped escape was a woman he met between Maysville, Kentucky, and the little town of Washington, four miles south. She was trudging along with a carpetbag in her hand. He put her on a steamboat at Maysville and traveled with her to Pittsburgh, then returned to Cincinnati where he ferried fourteen slaves across from Kentucky. Soon after, he was called to Lexington to bring out a man, his wife, and their three children, who had made it that far from eastern Tennessee. Guiding them at night by compass and bull's-eye lantern and sleeping by day in cedar groves, stealing from cornfields and surreptitiously milking cows, he brought them in four days to the Ohio, then improvised a raft of slabs and planks.[14]

Fairbank enrolled in a Methodist seminary in Lima, New York, in 1839, acquiring a license to preach in 1840. At some point in the early 1840s, however, he was attracted to Oberlin Theological Seminary in Ohio, a more strongly antislavery school, and continued his theological studies there, graduating in 1844. He apparently spent his summer vacations perfecting his slave stealing techniques. Clergyman though he was, he was prepared to use force when necessary, as an episode in June of 1842 reveals. The way he tells the story suggests that his religious calling did not prevent him, either, from acknowledging a strong attraction to the opposite sex. Having insinuated himself into the household of an octogenarian slaveholder in Montgomery County, Kentucky, he spent two weeks there as a guest "made . . . welcome to anything I desired. I became interested in a young slave girl of fifteen, who was the fifth in direct descent from her master, being the great-great-great-grand-daughter of a slave whom he took as his mistress at the age of fourteen." She was next in line to become her owner's concubine. Deciding to come to the defense "of as lovely a young woman as there was in Kentucky," Fairbank drove her away in his carriage in the dead of night. On their way to Lexington, a man jumped out of a bush and aimed a shotgun at Fairbank's head, "but I thrust it aside in an instant, and covered him with a Colt's revolver." The journey resumed with no further incident, Fairbank and his charge boarding the train from Lexington to Frankfort, and from there took a steamer down the Kentucky River and up the Ohio to Cincinnati.[15]

In May of the following year he was passing through the courtyard of "Megowan's Hotel," Lexington's combination jail and slave pen, when his attention was drawn to a tapping sound that seemed to come from an upper-floor window. There beckoned "one of the most beautiful and exquisite young girls one could expect to find." The recipient of a finished education in literature and the social graces, and but one sixty-fourth black, Eliza was to be sold to satisfy her father's creditors and a stepmother's jealousy. Fairbank called upon her in her cell, then sped to Cincinnati, returning with two thousand dollars contributed by Levi Coffin (self-styled "President of the Underground Railroad"), Salmon P. Chase (who later became chief justice of the United States), and Nicholas Longworth (an immensely wealthy businessman and patron of the arts). Her sale attracted an immense crowd that included Lexington's elite. Having been removed from a setting where she had known only comfort and delight and forced to contemplate a lifetime of bondage, Eliza trembled with apprehension as she stood on the block.

Fairbank had but one serious competitor in the bidding, "a short, thick-necked, black-eyed Frenchman from New Orleans" who was in cahoots with the girl's stepmother to remove her from the household. The auctioneer, clad in the customary long hammer-tailed coat, fancy plaid vest, and broad-brimmed beaver hat, called particular attention to those qualities of his merchandise that would make her an exquisite mistress for a gentleman of refined tastes. When the little Frenchman demanded how high he was intending to bid, Fairbank shot back, "Higher than you, Monsieur." Eventually, the pace of the bidding slowed. Fairbank bid fourteen hundred fifty, and the Frenchman had not answered it. Unwilling to let her go for such a paltry sum, the crier decided upon a theatrical gesture. Interrupting his hammer in mid-fall, he suddenly reached over to Eliza, ripped open her dress and displayed to the throng what Fairbank would in later years recall as her "superb neck and breast." Horror-struck, the cream of Bluegrass aristocracy cried out for shame at such indelicacy. Bidding resumed, though yet at a snail's pace. Still frustrated in his effort to get a fair price for such a fine piece of goods, the auctioneer tried one more ploy. Turning her around so that her profile was in full view, he lifted the girl's skirts as high as they would go, laying bare "her beautiful, symmetrical body, from her feet to her waist, and with his brutal, sacrilegious hand smote her white flesh," once more calling for a higher bid. Like public executions, such an indelicate strip-tease, though carried out in the interests of an everyday commercial transaction, must have provided a rare moment for reflection for the assembled Lexingtonians. Such denuding was not unheard-of in the sale of attractive female slaves (though most often it transpired in the privacy of Lewis Robards's private viewing gallery); but this time the body belonged to what to all appearances was one of their own. Fairbank finally triumphed, at a cost of fourteen hundred and eighty-five dollars. "You've got her damned cheap," said the disappointed auctioneer.

"What are you going to do with her?" "Free her, sir," he replied, and a cheer arose from the crowd, who though not converted to emancipation thought it appropriate in this instance. Eliza was placed in the carriage of Robert Wickliffe, the "Old Duke," one of the state's largest slaveholders and a leading apologist for the "peculiar institution," and escorted in style by the elite of the local gentry to be awarded her freedom papers. Fairbank subsequently conveyed her to Cincinnati, where she married into high society, only her husband and a few close friends ever aware she had once, however briefly, been a slave.[16]

The intense religious feeling to which Fairbank bore witness, and which led to his double career as Methodist minister and underground railroad conductor, was not equally evident in what is known of Delia Webster's youth, though it is true that in 1831 she joined the Congregational Church of Vergennes, and that the church's pastor "esteemed her as a young lady of correct, moral and religious principle; and unexceptionable, and consistent Christian deportment."[17] She was born December 17, 1817, to Benajah and Esther Webster, in a Lake Champlain valley town named for the Count of Vergennes (1717-1787), who as Louis XVI's foreign minister was instrumental in securing French support for the American Revolution. The town's name, originally First Falls of Otter Creek, was changed to honor his contribution—as Fayette County, Kentucky, of which Lexington was the seat, was named to glorify a more widely known French hero of the struggle for independence, the Marquis de Lafayette.

Vermont had the honor, by its constitution of 1777, of being the first state to prohibit slavery. Slaves captured from the British when Ethan Allen and the Green Mountain Boys took Fort Ticonderoga were set free with the declaration that "it is not right in the sight of God to keep slaves."[18] Equally well known to Vermonters was the decision rendered in the early years of the nineteenth century in Middlebury by Judge Theophilus Harrington. When a slave owner presented the standard proof of ownership in court, the Judge asked for more evidence. "The claimant, asking what further evidence could be necessary, was told that he would have to present a 'bill of sale from Almighty God.'"[19]

Despite these shining instances of antislavery sentiment on the part of some, not all Vermonters were ready to hide fugitives in their closets or give a warm welcome to abolitionist lecturers. Frederick Douglass, the slave who escaped from Maryland to a career as one of the most outstanding orators in American history, recalled a speaking tour he made there in 1843: "Those who only know the State of Vermont as it is to-day can hardly understand, and must wonder that there was forty years ago need for anti-slavery effort within its borders. . . . The several towns [we] visited showed that Vermont was surprisingly under the influence of the slave power. Her proud boast that within her borders no slave had ever been delivered up to his master, did not hinder her hatred to anti-slavery." In Middlebury, for example, "the opposition to our anti-slavery convention was intensely bitter and violent. . . . Few people attended our meeting, and apparently little was accomplished."[20]

Interestingly, one town stood out in Douglass's estimation as an exception to the state's general hostility to abolition: Ferrisburgh, which together with the nearby town of Vergennes, was Delia Webster's native soil. "In . . . Ferrisburgh the case was different and more favorable. The way had been prepared for us by such stalwart anti-slavery workers as Orson S. Murray, Charles C. Burleigh, Rowland T. Robinson, and others."[21] Rowland T. Robinson and his wife sheltered fugitives in a hidden east room of their house. The "Central Vermont Railroad" of the underground route passed through Middlebury, Vergennes and Ferrisburgh on its way to Canada.[22] On at least one occasion a Southerner appeared in Vergennes, hot on the trail of a fugitive who had just left the Robinson farm.[23] Rowland E. Robinson, born in 1833, witnessed several such incidents in his parents' house and described them in short stories he wrote in the 1890s. With particular poignancy "Out of Bondage" tells of a slave who dies of exhaustion just as his pursuers arrive.[24] Delia Webster thus hailed from the one hotbed of antislavery sentiment in the whole state of Vermont.

Webster only rarely spoke of her interest in abolition and almost never of helping slaves escape. She did describe herself as an impassioned educator, which no doubt she was. When beginning her first class at the Vergennes Classical School, "I became much attached to my little pupils, and soon acquired a love for teaching, which continues unabated in its ardor to the present day."[25] Like Fairbank, she had attended Oberlin College. Her studies there were cut short by some apparent impropriety whose content remains a tantalizing mystery. Replying in 1856 to a letter seeking information about Webster's standing when a student there, Hamilton Hill, treasurer of the school, stated that "she appeared to be a young lady of some energy and self-reliance, but for some reason she failed to secure the confidence of her teachers and many of her fellow pupils. Unfavorable reports were circulated with regard to her conduct in some respects. Her moral character was not impeached but there were circumstances which gave rise to apprehensions of her honesty."[26] It is not clear whether these apprehensions on the part of the Oberlin community were based on a philosophical disagreement about the morality of lying to a slave hunter in order to protect a slave or whether her professors had detected what they took to be some flaw in her character. It would not, in any case, be the last time she became the target of rumor.

Yet her reputation in Lexington in September, 1844, must have been beyond reproach, for not only had she made her name as a pedagogue to whom the most upstanding parents of the city entrusted their daughters but she had also recently been elected president of the Lexington Female Missionary Society. That organization was to hold its regular weekly meeting that very Saturday, the 28th, and it was her turn to prepare the sewing. The meeting went ahead as planned, but Webster adjourned it one hour early to make the planned excursion in the hack Fairbank had rented. The outing was no secret; she had even taken the precaution, though a risky one, of inviting other ladies from the boarding house to accompany them. Fortunately, the weather took a turn for the worse and the ladies declined; one can only presume that Webster knew it would. She was no doubt reasonably certain they would not accept for another reason: it was to be an overnight journey. But she tempted fate once more at the moment of climbing into the carriage by saying to Mrs. Glass that she would enjoy her ride much better if she too would come. The landlady then said she would be very happy to accompany her, "if it were consistent with her household duties." It was, fortunately, not consistent with those duties. "She then asked me if I thought I should get back by nine, on Monday morning, to which I replied in the affirmative, and requested her to detain my pupils."[27]

It was Fairbank's cover as a Methodist minister that formed the basis of the public justification of the journey. "On one or two occasions," Delia Webster would later recount, Fairbank "preached on the Sabbath" in Lexington that September.[28] Webster told her fellow boarders and the ladies of the missionary society that Fairbank was obliged to make frequent trips to neighboring counties on "church business," and was sometimes absent two and three days at a time. At least one of his trips, however, had quite a different purpose. Earlier in September Fairbank had crossed the Ohio River on a ferry to Ripley, a southern Ohio town some seventy miles north of Lexington, to scout out stations for his prospective passengers. Passing just upstream was a man in a skiff, whom Fairbank correctly identified as a "patroller," hired by slave owners to keep a look-out for runaways and their abettors—an unimpeachable source of information, surely. Hailing him from the ferry, Fairbank pointed to Ripley and asked, in a southern accent, "What kind of place is this?" "A black, dirty, Abolition hole," the answer came back. "Is not this a great hiding place for runaway slaves?" Indeed it was, the man replied. "Well, I've come from Lexington," said Fairbank, "and I'm interested in discovering the hiding places among the Abolitionists." The man was most cooperative: "Well, sir, you see that red house there? There Eli C. Collins lives, and in that other house over there lives Levi Collins, and Dr. Rankin occupies the one on the hill." With unintended irony, he told Fairbank he had better try "to pass for a good Abolitionist" if he wanted to gain entry into those houses.[29]

Fairbank bore no letter of introduction that could have convinced the Collinses or Rankin he was the genuine article (though unhappily, as it turned out, he was not always so careful); nor would it have been wise to have had a letter sent from his friends in Oberlin or Cincinnati to alert them to his arrival. So he really was under the necessity of doing exactly what the patroller said. In effect he was an underground agent posing as a Southerner posing as an underground agent. As a result, he had only mixed success. Though he made a reasonably good impression on Eli Collins, unfortunately Collins's hotheaded son had seen him talking with the man in the skiff, whom he recognized as the notorious patroller Pete Driscol. Fairbank had succeeded only too well in making Driscol, and Collins's son as he listened in on their exchange, believe he was a Southerner. Young Collins ran up the hill above the town to warn the Reverend John Rankin to be on his guard should the suspicious stranger come calling there. When Fairbank did approach Rankin, the clergyman was so reticent Fairbank concluded his house was not really an underground station. Yet it was in fact the most important by far of the several in Ripley, shepherding some two thousand to safety between 1828 and Emancipation. In 1852, Harriet Beecher Stowe would immortalize the true story of Eliza Harris and her child, who accomplished the miracle of walking across the ice-bound Ohio in the winter of 1838, guided by the light in Rankin's window.

Unable to make contact with Reverend Rankin, Fairbank went back to Eli Collins, who invited him to stay for supper. But the meal was interrupted by Eli's son, who burst in "with fury in his manner" and "ordered me to leave the house," denouncing him as a slave hunter and a spy. "He was plucky, but I finished my dinner, and afterward tried to convince them of my oneness with them in the cause." Eli Collins had the final, if tentative, word: "Maybe he is a friend. We will see when the time comes." Then, addressing Fairbank: "We will give you our help when we see you return with the trophies of victory." Ripley was "altogether an unpleasant experience, for I came near being mobbed by the girls of a hotel"—poor man!—"and only escaped by hastening away from the house." He was threatened, too, by "some wild fellows [who] were going to egg me . . . but they will help me when they see me come with the trophies of victory," he confided to a friend.[30]

The trophies would not, as events developed, be Berry's wife and children. That mission had aborted, as Fairbank in fact seems to have suspected it would even before he left Oberlin. He had a premonition that, despite forty-three successful missions, this time his luck was going to run out. "There is the darkest cloud I ever saw, rising higher and nearer," he wrote on September 24 to an Oberlin friend in a letter that was never delivered. "It seems to threaten me sometimes with utter destruction." He was well aware of the consequences of capture, of exposing himself "to the barbarous laws of this State, or the 'Lynch law,' which might pierce my heart with a leaden bullet and prostrate me in death." The foreboding deepened as the doubts he originally felt about Berry's honesty proved all too accurate. Berry had assured him that he had left money with two men, money Fairbank would need to underwrite the rescue—to rent the carriage, to pay his own expenses until the deed was done. But the first man said he had been given no money, and the second—Berry's uncle, who was supposed to be holding some $280 for Fairbank—had been dead for three months. In the September 24 letter Fairbank reminds his correspondent, "You well know, that I, before I left, expressed some doubt as to his [Berry's] honesty." The "unkindest cut of all," he goes on to say, was not that the money wasn't there but that "he said that I could find it, when he knew full well he lied." On top of this, Berry's wife failed to show up for her appointed rescue. She must have been detected, Fairbank concluded, or so closely watched that she didn't dare to come.[31]

Thus Fairbank was in the heart of slave country with no mission, and no money to remain there or to accomplish a mission should one arise. It was a slave, and Delia Webster, who came to his rescue: "I have spent my money searching for his children and his wife," he wrote his Oberlin friend, alluding to the Berry family. "I am now living upon the money of one Lewis, whom, in consequence of this failure, I intend to fetch with me, likewise his wife and child—a very active man, worth ten of Berry." It was Delia Webster who had introduced them: "In the meantime, Miss Webster told me of a slave man named Lewis Hayden."[32] Hayden was the joint property of Thomas Grant and Lewis Baxter. Grant, as Hayden later wrote, was "engaged as tallow chandler & oil manufacturer and dealer," while Baxter "was a Clerk in an Insurance Office in Lexington."[33] They in turn hired him out to work in John Brennan's Phoenix Hotel, Lexington's most prestigious inn. In its time it had seen such distinguished guests as Aaron Burr, James Monroe, Andrew Jackson, and Lafayette.[34]

It was common practice for owners to hire their slaves out and give them a share in the earnings. "Rented bondsmen," writes Marion B. Lucas, "played a crucial role in Kentucky's service industries. Often indispensable to owners of hotels, restaurants, and taverns, they served as cooks in the kitchens, waiters and bartenders in the dining rooms, and housekeepers. They also chopped firewood, stoked fires, carried luggage, and ran errands for both the owners and their guests." Though the state's 1798 slave code forbade owners to allow bondsmen to hire themselves out, "many owners disregarded the law by permitting slaves . . . to engage in whatever business they desired, provided they paid them a specified weekly or monthly sum." With wages rising in the 1840s, "hired slaves brought annually between 12 and 15 percent of their total value," while their upkeep was at the expense of the employer.[35]

Hayden had persuaded Grant and Baxter to purchase him with the understanding that he could earn enough money at the Phoenix Hotel to buy his own freedom.[36] Evidently his share was what Fairbank was living on for the moment and would pay for the carriage the latter would hire for the journey north. Hayden lived at the hotel, where he was hired by the month. His contract was to expire on September 29, so the flight to Ohio had to be scheduled before then, to take advantage of this temporary freedom of movement.

When they first met, Fairbank asked: "Why do you want your freedom?" Hayden's reply was quick and to the point: "Because I am a man." "I was deeply interested in him," recalled Fairbank, "and at once began to plan a way for his escape."[37] One can appreciate that deep interest when one learns what it was Hayden told him of his life, which was surely what he would later tell Harriet Beecher Stowe in a letter she published in *A Key to Uncle Tom's Cabin*, a collection of facts to back up the claims of her novel. Lewis Hayden was born in 1811 to a father who was sold off early and a mother of mixed Indian and white blood. A woman of stunning beauty, she was working in her master's dairy behind Transylvania University and near the Masonic lodge when a Mason, Hayden would later recount, saw her there and "made proposals of a base nature." She made no reply. He "told her that she need not be so independent, for if money could buy her he would have her." Money of course could indeed buy her, since she was a slave, and the man could afford himself this pleasure and made the purchase. But "she would not consent to live with this man, as he wished; and he sent her to prison, and had her flogged, and punished her in various ways, so that at last she began to have crazy turns." She tried to kill herself, once with a knife, another time by hanging. The jailor promised her that if she would calm down, he would let her see her children. "They let her out one time, and she came to the place where we were. I might have been seven or eight years old. . . . I came in and found her in one of the cabins near the kitchen. She sprung and caught my arms, and seemed going to break them, and then said, 'I'll fix you so they'll never get you!' I screamed, for I thought she was going to kill me; they came in and took me away. They tied her, and carried her off."[38]

Hayden had originally been the property of the Reverend Adam Rankin, a Presbyterian minister of whom "It was commonly reported,"

Hayden told Stowe, that he "had said in the pulpit that there was no more harm in separating a family of slaves than a litter of pigs." Ironically, this Rankin was a relation, though distant, of the other Reverend Rankin, the Ripley abolitionist on whom Calvin Fairbank had made such a bad impression.[39] The Lexington Rankin apparently had no more compunction about separating his flock than he did his slaves or his livestock, for one of his first accomplishments after settling there in 1784 was to split his church over the issue of how best to sing the Psalms. Known as "a talented, intolerant, eccentric, and pious man," he could not countenance Isaac Watts's newfangled, if more melodious, setting of psalmody in use at the Mount Zion Church at the time of his arrival.[40] He preferred the older, literal version, and was accused of having turned away from the Lord's Table those who sang them differently, ultimately taking a portion of his congregation away to form his own church. After a consistently stormy career the cleric declared in 1827 that he was leaving town and "going where the Lord directed him," which turned out to be the Holy City itself. He never made it to Jerusalem, dying in Philadelphia later that year.[41] When Rankin was preparing to leave Lexington for Pennsylvania, wrote Hayden, "he sold all my brothers and sisters at auction. I stood by and saw them sold. When I was just going up on to the block, he swapped me off for a pair of carriage-horses. I looked at those horses with strange feelings. I had indulged hopes that master would take me into Pennsylvania with him, and I should get free. How I looked at those horses, and walked round them, and thought for them I was sold!"[42]

Lewis Hayden's quest for freedom began with a kind of anointment by a dazzling historical personage, the Marquis de Lafayette. The hero of both the French and American Revolutions visited Lexington on May 16, 1825, under a full military escort led by Henry Clay. As the parade passed the fence where fourteen-year-old Hayden was perched, Lafayette bowed to the fence. The remarkable thing, as young Hayden suddenly realized when he looked around him, was that there was no one else on the fence. So that Lafayette must be bowing personally to him! Frightened and embarrassed, all he could think to do was to tumble off the fence and run away as fast as his legs would carry him. As luck would have it, he collapsed with exhaustion just under the mouths of the cannons about to fire the salute. "You can imagine how I felt," Hayden wrote Stowe, "a slave-boy to be favored with [Lafayette's] recognition. . . . I date my hatred of slavery from that day." Lafayette's nod gave young Hayden a sense of self worth: in the eyes of this distinguished visitor, he was no longer an invisible boy.

After the Jerusalem-seeking psalm-singer who sold him for a pair of horses, Hayden found himself the property of a peddler of clocks, whose journeys the length and breadth of the state afforded young Lewis a rare opportunity to listen in on travellers' tales and political debates. From conversations overheard in taverns and hotels he learned that not all white people thought entirely alike and, in particular, that there actually were some (perhaps spoken of at second hand) who thought slavery was a crime. Under yet another master in the 1840s, who tried to get the most of his investment by frequent applications of the lash, he taught himself to read by studying the Bible and whatever old newspapers he could find.[43]

Hayden had been contemplating plans for escape since 1842, after his marriage to Harriet Bell, but had not yet found one that made provision for his wife and son. Not until Delia Webster, that is, introduced him to Calvin Fairbank. The irony as far as Fairbank was concerned was that, while it was Webster who found for him in Hayden both a source of funds and a mission to accomplish, and her involvement made the venture possible, it also made it more dangerous.

Depending on whom they talked to, Fairbank and Webster had three different cover stories to account for the trip. Fairbank had to tell Parker Craig, from whom he rented the hack, the horses and the driver, that he was going as far as Maysville, over sixty miles away, because he needed to know from Craig if the horses could make it that distance and back. It would have been highly suspect, in a state where slave owners lived in dread of someone stealing their slaves, for a Yankee to make such a journey alone for no stated purpose. Therefore, he also told Craig that he would be accompanied by "a young lady from Mr. Glass," and he must have said, or at least hinted at, enough else for Craig to believe that he was going "off with this lady to get married."[44]

But Delia Webster had told the Glasses and their boarders that Fairbank had invited her to accompany him on a ride in the country on church business, and only as far as Versailles or Georgetown (each only about twelve to fifteen miles distant). "Having been closely pent up in the smoky atmosphere of a crowded city during the heat of summer without any recreation," Miss Webster found such a proposal to her taste. She had even risked inviting, earlier in the week, some of the other female boarders to accompany them. When they declined, and when Fairbank then said he would like to "change the route, and go through Paris, to meet some friends of his, who were expected to be there on that day," she replied, in a conversation evidently staged for Mrs. Glass and her boarders, that "My object being the benefit of a ride in the country air, it of course made no material difference with me, what particular road we took, provided I could return at the time specified." The specified time was nine o'clock Monday morning, when her classes in the Lexington Academy would resume. She would later write (in *Kentucky Jurisprudence*, her 1845 account of all that happened in the fall of 1844), in justifying and giving her own interpretation of all that was to transpire, what she surely would have said to Mrs. Glass and her boarders had she returned: "The next day [the day after their departure] was the Sabbath. I was deceived in the distance, somewhat fatigued and being unwilling to spend the whole day either in riding or visiting, Mr. F. left me at a private house, where I remained until late in the evening, when he returned."[45] In other words, though she indeed knew how far Fairbank intended to go, she would have maintained to Mrs. Glass (as she would to the readers of *Kentucky Jurisprudence*) that she had not.

Once the Haydens were safely in the hack, however, the story would change once more. Concealed by cloaks and their faces and hands disguised by a generous application of flour (with their young son Jo hidden under the seat), Lewis and Harriet Hayden were to become a white couple, Mr. Allen and Miss Smith of Paris, Kentucky, whom Webster and Fairbank were helping to elope to Ohio to get married.[46] These, evidently, would be those "friends of his" whom Fairbank wanted to meet in Paris in the story he told at the boarding house.

Delia Webster's presence in the hack made the journey less suspect, whether in the eyes of Parker Craig, of the Glasses and their boarders, or of anyone who chanced to look into the carriage en route. Yet she imposed a condition that made the venture significantly more dangerous than it would otherwise have been. "Miss W. will not come away," Fairbank wrote to an Oberlin friend on September 24, "but will come across the river with us; then I shall have to put these on the underground line and send them on, till I go back with Miss W. I must go back with her, because the people will suppose us to have gone riding, or rather to spend the Sabbath in another place, and it would create suspicion if I were not to return with her. . . . I have been cautious. . . . No apprehensions have as yet been entertained of me or her."[47] Had she been willing to "come away" to Ohio, to abandon her school in Lexington—or perhaps to abandon any other projects of slave rescue she may have had in mind, though no evidence has come to light of any other such ventures at this point in her career—then Fairbank, who himself had no reason to return to Lexington other than to facilitate Miss Webster's return, could have returned safely to Oberlin, free to carry on the fight another day, in another part of the South. As events would prove, however, the Haydens were the last he would be able to rescue for quite some time.

Shortly before five o'clock that Saturday they left the house on West Second Street, but despite their declared intention of making a country excursion they did not immediately leave the city. Instead, Fairbank instructed the driver—Israel, a slave he had rented with the carriage—to proceed to the Dudley House hotel, where two trunks he had left there four days before were loaded into the vehicle. They must have made at least one more stop before leaving Lexington, for a witness later recalled having seen "a negro man take a negro boy out of a window at Mr. Bain's, on the night the negroes left." Though this witness "did not see any carriage at that time about the place," Parker Craig would later claim he recognized the track of the coach he had rented to Fairbank and to have seen that track outside Bain's house.[48] Harriet Hayden belonged to Patterson Bain, as did the Haydens' son, Jo. Craig may have been exaggerating his powers of observation, for Fairbank would later recall that it was "near the residence of Cassius M. Clay" that he and Miss Webster had waited in the hack for the Haydens.[49]

Fairbank, Webster and the Haydens finally departed Lexington at eight o'clock.[50] An "inclement night," in the words of one of the toll collectors on the Maysville Road, its cold and rain hardly fit the notion Webster had bruited of a pleasant drive in the country.[51] The Maysville-Lexington Turnpike, financed by the state and by private contributions after Andrew Jackson's politically motivated veto of Henry Clay's Maysville Road Bill in 1830, was the first road in the United States west of the Alleghenies to be "macadamized," a significant improvement that involved layering the road-bed with six-ounce stones. Opened to the public in 1835, it stretched for sixty-four miles and featured thirteen toll houses and six covered bridges. On the Lexington-Maysville run a coach could average eight miles an hour, including stops for toll.[52] As their ultimate destination was Ripley, Ohio, some nine miles beyond Maysville, Fairbank, Webster, and the Haydens had some hard driving ahead.

At Millersburg, twenty-four miles into the journey, disaster struck. One of the horses took sick. Israel diagnosed it as "bots," a common equine affliction caused by the parasitic larvae of the botfly, and said he had observed that the horse had been ill before they left Lexington.[53] Calvin Fairbank may well have thought it more useful had he shared that knowledge before they set out, but history does not record his response. How could they now continue with but one horse to pull a coach that required two? Fairbank had stepped out of the carriage, and as he and Israel were discussing the problem, a Mr. Holloway, owner of the tavern where they had halted, came out to ask what was the matter. This was just the sort of encounter Webster and Fairbank wanted to avoid, for if Holloway were to look inside the carriage to strike up a friendly conversation, the Haydens could hardly avoid notice. Would their disguise hold? Indeed, as Fairbank would later attest, the tavern keeper did speak "to the persons within and asked them if they would not get out, and entered into a short conversation with them." Holloway even opened the doors of the hack, which would have given him an unobstructed view of the interior. Yet the flour and the cloaks must have done their job

Maysville, Kentucky, from Lewis Collin's Historical Sketches of Kentucky, *1847.*

well, for Fairbank would later state in an affidavit that "I have reason to believe he will state them all to be white persons as I verily believe he saw them."[54] The word "as" in the affidavit may have had a double meaning, the public one being "because," the private, and more revealing (yet hidden), one being "he saw them as white." Delia Webster adds in her account of the scene that Holloway "brought a pitcher of water to the carriage."[55] Holloway was so helpful that he provided not only refreshments but a new horse, agreeing to let them borrow one of his own and to take care of the one that had fallen sick. All told the delay cost them "nearly an hour," perhaps as long as "an hour and a half."[56]

Despite the seemingly benign outcome, the episode had one catastrophic result: Webster and Fairbank were recognized. Not by Holloway but "by two colored men from Lexington. On their return they unwittingly started the report" that would lead Patterson Bain and Parker Craig to connect the disappearance of the former's slaves with the rental of the hack.[57]

Fairbank, Webster, and the Haydens drove on through the night of September 28, passing through Blue Licks, Fairview, Mays Lick, and Washington, where H.G. Musick would recall that a hack passed his tavern on Sunday morning, driven at breakneck speed with all the curtains down. By nine a.m. Sunday, they had arrived in Maysville and were aboard a ferry crossing the Ohio to Aberdeen. The ferrymen would later say that they saw "no person of color but the driver," that as soon as the carriage came onto the boat the door was opened, a man got out and did not get back in until the carriage was on the other side—Calvin evidently, his eyes on the opposite shore.[58]

As he stood there outside the carriage on the ferry in the mist that on most mornings at that time of year enshrouds the river at Maysville, Fairbank may well have been thinking of how often rivers are fated to mark the frontier between bondage and freedom. For his grandmother, as he would later recount the tale, had been captured by Indians on the western frontier of New England settlement, and abducted across the Connecticut River twenty miles into the wilderness. Yet she managed to inebriate her guard by pretending to join him in the consumption of firewater; once her captors were asleep, she saddled up her old white horse, which had been captured with her and knew the way home. When her mount reached the river, he "plunged fearlessly in and, swimming with vigor, soon reached the opposite bank, leaving between him and his savage, disappointed pursuers the broad swift current of the stream. He bore his precious burden safely up the bank, and as she appeared through the brush, a shout of joy rang out on the morning air."[59] It is not unlikely that Calvin enjoyed the fleeting recollection of this family legend as he guided Lewis, Harriet and Jo to safety, and found that he had inherited some of what he called "sanctified pluck" from his eighteenth-century grandmother.

Having evidently been able to make contact in Ripley only with Eli Collins, Calvin could not leave the Haydens at the Rankin house, but had to go "back four miles to Hopkins,'" as he would later recount the event, probably alluding to Gordon Hopkins, an underground agent in Red Oak, four miles northeast of Ripley.[60] He apparently did enjoy sufficient confidence from Eli Collins to be able to leave Delia at his house until he returned from Red Oak later in the day. Lewis, Harriet, and Jo continued north to Oberlin, though when news of their escape broke, they were warned of pursuers hot on their trail, and made for Sandusky, from where they crossed into Canada.

In the evening Calvin returned to Ripley, picked up Webster and began the journey back to Kentucky, stopping around midnight at Mr. Musick's inn in the little town of Washington, just south of Maysville. The horses were very much fatigued, Mr. Musick later said. According to one account, Musick said that he left Miss Webster and Fairbank alone to go see about the horses, and that when he returned their door was locked, and remained so till about four in the morning, when they came out to start. There was no bed in the room, and Mr. Musick, "thinking they were a runaway couple, laughed at them a little about it"—apparently about their being an eloped couple unaccommodated with a bed. They neither acknowledged, said Musick, nor denied being married.[61] In another version of his recollection of events (or in another version of the trial testimony, the one Delia Webster printed in *Kentucky Jurisprudence*), Musick did not speak of any locking of doors, but recalled that "I sat in the room with them till morning. . . . I conversed with them in relation to runaway matches; the drift of our conversation was about marriage. They did not say they were married, or were not married, but I inferred they were."[62]

By daybreak Fairbank, Webster, and the coachman Israel were once more on their way. At the turnpike gate just south of Washington, the keeper told them of the escape of some Lexington slaves, showing them a handbill announcing it, little knowing that they were the ones responsible.[63] One can imagine the apprehension with which Webster and Fairbank drew closer to Lexington, realizing that the slaves' disappearance was now common knowledge.[64]

Near Mays Lick, they began to notice a riderless horse following the hack. At the next tollgate, the keeper demanded toll for the horse, but they denied ownership and requested him to drive it back. This was repeated at the next tollgate. At Blue Licks, they stopped for an hour, and the horse reappeared. This time it occurred to Israel that he knew the horse as belonging to one of his master's neighbors, and they decided to pay its toll and return it to Lexington. This seemed providential, for when they arrived again in Millersburg, Holloway told them the horse they had left with him had died; they decided to hitch up the horse that had been following them and thus avoid having to keep Holloway's substitute horse in harness until Lexington, and be subsequently obliged to bring him back to Millersburg.

When Patterson Bain had discovered that Harriet and Jo were missing, he began to ask around town what hacks had been rented, and ran into Parker Craig. The livery stable owner inspected the track of a coach that had turned around in the street by Bain's house, and said he could tell it belonged to the one he had hired out to Fairbank "by the peculiar conformation of the tire." Craig and Bain then started for Maysville, meeting up with the returning hack between Millersburg and Paris. Fairbank asked Craig if he recognized both the horses. Craig said he knew one, but not the other. Calvin explained what had happened concerning the horses. "Craig then asked him where they had been," and Fairbank "replied, to assist a runaway couple to be married. What were their names? asked he; when Miss Webster told Fairbank not to answer that question."[65]

They continued to Paris, where the conversation was resumed. Parker Craig began to insist that Fairbank pay for the horse. Calvin replied it didn't seem right to have to pay for a horse that was sick before he got it; and besides, he had rented the coachman too, so he was surely absolved of responsibility for the horse. Craig answered that *he* didn't know the horse was sick, and anyhow couldn't afford to lose him. He demanded a hundred dollars. Calvin proposed arbitration.[66]

On this note, they proceeded to Lexington, closely followed by Craig and Bain. They had nearly reached the Glass boarding house when Parker Craig climbed out of his carriage and clambered up into the driver's seat of the other carriage, took over the reins, and directed the horses to the "Megowan Hotel." When they arrived there, Craig descended, opened the door of the coach, and began again to demand payment for the horse. By this time a crowd had gathered, partly from the noise of the argument but partly too because word had spread of the missing slaves and of the likely involvement of the Yankee couple in their disappearance. Fairbank emerged from the hack, and Craig grabbed him by the collar and shouted, "Bring a rope quick. I've got the man that killed my horse."[67]

"Till now," Delia Webster would later write, "I had been silent. My heart was pained with the horrid imprecations that rent the atmosphere, and knowing how lightly human life was esteemed, especially by an infuriated mob, and how slight an offence would provoke the dark and fiendish spirit of those enemies of God and man to draw the dirk, pistol or bowie knife upon their defenceless fellow, I feared the result." But she did venture to assert to Parker Craig, "Though I may be a stranger to you, sir, I have for some time been a resident of this city, and am well known as principal of the Academy. My name is Webster, and my patrons are of the first class in the community. Your demand seems to me, sir, unreasonable; but if Mr. Fairbank wishes to satisfy it, I can loan him the requisite sum." Craig "respectfully and mildly replied" that he was simply angry at Fairbank because he had not seemed inclined to pay, even if he had the money. Webster explained that Fairbank was a stranger in town, "not accustomed to our usages," and offered to pay for the horse herself.[68]

Craig then said he needed to talk with Fairbank for a few minutes more, but told Israel he could drive Miss Webster back to her boarding house if she wished to go. As the horses started, the crowd surrounded Fairbank, who was heard to say, "Gentlemen, it is not necessary for you to tie me. If you wish me to go in, I will do so." He was dragged into the barroom. The mob rushed after him but were turned back at the door, which was locked. "I ordered the carriage to stop," she recalled, "but no sooner was I obeyed than I found myself literally enveloped by a mob of several hundred." James Megowan rushed up to protect her, offering her safe haven in his parlor, but she declined, saying she was expected back at the boarding house. After some delay, Megowan escorted her home. "Supper was over, but mine was immediately brought up and I sat down to relate the incidents of my unfortunate ride. . . . When I retired to my room, I requested Mrs. Glass to accompany me, which she did. Immediately upon opening the door, I perceived a slight change in the location of several articles and inquired of Mrs. G. who had been in my room during my absence." No one had, she claimed. Webster pointed out that surely she could remember seeing her close and fasten the shutters before she left. Maybe it was the wind, the landlady replied, that had blown them open. In point of fact, Mrs. Glass, having heard that her lodger was suspected of stealing slaves, had taken a passkey and entered her room. In one of Webster's trunks she found several letters from Oberlin, including one from Fairbank, proposing to come over and assist her in running off slaves. Meanwhile, those interrogating Fairbank at Megowan's had by now discovered the letter in his pocket that he had never sent and in which he had written so incriminatingly of a certain "Miss W."[69]

"Late in the night we were aroused by a heavy rap at the door, which was several times repeated each time louder and heavier." Only with reluctance did Mrs. Glass, accompanied by Miss Webster, go to the door. Who was there? A voice answered, "Friend." She asked for a name. No reply. Several voices then asked for Mr. Glass. When they learned he wasn't at home, they left, bidding a pleasant "good evening." An hour later there was another knock. This time, when admitted, "a company of persons entered in the garb of gentlemen, whose object, as the sequel disclosed, was the capture of an unprotected female. . . . I was desired to return to the 'Megowan Hotel.'. . . My walk was quiet and somewhat agreeable. It was a beautiful moonlight night, though cool for the season. Some few clouds mantled the horizon, and the murmurings of a gentle breeze added romance to the occasion. Nought else was heard, save low whisperings and the tramping of footsteps on the pavement." Escorted by some forty men, at intervals Delia Webster passed by small groups of ten or twenty persons, "apparently engaged in earnest consultation. Whether they were planning a project of humanity or meditating some deed of darkness, was not in my power to determine." At Megowan's "hotel," she was ushered upstairs to the "Debtor's Room," which occasionally also served as hotel accommodation for travellers, and the door was locked behind her. Not a word was spoken. "This eventful night," she would later write, "was the commencement of a new era in my history."[70]

2

"PERHAPS YOU CAN DECIPHER ITS CONTENTS"

Though she could hear the key being turned in the lock, Delia Webster, if she can be believed, did not realize she was in jail. The building was called "Megowan's Hotel" partly by way of a joke and partly because it really was, in addition to a jail, a hotel. There were perhaps as many as a hundred regular boarders, who in fact outnumbered its prisoners. Thomas B. Megowan, in any case, was the jailor of Lexington. For as long as she had been in the city, Webster later wrote, "I had no idea in what part of the town the jail was located, never dreaming of its being in any way connected with the 'Megowan Hotel.'" Its outward appearance could well have been deceptive, for the two-and-a-half-storied and five-bayed brick and stone structure with two chimneys on each gable end, standing on the northwest corner of Limestone and Short Streets, "resembled a residence of the period," according to Clay Lancaster in his architectural history of Lexington.[1] The room into which she had been placed was quite possibly, as Mrs. Megowan had assured her, "as good a room" as the establishment afforded. "Large and rather commodious" in Webster's words, it may have served alternately as hotel accommodation and the genteel confinement for debtors.[2]

The next morning, as the door was still locked, Delia Webster looked around for a Bible to occupy her attention before the hour of school—for she fully expected to be released in time to resume her classes at the Lexington Academy. A thorough search turned up but one book in the room, "which I eagerly seized, but discovering it to be a 'novel' I laid it down unopened, and returned to my meditations." A servant brought in her breakfast, then left in total silence, locking the door behind her. This was puzzling, she thought, for it seemed to imply that someone thought her too ill or incapacitated to take her breakfast with the other boarders. She dressed, and began looking about the room. Carelessly drawing aside the curtains, she discovered, to her hor-

Megowan's Hotel, where Webster and Fairbank were imprisoned to await trial in 1844. J. Winston Coleman Photographic Collection, Transylvania University Library

ror, that the window was barred. "I gazed in silent amazement, and thought for an instant it must be the delusion of a dream, from which I should soon awaken." The other window was likewise barred, and the view from both was spoiled by an enormous brick wall.[3]

She studied the massive lock on the door, then laughed at the incongruity of it all. "I sat down to my breakfast, thinking it folly to puzzle my brains in trying to unravel what eluded my comprehension, as it was impossible long to be kept in suspense. I was not long in suspense." Shouts laced with profanity came up from the courtyard below. She went to the window and, despite the wall, was able to see Calvin Fairbank surrounded by a group of well-dressed gentlemen taunting him with all sorts of names, chief among which was "Vile abolitionist." They also threatened his life. "Let's hang him and be done with it, and let Miss Webster go back to her school," some proposed. Others protested that both of them should be publicly decapitated and their heads paraded through the streets of the city. A bowie knife was presented, aimed at his heart. Fairbank is reported to have replied, "Gentlemen, think not to frighten me with such sights." Tearing open his coat, he exclaimed, "I am prepared to die. But remember there is a God in Heaven! And if I fall a victim to your violence, remember that that man who sheds a drop of my blood, will lose his soul in Hell."[4]

This seemed to calm the crowd somewhat. Fairbank asked after his companion, saying he wished to see Miss Webster. Some of the men had seen Webster's face at her window from the start, and now told him to direct his gaze upward. She called down a cheerful "Good morning," but he was immediately taken away. It was, coincidentally, at the same window a year and a half before that Fairbank had heard a tapping sound and looked up to behold the beautiful face of Eliza, whom he subsequently rescued by buying her at auction. She, too, had been housed in Megowan's debtor's cell as she awaited her fate.

At this point, Mrs. Megowan barged into Delia Webster's room and ordered, "You are not to look out of that window nor the other." Webster told her she would have to leave soon, as it was almost time for her classes at the Lexington Academy. "You will be kept here two or three days, school or no school," Mrs. Megowan replied.

"Then I would like to see Mr. Clay, as it is really inconsistent with my duties to spend so much time in this place."[5]

"You have already had business enough with Mr. Clay, in stealing negroes. He ought to be in jail himself; and will be arrested before night."

"Might I have the privilege of sending a note to him?"

"No."

"May I send a note to my school?"

"You may not."

"I have no books with me and have nothing to employ my time. Might I at least have the loan of a Bible?"[6]

This met with the same refusal, and Mrs. Megowan shut the door before Webster could think of what to say. By her account, she then began to pray, thanking her Creator that at least the right to do that was not denied the prisoner. But her prayers were soon interrupted by "the commingling tones of pleasure and pain": Fairbank had been led into the courtyard again, and was being put into irons. The cries of pain were his, as his captors pounded the metal into shape around his wrists and ankles; those of pleasure were evidently of those who "seemed to delight in his torture"—as well as from those of their number who proclaimed their interest in having Miss Webster fitted out in the same manner. It was with great difficulty that she restrained herself, remembering Mrs. Megowan's injunction, from looking out the window. In the end she succumbed to the temptation, but gives no indication of being seen by those below. The ironing procedure was not only painful, but "long and tedious."[7] At last, Fairbank was led away once more, to the "dungeon" in the cellar. The "stiff irons," he later recounted, weighed twenty-four pounds.[8]

Peace returned, writes Webster, "and I availed myself of the quietude to calm my agitated bosom." Then suddenly it sounded as if all of Satan's demons had broken out of hell. A crowd of men rushed into the yard, dragging with them old Israel, the driver of the hack in which the escape had been made, to be whipped into confessing his part in carrying off the slaves. He dropped to his knees, begging for mercy, for his life. He was told to take off his shirt, but would not, knowing too well that "his skin would come off next." Lashes to his face accompanied the command. His master, as if touched by pity, spoke in a gentle voice: "Why then don't you take off your shirt?" Habituated to a lifetime of obedience, Israel automatically did as told, and received, by Webster's count, fifty stripes on his back. The cries for mercy gradually subsided to "deep and stifled sobs." All this time Webster gazed down from the barred window, unnoticed. She seemed strangely unmoved: "With purpose fixed, I gazed in silence on the spectacle before me. My heart was riven, but my cheek was dry. This was no time for tears." But then her legs started to tremble, and she grabbed the bars to keep from falling to the floor. The upward motion of her hands caught the attention of someone's eye below. "Stop! Stop! Miss Webster is looking on! Take him out of sight! Take him to the barn!"[9] Chivalry required that she be spared the sight of such torment.

Jailor Megowan came in, shut the window, and left. Then a group of gentlemen entered bearing her trunks and demanded that she open them. Standing upon ceremony, or legality, she refused, but held out the keys and told them to take on that responsibility themselves. None did, so she set the keys on one of the trunks and retired to a chair. Megowan ordered her to unlock them. She complied, but without opening the lids. They asked her if any of the trunks held letters. She said yes, and told them which one. "Open it." "It is unlocked." "Raise the lid." She acquiesced, but refused to do more. She did point out her letter box, but questioned the lawfulness of their perusing its contents. Peruse them however they did—"with a greediness," wrote Webster, "truly amusing." When she told them that this was "not a hundredth part" of the letters and papers in her possession, the rest being back at the Glass house, they demanded, and got, the key to her room there. As they were still rifling through the letters at hand, Mrs. Glass walked in and presented them with a letter she had taken it upon her own initiative to ferret out.[10]

Later that morning, Israel emerged from the barn, having made a confession, and was placed in the dungeon. The men who had forced it out of him ran up the stairs in triumph, and burst into Webster's room to announce the good news. "Well, we've got it out of him! Rather than die, he has at last come out and told it! We knew he would. And now Miss Webster, if your statement should correspond with his, you will save Israel's life, and yourself from sixty years in the penitentiary! There is no hope for Fairbank, but no one wishes to imprison you. Neither do we wish you to stand trial. It is in your power to clear yourself. You can do so as easily as you can turn your hand over; and then you will not be kept here an hour. The doors will be opened, and you can return to your school." She refused, demanding justice and refusing mercy. "Whatever assertions Israel may make, I shall neither admit, or deny." She was holding out for a trial. This wish was granted, as later that afternoon she was duly served with four indictments and held under five thousand dollars bond.[11]

The day's excitement, she later wrote, had given her "a fine appetite." When supper was brought up, it looked inviting, but there was no silverware. She demanded a knife and fork. The servant said the jailor had expressly forbidden it. "Very well," she replied. "I had a good dinner at noon, and that will suffice. I will drink the milk, and then you may take away the tray."[12]

Welcome sleep arrived. "I was soon lost in imagery bright and invigorating." In the morning, she awoke refreshed. Breakfast was brought in, this time with the proper utensils. The stillness was broken by a noise of clanking below. It was Fairbank in irons, chained to two black prisoners scheduled for execution in the coming weeks, all led out to take their breakfast in the yard. Fairbank's feet were bound so close together that he fell several times. He seemed "low and disconsolate." Delia bid him "Good morning and asked him how he enjoyed his mind." He shook his head as if to plead with her not to draw down the jailor's wrath. But it was too late. Megowan ordered that Fairbank be chained to the dungeon floor and not permitted to see the light of day.[13]

One of the two condemned prisoners chained to Fairbank that morning was Richard Moore, who on August 22, 1844, had strangled his mistress to death. Had he not been a slave (or black), Moore might have been able to plead insanity—hers. A Boston blueblood, Caroline Turner had lived in Lexington since the mid-1830s as the wife of retired judge Fielding Turner. Theirs was a house of considerable wealth, boasting more household servants than any other in the city. "A woman of strong muscle and fierce temper," Mrs. Turner was known to frequently take the whip to her slaves.[14] In the spring of 1837, she was flogging a young boy when, overcome with rage, she threw him out of a second-story window. He struck the stone courtyard below, broke an arm and a leg, and so injured his spine that he was crippled for the rest of his life. Soon afterward, declaring that "She has been the immediate death of six of my servants by her severities," her husband had her forcibly committed to the city's lunatic asylum. She did not go quietly, demanding that a jury be convened to decide if she was indeed insane. Before the jury could do its work, however, the asylum directors, having examined her and finding nothing particularly wrong with her faculties, set her free. History does not record the effect of this event on her marriage, except that she returned to her former ways with regard to her servants. Before the judge died in 1843, he stipulated in his will that all his slaves become the possession of his children. "None of them are to go to the said Caroline, for it would be to doom them to misery in life & a speedy death." Undeterred, Mrs. Turner renounced her husband's will, and got possession of several of the slaves—though these did not include Richard Moore, whom she purchased from a James Jones of Fleming County. Moore was described as "about 24 years of age, of yellow complexion," and six feet in height. "He can read and write, and is very sensible and plausible."[15] On the morning of August 22, she chained him to the wall and was flogging him in her accustomed way when he managed to break loose, seized her by the throat, and broke her neck. He fled. A reward of five hundred dollars was offered for his capture. Captured in neighboring Scott County and brought to Lexington for trial, Moore was found guilty of murder and sentenced to hang from the gallows in the jail yard where Delia Webster had seen him shackled to Calvin Fairbank.

Chained together in the cellar, Fairbank and Moore plotted escape. Years earlier, some prisoners had once broken out through the north wall of the yard. The hole they made had not been entirely repaired. The stones were put back, but without mortar; oak planks with iron bars covered the stones. Fairbank discovered that the planks, now warped and cracked, could be dislodged and the bars that held them broken. Working in concert with five other prisoners, they set the date of their escape for the first Sunday in November. During breakfast that day one of the other five broke the bars, removed the planks, took out some of the stones, and then put everything back until dinner time, when all but Fairbank and Moore made their escape. One of them, John Minnis, had been jailed on suspicion of longing for freedom; seeking perhaps to prove his innocence, he used his escape to return to his owner. Another had been arrested in Ohio on his way to freedom, and brought back to jail for eventual sale. Soon after his escape, he wrote a letter to Fairbank and Moore bragging of earning a dollar and a half a day and "smoking Spanish cigars at night, and no master to thank for it all." Moore and Fairbank were not so fortunate. They struggled with the stones all night, but could not break through, even though "the palms of my hands," wrote Fairbank, were "worn to the naked tendons by the iron instrument with which I attempted to break the wall."[16] At dawn, they were discovered. On the day Moore was to hang, wrote Fairbank, "when the military arrived, and the door swung open, we were found on our knees, commending that soul to Him who had given it, and the armed men stood silent and awestruck in the presence of Jehovah, and the pleading dying man. He finished his course in peace."[17]

On October 1, the first evening of his captivity, Fairbank wrote a letter to "Bro. Herman Safford, John Brown, and all others of my friends" in which he speaks of his incarceration but refrains from confessing his crime. On the other hand, nothing he writes is at variance with the facts. "Having taken a ride to Maysville with Miss Delia A. Webster and crossed over into Ohio to Aberdeen, and having started on my return, I was informed of some runaway slaves viz. Lewis, his wife and child. . . . I am accused of taking those persons away." He mentions the encounter with Parker Craig which led to his arrest. Then he brings up the reason for his letter: A "Brother McCowen" of Lexington, a Methodist preacher, had learned that he was a Methodist "licentiate" and asked for proof of his rank. Fairbank requests of Safford and Brown that they send a letter attesting to his standing in the church. "Brethren do not forsake me here in captivity," he adds, and asks them as well to help him raise bail. "I have been here one night it does not seem very pleasant, yet these several Negroes shut up here with me who are to be sold, and taken South or some other place: they are pretty good Methodists; we have good prayer meetings & enjoy ourselves well."[18] Fairbank well knew that every word he wrote would be intensely scrutinized for evidence of guilt, and consequently he speaks of the slaves as if he knew nothing personally about their escape. He apparently believed that if his credentials as a Methodist preacher could be established, his captors might show him a little more respect. The haste, and no doubt trepidation, in which he wrote the letter is apparent.

On October 5, Fairbank wrote another letter, this time under evident duress. His captors apparently wanted him to do what he could to get the slaves back. While the letter, addressed to "John Rent, a Friend, Buffalo, New York," appears to indicate that he caved in to pressure, it no doubt also served the purpose of alerting the Underground Railroad that the slave catcher Ben Wood was hot on the Haydens' trail.

Lexington, Ken., Oct. 5, '44.

Dear Sir:—

Let me ask of you in a hasty letter which will render to me a few favors at present. Mr. Wood is a gentleman in office in this city and has come to you to ascertain where one Lewis is with his family, viz, his wife and son. I am in jail for being sent to his assistance in escaping from this place. I am in jail with irons on which makes it quite uncomfortable for me.

Now if you can be of any service to me in this thing you will aid Mr. Wood in finding his property. If this can be done I shall be released very soon; but [if] not, it is probably that I shall most likely spend a long and heavy twenty years in prison, if found guilty. I am well in jail, books and plenty of company, eighteen of us and but three Whites; we sing and pray and have pretty good times.

Yours in haste,
Calvin Fairbank[19]

Writing this letter, he readily admits, will be worth "a few favors"—such as, one might imagine, a loosening or even a removal of the irons. The wording of the third sentence ("I am in jail for being sent . . .") is strange, so carelessly put as almost to amount to a confession. Fairbank's fatigue is evident here. Had he not been under such pressure, and torture, he would have found a more circumspect turn of phrase.

Put in the same situation—though without the attendant physical torment of being bound in irons in the cellar—Delia Webster showed a cooler head:

Lexington jail, Oct. 7th, '44

Mr. [Mason]

Dear sir: The object of this epistle is to introduce the bearer, Mr. Wood of our city, hoping and believing as I confidently do, that you will be his friend and protector as far as lies in your power.

Mr. Wood is in search of absconded property which it is supposed, have taken refuge in *Buffalo* or *Canada*; knowing as I do, that your community are violently opposed to servants, who have eloped from their masters, finding an asylum in Oberlin, I have given Mr. W. a letter of introduction to Pres. Mahan, but in that letter did not say half what I wished to, as my candle went out, and the stage which took the letter left before day. I wish not only yourself and the President, but *every* one who may see Mr. Wood to treat him with all kindness, and aid him as far as *consistent*, in apprehending said property. This, in my opinion, you can do, sir, (that is if they passed through Oberlin, or that way, to the lake,) by giving him information as to the course they took—where they may have been seen—where they stopped—whether they went to *Buffalo*—whether they crossed immediately into *Canada*—or whether (as is thought) they stopped a while to rest in Cleveland, at which place they may be found at the present time.

Now, Mr. ———, you know that I am an ardent friend and well wisher to Kentucky. You know that in principle I am a colonizationist. You know that I have ever disapproved of the course pursued by Northern abolitionists; and, sir, it is my rule of life and action, to do in *all* cases, as I would wish to be done by. This, sir, ought also to be your motto. Now, sir, please tell me, ought you not, as a gentleman and Christian, mount your *horse*, and manifest your friendship to *Mr. Wood* by going *with* him, at *least* as far as *Cleveland*, and if said property is not found *there*, and you cannot possibly go farther, then give him letters of recommendation to some of the most influential men in

Buffalo or *Canada*, else I would most certainly give him letters myself, as I do most sincerely hope his journey will be both a prosperous and *profitable* one.

I would like to say something in regard to myself, and circumstances, but if I were to commence, I would not know *when*, or *where* to stop; and as my time is *limited*, I will devote a few lines to my unfortunate fellow prisoner, Mr. Fairbank, who, if I may be allowed to judge, I think to be a very unhappy man. His *real case* is bad enough I do assure you, *sir*, but I do not think it a circumstance to which *he* imagines. I never viewed him as *polluted* with the foul blot of abolitionism. From my *earliest acquaintance* with him he never hinted to me that he entertained any such sentiments. Neither do I believe a person can be found, who has the remotest right to think him guilty. And were it not for the tremendous excitement that exists upon the subject, which it is said never was equalled west of the Alleghany mountains, I would say to him, "be of good cheer." We are urged to have our trial immediately, in the midst of the excitement, *but, sir, we shall not* do it. The Judge informs me that we may have our trial on any day between this and next March. It is impossible for them to prove any thing against us without false witnesses. But I have no doubt there are hundreds here of that character, ready at the twinkling of an eye to seize even a suspected abolitionist by the throat without regard to law or gospel, judge or jury. As one uncouth fellow remarked, (whom I have never seen) that he would gladly go *two hundred miles* to be a witness against Miss Webster.

I am solicited by very many respectable witnesses of this place, professedly my friends, to clear myself; but, sir, if I am cleared, I shall be cleared by the laws of my country. I am very cheerful, composed, and happy, and await, with patience, the extreme justice of the law.

I often tell my accusers, jurymen or others, that I defy any individual in the State, bond or free, black or white, to prove that they have, or ever had, the slightest grounds for believing me to be an abolitionist.

If it be a possible thing, let me *entreat* you to secure aid for Mr. Fairbank. Our bail, jointly, is ten thousand dollars. If you can secure bail for *him*, ($5000,) I will be very content to remain.

The grand object for which the return of the servants, (viz: John or Gilson, Lewis, his wife and child) is so strongly desired, is, I am credibly informed, *not so much for* the intrinsic value of the *property*, as to make their *punishment* operate on the minds of other servants, and preclude all idea of further elopement among the blacks.

Please introduce Mr. Wood to the tavern keeper, and desire for him his protection and friendship.

Again let me entreat you to see to it, that Mr. Wood meets with all those kind attentions, and civilities due to a gentleman from a sister

State—I shall tremble for his safety, unless, sir you keep down your black population, which acts from the impulse of the moment, without regard to consequences.

Excuse this hastily written scrawl; I *fear* it is so illegible you will hardly be able to read it, but if you are from the old Granite State, perhaps you can decipher its contents.

A certain *John* or *Gilson*, or whatever his name be, ran off very much in my debt. If you can hear any thing from him, and secure my money, you will confer a favor. All letters which I receive or write, are subject to close inspection.

Please write immediately, and use *great caution*, as every letter is carefully read before it is brought into my presence. Please direct your letters to Delia A. Webster, to the care of *Hon. H. Clay* and *Gen. John M. McCalla*, my counsel.

Yours in haste,
Delia A. Webster

N.B. A letter of mine, written by Mr. J. Brown, an Eastern gentleman, is now in the hands of my accusers. Brown was in or near Oberlin when he wrote the letter, and some are trying hard to prove that he is a colored man; but if they can prove *Brown black*, they can do great things. I have said to them repeatedly, that Brown is not black, but they hardly believe it.[20]

This version of the letter is copied from the November 13, 1844 issue of the *Ohio Statesman*, a Columbus Democratic newspaper vituperous in its denunciations of the Whig presidential candidate Henry Clay. The *Statesman's* principal interest in publishing the letter was to prove that Fairbank and Webster were indeed in the Lexington jail (apparently the Whigs in Ohio were claiming they were not) and that Clay was Delia Webster's lawyer, or at least letting people think that he was: "To put to rest forever the denial of the Whigs that Mr. Fairbank and Miss Webster are in the Jail at Lexington, we publish a letter from her, written in jail, to a gentleman in this State. The italics are all hers, and it will explain itself. . . . Mr. Clay, for political capital in Ohio, if for nothing else, seemed willing to have it known here that he was her attorney!" As the headline indicates, the paper was somewhat misinformed as to her identity: "Letter from Miss Delia A. Webster, Niece of Daniel Webster."

In a letter she would write on August 30, 1845 to William Garrison, editor of the abolitionist newspaper the *Liberator*, Webster would feel obliged to explain this embarrassing document: "You allude to some letters written by me in jail, which you say 'disgusted the abolitionists.' I suppose you refer to the letters to Rev. Mr. Leavitt of Vermont, and Mr. Mason of Ohio, as I know of no others that were published during my incarceration." The Leavitt letter, though embarrassing, would prove to be so much less so than the Mason letter that Webster would have no qualms about publishing a substantial portion of it in the account she was to write of her trial in 1845. The Leavitt epistle was very widely reprinted in the abolitionist press, and was in fact used to elicit sympathy for the writer. The Mason letter (although the *Ohio Statesman* left the addressee's name blank, it is clear that this is the letter to which she alludes), as far as can be determined, received much less general distribution, and was not of a nature to make abolitionists feel kindly toward its author.

In her response to Garrison, Webster would say of both letters that they were private communications "addressed to individuals who for a long time had known my sentiments too well to be deceived." The Mason letter in particular bore some secret marks that its recipient would have known how to decipher: "The printer [presumably of the *Ohio Statesman*] omitted some stenographic characters, which he probably did not notice, (and that were *not intended* to be noticed by the careless observer,) which would have made a material difference in the sense of the letter."[21] The third paragraph from the end of the letter is clearly a warning to the reader that the letter is in need of decipherment: "if you are from the old Granite State, perhaps you can decipher its contents."

Underground Railroad agents were well skilled in writing letters that conveyed one message to the outside reader, but another to the actual correspondent. Laura Haviland, for example, a contemporary of Delia Webster (and who would one day be mistaken for her), tells of being constrained by slave catchers to write a letter home that would result in the entrapment of a family of escaped slaves.

> Now my intention in writing to Hamilton was to serve these slaveholders by defeating them. I knew, too, that disguising my handwriting was not enough to reveal to the Hamilton's that the letter was a sham, and whatever I wrote would be subjected to the perusal of my employers before it was sent. . . . It came to me like a flash, and I cheerfully wrote all they dictated. . . . I requested permission to add a few lines on my own responsibility, which was readily granted, as I explained to them that Elsie would not be prepared with regard to clothing. . . . "Indeed, madam," said the son-in-law, "that will be very kind in you. They can get ready so much quicker." So I added to my letter to Willis as follows: "Tell Elsie to take for herself the black alpaca dress in the south bed-room, and the two pink gingham aprons and green striped flannel dresses in the bureau in the west room for the little girls."[22]

The deception had the anticipated effect, for its recipient drew the desired conclusion: "I believe the slave-holders wrote it themselves," said Elsie when she read the letter. "They thought, as [Mrs. Haviland] was a widow, she'd have a black dress, and you know she hasn't got one in the house. And where's the pink aprons and green striped dresses? And there's no south bedroom in this house. It's all humbug; and I sha'n't stir a step until I see Mrs. Haviland."[23]

Now Delia's postscript to the Mason letter served the same purpose as Laura's, for it is evident from Calvin Fairbank's autobiography that the "J. Brown" in question is the very man who sent him on his mission to Lexington to bring out Gilson Berry's family (and one of the addressees of Calvin's letter of October 1, 1844). "I was passing Chapel Hall at Oberlin, Ohio, in August, 1844," Calvin writes in his autobiography, "when a call from an upper window drew my attention. 'Brother Fairbank!' It was John M. Brown, now Rev. John M. Brown, D.D., a bishop in the African Methodist Episcopal Church."[24] Webster would have known John Mifflin Brown (1817-1893) in Oberlin when they were both students there in 1842; in 1844 he was studying in Detroit, though from Fairbank's autobiography it is clear that in August of that year he was back in Oberlin.[25]

Brown, of course, *was* black. So when Delia Webster affirms that "Brown is not black" she was essentially saying that black is white, and thus adding the postscript that, like Laura Haviland's, deconstructs the letter.

The letter contains at least one other untruth, obvious to the recipient if not to others. The addressee is evidently an inhabitant of Oberlin, Ohio; the President Mahan therein mentioned was at that time president of Oberlin College (and would so serve until 1851). For Webster to write "knowing as I do, that your community are violently opposed to servants, who have eloped from the masters, finding an asylum in Oberlin" is like saying John Mifflin Brown is not black. It is so incongruous a statement that one wonders how Ben Wood and Thomas Megowan could have been fooled by it. As Nat Brandt writes in *The Town That Started the Civil War* (the town being Oberlin), "For nearly a quarter-century until 1861, a constant stream of runaway slaves passed through. . . . Harboring and helping the runaways were standard practice. . . . In fact, six well-established routes of the Underground Railroad ran through Oberlin. . . . As many as three thousand escaped slaves were said to have found a haven, at least temporarily," in the town.[26] The college had been founded in 1834 by students and faculty from Lane Theological Seminary in Cincinnati who were frustrated by the refusal of Lane's board of trustees to allow open discussion of abolition. Harriet Beecher Stowe's father, Lyman Beecher, was President of Lane at the time and did not provide adequate leadership to prevent the departure of most of the seminary's students and its resultant demise. "The institution never fully recovered," writes Joan D. Hedrick. "Between 1836 and 1840 the average class size dwindled to five students. There were no students at all in 1845."[27]

While on the underground route in Ohio, "the Haydens were warned that slavecatchers lay in wait along their anticipated route of flight toward Oberlin," with the result that "their course was rerouted to Sandusky, Ohio, where sympathetic Quakers nourished them until they crossed the Canadian border."[28] Webster writes to Mason of another letter, addressed to President Mahan (the one in which she "did not say half what I wished to"), that she had mailed earlier; the Mason letter, on the other hand, was not mailed, but went with its "bearer, Mr. Wood." Evidently Webster's letter to Mahan constituted the warning that saved the Haydens. Fairbank's letter could have served that purpose, too, but is less likely to have done so, as it was addressed to Buffalo, not Oberlin. His letter is dated October 5, while her letter to Mahan was apparently mailed some time before October 7 (thus at most a day after Calvin's, on October 6); therefore the news it bore of Wood's impending arrival would have reached Mahan before word could have arrived from Buffalo.

In her letter to Garrison, Webster would also say of the Mason letter:

> [It] was taken to the press by a slaveholder, who knew my sentiments, and who was one of my most vigilant enemies. He was, at the time, under the influence of powerful excitement, vexation and disappointment, having been defeated in his infamous design to murder a prominent abolitionist. I afterwards heard him say that his defeat was the result of fears of losing his own life by a mob of runaways. What he wished to accomplish by the publication of the letter, I never knew. Said letter savored more of *policy*, perhaps, than would be approved by some. But as there was no wish, expectation or purpose to deceive the person to whom it was addressed, and as none others had a right to its contents, I do not censure myself for penning it, and only regret its publication, lest the Southern slaveholder draw the inference that I think the North ought to deliver up fugitive slaves, which is not the fact.[29]

It would appear that the "prominent abolitionist" was none other than Cassius Clay, and the slaveholder Robert Wickliffe, Jr., son of the man who escorted Eliza from the auction where Calvin Fairbank bought her freedom in 1843. An incident at Russell's Cave in which Clay was assaulted by Sam Brown ("Clear the way, and let me kill the damned rascal"), and escaped with his life only because Brown's bullet struck Clay's bowie knife scabbard, just above his heart, had in Clay's estimation been orchestrated by Wickliffe.

Clay had challenged the veracity of a handbill Wickliffe had been waving in his stump speech (he was running for Congress, while Clay was supporting his opponent) when Brown took aim. According to Clay's memoirs, at the subsequent trial Brown had deserted his proslavery friends and become "my principal witness. He proved that there was a consultation . . . between himself, Wickliffe, Prof. J.C. Cross . . . , Jacob Ashton, and Ben. Wood, a police bully; that the pistol with which I was shot was loaded in advance; that he was to bring on the affray, and they were to aid; that the four went in the same hack to Russell's Cave, and there all took part in the fight."[30]

What makes it especially likely that Clay and Wickliffe are the persons to whom Webster refers is the presence on the scene of "Ben. Wood, a police bully"—the same Ben Wood for whom Webster and Fairbank were writing their letters of introduction. If Wood and Wickliffe were co-conspirators in the attempted murder of Cassius Clay, they could well have worked together, as Webster charges that they did, to publish her letter to Mason in the *Ohio Statesman*. Wood had possession of the letter, as is apparent from its first line. The incident at Russell's Cave had taken place just the year before, in 1843; Wickliffe could thus have still been, "at the time, under the influence of powerful excitement, vexation and disappointment." Delia's remark that Wickliffe was "one of my most vigilant enemies" takes on added significance with the realization that the Glass boarding house was directly across Second Street from "Glendower," the Wickliffe mansion.[31] If Wickliffe was that vigilant, she must have imagined that her comings and goings at the Glass residence were the object of some scrutiny.

It is apparent from Webster's letter to Mason that not only the Haydens, but Gilson Berry as well would be the object of Ben Wood's search. It was Berry, it will be remembered, who was responsible for Calvin Fairbank's being in Lexington in the first place. He had persuaded him to go to Kentucky to rescue his wife and other members of his family; the rescue proved impossible, and the money he had promised Fairbank was not to be found. In no other document extant from Webster's hand is there any mention of Gilson Berry. She always denied as well, at least on paper, that she had any part in the Hayden rescue, but of course Fairbank's writings make it clear that she did.

But to realize that she had anything to do with Berry comes as a surprise. The absence of any reference to Berry is due to the fact that her involvement in his rescue did not come up at her trial, at least not in the record of it—which of course is almost entirely *her* record. Yet, apparently an incriminating letter on this subject was presented to the grand jury, where the rules of evidence are less stringent. According to the *Lexington Observer and Reporter*, "A letter was found in her trunk, on her arrest, from a man in

Ohio, returning her the thanks of a negro man, belonging to Mr. Berry, in the neighboring county of Clark, for her assistance in procuring for him his freedom, and giving her directions in what manner to proceed to ensure the freedom of his wife, his mother, and sister. The letter was proven to have been brought to her from Oberlin, Ohio, by a Mr. Smith, of Jessamine, and delivered to her, but could not be read as evidence in the case for which she was then held on trial."[32]

In her account of the trial, Delia does record the moment when the prosecution tried to introduce the letter, but nowhere does she reveal its contents.

> Smith: I delivered a letter to Miss Webster, and think this (Brown's) is the same; I got the letter from a young man in Ohio, in a book store, in Oberlin. (Brown's letter offered by Commonwealth, and *rejected*.)
>
> Coons: The letters now shown to me were *first* placed in *my* hand by *Mrs. Glass*, at her house; I saw Miss Webster, and she admitted the reception of Brown's letter, and said she intended showing it to Mrs. Glass, but failed; she denied having any thing to do with the escape of the negroes, and also that she knew any thing about it. —(Letters referred to here, *rejected*.)[33]

(This of course is the J. Brown—John Mifflin Brown—to whom she alludes in her postscript to the Mason letter.) Given that Webster would sedulously omit any mention of Gilson Berry in the future it is remarkable that she should make such a potentially self-incriminating statement as this, that "*Gilson*, or whatever his name be, ran off very much in my debt." She evidently lent him money to further his escape. But why she would admit any acquaintance with him in a letter she was giving to Ben Wood is something of a mystery. Perhaps she intended to concoct a story that would have got her off the hook if the Brown letter should prove admissible in court: that she simply lent Berry money, which without her knowledge or intent made possible an escape for which she was not responsible. Perhaps she in reality lent him no money at all, but did help him escape, and would later be able to say that the gratitude he expressed through Brown's letter was for the loan of the money, which in his mind was equivalent to his ticket to freedom.

Another letter bearing news from an escaped slave would soon arrive in Lexington, though in this instance it would come directly from the former slave himself. Dated from Amherstburg (West Canada—now Ontario) October 27, 1844, it was addressed, in care of "Lewis Postlewait Esq.," to Lewis Baxter (with Thomas Grant one of the writer's two former co-owners) and its author was Lewis Hayden. The delight Hayden felt in having achieved his escape is evident. So too is his desire to tell his masters what he had been really thinking all those years he spent pretending to be the happy slave, grateful for the mildness of Kentucky bondage. "Sir, you have already discovered me absent. This will give notice where & why. I never was a great friend to the institution of robbing & crushing slavery & have finally become sick of the whole concern & have concluded for the present to try freedom & how it will seem to be my own master & manage my own matters & crack my own whip."[34] Slavery, in Hayden's estimation, is fundamentally robbery, and now that he has recovered the self that had been stolen, he is ready to make up for lost time: "I may not, even though a Freeman, expect at this late date, to become familiar with the Arts & Sciences as if I had never been robbed, & even now I have to get an *Amanuensis* to pen down my broken, irregular & incoherent thoughts but I am now sitting with writing implements in my hand & have been already at school & mean to go more & my little Son is going to school and I intend shall be able to wield his own pen at the instance & impulse of his own swelling Soul."

Dignity is what Hayden desires, and the chance to develop his own sense of self. "I once heard of a poor slave, who in passing by a swine's residence, wished himself a hog, because, said he, he eat, he drink, he walk about like a gentleman. I also have at length concluded to try how it will seem to walk about like a gentleman *my share* of the time. I am willing to labour, but am also desirous to act the gentleman, with all the important mien that attaches to a man, who is *indeed*, in truth, *himself*, the self, identical I. The very living being of whom Locke wrote in his essays." Surely few slave narratives move with such ease from the barnyard to John Locke's *Essay Concerning Human Understanding*. Did this book figure among those Hayden read inthe time he could steal from his duties at thePhoenix Hotel? Or did his "amanuensis" slip in the reference?

"I should not have left so soon," he continues, "had I not expected my sale might possibly be on hand, which I expected soon to take place in consequence of the death of one of my joint owners, your Colleague." Since the letter is addressed to Lewis Baxter, he must be alluding to Thomas Grant. Grant did not commit suicide, though Hayden seems to have thought he was going to: "Like many other poor wretched Slaves [he] became tired of wallowing in sin & concluded to throw off the burden by dashing into the presence of the Omniscient Judge."

He likewise harbors ill feeling toward the man to whom he was hired out, Lewis Postlewait, who "was so very full of grace & Methodism as to come & open our poor People's meeting by singing & Prayer, but yet forbid me going to meeting & declare if I did, he would make me feel the power of his wrath." Hayden's ambiguous attitude toward Christianity, on which his friends would comment in later years, is already evident here: "For going &

trying to serve my God, that old blue Methodist Professor was either about to flog me or take from me my head. I thought if that was Religion I would be off & more than this I think such an one better prepare to fight than pray, & so am I & I could fight him with a good stomach til I have taught him manners if no more."

The fight he anticipates with Postlewait arises from a fantasy of making war on the United States slavocracy in an alliance with Canada and Mexico. It would make possible a triumphant return to the Bluegrass: "In my leisure walks I have had occasion to inspect the solid, regular-angled piles of cannon balls & I thought Old John Bull's blue Pills, would be rather severe even for a well man, & if one dread sickness, like the Grecian Youth who refuses to meet a Physician lest he should get sick, they must shear off & should John Bull not be able to do sufficient execution, we can swing around the corner & file in with Mexico to oppose the Texian annexation. This will perhaps be the only way I can ever avenge my wrongs, & then I should perhaps meet with Capt Postlewait."

Hayden has greetings, too, for "my Brother Whig, the Editor of the Observer & Reporter." Though he may just be exaggerating the extent of his circle of friends, he could have made the editor's acquaintance in the dining room of the Phoenix Hotel. Tell him, Hayden writes, that "I started electioneering for the honorable Mr. Clay" but that "in my jolting & jarring as I crossed the Old Bridge & came into the before invisible state of Freedom . . . my exit [was] so sudden as to shake all the Whigism out of me." And now that he is "in a Birney state, all in the Whig state is perfect invisibility. So that my brother Whig Editor is perfectly lost in the distance & the Fogs that envelop that whole system." James G. Birney was originally a Kentuckian, having been forced to leave the state in 1835 when he attempted to publish an antislavery newspaper in Danville.[35] In the fall of 1844, he was the Liberty Party candidate for president, running against Democrat James Polk and in particular against Whig candidate Henry Clay. Hayden's interest in politics was longstanding. While traveling with one of his previous owners, the clock-peddler who took him about the state, he had gleaned much from overhearing tavern conversations about parties and candidates. He once told Judge Tom Marshall that he was a Democrat because Andrew Jackson "put an end to the United States Bank, and by that means broke up the slave trade."[36]

The letter is laced with irony. The story of the slave who wished himself a hog, for example, is subject to more than one interpretation. Is it testimony to the degradiation of slavery, to say that a hog leads a better life? Or is it that slaveholders who think themselves gentlemen are really swine? Or is it just self-deprecating humor? I know that to be a gentleman is swinish, but I want to be one all the same.

Could he have sincerely meant the letter's closing? "So farewell to you, but yet still remain your affectionate Friend." He was indeed in some uncertainty at the moment he signed (or dictated) his signature. "Lewis Hayden" is marked out, replaced by "Lewis Grant." He did not become Lewis Hayden until his arrival in Canada, having been known in Lexington as Lewis Grant. Slaves customarily were given the last name of their owner when they were allowed any last name at all; Thomas Grant of course was, with Lewis Baxter, one of Hayden's owners at the time of his escape, though he had had other owners before then. The reason for the crossing-out may have been that he was not yet certain what name he was going to adopt, or that he intended to live as Lewis Hayden while in Canada but realized that he did not wish to share that knowledge with his former owners, in order to avoid recapture should he venture back into the States. Lewis's hesitancy about whether he should be known as Hayden or Grant may also reflect a genuine search for personal identity, as his expressed desire to become "in truth, *himself,* the self, identical I" reveals.

Though "robbed," in his words, of his time, his labor, and his chance for an early education, Lewis Hayden nevertheless had a remarkable career yet before him. The hopes he held out for his son would prove attainable for himself as well, for he too would in years to come have the opportunity to exercise his powers of argument and "wield his own pen at the instance & impulse of his own swelling Soul."

3

"PARTNER OF HIS GUILT"

Meanwhile, Delia Webster was demanding to see a lawyer. Beseiged by visitors, some prying for incriminating information, others offering unsolicited advice, she insisted on having her day in court, but insisted too on obtaining the services of competent counsel. She was told it didn't matter, the court would appoint her one. Only after she had interested the deputy sheriff, Waller Rodes, in her behalf was she able to get word out to General John McCalla, who agreed to take her case. Her first choice had been Henry Clay, which was only natural as Clay had the reputation of near-invincibility as a trial lawyer in his native state. Though he was the Whig candidate for president in 1844, Clay remained in Lexington for the duration of the fall campaign. But it is difficult to imagine that he would have allowed himself to be distracted from the presidential contest to take up Delia Webster's defense. His distant kinsman, Cassius Clay, was out on the hustings on his behalf in New York and New England. Well regarded among Northern abolitionists, Cassius sought to persuade members of the Liberty Party, who had nominated James G. Birney, that his cousin Henry was their best chance of electing a president who would stop the expansion of slavery into Texas.

Typical of his national role as the "Great Compromiser," Clay adopted a middle-of-the-road position on slavery. He was founder and president of the American Colonization Society, which advocated gradual emancipation and resettlement of blacks, with their consent, in Liberia. Clay apparently believed, according to his recent biographer, Robert V. Remini, "that the ultimate end of slavery would come if the laws of economics and population were permitted to operate." Eventually, free labor would become cheaper than slave labor, and the southern states "would free their blacks and presumably ship them back to Africa."[1] Colonization was an inherently racist idea, based as it was on the notion that the real problem was the presence itself of blacks in American society. Cassius Clay, though no colonizationist, based much of his argument for emancipation along similar lines, that free labor was more efficient than slave, repeatedly citing the greater prosperity of Ohio farms compared to their Kentucky counterparts. Despite the fact that Democratic candidate James K. Polk of Tennessee was an out-and-out Southerner on the slavery issue and favored the annexation of Texas, Cassius was not able to win New York for the "Sage of Ashland," and it was precisely the New York vote for Birney that would deny Clay the presidency on November 5, 1844. Delia Webster's plight, as reported in the abolitionist press, contributed in at least some small way to Clay's defeat. Her arrest and imprisonment was certainly an embarrassment to the Whigs, as may be judged from these impassioned words in the *Emancipator* for November 20, 1844: "For the elevation of the great embodiment, Kentucky's favorite son, they are billing and cooing for abolition votes, upon the alleged ground, that he is no enemy to the cause; while, at the same time, a fair daughter of the Green Mountains tenants a *Kentucky prison*, almost in sight of Ashland, upon a charge of being friendly to the cause. This is the sympathy of Henry Clay's friends at *home* for abolitionists. Let every true abolitionist remember this fact, when he is entreated to trifle with his vote by casting for the Whig candidate for the presidency."

Though Delia Webster wanted Henry Clay to be her lawyer, jailor Megowan "objected to my sending for Mr. Clay," and so she settled for John M. McCalla. Commended for "distinguished" service in the First Battle of the Raisin in 1813, which saw Kentucky's six companies of volunteers go down to ignominious defeat at the hands of the British and Indians, McCalla, according to Lexington historian George Ranck, writing in 1872, "was well known for his bold and skillful support of the Democratic party. He was a clear, astute, and efficient political debater, and is well remembered for his earnestness, energy, and integrity."[2] Remini paints a rather different picture. In the 1844 election McCalla, together with Robert Wickliffe and James Guthrie, "formed a particularly vicious group of Kentucky scandal mongers. . . . McCalla, for example, circulated tales that Clay had gambled on board the steamboat from Wheeling to Maysville every time he returned from Washington. . . . And when Clay went to Blue Licks in Nicholas County for a few days of rest in late August, McCalla spread the word that he had won several hundred dollars at the gaming tables instead of taking the waters as he claimed."[3]

Webster succeeded in acquiring McCalla's services in the nick of time, for Megowan had just completed arrangements for putting her in irons and consigning her to the dungeon, where she would not want for company, but would be compelled to sleep on the naked floor. McCalla intervened, offering to pay for the room she had been occupying. Megowan refused. When McCalla, back in his law office, was narrating his difficulties with Megowan he was overheard by "a gentleman of high standing and influence from Alabama." Though a slaveholder, the Alabaman entertained certain chivalric ideals, and thus immediately leaped out of his chair and rushed to Judge Buckner to express his indignation at behavior he found to be "beyond all the bounds of propriety, and an outrage upon humanity." The judge subsequently informed the jailor that Miss Webster was to remain where she was, be treated with all due respect, and be relieved of further annoyance from uninvited visitors.[4]

Among those visitors was a journalist from the Lexington *Gazette* who reported: "We have conversed with both of the prisoners, and find them to be well-educated, and very intelligent. Miss Webster, the accomplice of Fairbank, is uncommonly well-educated, and has for some time past been teaching a female school in this city. Their crime is evidently the result of a deep seated fanaticism, which has led them to believe they were doing good service to God and humanity by stealing their neighbor's property."[5] The rival *Observer and Reporter* took a milder view of Webster's involvement, assigning all the blame to Calvin Fairbank: "Facts which have been developed are such as to leave no doubt of his guilt; and to produce the impression, that his object was mercenary, his design being to obtain such funds as the servants by prudent economy had laid up, and then, to dispose of the servants themselves for his own advantage. We understand that to cover his designs, he induced a young lady of this city to become partner of his guilt, by a pretense of a runaway matrimonial connexion with her, to be consummated at Aberdeen, Ohio."[6]

In a letter of October 12 addressed to Reverend Harvey F. Leavitt, her pastor back in Vermont, Webster provides, not without some irony, a description of her cell. It was, she writes, "very pleasant . . . being retired from the noise and bustle, though near the centre of the city. My room is large and commodious, being nineteen feet by twenty-five. It has two large windows, and a grate for burning stone coal. . . . Have a fine opportunity for reading and meditation. My food, though not of the plainest kind, has a good relish, and digests well. My sleep was never more sweet or refreshing. My dreams never more pleasant. I dance a little every day, which is the only exercise I have, except making my own bed and sweeping my room. . . . Uniformly cheerful and in good spirits[,] I seem to be a novelty to all my visitors." Fairbank, she goes on to say, is much less well treated. "It is fortunate for the present, that we are in prison, for public excitement is raging to such a height, that were we let out, I presume it would not be ten minutes before we would be inhumanly butchered in the streets, without judge or jury."[7]

This may not have been an exaggeration, for a notice appeared in all the Lexington papers on October 5 alerting the public to an "Alarming Discovery," and urging the citizens of Fayette County and the city of Lexington to attend a meeting at the courthouse on the 7th "to consult upon the means necessary to counteract the schemes of those who are striking at their interests and rights." The discovery in question was that of "the concerted action between individuals in this vicinity, and the abolition party in Ohio, by which much valuable property has been lost, and more endangered. Two of the agents have been arrested and are now in jail. . . . It is hoped that there will be a full attendance, without distinction of parties."[8]

What is more remarkable is that on November 2, the Lexington *Observer and Reporter*, a Whig paper, accused General McCalla of having written the notice himself, in complete disregard of the interest of his clients, in order to advance the fortunes of the Democratic Party against Henry Clay. Earlier in the same article, which bears the title "The Crowning Act of Infamy in the History of John M. M'Calla," the *Observer and Reporter* quotes a Democratic paper in Ohio as "representing Fairbank and Miss Webster, the negro stealers, as 'imprisoned, ironed and manacled within sight of the shades of Ashland' [Henry Clay's Lexington estate], and making it the ground of an impassioned appeal to the abolitionists against Mr. Clay." McCalla, the paper further reported, obtained a certificate from jailor Megowan attesting that Fairbank and Webster were indeed imprisoned; according to the writer of the article, McCalla pretended to obtain the certificate in order to prove to the prisoners' friends that they really were in jail so that they might contribute money to their defense, but his real object was to use it to embarrass Henry Clay in the eyes of Ohio abolitionists. In other words, "While he is engaged as the lawyer of the prisoners, counseling and advising them, and secretly writing to their Abolition friends in Ohio to excite them against Mr. Clay, he is at the same time playing false to his clients by endeavoring by the most inflammatory appeal to create public excitement and indignation against them here, that it may produce a political effect against Mr. Clay abroad."[9] As James Hillary Mulligan, born that year, was to write in his ode to the state: "Songbirds are sweetest, in Kentucky, / Thoroughbreds the fleetest . . . / The landscape is the grandest, / *And politics the damnedest,* / In Kentucky."

While Lexington's Whig newspaper was claiming that the Democrats through McCalla were trying to make political hay out of Fairbank and Webster among Ohio voters, the city's Democratic paper was trying to tar Clay with the brush of having Fairbank and Webster for friends. Fairbank, the *Lexington Gazette* claimed, had spoken in a letter discovered on his person "of having visited Mr. Clay, and of his intention to visit him again." Another letter, the incriminating one signed "Frater" quoted in the previous chapter, was "written upon a sheet of paper having the miniature of Mr.

Clay upon one corner. All these circumstances show that Fairbank is an ardent Whig. . . . These abolitionists," the paper continued, alluding to Fairbank and Webster, "are what they profess to be, Whigs. The great desire of their hearts may be comprised in two words: stealing Negroes and electing Clay."[10]

In the *Gazette* on November 9, 1844, McCalla answered all the charges made against him in the *Observer and Reporter*. Yes, he had penned the notice, but he was not the author. Thomas Megowan, the jailor, was. McCalla had merely, at Megowan's request, put it into proper wording. It was Megowan and Captain Henry Johnson who "suggested the propriety of a public meeting. . . . They came to my office, not even to consult me on its propriety, but as my office was near at hand, to ask me to shape such a notice and put it on paper as would meet Mr. Megowan's view." Furthermore, at that time he was not yet the lawyer for Webster and Fairbank. "It was not until one or two days after I had written that notice for Mr. Megowan, that I was sent for by [Webster and Fairbank], and agreed to appear for them as their attorney."[11] The certificate had been obtained at the request of his clients; that someone may have stolen it to further political designs of their own was none of his affair.

The Whig paper, seeking to have it both ways, had not only accused McCalla of betraying his clients but also taken him to task for being their lawyer in the first place. "This man is one of the electoral candidates for the state at large upon the loco foco [i.e., Democratic] ticket, and we find him the friend, counselor, and adviser of abolitionists, who have been caught in the very act of stealing the negroes of our citizens."[12] In answer to this, McCalla thundered back: "Honorable members of the legal profession, when applied to by persons under charges of any kind, always give them their professional aid, no matter how much they may be opposed to the crimes with which they are charged. . . . The accused may be innocent, the law presumes them to be so until they are convicted, and the duty of their counsel is to see that they are not condemned except according to law and evidence."[13]

Yet by December 2 McCalla had withdrawn from the case, citing the necessity of leaving Lexington for Washington, D. C. In a letter bearing that date, Webster writes to Madison C. Johnson requesting that he join her defense team to replace McCalla. That team already included Leslie Combs and his colleague Samuel Shy since at least October 12. This circumstance suggests not only that she had lined up an impressive array of legal firepower but also that the proceedings of the law make for strange political bedfellows indeed. For Leslie Combs was as ardent a supporter of Henry Clay as McCalla was an enemy; indeed, Combs was a candidate for presidential elector pledged to Clay, as McCalla was a candidate pledged to Polk.[14] That Webster was aware of the political significance of her bipartisan team is evident from her letter to Reverend Leavitt: "Please tell my father, that Gen. John M. M'Calla, a particular friend and patron of mine, and the celebrated Democratic elector of this State, together with the famous Gen. Coombs [sic], the Whig elector, and his partner, Mr. Shy, are my counsel."[15] Given the vituperation that filled the air in that political season, it is interesting to imagine McCalla and Combs sitting down together to plan Delia Webster's defense.

Combs was as distinguished a Kentuckian as McCalla. Born in 1793, he too had fought with the Kentucky volunteers in the War of 1812. On one occasion Combs crossed a hundred miles of ice and snow to carry a dispatch to William Henry Harrison. On another, he volunteered to carry the news from Fort Defiance to Fort Meigs, besieged by the British, of the impending arrival of relief forces under General Green Clay (Cassius's father); he managed to get within sight of the fort when Indians attacked his party, and he was forced to turn back. At Dudley's defeat on May 5, 1813, at the Second Battle of the Raisin, Combs was taken prisoner by the Indians and made to run the gauntlet. This "boy-captain of 1812" settled in Lexington and was admitted to the bar in 1818. Nineteenth-century local historian George Ranck characterized Combs, "lawyer, trustee of Transylvania University, member of the legislature, railroad pioneer," as "a brilliant and sparkling speaker."[16]

Whether Combs and McCalla planned it together or whether it was Delia Webster's idea, her defense was clearly going to be that she was not guilty of stealing any slaves. In the letter to Reverend Leavitt, she addresses her pastor in filial terms of endearment, writing: "Your daughter Delia is at this awful moment within the confines of the city jail. For what? . . . For nothing, I reply." Nothing, that is, except suspicion "of being tinctured with the foul blot of abolitionism." She is no abolitionist, she writes, but a colonizationist (so too was Henry Clay). She then recounts the carriage ride with Fairbank, says nothing of picking up any slave passengers, but does relate that at about the same time three slaves were discovered to be missing; suspicion naturally fell upon Fairbank and her. Her letters were seized. One was found "addressed to me, written, as is supposed, by an abolitionist. It is on account of this letter that I am retained in custody." An article in William Garrison's *Liberator* of November 29 adds some helpful detail about that letter: that it mentioned "her acquaintance with Mr. F." At her trial Webster would maintain that she had not made the acquaintance of Fairbank before his arrival in Lexington.

In her letter to Leavitt Webster engages in some extraordinarily wishful thinking. "The Hon. Henry Clay has also given me encouragement of appearing in my behalf. If he does, all will be well, as he is a great favorite in this community. . . . I am advised to employ the Hon. Daniel Webster, but the want of funds prevents my writing to him." As the *Emancipator* commented,

"Think of Henry Clay and Daniel Webster defending this woman! The two very foci of the forensic skill and eloquence of this republic, could they have a worthier client or a weightier cause?"[17]

The *Emancipator*'s defense of Delia Webster's conduct was not universally shared among the abolitionist press. The *Spirit of Liberty* comments on her letter to Reverend Leavitt: "With full appreciation of the unpleasant position of this lady . . . we must decidedly condemn the spirit which she manifests in speaking of the 'chivalrous' Kentuckians. . . . Surely she cannot be a true Yankee woman. . . . The stones of her prison walls should cry out before she should give utterance to praise of the Vandal Slaveholding women-whippers, whose vengeance she provoked by daring to be a friend of poor Fairbank, who, it appears, is an Abolitionist, unequivocally, and therefore cannot hope for mercy."[18] Webster's hopes for mercy are evident in her praise of Kentuckians' native chivalry, to which this writer took offense. "Kentuckians little know the friendship they are abusing," she wrote Leavitt. "This gallant State is not aware of the strength of my attachment. She little thinks she has a warm-hearted friend and advocate in her inoffensive, submissive prisoner. And though I am doomed, through mistaken apprehensions, to finish out my three score years in yonder den of criminals and felons, still, sir, *I love Kentucky* . . . as though it were *my own dear native land*. . . . After this hand has ceased to move, may this testify to the *manly bravery, noble generosity, the zealous patriotism, and chivalry of proud Kentucky*."[19]

One can well imagine that such words as these formed the gist of her defense to the Lexingtonians who visited her in her cell. By her own admission she told them this as well: "Tell my beloved father it seems to have a very happy influence on the minds of the people, when I tell them that I was not brought up to be an abolitionist. . . . If . . . they could know to a certainty that my father is pro-slavery, and had ever been an enemy and strenuous opposer to the abolition cause, I have no doubt it would operate greatly to my advantage."[20] Benajah Webster, according to the *Emancipator*, "is well known by the citizens of Vergennes and Ferrisburgh, to have been always hostile to abolition in any form; indeed, has been noted for his ultra opinions on this subject."[21]

The citizens of Ferrisburgh, Vermont, which neighbored Vergennes, came to Delia Webster's defense. A public meeting was held November 13, 1844, to consider her case, and in particular the "reports . . . in circulation through the public prints, prejudicial to [her] character." A committee was appointed, which included Rowland T. Robinson, agent of the Underground Railroad at "Rokeby" and the father of writer Rowland E. Robinson, to ascertain, "through authentic sources, the facts in relation to the character and standing of said D.A. Webster, embracing so much of her past history as may have any bearing upon her present circumstances." The investigative committee reported that she had united with the Congregational Church in Vergennes at an early age, "and remained in full fellowship" until her departure for the Southwest, "being regarded as one of more than ordinary piety and conscientiousness." They allude to "her unblemished character," and add that "both as a school teacher, and as a member of civil and religious society, her deportment has been such as to gain the esteem of a large circle of friends, who deeply sympathize with her in her present unhappy condition."[22]

Webster's health began to suffer from the strain of her imprisonment. She particularly regretted Megowan's decision to screw her windows shut so that she might have no further communication with Fairbank. In her December 2 letter to Madison C. Johnson, she complains that while God freely bestows his gift of "pure and invigorating atmospheric air" on all creatures, she is denied it. Denied, too, "the varied beauties of the horizon,—the blushes of the morning, the radiant clouds of twilight, the rising or the setting sun," all of which "never smile upon my casement."[23] By October 28, she had fallen ill, and between November 7 and December 5 was "unable to sit up for my bed to be made" (though not every prison inmate has been able to enjoy maid service). On December 10, her father, Benajah, arrived in Lexington, having left Vermont thirteen days earlier, as indicated in a letter from her mother, Esther, printed in the December 25, 1844 issue of the *Emancipator*: "My mind is so much agitated I can hardly use my pen. My husband started for Kentucky Nov. 28th, an aged man with slender health. It was thought by some imprudent to undertake a journey of 1000 miles at this season of the year, but he could not rest by day or night, and said he would go and see if there could be anything done to relieve our unfortunate child. . . . The people here have much sympathy for our distressed daughter, and wish to do something for her relief. I hope we shall not remain in suspense long."

In her letter of November 23 to the Honorable Richard Buckner, who was to preside at her trial, Webster requested a dismissal of the case or, failing that, a speedy trial. She was by then aware than McCalla would be drawn out of town by business in Washington the following week, and said she wished her trial to take place while he could still defend her. But the Commonwealth's attorney was not ready, so Buckner fixed the date for December 17, Delia Webster's twenty-seventh birthday. She secured the services of Madison C. Johnson to replace McCalla; Combs and Shy remained on the defense team.

At ten on the morning of Tuesday, December 17, 1844, proceedings began. The brick courthouse was filled to capacity with the outraged and the curious. It was, writes J. Winston Coleman, the first case of its kind in city's history. "For five days excited men and women packed the circuit court room, crowded the aisles and stood with craning necks in the corridors, as the distinguished lawyers for the defense made a vigorous fight for their two abolitionist clients."[24] Coleman may have been wrong about the women, if Webster is to be believed: "It was expected that the audience would consist principally of ladies, it being generally known that they had made their arrangements to attend. But the day previous to my trial, reports were circulated that the facts developed in evidence would shock the delicacy of females, and that it would be unfit for them to attend. . . . The ladies . . . were thus kept away, and not another female entered the Court house" except for two female witnesses.[25]

To Delia Webster's discomfiture, Calvin Fairbank was led into the courtroom. They were to be tried together. Her lawyers objected, fearing the general sentiment already evident against him would prejudice her case. "Beside this, the testimony in his case was of an entirely different character from that in mine."[26] The evidence against him, that is, was much more compelling. After all, the prosecution had the "Frater" letter they had found in his pocket. In the letter, dated September 24, 1844, and addressed to a friend in Oberlin, Fairbank speaks of all his difficulty locating Gilson Berry's wife and child and the money Berry had promised; his making the acquaintance of "one Lewis," and of his plan to effectuate his escape and that of Hayden's wife and child. Most damagingly for Delia, he writes of a "Miss W.": "Miss W. will not come away, but will come across the river with us; then I shall have to put these on the . . . underground line and send them on, till I go back with Miss W." Keeping the unsent letter on his person seems out of character for the experienced and prudent Fairbank, but keep it he did—until Megowan found it. Though he had signed it "Frater" instead of with his name and claimed it was not in his handwriting, the letter was devastatingly incriminatory.[27] It sealed his fate, and would seal Webster's—unless she could prevent the prosecution from introducing it in court. The prosecution would have first to prove a conspiracy between her and Fairbank before they could introduce it in evidence against her. The Commonwealth's attorney was also in possession of a letter from Fairbank to Webster "proposing to come over and assist her in running off slaves." Mrs. Glass, the landlady, had found it in her diligent search of Webster's trunk. But the rules of evidence forbade the introduction of this letter, "on the principle laid down in Greenleaf . . . that the mere possession of letters, not proved to be answered, is no evidence of acquiescence in their contents.[28]

Webster won the right to be tried separately. Fairbank then applied for a continuance, stating that "some of his most important witnesses were absent, particularly a Mr. Allen, of New York, by whom he expected to prove that there were no negroes in company with him on his journey to Maysville."[29] The *Emancipator* of March 19, 1845, would report that a son of the Reverend John Rankin, who operated a station on the Underground Railroad in Ripley, Ohio, wrote a letter to the *Cincinnati Herald* in which he declared "That Mr. Allen and Miss Smith accompanied them to Ripley, Ohio, and were married by Rev. John Rankin, I know to be false. Mr. Rankin has never heard or or seen Mr. Allen or Miss Smith." These were the names assigned to Lewis and Harriet Hayden, who were made up to pass for white in the carriage. Thus what Fairbank had in mind in asking for a continuance so that a Mr. Allen of New York could be sought was apparently to suborn a white friend who would pretend in court to be the Mr. Allen of the eloping couple. Either that, or—more likely, since when Fairbank did come to trial he pled guilty and threw himself upon the mercy of the court—he wanted to further Webster's defense by giving some color to her claim, should she choose to make it, that there were no persons with them in the hack but white persons.

In pleading for a continuance, Fairbank also said that his lawyer John M. McCalla had recently departed the city, and that he had no other counsel (evidently he did not share in Webster's representation by Johnson, Combs and Shy). The court then appointed William B. Kinkead as his counsel, and granted his application; Fairbank was remanded to jail.

Delia Webster was asked how she pled to the charges: not guilty. Selection of the jury began. Her lawyers did their best to avoid the obviously prejudiced; but there was possibly no one eligible to serve who had not heard of the case and already formed an opinion. By one o'clock only one juryman had been chosen. After a half-hour break for dinner, the examination of jurors resumed, and consumed the rest of the afternoon. "By being a little less particular," writes Webster, "we accepted eleven more," so a complete jury was found by the time the court adjourned as darkness fell. When the trial resumed at ten on the morning of December 18, the parade of witnesses began. Thomas Grant was called to the stand to say that he and Mr. Baxter were the owners of Lewis. "He left on Saturday after the races at Lexington; I have not heard from him or where he is, since he left." H.G. Musick, the Washington innkeeper, testified that Fairbank and Webster stayed at his house from midnight Sunday night until daybreak, and that he sat with them in the room the whole time. They talked of runaway matches and marriage. "They did not say they *were* married . . . but I inferred they were." (Perhaps this was the kind of testimony calculated to frighten away the ladies.) One of their horses looked fatigued; they said nothing of having gone to Ohio. But he did recall having seen the same hack on the way to Maysville earlier that day.[30]

Mrs. Glass said that Webster left with Fairbank on Saturday saying she was going to Versailles and inviting her daughter to accompany her. On her return, Webster told her she had been with Fairbank to assist a runaway match. Contradicting herself, at one point she testifies that she did not look in Webster's room for letters until after her arrest, then later that "before Miss Webster's return"—that is, before her arrest—"I opened her door with another key, and myself and daughter went into her room." Her husband then testified that upon their first meeting Fairbank and Webster appeared to meet as strangers. "He said he wished to talk with her and they went into another room; I think bedroom." Mrs. Glass then returned to the stand to correct her husband: It wasn't a bedroom but a parlor.[31]

Parker Craig was called to establish that Fairbank rented the hack and driver from his livery stable on September 28, that he and Patterson Bain met them on their return in Paris, saw that one of the horses was not his, argued about who would pay, "asked Fairbank why he went off with this lady to get married" and was told he had not but had helped a couple from Paris elope.[32] Missing from Webster's version of the trial, but present in that of the *Louisville Journal*, copied in the *Western Law Journal*, is the interesting exchange that then followed, according to Parker Craig. Craig asked Fairbank what were the names of the eloping couple "when Miss Webster sharply told Fairbank *not to answer the question.*"[33] It is significant that this passage of Craig's testimony should be omitted from Webster's account, as it not only casts a shadow on her claims of innocence but, more intriguingly, suggests a quite different sort of relationship between her and Fairbank than she would have us believe. In her version of the story, she is consistently portrayed as a submissive, not to say ignorant, female; in the fuller picture, at that particular moment at least, it is she who calls the shots, telling Calvin to shut up, almost as if she were the mastermind of the whole adventure.

Patterson Bain then testified that his property, the slaves Harriet and Jo, were discovered missing on September 29. He sent two slave catchers, Mssrs. McLaughlin and Wood, to Ohio to fetch them but they came back empty-handed.

The examination of these and other witnesses took up the second and third days of the trial. The prosecution kept trying to introduce the "Frater" letter but the defense's objections were consistently sustained. "One of the prosecuting attorneys," writes Webster, "urged the admission of the letter, and with much warmth, declared that unless it were admitted, he could not argue the case, as there was not ground for argument."[34] Finally on the fourth day of the trial, "to our surprise," she writes, Judge Buckner "admitted the letter." Webster does not, in her account of the trial, explain why the judge changed his mind. But the *Louisville Journal*'s account, as reported in the *Western Law Journal*, does: The prosecution finally figured out a way to establish the existence of a conspiracy between Fairbank and Webster. It turned upon the fiction Webster had put forth in conversation with one of those incessant visitors to her Megowan Hotel cell, a fiction she wisely chose not to try out at her trial, about the eloping couple. Nevertheless the tale of the runaway match did come out in the trial:

> Jas. Keiser: (Called a second time by Commonwealth.) Had talked with Miss Webster in jail and she said there were persons got in the hack between this place and Paris.
> H.B. Franklin: States that he was present in jail when Cunningham was talking with Miss Webster, and heard her say in response to his questions, that three persons got into the hack between this and Paris—a man, woman, and child; but they were all white persons. . . .
> Cunningham (introduced by defendant): States that he was talking with Miss Webster soon after her arrest, and Mr. Franklin was also there. She denied that any negroes got into the hack. She said she knew nothing of their escaping, and if Fairbank was guilty, he had imposed upon her. She also stated that she thought she was going to Versailles, and had been decoyed on by Fairbank, on missions of business in preaching, &c.[35]

Unfortunately, verbatim transcripts of court proceedings were not kept in 1844, and Delia Webster's *Kentucky Jurisprudence: A History of the Trial of Miss Delia A. Webster*, which she published in 1845, is the closest we can come to a complete record of the trial, untrustworthy as it may be. Webster claims that she reproduces in *Kentucky Jurisprudence* "all the testimony which was introduced[,] a copy of which is now in the possession of Governor Owsley, and was approved of by the attornies for the Commonwealth, and certified by Judge Buckner" (the governor's copy has not survived).[36] Yet there are some points in which it differs from the summary given in the *Louisville Journal* and reprinted in the *Western Law Journal*—Musick's testimony, for example, about whether Fairbank and Webster were locked alone together in his inn or he was present with them all night, and Craig's claim that she spoke "sharply" to Fairbank telling him not to give the names of the eloping couple.

Most significantly, the *Western Law Journal* summary states that "It was then proven that in a conversation held subsequently to her arrest, Miss Webster had declared that she had gone with Fairbank to assist a runaway couple to get married. . . . In another conversation, she was asked where the negroes got into the hack. She answered, no negroes got in. But between this place and Paris three persons, a man, a woman, and a child . . . got into the hack; but added, they were all white persons, to her unknown."[37] Only the second of these two conversations reported in testimony at the trial is reproduced in Webster's version. The second, with the child as a third passenger, seems not likely to have had anything to do with a runaway match. Thus Webster in *Kentucky Jurisprudence* is suppressing the testimony concerning the supposed elopement. The *Western Law Journal* account at that juncture goes on to say, "The Commonwealth, having previously several times attempted to read the letter of Fairbank, was now permitted to do so."

One or both of these cover stories apparently sufficed to persuade the Court that a conspiracy did exist between Webster and Fairbank. The elopement story, at least—even if everyone knew it was false—established that there was a prior conspiracy, that is, a conspiracy to help the couple elope. The "Frater" letter, with its incriminating mention of the role to be played by a "Miss W.," was read aloud to the jury.

Friday, December 20, was given over to the final pleas of defense and prosecution. In her account, Webster gives praise all round. Samuel Shy began "with an address, deep, impressive, and full of feeling." He was followed by the second of her three lawyers, Madison C. Johnson, who made a "profound, disinterested and noble plea." The prosecution, though outnumbered three to two, then got a chance to speak in the person of A.H. Robertson, making "an eloquent appeal for the Commonwealth" that "would do credit to the greatest talents." General Leslie Combs, "true patriot and philanthropist," made the final appeal for the defense. "The natural dictates of his superior mind—the generous effusions of his warm heart, aided by the solemnity of the twilight hour, seemed to open the channel of feeling, and brought tears from the eyes of many of his auditors." Richard Pindell's closing speech for the prosecution was so good, wrote Webster, that she "could hardly suppress the rising wish that he, too, had been employed for the defendant. . . . His every breath seemed to inspire them with his own sedulous care for the safety of the Commonwealth."[38]

In his instructions to the jury, Judge Buckner told them to consider the letter only if they should previously decide that there was a conspiracy. On the evening of December 20 the case was given to the jury, who did not deliberate in secret, according to a complaint made by Benajah Webster. They were boarding at the Megowan Hotel, as was he, and "even after the case was given them, they were in the house mixing with the company indiscriminately," taking their meals with the other boarders, of whom there were "about one hundred." On Saturday morning the jury returned a verdict of guilty, recommending a sentence of two years in the state penitentiary.

But the jury did one thing more. They presented Delia Webster with a letter, signed by all twelve, addressed to the governor of Kentucky, William Owsley, "praying him to interpose his executive power in my behalf, and grant an immediate pardon, before the sentence should be pronounced." Something in her plight must have moved them to seek a way to extend mercy. As the *Frankfort Commonwealth* put it, "The Jury signed a petition to the Governor, praying her pardon on account of her sex."[39]

Webster, however, did not want a pardon; she wanted a new trial. To get a pardon she would have to ask for it, and to ask for it normally involved an admission of guilt. Furthermore, she had only been tried on one of the indictments against her, that of the theft of Lewis Hayden. Other indictments still stood, accusing her of stealing Harriet and Jo.[40] It would be hard indeed, she wrote, to spend two years in the penitentiary only to be tried then on the other indictments, "at which time my witnesses might be in foreign lands, if not in the world of spirits." So Combs and Shy did move for a new trial, principally on the grounds of the defendant having been surprised by evidence introduced by the prosecution (principally the "Frater" letter) and of improper evidence (again the letter) having been given to the jury. In her affidavit requesting a new trial Webster stated that her counsel had advised her against calling Fairbank as a witness at the first trial but that at her second trial she would like to, so that he could either say he was not the author of the "Frater" letter, or if he was could explain how her name (as "Miss W.") was used in it without her consent and knowledge. She also wanted to call as new witnesses the ferry boat operators at Maysville, who would testify (and subsequently did affirm in affidavits) that they saw no one in the hack but white persons.

In a rather surprising revelation she attests that she had been so sick before her trial that during the time she was bedridden "she made no disclosures to her Counsel of the facts in her case." She claims that the reason was that she thought her illness so grave it was "very doubtful whether she would live to see the day of her trial." Only "some few days before her trial" did she tell them very much about it, and by then it was too late to get the ferrymen down from Maysville.[41]

Webster speaks in the affidavit of her regret at having spoken so freely with her unofficial interrogators during those days when her room at the Megowan Hotel was flooded with visitors. "She conceives that the conversations which were used against her"—in particular Franklin's testimony in the trial that she had told Cunningham that a man, woman, and child got into the hack between Lexington and Paris—"were not obtained from her fairly," but "in consequence of her ignorance. When first arrested, she was laboring under the belief that she was bound to answer all questions that were asked her" and for the first several days did so, until a Judge Davis told her she was not obliged to. "Some of these conversations she is sorry to say, have been misconceived to her injury."[42] She does not explain, of course, what exactly the misconception was; interestingly, she seems not so much proclaiming her innocence as arguing that no one could legally prove she was guilty.

While all that was necessary to move for a new trial was going ahead, Webster, despite her unwillingness to seek a pardon, did allow herself to be persuaded by her father and her lawyers to forward the jury's request for a pardon to the governor. Several prominent citizens—including, Webster claims (though no record of it survives), Henry Clay—sent accompanying letters "praying an immediate pardon." The one difficulty was that Webster herself would have to write a letter too. She managed to do so without admitting guilt: "Although it is humiliating and mortifying in the highest degree to the feelings of your petitioner to have such a verdict rendered against her, and much more so for her to be compelled to ask a pardon, for an offence of which she is not guilty, yet notwithstanding her feelings revolt in asking a pardon, she supposes she must, from necessity, ask it. Therefore, will you look at the evidence in her case, and extend to her such clemency as her case will justify, and her condition and sex merit," she wrote, referring to herself in the third person.[43]

At the same time, however, a hundred and twenty citizens signed a "remonstrance" urging the governor *not* to pardon Delia Webster. "We, the undersigned, citizens of Fayette County, having learned that application has been made to the Governor to pardon Delia A. Webster . . . beg leave respectfully to remonstrate against a pardon; and hereby express to the Governor our conviction that the law should be permitted, in this case, to take its regular course."[44]

The governor, for the moment, did nothing.

The court was to reconvene on January 4, 1845, after a two-week break for Christmas and New Year's. On that day her lawyers were to make the motion for a new trial. Webster claimed she had no doubt as to the outcome. But "some of my enemies boldly declared they would mob and lynch the Judge himself, if he suffered me to have another trial; and at the very moment, when I was looking for the realization of my hopes, I was ordered to rise and receive my sentence which was two years confinement at hard labor in the Penitentiary of Kentucky."[45]

At two o'clock on Friday, January 10, Delia Webster was escorted on to the train to Frankfort, site of the state capitol and of the penitentiary. In the train she meditated on her fate. "I was about to enter that living tomb; where, in addition to all other grievances, I should be in the case of such a

The Kentucky Penitentiary, from Sneed's History and Mode of Management of the Kentucky Penitentiary, *1860.*

hostile keeper as Capt. Newton Craig had been represented to be." What worried Webster was in part the web of kinship that linked the keeper of the state penitentiary to her persecutors: His wife was jailor Megowan's cousin; Craig himself was cousin to "my most vigilant enemy," Parker Craig, the livery stable owner who had hunted down Webster and Fairbank in Millersburg and "had done me so much injury through Fayette county"; on top of that, Craig's wife was Parker's sister (and thus Newton's own cousin too). "To say nothing of the Captain's feelings toward Abolitionists in general, and the thousands of dollars he has expended in consequence of their invasions," he had "the most inveterate hatred" toward "Negro stealers."[46]

"It was twilight," Webster writes, when the train reached Frankfort. She expected at any moment to meet Samuel Shy, her lawyer. But "who should appear but Capt. Craig himself, the very man of all the world I most dreaded to see." They were introduced, "and I scrutinized his every feature as closely, as the lingering rays of twilight would permit. I could see nothing in him to condemn or approve ... but still I felt an aversion not easily overcome. I entered the walls of the Penitentiary at 5 o'clock P.M., Jan. 10, 1845."[47]

4

"ON ACCOUNT OF HER SEX"

Newton Craig, born September 16, 1807, was the grandson of Joseph Craig (1741-1819) who, with his brothers Lewis and Elijah, was persecuted for professing the Baptist faith in eighteenth-century Virginia, where the Episcopal religion had the force of law. They suffered repeated imprisonment for stubbornly holding their "unlawful conventicles" and preaching without a license. Once arrested, they would lustily sing hymns through the bars of their prison, attracting large and solemn crowds.[1] Joseph, however, was a little less zealous than the others as far as imprisonment was concerned. Thinking it "no dishonor to cheat the devil," he managed on more than one occasion to escape the clutches of the law.

Lewis Craig, accompanied by Joseph, led the "Traveling Church," a congregation of five or six hundred souls, into Kentucky in 1781, where Elijah later joined them.[2] "Remarkable for his eccentric manners," Joseph was said to be "cracked some times" and a "curious sort of man." In response he said that he must have been "cracked on the right side of the head" because he "got the richest of any of the Craigs, but it was by farming," not preaching.[3] Joseph was "not as talented as . . . Lewis and Elijah" but "was very prudent in his financial concerns and was very industrious." He always had corn to sell in scarce years and "learned his children to work."[4] One of those twelve children (six sons, six daughters) was Reuben (1763-1837), who married Frances Twyman (1768-1849) in 1787. Born next to last among Reuben and Frances's nine children was Newton, who would grow up to be as prosperous as his grandfather, owning some thirty thousand acres of Scott County farmland by the time of the 1850 census and, like Joseph and his brothers, would gain an intimate knowledge of prison life. Like them he preached in jail, but it was his own, and to a captive audience: "At 9 o'clock on every Sabbath morning, a lecture is delivered in the familiar manner of domestic worship, endeavoring, by friendly counsel, to win the wicked back to purer thoughts. The apparent good effects produced by this course, are highly gratifying to my feelings."[5]

Calvin Fairbank had his own opinion of the value of Craig's Sunday School talks, which would sometimes go on for as long as three or five hours. "Invariably he poured his invective and tirades upon me over Northern Abolitionists' backs in his Sunday lectures until I became entirely disgusted." On one Sunday, Craig had been as usual devoting his Sunday School lesson to the castigation of abolitionists when Fairbank decided he had had enough and took refuge behind a pillar in the room to read a book. At length Craig took note of his lack of attention. "*Fairbank*! What are you doing?" "Reading, sir." "What are you reading for?" "Because, sir, I don't want to lose all my time here." "But, ain't I talking to you?" "Yes, sir, but I don't want to hear you talk." "What is the matter, Fairbank?" "Sir, you abuse me, and my people." "I do? Well, come out here, and sit on this front seat." He meekly obeyed. "Now, Fairbank, let us do better." Expecting to be locked in solitary and whipped with the rawhide strap, Fairbank was surprised to escape it.[6]

From 1844 to 1854 Newton Craig would serve as "Keeper of the Penitentiary" in Frankfort, having apprenticed as assistant keeper in 1833-34. The post was granted by the legislature and was in principle a profitable one. Craig and his partner William Henry were to keep a third of the profits over five thousand dollars from such prisoner-made products as hemp bagging for the New Orleans cotton market and rope, carts, carriages, sleighs, wagons, bedsteads, buckets, rocking chairs, cane-bottomed chairs, infant chairs, barrels, tongs, shovel handles, handcuffs, bridles, martingales, harnesses, trunks, saddles, boots, shoes, slippers, windowsills, and tombstones. The woodworking must have been of some sophistication, for the paint shop included such items as "Red Lead, Venetian Red, Terra de Sienna, Chrome Green, Chinese Vermilion, Gold Leaf, French Leaf, and Copper Bronze."[7]

But a disastrous fire on the night of August 30, 1844, less than six months into his term, considerably imperilled Craig's financial situation. According to William C. Sneed, the prison physician, the fire may have started by "the accidental catching of the partition, in a room, from a candle stuck against the same, by a female convict who was sleeping in the room (there being then no female prison within the walls)."[8] Unfortunately, the supply of water from the Kentucky River had been shut off that night, and it was exceedingly difficult to fight the flames. All the workshops were destroyed, with their machinery and tools. The cells were spared, but for a while it had looked as if the prisoners were going to be roasted alive. The governor appeared at the prison gates and demanded that they be released. The guard refused, saying he would shoot any man who tried. Newton Craig was sent for. He had been busy emptying the steam boiler of water so that it would not explode, as well as removing sixteen kegs of powder that had been stored in the prison yard. Craig went into the cells and calmed the inmates. Some of the more trustworthy were let out to help save the other buildings and their contents. Losses amounted to over $22,000 (the equivalent of several hundred thousand today).[9] To resume operations, Craig and Henry invested over $5,000 in the construction of a brick building 220 feet long by 40 wide to house the rope and bagging factory, in hopes the state would reimburse them.

It was to such a prison that Delia Webster was brought on the evening of January 19, 1845. A small one-room frame structure, made of "rough and plain weather boarding" had been built to house her, the only female prisoner, in the middle of the yard.[10] She was happy to note that it had five windows, and that they were not screwed shut as had been those of the Megowan Hotel. Several gentlemen of respectability escorted her to the little house, where Newton Craig read her the "Prison Rules": "At the ringing of the first bell at daylight, the prisoners will rise, dress themselves, put in order their rooms, and be in readiness for business. At the second ringing, the cell doors will be thrown open, each prisoner will then station himself at his cell door, observing profound silence." At the third bell, they were to hasten to their appointed place of labor. "Every man is required to remain in his place, nor is he permitted to leave for materials, water, or under any pretense, save to the privy, but must ring the bell for the Waiter or Foreman, who will, in all cases, provide for his wants." It was forbidden to stare at passersby. Meals were taken in silence, with a system of coded signals to indicate which dish or eating utensil was wanted: a raised hand for bread, a knife for meat, a fork for vegetables, a cup for "water, coffee, or milk (when we have them)," for soup a spoon. "When any sign is made, and not noticed, the knife, &c., may be rattled on the table and held up again."[11]

Craig made it plain that the rule against any conversation with outsiders would apply strictly in Webster's case. "If my Father should enter my house in the morning I was neither to speak to him, or pay any more attention to him than as though he were a stone, without permission from an officer." Craig asked if she saw anything to object to in the rules. She did not, and assured him that she desired no partiality. He told her that "sooner should his blood be spilt, than I should receive any abuse or unkind treatment while in his care." He concluded his remarks "with a short but very able and touching address, during which my prejudice vanished, and I came to the conclusion that if he were not a christian, he certainly appeared very much like one." Newton Craig and the gentlemen departed, and Delia Webster was left alone with her thoughts. She was afraid that, despite his sense of fairness, he bore a prejudice against her, given all the vicious rumors that had assailed her reputation. Yet she felt "happy in the thought that my *new keeper had a heart.*"[12]

On the next day, her lawyer, Samuel Shy, came to call. Webster confided in him her fear that such was the strength of Craig's prejudice against her "that any effort on my part to conciliate his feelings would be worse than useless."[13] Though it may seem unusual for a new prisoner to be so concerned about conciliating the feelings of her warden, such was the personal approach Delia Webster consistently adopted. It would eventually bear fruit.

Shy answered by saying that Craig was an independent thinker, capable of forming his own opinion of her despite what anyone else said. And he held out hope that whatever the Keeper presently thought of her, once he was made aware of all the facts "he was sure to be my friend." Webster apparently played upon Craig's paternal instincts (though he was only ten years her senior). Webster's Vermont pastor, Reverend Leavitt, assured a friend that "the keeper assures her she shall be as sedulously protected against insult as if she were his daughter."[14]

On Sunday the local ministers came calling. Soon, all of Frankfort society was beating a path to her door. These conversations, wrote Webster, "contributed very much to my enjoyment. The Legislature was then in session, and most, if not all the members of both houses called on me, and I am happy to say, expressed to me their warmest sympathies." Her social prominence was noted two weeks after her arrival by a correspondent for the *Cincinnati Gazette*: "Among the lions, or rather lionesses, here, is Miss Delia Webster."[15]

With her conviction in December, Delia Webster had again attracted national attention. W.H. Burleigh editorialized in the Hartford, Connecticut, *Christian Freeman*, an organ of the Liberty Party: "In the roll of Liberty martyrs, her name will occupy a proud eminence as the first of her sex to suffer imprisonment at the demand of that curse of curses, American Slavery."[16] The distinguished poet John Greenleaf Whittier penned a note to the *Emancipator*: "Miss Webster, the daughter of a New England farmer, is suspected of being a friend of freedom. . . . For ought we know, innocent as the angels—in a land of strangers, not to say barbarians—thousands of miles from her native mountains—this young WOMAN is cooly convicted of abolitionism . . . [and] sentenced to the penitentiary for two years!"[17] The *Broadway Journal*, for which Edgar Allan Poe had recently begun to write, featured an article dripping in sarcasm. Commenting on Webster's complaint that she had only $110 to pay legal bills amounting to $750 and to her indication that her lawyers "expose themselves to great censure by appearing at all on this exciting occasion," the writer takes a stab at Gotham wit: "Great censure probably from the other members of the profession for working so cheap." The article concludes with a comparison between Lexington, Kentucky, and Lexington, Massachusetts, site of the first battle of the Revolution. "It was very proper . . . that the first imprisonment of a helpless woman

Newton Craig. Courtesy Mrs. Galey Coleman

for her sympathies in the same cause"—that of American Independence—
"should take place in a town of the same name. But lest future historians
should confound the two places, in narrating these illustrious events, we
think that the name of one of them should be changed."[18]

Webster and Fairbank's plight—along with that of other imprisoned
martyrs—had even inspired "A Song for the 'Slave-Stealers'":

Thompson and Torrey,
Miss Webster, Work and Burr,
Lane, Fairbank—don't their story,
The soul of freedom stir!
Weary and dreary,
In dungeons they must pine,
That pirates may be cheery
With idleness and wine.[19]

The Liberty Party convention in Albany, New York, on December 4-5,
1844, made an "Address" to the nation that identifies the imprisoned heroes
(and one heroine) celebrated in the song: "We deeply sympathise with John
D. Lane in the State Prison of Virginia; with Burr, Thompson and Work, in
that of Missouri; with Charles T. Torrey in the jail of Baltimore . . . and with
Mr. Fairbank and Miss Webster, in jail at Lexington, within sight of the
groves of Ashland—all for the alledged [sic] CRIME of having aided their
fellow-beings, according to the dictates of humanity and the principles of the
Gospel, to escape from cruel, unjust bondage."[20]

Meanwhile, Calvin Fairbank's case was coming up for trial. He had petitioned the legislature for a change of venue to Paris, north of Lexington in
Bourbon County, in hopes that the change of locale and the delay would
allow for a trial less menaced by popular sentiment inflamed against him. "I
had obtained a change of venue . . . by which I had expected to avail myself
of all privileges to prolong the trial of my case for at least one year, upon the
assurance of acquittal by explanation of the 'Frater' letter, by Sam Shy."[21]
Fairbank succeeded in getting a bill for the change of venue passed by both
houses of the state legislature, but then he learned that Governor Owsley
intended to pardon Delia Webster only after his trial was completed. Furthermore, Owsley apparently did not want Fairbank to call Webster to testify at his trial for fear it would heat up public opinion against her once more,
making it impossible to grant the pardon.[22] "I therefore requested him not to
sign the bill, notified the Court of my willingness to go into trial and plead to
the facts as soon as possible, assume the responsibility and procure her re-

lease."[23] The correspondent for the *Emancipator* wrote that "The feeling seems to be in favor of pardoning Miss W. and making an example of Fairbank; and punish him the more severely as a sort of set-off. . . . When I left Frankfort the governor had not yet released her, though he had promised her father and counsel to do so as soon as Fairbank should be placed in the penitentiary."[24]

At the trial, held on February 13, 1845, Fairbank initially pled not guilty, but after the jury was chosen changed his plea to guilty. The commonwealth offered no testimony, agreeing to allow him to make his own defense. He threw himself upon the mercy of the court, pleading: "Gentlemen of the jury, 'but for the grace of God there goes John Bunyan,'" alluding to the author of *The Pilgrim's Progress* (1678), who—like Newton Craig's ancestors—had been imprisoned for preaching a dissenting religion. "Had I been born and educated here," Fairbank continued, "I might have been as you are. But thank God I am what I am, and I would that ye all were as I am, except these bonds."[25] He said he expected to be convicted, though he did make an attempt at legal exculpation, arguing that slavery is technically not legal in the United States. But his principal argument was that "though I had knowingly violated the law, and laid myself liable to the full penalty, yet I pleaded an abatement on the ground of conscientious convictions of duty."[26]

The version reported by the *Louisville Journal* adds a nuance of contrition not present in Fairbank's own record. "He protested the conscientious sense of duty under which he then acted, the result of his early education; said that he now believed that he was wrong; that he had found that the efforts of the abolitionists, instead of ameliorating, had only served to embitter the fate of the slaves, [who] were more comfortably situated here than any of their comrades who had escaped, and concluded by imploring their clemency."[27] The *Frankfort Commonwealth* reported similarly: "He made a short address to the jury . . . stating that he had been religiously educated an abolitionist, and thought he was but obeying the mandate of religion and humanity in aiding slaves to escape bondage. He had now learned, he said, from personal observation, that the condition of Kentucky slaves was far happier than he supposed it at a distance."[28]

The jury, taking little notice of these appeals for understanding, returned a verdict of guilty, after deliberating only half an hour, recommending a term of fifteen years, five for each of the three slaves he had stolen. Fairbank's counsel, Kinkead and Shy, then tried to argue that the abduction of the three slaves "constituted but one single felony—reasoning by analogy from the case of a number of articles being stolen at the same time, but constituting a single act, and punishable but once." Had this motion been successful, Fairbank would have had to serve but five years. They also argued for the three five-year terms to run concurrently, which would have had the same effect. Both motions were denied.[29]

Judge Buckner, who had presided at Delia Webster's trial, addressed the prisoner: "Stand up, Calvin Fairbank. . . . The crime of which you have been guilty is a grave and heinous one [which] not only injuriously affects the persons whose property you have stolen, but . . . in a high degree, this whole community, [striking] at its peace and tranquility, nay, at its very existence." The judge raised the specter of slave revolt, encouraged by abolitionist meddlers. Nat Turner's 1831 uprising in Tidewater Virginia had not been forgotten: "You have placed us in danger of our lives; you have endangered the very existence of our community as a community, by the efforts of yourself and your fanatic co-laborers to sow discontent among our slaves; to incite them to insurrectionary movement in order to regain their liberty." Yet, as Marion B. Lucas points out, there never had been any slave insurrections in Kentucky, though rumors of them "ran rampant, creating hysteria among Kentucky's whites." When such scares erupted, "the white community, almost unanimously, concluded that abolitionists were the major instigators." Abolitionists were thought to be moving secretly among the black population distributing their tracts and "inciting the slave population to rise against their masters."[30]

The judge admonished Fairbank to be grateful for "so slight a punishment," as the jury might have chosen to condemn him to sixty years. "I was pleased to hear you express regret for the course you have pursued. If what you said to the jury were your real sentiments, and you still retain them, it may be that the executive will see fit . . . to remit some portion of your punishment. As you have professed your penitence, I hope he will." He then pronounced sentence: "That you be taken hence to the jail and penitentiary house of this commonwealth, there to remain at hard labor for the term of five years upon each one of the indictments against you, making the full term of fifteen years."[31]

Fairbank was remanded to the Lexington jail. On February 18, 1845, he was transported in chains to the Frankfort penitentiary. His head was shaved close, he was given the prisoner's uniform of a woolen cap and striped shirt and pants, and immediately put to work sawing stone. The correspondent for the *Emancipator* was in Frankfort at the time, and "lingered about the penitentiary some half an hour or more, looking upon him between the iron bars of the prison gate, while he was performing his first day's labor." On the next day, the reporter entered the prison and asked for Fairbank, but was told that he was in the hospital. "I fear poor Fairbank will have a hard time of it. God only knows what will be his fate. The keeper of the penitentiary declared before he was convicted, that when he came into his possession, he would flog him till he had disclosed every particular with regard to the escape of the slaves."[32]

Whatever Newton Craig may have said before Fairbank's arrival, once the prisoner was in his care he treated him "much better than I had expected he would, giving me a choice of labor, and in many other ways treating me with respect."[33] For her part, Webster spoke of Craig and his wife as "magnanimous spirits" whose care for her exposed them "to the censure of ignorant and narrow minds."[34] The reporter for the *Emancipator* who had peered through the prison gate for half an hour at Fairbank sawing stone wrote of Delia Webster that she "occupies a little shanty, in the prison yard, which seems to have been erected for her own special use, as she is the only female prisoner. She wears her usual dress, and is employed with her needle making shirts."[35] Webster is careful to point out that she was not "*required* to perform any kind of labor; but some light sewing was brought in for my own amusement."[36] It might be recalled that in Lexington she had been in charge of the sewing for the Lexington Female Missionary Society on the day the Haydens escaped.

Indeed, her treatment was remarkable. She was "furnished with a fine library" to which she had free access. To Mrs. Craig, the woman of whom she had entertained such apprehensions upon learning that she was the sister of Parker Craig, the man responsible for their capture, she became "most ardently attached." Mrs. Craig "often visited me in my room, and sometimes invited me to walk out with her"—presumably in the streets of Frankfort. Mrs. Craig made sure that her food was of the "most delicious quality, and prepared with neatness and elegance." Delia Webster felt herself to be in "a land flowing with milk and honey." Mrs. Craig, she concludes, "is a lady of strong and well balanced mind and appeared perfectly regardless of the flying rumors assailing my moral standing."[37]

As early as January 25, 1845, just two weeks after she had entered the penitentiary, a pardon from Governor Owsley nearly came through. But, according to Webster's account, the rumor circulating that her release was imminent "greatly incensed that portion of the populace who were my enemies." She accordingly sent a message to the governor "saying, I was not so selfish as to wish a pardon, if he, in granting one, would expose himself to censure, or endanger the interests of the State."[38] Owsley, listening to the advice of his friends, decided on postponement.

The governor made several visits to Delia Webster, which were facilitated by the fact that the penitentiary and the seat of state government were located in the same town, "and continued to manifest a friendly feeling during my incarceration." Feeling pressure not only from those opposed to her release but from the "large number of the members of the Legislature, of all political parties, and embracing every member of the committee on the Penitentiary in each House, praying her pardon," Owsley had to find some middle way.[39] As he expressed it to Webster, "he was assured if he were to pardon me without any compromise on my part, the people would not be satisfied. He admitted the requirement to be hard, but said he must act for the people."[40] The correspondent for the *Emancipator* was somewhat more critical of the governor. He mistakenly reports that Owsley succeeded in exacting a promise from Webster never to return to Kentucky, "but still he is not satisfied. He says he wishes her to appear more humble." It is not that he wants to make her confess to the crime, writes the correspondent, "but he wishes her to beg, shed some tears. . . . It seems that it would be a great satisfaction to the governor to see a woman cry; but as she is not one of the sniveling sort, I think he will hardly succeed."[41]

Webster writes that, in his attempt to find some compromise, the governor first did try to get her to promise to leave the state and never come back, but that she steadfastly refused. "All my feelings revolted at such a compromise, and inasmuch as I could not act in it heartily, rather than submit to conditions that could be construed unfavorably to my sincerity, I would stay and serve out my sentence. . . . I might never desire to return to Kentucky, and probably never should; but if I wished to return and resume my school, or visit a friend, I would not be debarred the privilege."[42] After recounting the false hopes raised of a pardon back in January, Webster then writes that a "Free and Full Pardon" suddenly set her free on February 24, as if it came as a total surprise—and as if the governor had given up on finding any ground for compromise. Yet while the reporter for the *Emancipator* declared her pardon unconditional ("Miss Webster was released by the governor on Monday last, unconditionally, she having most heartily retracted the promise which he had drawn from her, to leave the State of Kentucky, never to return"),[43] the *Frankfort Commonwealth* reported that there were certain "grounds" for the pardon that were made clear in an "interview between the Governor and Miss Webster" which, "having witnessed . . . we are enabled to repeat":

> It is her voluntary purpose to return forthwith to Vermont and set about her exculpation from the charge of which she has been convicted. She declares that, although opposed to slavery in the abstract, she is not and never was an Abolitionist. She is in favor of Colonization. She believes that the interposition of exterior influences in regard to slavery in Kentucky, is wrong in itself, as well as illegal, and results not merely in the injury to the slaveholders, but to the detriment of the slaves themselves; and seriously retards the progress of sentiment in this State in favor of ultimate emancipation. She is, therefore, hostile to all

agitation of the slave question, except by the people in the Slave States, and designs to make the attempt to convince the agitators of the North of the illegality, the folly and injustice of their intermeddling with the question in any way whatever. She has a high respect and regard for the people of Kentucky and particularly admires their generous spirit; she believes it will be in her power, as it is her purpose, to convince them not only that she is innocent of the crime of slave stealing, but that she is entitled to their confidence and respect. She manifested a most intense solicitude to recover the good opinion of a people so generous and for whom she retains, even in her misfortune, so high a respect.[44]

This has every appearance of having been hammered out through intense discussions between Webster and Owsley, though Webster's father very likely played a leading role in the negotiations. This is particularly probable in light of later revelations that the book she would write in which she would say what she promised to say about her innocence, her anti-abolitionist beliefs, and her love for the people of Kentucky, was written under paternal duress.

It may appear strange that the first point made in the reporter's account of the grounds for the pardon was that the prisoner intends to set about proving her innocence. After all, in the normal course of events to accept a pardon is to accept guilt. Such indeed had been her reason back in December for preferring a new trial to a pardon. "It strikes us as very odd," commented the *Emancipator*, "that Miss Webster should go away to Vermont to convince the 'generous' people of Kentucky that she is innocent of the crime of aiding slaves to be free. The natural course would be to disprove a charge in the neighborhood where it is laid, and where all the witnesses are. . . . The only explanation we can think of is, that the 'generous spirit' of the Kentuckians will only be convinced of her innocence by the zeal with which she shall labor to defeat abolition in Vermont, and build up the Whig party."[45]

But here the issue of guilt and innocence is all caught up in the declared desire to regain the confidence and affection of the offended party, the people of the state of Kentucky. If this is her chief goal, then it is indeed in her interest to declare, as she does, that she is not an abolitionist but a colonizationist. Henry Clay and a great many other distinguished Kentuckians were colonizationists. It was an acceptable way to express one's opposition to slavery. It is likewise in her interest to agree to be, as the *Emancipator* put it, "a missionary to the abolitionists, to convert them from the error of their ways."[46]

Delia Webster's account of her trial, *Kentucky Jurisprudence: A History of the Trial of Miss Delia A. Webster* (1845), closes with some "Thoughts on Slavery." This, in the book she promised she would write when she was pardoned, would be the statement the Kentuckians were waiting for in which she would declare herself to be a colonizationist, never an abolitionist. Yet, there is a nuance: "It is true," she writes, "I denied being an Abolitionist in the sense of Kentucky construction, and I still deny it; for I am, and ever *have been*, as bitterly opposed to what is termed '*Negro Stealing*' as Kentuckians themselves." She is an abolitionist therefore in the Northern sense, in favor of the abolition of slavery—but by law: "I would have it done legally and with a sacred regard to the preservation of our Union and the Constitution of our beloved Country." It is her hope, she writes in these concluding "Thoughts on Slavery," that the Southern state legislatures would themselves abolish it. And she opposes enticing slaves to run away: "I believe the zeal of those who would seduce the slave from his master, is altogether misdirected. For though the condition of individual slaves may thus be greatly improved, the chains of thraldom are riveted tighter than before on the remaining thousands."[47]

Slaves in Kentucky, she writes, are relatively well treated. There, "public feeling is opposed to cruelty. The slaves are generally faithful and much attached to their owners who treat them with as much liberality as servitude will bear." Kentucky slaves appear to be "well fed, well clothed and cheerful as could be expected." She concludes with this summing-up: "I am not conscious of any change having been produced in my mind during my residence in the slave states, except that I acquired more sympathy for the slave, and more for his master."[48]

The *Frankfort Commonwealth* cited two more reasons for the pardon. One dates back to the disastrous fire of August, 1844: "The condition of the Penitentiary, owing to the destruction of the buildings by fire, made it extremely inconvenient to retain her in confinement, even if other considerations had not fully justified her release." The other reason was that "the moral effect of the conviction had already been secured by the confinement she had already undergone; and it was believed the generous people of Kentucky could take no pleasure in her further suffering."

Delia Webster departed with her father, Benajah, for Cincinnati, doubtless taking the customary route by steamboat up the Kentucky River, which passes through Frankfort, to the Ohio, and from there east to Cincinnati. The *Cincinnati Atlas* interviewed Webster and her father at the Franklin House hotel. Her first order of business was evidently to dispel the rumor that she had spent the wee hours of the morning of September 30 *locked* alone with Calvin Fairbank in a room in Mr. Musick's Washington, Kentucky, inn. The reporting of the *Louisville Journal* was here at variance with the copy of the trial testimony certified by her attorney. According to the latter, Mr. Musick testified that he sat in the same room with them the whole time.

That rumor dangerous to her moral reputation put to rest, Webster now gave the Cincinnati reporter her version of events. It is interestingly quite divergent from the account she would give a few months later, when she wrote *Kentucky Jurisprudence*. "Her story is, that Fairbank invited her to attend the wedding of Mr. George Allen, a friend of his, who was about to be married to Miss Emma Smith, then in the neighborhood of Paris, Kentucky—that after declining the invitation several times, she at last consented to go—that, near Paris, Mr. Allen and Miss Smith got into the hack with them, and drove on to Maysville and crossed the Ohio—that, finding herself deceived in the distance, she refused to go any farther—that Fairbank returned in a few hours after leaving her, and reported that they were married by Rev. Mr. John Rankin, of Ohio, and that they then returned to Lexington." And that there were no slaves with them in the hack nor did she see any nor have have any knowledge of a slave abduction.[49]

Webster decided not to use this story in *Kentucky Jurisprudence*. The reason may be what readers of the *Cincinnati Herald* would discover a few days later, when Reverend John Rankin's son, Samuel Gardner Wilson Rankin, published a letter in which he pronounced her a liar. The elder Rankin, it will be remembered, ran a station on the Underground Railroad in Ripley, Ohio. Calvin Fairbank had attempted to contact him before he arrived with the Hayden family. It is not known whether he used Rankin's good offices in the escape itself; indeed, he may not have, for he does say that he left them not in Ripley, but "at Hopkins'" (in Red Oak). Yet Delia Webster must have thought that Rankin would not object to a little chicanery to preserve her reputation in the eyes of the Kentuckians. Perhaps he did not, but his son certainly did. "In reference to her story," the younger Rankin writes, "I am prepared to say . . . that it is not true, from beginning to end. That Miss Webster did accompany Fairbank to Ohio, I know to be true; but that Mr. Allen and Miss Smith accompanied them to Ripley, Ohio, and were married by Rev. John Rankin, I know to be false. Mr. Rankin never heard or saw of Mr. Allen or Miss Smith. In regard to her not knowing of any abduction, and never seeing the slaves, or riding with them in the hack, together with Fairbank, I am prepared to prove, when necessary, that she did ride with the slaves, and that she did see them."[50]

Not yet aware of the denunciation young Rankin would make, the *Atlas* reporter fell totally under Miss Webster's charms, finding her to be "A young lady of irreproachable character—of good education—lady-like manners—and high intellectual endowments."

For evidence of what genteel Kentuckians may have thought of Delia

Webster, one could look at the extended mention of her pardon and departure for Vermont that James Lane Allen wrote into his novella *Aftermath*, published in 1895 but set in the Bluegrass region during the mid-1840s:

> I turn my conversations with Georgiana as gayly as I can upon some topic of the time. . . . "Well, Georgiana," I had said, "Miss Delia Webster has suddenly returned to her home in Vermont."
>
> "And who is Miss Delia Webster?" she had inquired, with unmistakable acidity.
>
> "Miss Delia Webster is the lady who was sentenced to the State penitentiary for abducting our silly old servants into Ohio. But the jury of Kentucky noblemen who returned the verdict—being married men, and long used to forgiving a woman anything—petitioned the governor to pardon Miss Delia on the ground that she belongs to the sex that can do no wrong—and be punished for it. Whereupon the governor, seasoned to the like large experience, pardoned the lady. Whereupon Miss Webster, having passed a few weeks in the penitentiary, left, as I stated, for her home in Vermont, followed by her father, who does not, however, seem to have been able to overtake her."
>
> "If she'd been a man, now," suggested Georgiana.
>
> "If she'd been a man she would have shared the fortunes of her principal, the Reverend Mr. Fairbanks, who has *not* returned to his home in Ohio, and will not—for fifteen years."
>
> "Do you think it an agreeable subject of conversation?"[51]

5

"THE ERROR OF
A WOMAN'S HEART"

Despite James Lane Allen's gibe, Delia Webster did not hurry home any sooner than her father. Benajah Webster and his daughter took a steamboat up the Ohio from Cincinnati, passing the river towns of Ripley, Aberdeen, and Maysville, stations along the fateful journey she had taken six months before with Fairbank and the Hayden family. From Pittsburgh they traveled to Philadelphia, as can be learned from the Covington, Kentucky, *Licking Valley Register* of March 22, 1845 (with an understandable delay in those days before the telegraph was in widespread use). The paper reported to its readers, who were apparently aware of her notoriety in Lexington and her recent visit to Cincinnati, that "Miss Delia Webster is now in Philadelphia." Her course may be further plotted from the *Boston Courier* of March 13: "Miss Delia Webster . . . arrived in New-York from Philadelphia on Tuesday [March 11], on her way to her friends in Vermont. Governor Davis of Massachusetts and Mr. John P. Hale of New-Hampshire, were at New-York the same day." Webster's celebrity was so considerable, it seems, that either she met the governor or he at least reported her presence in the city to his Boston friends.

Upon her arrival in Vergennes on March 14, 1845,[1] the first order of business appears to have been to begin work on her account of the trial, for on March 19 the following notice appeared in her hometown newspaper, the *Vergennes Vermonter*: "Miss Webster takes this opportunity to inform her friends and the public generally, that a full statement of her trial as certified by the judges and admitted by the prosecutors to be correct, will very soon be laid before them, that each one may be enabled to form his own opinion of her guilt or innocence from the facts."[2] The eighty-four-page book was evidently completed in little more than a month, for Benajah Webster is recorded as having deposited it for copyright purposes with the Clerk of the District of Vermont on April 23.[3]

70

The title page bore these words:

KENTUCKY JURISPRUDENCE,
A HISTORY of THE TRIAL OF
MISS DELIA A. WEBSTER
At Lexington, Kentucky, Dec'r 17-21, 1844,
BEFORE THE HON. RICHARD BUCKNER,
On a charge of aiding Slaves to escape from
that Commonwealth— with Miscellaneous Remarks,
including her views on American Slavery.

WRITTEN BY HERSELF.

"He that filches from me my good name,
Robs me of that which not enricheth him,
And makes me poor indeed." —— *Shakspeare's Othello.*

VERGENNES:
E. W. Blaisdell, Printer.
1845

The claim to truthtelling that the Shakespeare quotation might appear to enforce is somewhat undercut by the fact that the words are actually spoken by Iago, a villainous liar, at the very moment he is lying (Act III, Scene 3). On the other hand, these lines were customarily employed in the nineteenth century, and later, for the very reason Webster appears to be quoting them: to preface an appeal in justification of one's public reputation. Yet Delia Webster would have to go to great lengths to explain just what she meant by some of the things she said in *Kentucky Jurisprudence*. And Calvin Fairbank would have occasion to write in a letter to William Garrison's *Liberator*: "Her book was written under the influence and by direction of her father. . . . This is the man . . . who, after his daughter had lain down her pen for four weeks, clearly convinced that she should destroy herself if she wrote what she afterwards did write, and would prove false to truth, coerced her, saying, 'That book must be written as I want it, or it can't be published.' At the same time, he argued to make it appear that it was in keeping with truth. You know the influence that a father can exert over his child. I disapproved of that book."[4]

Fairbank's mention of a four-week hiatus during which Delia refused to complete the book helps fill in some of what must have transpired in her father's house in March and April of 1845. She arrived home, as she said, on March 14, and it is clear that the manuscript was completed by April 23, when Benajah deposited a copy with the clerk. Between mid-March and mid-April, therefore—if Fairbank is right—she and her father must have been engaged in a four weeks' dispute over what she would write. From what Webster was to say in a letter that would appear in the January 8, 1846, issue of the *Green Mountain Freeman*, a further detail emerges: "At the time it was written I was confined to my bed by serious illness, and was hardly able to move my pen, having been prostrated some twenty days." By about April 15 she must have capitulated to her father's wishes, and wrote the entire eighty-four pages, still sick in bed, in the space of a week between the 15th and the 22nd of April.

In the same letter that appeared in the *Green Mountain Freeman* she goes on to say that "as I was impatient to get the work before the public, and as it had already been delayed some time, I concluded it hastily without weighing my language as I ought, and without the same degree of scrutiny and care that I probably should exercise in a state of health." In another passage in that letter, alluding to having included in *Kentucky Jurisprudence* an affidavit from Fairbank denying she had any knowledge of escaping slaves, she declares "it was forced in there by my father against my will, and entirely without my consent."[5] These admissions, together with Fairbank's contention in the 1850 letter published in the *Liberator* that Webster knew that what she wrote "would prove false to truth," really do make one wonder if she might indeed have been conscious of the double meaning of Iago's words on her title page.

Her motives for writing the book were in any case mixed. First, among the grounds for her pardon was apparently a promise on her part to exculpate herself and justify the good opinion that some Kentuckians, at least, and some very prominent ones, had of her. The book is certainly an exercise in self-exculpation. Secondly, these Kentuckians expected her to speak well of their treatment of their slaves, to show how much milder it was there than on the cotton plantations farther south. Thirdly, her father wanted even more strongly to clear her name, to the point of forcing her to lie. Finally, she needed the money. "My persecutions at the south had thrown a debt upon me of more than one thousand dollars. I have been at the expense of getting up my book, not only to give the world a sample of southern jurisprudence, but hoping to realize something from the sale of it that might relieve me, to some extent at least, from this burden."[6] From these words, written to defend herself from an attack by Amos Phelps in the *Anti-Slavery Reporter* in November, 1845, it is apparent that she was writing for two distinct audiences. While she may have wished to reassure the Kentuckians of her affection and respect for them, she wished to complain to northern readers of the abuses she suffered at the hands of the Kentucky legal system. To the Kentuckians she wished to prove she was not guilty of taking part in the Haydens' escape; to abolitionists she wished to show that, while she did aid in their escape, she was unjustly convicted of doing so because evidence was lacking and what incriminating evidence did exist was illegally introduced at her trial.

Kentucky Jurisprudence begins with a sentence that seems to echo the self-contradiction evident in the title page's display of Iago's claim to innocence. "The time is now come," writes Webster, "when every breeze seems to whisper in monitory tones, that it belongs to me to remove a weight from the public mind, imposed on them, by a certain class of persons, whose motives I have no wish to impugn, and to whose low innuendoes and foul detractions I shall not condescend to reply"—for it is difficult to imagine how characterizing their detractions as "foul" is not in fact to "impugn" their motives for making them. Webster goes on to assert that those who possess the facts—meaning herself—have the obligation to "unprejudice the minds now biassed by falsehood." Duty thus compelled her take up her pen—though, in a surprising aside, she writes that it is a task she had "hoped to have seen done by a much abler hand."[7] One wonders by whose hand? Her lawyers'? Henry Clay's? Or some potential champion not yet on the scene?

Aware that her readers would want to know why she left the peace and security of Vermont's Green Mountains to venture into a land of slavery, she gives some account of her life and travels: the discovery of a teacher's vocation at the age of twelve at the Vergennes Classical School, where she was also a pupil, the departure in 1835 at age seventeen for a teaching post in a neighboring town, and then a grave illness in 1839. Medicines having run their course with no effect, as a last resort the doctors suggested a change of scenery. Her father accompanied her to Saratoga Springs, New York, leaving her there in the care of a sister. "The water agreeing with my health, I remained there so long as I seemed to acquire strength from its use," then journeyed to "Montreal, and several other places in Canada" in the company of another relative.[8] The Canada sojourn is intriguing, since she would later claim that her persistent lung ailments drew her south, not north. "The long, cold winters, and the bleak, inclement winds of her mountain home, first drove Miss Webster to seek her health under the more genial skies of Kentucky," she would write in a later account. The Commonwealth's "salubrious climate" better suited her "frail constitution."[9] Canada, in other words, would not have been a particularly appropriate destination if concerns of health were uppermost. If her interests, however, had already by this point extended to the Underground Railroad, then visiting its northern terminus and some of the thousands of fugitives dwelling there may have been appropriate.

Conspicuous by its absence is any mention of Oberlin College, where she was a student for a few months in 1842—and where, as previously mentioned, "unfavorable reports were circulated with regard to her conduct."[10]

Webster dates her first visit to Kentucky in early 1843, mentioning her companions Mr. and Mrs. Spencer and the painting classes she gave "in the vicinity of Lexington." In July of that year the three of them began a class in Lexington that blossomed into a "high school," upon the insistence of Presbyterian minister Nathan H. Hall and other prominent citizens. When the Spencers fell ill of "intermittent fever" and left the city, Delia carried on alone.[11]

After listing twenty-four Lexingtonians of distinction who can vouch for her character, including her lawyers and both Henry and Cassius Clay, she proceeds to tell how she came to be falsely accused of stealing slaves. At several points in her narrative she substitutes a letter she wrote at the time for a more straightforward account, and does so here, at the very beginning of her story. Given the evident haste with which she put the book together, one can grant that it is a way to save time; yet one might also suspect that it is a way of avoiding a direct recital of certain crucial moments in her story, of shying away from addressing the readers of *Kentucky Jurisprudence*—by addressing instead the recipient of the letter. There is an ever so slight lessening of responsibility in such a procedure. Webster actually begins the story of the events of the fall of 1844 with two letters, one to a friend in Ohio, the other to one in Lexington, both of them purporting to show that all she wanted on September 28, 1844, was to take a drive in the country. Then follow seven pages of narrative detailing the journey to Maysville and back, the horse that died, the mysterious horse that followed, Parker Craig's anger, the return to Lexington, the men who came to get her at the Glass house. Then a passage, concerning her arrest, from a letter dated October 7 that may be the same as the one to an Ohio friend quoted earlier since it bears the same date. Then fifteen pages about her stay in the "Megowan Hotel," her importunate visitors, and the illness that laid her low for six weeks.

An eight-page extract from a letter of November 23 to the judge who was to preside at her trial recounts much of what has been told up to now. It is interesting that her approach to the man who was to be her judge should anticipate the one she would take two months later to the man who would be her jailer, Newton Craig. Look upon me, she begins her letter to Judge Buckner, "as one, who needs and insists upon your sympathy—your confidence—your friendship and your aid." She appeals to phrenology, the pseudoscience of the day: "The face is the heaven of the soul; and both Physiognomists and Phrenologists give me the character of being candid, ingenuous, frank, open-hearted and confiding."[12] Confiding she was, perhaps to a fault; whether what she confided was candid is another matter.

A narrative interlude recounts the setting of the trial date and speaks of McCalla's departure. A letter to Madison Johnson, requesting his legal services in the absence of McCalla, concludes the first forty pages of the eighty-four-page book.

Her record of the trial occupies the next twenty pages, beginning with the indictment asserting that "On the twentieth day of September . . . Calvin Fairbank . . . did willingly and feloniously entice and seduce [Lewis] to leave said owner and to escape [and] that Delia A. Webster on the nineteenth day of September did knowingly and feloniously incite, move, aid, abet, counsel, and command the said Calvin Fairbank to do and commit the felony aforesaid."[13] Thus the crime at issue—at least in this indictment, and she lived in fear of being brought to trial on some later date on the others—was not what happened on September 28 but the seducing and enticing that preceded it: both the seducing of the slaves (Webster sharing Fairbank's guilt here, even though she would succeed in separating his case from hers) and Webster's inciting Fairbank to perform the deed. Only in the wording of this indictment, and nowhere else of course in this exercise in self-exculpation, can one glimpse what may well have been Delia's actual role in the events of that September. The grand jury that drew up the indictment had access to one crucial piece of evidence that was not allowed to be introduced at the trial, and which Delia does not introduce into the record—the letter from John Mifflin Brown relaying Gilson Berry's thanks for her role in his escape.

The incriminating "Frater" letter Fairbank wrote on September 24, 1844, is then presented (in both the trial and Webster's account of it), the closing arguments summarized, followed by the guilty verdict, the jury's letter requesting a pardon, and her agonizing over whether to ask for one. Of particular importance for the controversy in the abolition press that would follow the publication of *Kentucky Jurisprudence* is the letter she wrote to the governor requesting the pardon.

The governor did not grant the pardon at the time the petition was made, and thus Webster's lawyers petitioned for a new trial. Principally their grounds were that the defendant was surprised by evidence introduced by the prosecution, that the "Frater letter" should not have been allowed to go to the jury, and that the defense had come up with new evidence. Among the latter was the testimony of the ferry operators at Maysville, who did not show up at the trial but who subsequently signed affidavits attesting that they did not see Webster in the carriage, nor did they see any passengers therein but white persons. A confusion that is not cleared up by any commentary from Webster is that the three ferrymen consistently refer to a date much earlier than September 29—"I think," testified one, "near the 20th, but at any rate on the Sabbath day." September 29 was a Sunday, but the man is speaking of something closer to the 22nd. Given that so much of what Webster and Fairbank were up to is undisclosed, one wonders if they had freed yet another slave or slaves the week before.

Webster then produces an affidavit from Calvin Fairbank in support of her petition for a new trial. In it Fairbank swears that "I do know, to a positive certainty, that Miss Webster is innocent of aiding and assisting Lewis[,] wife and child to escape." It was the fault of the weather, he attests, that they went to Maysville instead of Versailles; the rain kept the "other members of the [Glass] family" away. It is curious that while he is willing to lie to the extent of saying that Delia was innocent of helping the Haydens escape he was not willing to say that he had forced her to go farther than she wanted. "I did not oblige her to go against her will." Yet he does stress her unhappiness with being constrained to miss her Monday morning classes. "She seemed somewhat disaffected, —expressed regret at leaving home, and manifested much impatience to return; and if I recollect right, she two or three times spoke of returning in the stage."[14] This could well be true. Once the slaves reached Ohio, Webster's presence was no longer needed, and she could well have taken the stage back to Lexington and returned in time for her school. What might have been the result? Fairbank could have gone on to Oberlin; Israel could have driven the carriage back to Parker Craig without him. What Webster and Fairbank did not know at the time, however, was that they had been recognized in Millersburg on Friday night and word of their role in the Haydens' escape had spread through the city.

This affidavit from Fairbank is followed in *Kentucky Jurisprudence* by another, written earlier, when Calvin was asking for a continuance of his case. He maintains that the tavern keeper in Millersburg will testify that he saw no one in the carriage but white persons, likewise the ferry operator at Maysville, and that "I verily believe I can find some one who can give some explanation in relation to" the incriminating Frater letter, "if time is given."[15]

Webster then inserts some remarks of her own "which should have come in immediately after the remonstrance" of 120 prominent Lexingtonians against her petition for pardon—that is to say, eleven pages earlier— "but which were omitted by mistake." This awkward self-correction gives evidence of the apparent haste with which she put together the book. Here she maintains that Kentuckians are at heart good people, but are unfortunately sometimes carried away by "the impulse of the moment."[16]

These remarks are followed by an account of her lawyers' efforts for a new trial, the surprise of being sentenced on the day she had expected to be taken up with the motion for a new trial, her train ride to Frankfort, her apprehensions concerning Newton Craig, and her gratification at seeing her fears assuaged by the realization that her keeper "had a heart."[17] The narrative continues, as we have already seen, with a description of her stay in the penitentiary, of the arrival of her pardon, and of her departure with her father for Vermont by way of Cincinnati.

Kentucky Jurisprudence concludes with "Thoughts on Slavery," analyzed in the preceding chapter, in which Webster declares that she has never read any abolitionist literature, and that she is not an "abolitionist" in the Kentucky sense of the word, which is to say she is not a slave stealer, though would happily offer congratulations to the bondsman who made his own "voluntary and harmless escape." Summing up her Southern experience in an evenhanded way, she declares that "I acquired more sympathy for the slave, and more for his master."[18]

At the same time that Delia and Benajah Webster were returning to Vermont and Calvin Fairbank was beginning his fifteen-year sentence, Lewis Hayden and his family were leaving the safety of Canada to return to the United States. After Fairbank had left them in the care of Gordon Hopkins at Red Oak, they were fed and housed by Quaker Underground agents all the way through Ohio, changing their direction from Oberlin to Sandusky when they learned that slave catchers were hot on their trail. Patterson Bain, as his trial testimony revealed, had employed Messrs. MacLaughlin and Wood to recover Harriet and Jo. But as Wood testified, they "saw nothing of them." On October 27, 1844, Lewis "Grant"—still bearing the name of his owner—wrote to his former master from Amherstburg, Ontario, to say that he had arrived safely and was savoring the delights of freedom. But after six months of safety in Canada, Lewis and Harriet Hayden found that their conscience was troubling them, and decided to cross back over to join the growing black community in Detroit. Though they risked recapture by returning to the States, they wanted to work in the Underground Railroad to help others escape. Detroit was a major gateway into Canada for fugitive slaves, and Lewis Hayden felt there was good work he could do there. He spoke and raised money at black churches; he organized a school, and founded a church.[19]

On February 19, 1845, five days before Delia Webster received her pardon, the *Lexington Observer and Reporter* carried a notice of the impending appearance of the *True American*, an antislavery newspaper to be published by Cassius Clay (it was near his residence that Webster and Fairbank had picked up the Haydens). The first issue of Clay's newspaper appeared on June 3 of that year. Expecting trouble, Clay had fortified his printing office at Number 6 Mill Street with sheet iron, two four-pound brass cannons loaded with minié balls and nails, accumulating as well a stand of rifles, shotguns, and twelve Mexican lances. If his enemies came, he would be ready. Escaping through a trapdoor in the roof, he could set off the kegs of gunpowder he had hidden in a corner from outside the building. But he never got the chance. From July 21 he was incapacitated by typhoid fever. On August 14 a committee of citizens plotted strategy at the court house; on August 18 they succeeded in getting a judge to issue an injunction to halt publication. Clay was compelled by law to hand over the keys to his printing office to a city official. Later three men, including James Clay, a son of Henry Clay, and William B. Kinkead, one of Calvin Fairbank's defense lawyers, demanded the keys from the mayor, who surrendered them unwillingly. They carefully packed up Clay's printing press and shipped it to Cincinnati. In October, Clay began publishing the *True American* from Cincinnati, and continued for about a year. The following year Clay fought in the Mexican War as captain of the Lexington Light Infantry, was captured, and returned to Kentucky a hero.[20]

Delia Webster undoubtedly attended the wedding of her sister Martha to Simeon Goodrich, which took place in Ferrisburgh on June 4, 1845. Her name next surfaces in a story in the *Green Mountain Freeman* on July 4 as having responded to a call for a series of conventions of "anti-slavery Christians" to be held in various Vermont towns: "*Ferrisburgh*. Rev. C. Prindle, Rev. N. Day, Miss Delia A. Webster, and some 50 more." The call was issued May 13, and the article listing the names of the respondents is dated June 20. Two weeks later, the same paper reported that "Miss Webster's Trial" has at last appeared, priced at 25 cents. "Our thanks are due the authoress for a copy. We have not finished the perusal of the book," the editor writes, "but as far as we have gone, it is deeply interesting. It fully acquits Miss W. of the unjust aspersions cast upon her. . . . Miss Webster is not quite so much of an abolitionist . . . as we could wish; but that she is *anti slavery*, we think there can be no doubt. The book is richly worth purchasing. Where it is to be had we are not informed, but presume of the authoress, at Vergennes."[21]

Benajah Webster, who had made his daughter write the book, took an active part in its dissemination. "Mr. Webster, the father of Delia A. Webster," reported the editor of the Boston *Emancipator* on July 30, "called on us yesterday with a copy of the narrative just published by his daughter." In his conversation with the editor, Benajah Webster had evidently stressed the financial aspects of the situation. "Mr. Webster and his daughter have been put to an expense of nearly $2000 . . . and this book is offered for sale to reimburse a part of the loss. We ask a rapid sale. Some copies may be found at this office—also at No. 1 and No. 25 Cornhill [just down the street from the offices of the *Emancipator* at 7 Cornhill]. Price 25 cents."[22] The book's

combination of self-exculpation, both from the charge of being an abolitionist and that of the specific crime of aiding in the Haydens' escape, and a
perhaps too moderate expression of antislavery sentiments evidently made it
difficult for the editor of the *Emancipator* to render judgment. In conversation with him in the newspaper office, however, Benajah Webster's personal
powers of persuasion apparently pushed the editor toward approbation: "We
will take the occasion to remark, that on perusing the pamphlet, with the
explanations of the father," he adds, "we are satisfied that Miss Webster
is . . . entirely innocent" of the crime with which she was charged. As for her
fidelity to the cause, "She gives a very fair average of an anti-slavery creed."
As for the contradictions apparent either in the book itself or between what
she writes in the book and what she has elsewhere said (such as the story she
floated in Cincinnati about the eloping Mr. Allen and Miss Smith), "We
believe that any apparent inconsistencies in her letters and statements ought
in all charity to be set down to the extraordinary and most trying circumstances in which she was placed. . . . We have never given this opinion before, because we have felt a painful uncertainty about the matter, but this
misgiving has all given place to the deliberate judgment expressed above."[23]
    William H. Burleigh, editor of the Hartford, Connecticut, *Christian
Freeman*, took an intense interest in the Webster controversy. To defend her
from the charge of mendacity, Burleigh concocted a parable: Suppose a man
trudging through the wilderness, aware that he is being tracked every step of
the way by a hungry lion. When the man stops, so does his pursuer; when he
continues on his way, the predator follows, at a distance. The wayfarer knows
the beast is only waiting for nightfall to claim his dinner. That evening, the
man finds himself at the edge of an abyss—and thinks of a stratagem to save
his life. He cautiously places his cloak and hat on his staff, propping it on the
edge of the cliff, then conceals himself in a cavity in the rock to await developments. The lion approaches stealthily and then springs upon what he takes
to be the man, but thereby falls to his death over the precipice, while the
traveler devoutly thanks his Maker for his fortunate escape. Would this constitute an immoral deception? asks Burleigh. Of course not, he concludes.
But if it is ethically permissible to so deceive a bloodthirsty beast, would it
not also be if the pursuer were a human being with murderous intent? "Will
some of our over-wise moralists answer? Frankness, openness, sincerity, we
prize as highly as anyone—but when we are told that all deception involves
sin, we confess we are not prepared to assent to the proposition."[24]
    What occasioned this exercise in situation ethics was criticism like the
following, leveled at Webster by the *Watchman of the Valley*: "To deceive
slaveholders, to enter their houses as friends, and betray their hospitable
confidence . . . , to enter the service of slaveholders for the purpose of divid-

Benajah Webster. Courtesy Bard and Gina Prentiss

ing with them the earnings of their slaves . . . is both dishonorable and wicked."[25] Evidently the part about sharing the earnings of slaves was directed at Webster's having earned her living by teaching the children of slaveholders in her Lexington school (it is unlikely this critic would have known about Fairbank's having shared Lewis Hayden's earnings from the Phoenix Hotel). It was Webster's widely circulated letter to Reverend Harvey Leavitt, her Congregational pastor in Vergennes, that prompted the most criticism. William Lloyd Garrison would say of the letter that its "praise of the chivalry and humanity of the Kentuckians served to disgust the abolitionists."[26] But in Burleigh's estimation the letter, though "peculiar," should nevertheless be recognized as a "glorious piece of irony . . . reminding us of the language of the prophet of the Lord to the priests of Baal." He is alluding to the episode in I Kings 18 in which the prophet Elijah challenges the rival priests to set up an altar to their god, place wood beneath it, and pray to Baal for fire to come down from heaven to ignite the sacrifice. He would do the same (though, to make it more sporting, he doused his wood with water): the god that answered would be the true God. All day the priests prayed to Baal in vain. Then Elijah mocked them with magnificent irony: "Cry aloud," taunted the prophet, "for he is a god; either he is talking, or he is pursuing, or he is on a journey, or peradventure he sleepeth, and must be awakened."[27] If these words were quoted out of context, they would make Elijah look like believer in Baal. But, like Delia Webster's statement about Kentucky chivalry, they must be understood as ironical, according to editor Burleigh.

On another page of the same issue of the *Christian Freeman*, Burleigh quotes the *Boston Chronicle* quoting, in turn, a Harrisburg, Pennsylvania, paper that urged the governor of Kentucky to pardon her: "He should let this girl go free. At the most, she has erred only in judgment . . . and may we not pardon the error of a woman's heart? when, even if wrong, 'The light that leads astray, / Is light from Heaven.'" The Harrisburg editor is no abolitionist, but thinks "some abolition editors" ought to be "ashamed of themselves" for attacking her so cruelly.

Burleigh's defense convinced the *Northampton Herald*, for one, that they had been too hard on Webster. "The rebuke of our friend Burleigh . . . is just." She may have been guilty of "prevarications and falsehoods" but was nevertheless "suffering for an act of mercy to the helpless" and therefore "entitled to our sympathy and our help." Burleigh quoted the acknowledgment, but added the comment that as far as the falsehoods were concerned, "it seems but fair that she should be heard in defence, before she is condemned."[28]

Within two weeks, however, something happened to make Burleigh falter a little in his unflagging support of the maligned Delia Webster. Responding to a rival editor, Dorson Sykes, "the Pharisee of the Norwich Courier," who "reiterates the lie that 'we have defended and justified Miss Webster in the utterance of known, deliberate and unqualified untruths,'" Burleigh denies the charge of defending a lie, but goes on to make the admission that "We have *since* seen things which threw doubt upon her veracity."[29] It is likely that what Burleigh had recently seen that called her truthfulness into question was the article in the *National Anti-Slavery Standard* that quoted the *Lexington Observer and Reporter*'s revelation of the letter from Oberlin found in her trunk, but not allowed to be introduced at her trial, expressing Gilson Berry's thanks for her having rescued him from slavery. "To assist fugitives to escape is no crime," commented the abolitionist editor, "but to endeavor to conceal the fact by falsehood, is none the less an immorality." Miss Webster needs to "clear herself of the imputations against her character."[30]

A month later, however, Burleigh seems willing to believe in her once more: "A correspondent of the Boston Chronicle, who signs his name S. Haselton, says that he has a number of letters explanatory of the affairs in which this young woman was involved, and he fully believes her innocent of the accusations published against her. She is about publishing a pamphlet giving an account of her trial. . . . We shall be glad to see her clear herself of the charge of falsehood." He goes on to mention that "her father fears that he shall be compelled to sell his farm to pay the debt incurred" in her defense.[31]

While the *Emancipator* not only gave a mild endorsement of *Kentucky Jurisprudence* but published a lengthy extract from it on August 2 (the same passage, detailing Israel's flogging in the prison courtyard and the scene in which Webster's trunks are brought into her cell and their contents searched, would also appear in the *Green Mountain Freeman* of August 21), William Lloyd Garrison in the *Liberator* showed quite a different attitude. He rehearses the events well known to his readers, not neglecting to mention (though not specifically) the letter she wrote from Megowan's jail to Reverend Harvey Leavitt whose "praise of the chivalry and humanity of the Kentuckians served to disgust the abolitionists." He reports that immediately upon returning to her Vermont home Miss Webster has "been occupied in preparing a pamphlet, in vindication of her character." And now it has appeared. "A careful perusal of it satisfies us, as we presume it will every candid reader, that she was wholly innocent of the charge brought against her; that she is anything but 'a fanatical abolitionist,'" and that her conviction was a miscarriage of justice. Like the *Emancipator* and the *Green Mountain Freeman*, Garrison's *Liberator* quotes from the book, but does so in order to contrast Fairbank's cruel treatment (in the mob scene when he was torn from the carriage and in the account of being painfully put into irons) with the leniency shown Webster in Frankfort (the house of her own with no lock on the door, the freedom from prison garb and forced labor, the solicitude of Mrs. Craig). Garrison mocks the social lionization afforded Frankfort's most prominent inmate, pretending to give credit for courage and humanity to the ministers of the gospel who visited her in the penitentiary until he comes across Delia's claim to popularity among the elite: "Where ladies and gentlemen 'of the first class,' and the Legislature *en masse*, dare venture, it is to be taken for granted that the clergy will venture also," Garrison concluded.[32]

More substantial criticism is directed at her declaration that she had never read any abolitionist literature. "We would advise her" to do so immediately, Garrison cautions, for her opposition to slavery is too "abstract." Her protestations of respect for the Commonwealth of Kentucky he regards as "pitiable." How can she respect a state that forces its slaves to live together "without the sanctity of marriage"? Her claim that Kentucky herself is not to blame for her arrest and imprisonment is "absurd." Then he levels what must have been meant as a crushing blow: "She owes her deliverance, unquestionably, to the fact that she was not an abolitionist, but the apologist of slaveholders, rather than to being innocent of the act alleged against her."[33]

Garrison takes issue with Webster's declared opposition to a dissolution of the Union. Not all abolitionists shared his extreme view on this issue. The *Liberator* consistently proclaimed "No Union with Slaveholders!" and called the United States Constitution a "covenant with hell." He urged the North to secede from the South. Delia Webster's position in this instance was surely more in harmony with the general run of abolitionists than was Garrison's.

Finally, he observes that her description of Kentucky slavery as milder and less cruel than that of other Southern states must be based on limited knowledge: "Of the condition of plantation slaves she knows little or nothing by actual observation, but speaks of the appearance of those she has seen in Lexington."

Delia Webster would reply to Garrison's attack in the columns of his own paper, but first she wrote a letter to the *Green Mountain Freeman*, dated from Ferrisburgh, August 18, 1845, to answer those who had "derived from some portion of my remarks on slavery, the impression that I believe it is a *moral wrong* to aid in the escape of slaves." She regrets not having expressed herself more clearly and fully. "I merely expressed my opinion in relation to the *expediency* of first planning his escape, and seducing him away." Then she makes a curious declaration of ignorance (and thus of innocence). "It may be I am entirely mistaken in my views on this point, and I desire instruction." Perhaps I should be "better informed," she continued, before venturing an opinion on the question, "for my opportunity for observation has by no means been extensive."

She then addresses the issue of whether it is right to aid an escaped slave in Northern territory on his way to Canada. Never, she writes, has she questioned the propriety of giving aid in this situation. After all, one should do the same for any poor "wayfaring stranger, who is hungry, cold, or weary." She would have no reason to ask if he were a freeman or a slave. But if by chance she learned that he was the latter, "with tears of joy I would congratulate his successful flight, and bid him God-speed to the asylum of Canada." She would give him her last dollar, if need be. "I have done it once—yea more," she writes, telling us something we did not know about her past but are perhaps not surprised to hear, "and would do it again. Or, if he chose to dwell on the verdant shores of Champlain among our nominal mountains of freedom," she continues, tugging at the heartstrings of patriotic Vermonters who read the *Green Mountain Freeman*, she would "use my feeble influence (if need be, at the hazard of my life) to protect his rights."[34]

Having declared in *Kentucky Jurisprudence* that she had never read any abolitionist literature, she was not in a position to admit that she was a regular reader of Garrison's *Liberator*. Perhaps, indeed, she was not. In any event, she begins her four thousand-word reply, dated August 30, 1845, by saying that the August 1 number—"the first I had ever seen of *The Liberator*"—had come to her just "a few days ago." The principal purpose of her book had been to tell the facts of her arrest and trial, not to produce a treatise on slavery. Those closing remarks on the subject had only been inserted at the last minute, with the knowledge that very little space would be available for the purpose, to counter the spreading rumor that she was "the friend and advocate of slavery."[35]

Taking aim at Garrison's assertion that her opposition to slavery was merely "abstract," she quite justifiably, though at the risk of blowing her cover (the cover of innocence and ignorance that denies her actual involvement in freeing the Haydens, and before them, Gilson Berry), asks, comparing her antislavery activity to Garrison's, "do I not go farther?" Like "the great mass of anti-slavery advocates," including Garrison, she is "in favor of preaching against slavery—of praying against it—writing against it—petitioning against it—and [if women could vote] voting against it. . . . I not only go as far as yourself in approving the use of those means which, morally and legally, we have an undoubted right to use, to rid ourselves of the hydra-headed monster, but do I not go farther?" Later in her response she will come even closer to hinting at the true extent of her involvement in spiriting slaves out of the south: "Whether my sympathies for the injured slave were so active and uncontrollable as to induce me, at the jeopardy of my life, to effect the quiet rescue of a few individuals, or not, the Judgment-day will reveal."

Webster calls Webster—Noah Webster, the lexicographer—to her defense when Garrison takes issue with her declaration of "respect" for the Commonwealth of Kentucky. "By the term 'respect' here, I do not wish to convey to the mind more than that word expresses, which Webster says is less than reverence and veneration." To respect, that is, is not to revere. As far as "Commonwealth" is concerned, she notes that she had Webster's second definition in mind, not the state itself but "the whole body of people in a state." In other words, Kentuckians. "I consider that the body of the people [of Kentucky] possess some noble qualities which command respect. Are you, Mr. Editor, prepared to deny this?"

As for her professed "love" for the Commonwealth (evident in her widely reprinted letter to Reverend Leavitt: "though I am doomed ... to finish out my three score years in yonder den of criminals and felons, still ... *I love Kentucky*"[36]) on good Scriptural basis she argues that "in this command to love our neighbor, I do not understand that we are to love his sins, respect or partake of his vices. . . . We may love the individual, while we abhor his sins and rebuke his wicked practices. . . . Just so we may love a community, a Commonwealth, a nation." Here of course she was hitting Garrison close to home, for his whole identity as a radical abolitionist was based on denouncing the South as an unfit partner in the Union of states.

Webster shows that her attitude is more in keeping with the New Testament injunction to respect all members of the body than Garrison's.[37] St. Paul wrote in I Corinthians 13: 21-23 "And the eye cannot say unto the hand, I have no need of thee: nor again the head to the feet, I have no need of you. Nay, much more those members of the body, which seem to be more feeble, are necessary: And those members of the body, which we think to be less honourable, upon these we bestow more abundant honour; and our uncomely parts have more abundant comeliness." Echoing these verses, Webster writes: "Members belonging to the same body politic, are we not bound to 'have the same care one for another'; instead of the head saying to the feet, I have no need of you?" Responding directly to the aspersion Garrison cast on her sexual mores in his question, "How, as a virtuous woman, can she respect the Commonwealth which ... compels [thousands of its population] to live in a state of unmitigated pollution, without the sanctity of marriage ... ?", she continues, quoting I Corinthians 12: 23: "Even 'those members of the body which we may think less honorable,' because millions of their population are herded together as brutes, to live, using your own language, in a state of unmitigated pollution, without the sanctity of marriage, even those have a claim upon our kindness, nor have we a right to lift up our heel against them." Webster has found Garrison's Achilles' heel, as it were, namely, the confusion in his mind between the "less honorable parts"— the organs of generation—and the Southern states, evident in his horror at the "unmitigated pollution" of the sexual license forced upon the slaves and his citing that as a reason, perhaps the ultimate reason, for advocating that the North expel the South from the Union. Doubtless Garrison has in mind another verse of Scripture—rather at odds with Paul's words in I Corinthians—Jesus's advice to remove an offending member: "If thy hand or thy foot offend thee, cut them off, and cast them from thee; it is better for thee to enter into life halt or maimed, rather than having two hands or two feet to be cast into everlasting fire" (Matthew 18: 8). Nevertheless, Delia Webster, by confronting Garrison's sexual horror with the apostle's observation about bestowing more honor on the less honorable parts, seems to suggest that Garrison's abolitionist politics may have been predicated on a repressed desire for self-mutilation.[38]

6

"DID . . . ENTICE AND SEDUCE"

For three days, beginning on Wednesday, October 1, 1845, more than three thousand people thronged Boston's Tremont Temple to attend what was billed as the "Anti-Slavery Convention of the Eastern, Middle and Western States." The abolitionist movement had since 1840 been divided between the followers of William Lloyd Garrison, who renounced any attempt to reform the political system from within, and those who believed that political reform to put an end to slavery was indeed possible, and that the best avenue was a new political movement within the system—the Liberty Party, whose candidate James G. Birney had denied Henry Clay New York State and thus the presidency in the election of 1844. Birney was too ill to attend the convention, but the work of political action went on apace, with the preceding Tuesday devoted to the nomination of candidates for governor and lieutenant governor of Massachusetts. The three-day event that began on Wednesday, however, was national in scope. "Every free State and Territory in the Union, unless it be Indiana, together with the District of Columbia and Kentucky, were there represented."[1] "The convention appeared to be made up principally of persons not resident in the city [of Boston], and was exceedingly respectable in appearance and strong in numbers."[2] Such abolitionist notables as Gerrit Smith, Lewis Tappan, and the poet John Greenleaf Whittier were present. So too would be Delia Webster and Lewis Hayden.

The gathering provided Webster with an opportunity not only to sell copies of her book, *Kentucky Jurisprudence*, but to explain it. In the afternoon session of the second day, "Miss Delia A. Webster, of Vermont, was called for, and was introduced to the audience by Rev. Mr. Colver, of Boston." It appears, however, that she did not address the audience herself, but left that task to "Rev. N. Day, of Vt."[3] Women in the 1840s did not often speak to "promiscuous [i.e., mixed] audiences," though the Grimké sisters had in the decade before, and Abby Kelley, a Garrisonite, was doing so at that very moment in Ohio. Gerrit Smith, the chief financial backer of the

Liberty Party, and whose address on Texas was a major event of the convention, was evidently not opposed in principle to women speaking in public, for he had tried, without success, to persuade Abby Kelley to give a series of lectures in his home district in New York state in 1843.[4]

Webster was certainly not averse to addressing the public through the medium of print, as her open letters to Garrison and other abolitionist editors reveal. Yet communicating with the public solely through the written word afforded her the luxury of choosing her words with care and not having to answer questions on the spot. This would have been reason enough, whatever Gerrit Smith and his fellow Liberty partisans may have felt about women speaking in public, for her to rely on Reverend Day to answer those questions for her. Day "addressed the convention upon the subject of Miss Webster's imprisonment and trial—assuring them that she was, and had been for years, thoroughly anti-slavery, and it would yet appear so before the public, notwithstanding the reports that had been circulated to the contrary." Thus reported the *Green Mountain Freeman.*[5] The *Emancipator* recounted, similarly, that "Delia Webster was there, and her case was explained, by the Rev. Mr. Day, in a manner which told much to the disadvantage of the 'chivalry' of Kentucky, and the whiggery of Vermont."[6] It is likely that the whiggery at issue was her father's, given that Calvin Fairbank would describe Benajah Webster as a man "who to this day would immolate himself upon the altar of Whig-Websterianism."[7] The Webster in question here is Massachusetts Senator Daniel Webster, who at the time Fairbank made that comment on Benajah's politics had just revealed the full extent of what abolitionists saw as his betrayal of New England ideals in a speech of March 7, 1850, in which he gave his support to the Fugitive Slave Bill.[8] "Whiggery" itself could be defined as holding the Union as the highest national ideal, though it be at the cost of compromises that appeased the South. Henry Clay too was such a Whig.

A third account of Delia Webster's appearance at the convention, from the *Christian Freeman*, provides somewhat more information, giving specific mention of the issues that had been troubling many in the audience: "Miss Delia Webster took her seat, by request, on the platform, and explanations were made of her conduct in jail, and of the book which has been published giving an account of her imprisonment and trial, by Rev. Messrs. Colver of Boston, and Day of Vermont."[9] That she "took *her seat* . . . on the platform" and that explanations were then made makes it clear that she was not on the platform to speak but to be seen while others (Day and Colver) spoke. By "her conduct in jail" the reporter no doubt refers to the letters she wrote from prison—the one to Reverend Harvey Leavitt in which she spoke too highly of "Kentucky chivalry" for New England tastes, and the one to a

Mr. Mason of Oberlin, Ohio, that was really more troubling—though, curiously, less widely discussed. Its avowed intent was to serve as a letter of introduction for the slave catcher who was trying to recapture the Haydens but its postscript bore the clue that revealed its true meaning. The book she had published that summer did of course need a great deal of explanation, both with regard to her claim of innocence to the charge of slave stealing and its concluding words acknowledging a constitutional basis for Southern property rights, in particular, that of owning slaves.

The *Christian Freeman's* account differs from the other two in that it seems to imply that Colver participated as much in Webster's defense as did Day. The *Green Mountain Freeman* on the other hand has it that Colver introduced her while Day did the explaining. Colver was already on the platform anyway, having opened the afternoon session with prayer.[10] In any event, the fact that Colver presented her to the assembly no doubt gave, and was meant to give, the impression that he endorsed her defense. Colver, who occupied a Baptist pulpit in Boston, was not held in very high esteem by William Lloyd Garrison: "No man knows better how to strain at a gnat, and swallow a camel, than Nathaniel Colver," he would write in 1846.[11] Garrison found Colver too cozy with New England pastors whose opposition to slavery was lukewarm or in some cases nonexistent. Colver's greatest failing is his inconsistency (a charge remarkably similar to those leveled against Delia Webster), according to Garrison. Though he professes to be "an uncompromising Liberty party man" (and took part in the Boston Liberty Party convention) Colver actually voted, Garrison charged, not for the Liberty but the Whig candidate for governor of Massachusetts—"whether because Gov. Briggs is a deacon of the Baptist church in Pittsfield, or for some other reason, we leave those who know how strong are his sectarian feelings to decide." The Annual Report of the Massachusetts Anti-Slavery Society for the year 1845 reveals that Colver was not sufficiently firm of heart on the issue of the Baptist denomination's forbidding slaveholders to serve as missionaries. He had introduced a resolution at the meeting in Providence, Rhode Island, of the American Baptist Home Missionary Society to the effect that "the Board should not hereafter appoint Slaveholders as Missionaries," but later withdrew it upon receiving assurances that no slaveholder would be so appointed. "So that the Home Missionary Society avoided committing itself on the subject," thus comforting the southern Baptists but dismaying the abolitionists.[12]

Allusion had already been made earlier in the day on October 2 to what had taken place in Lexington in the fall of 1844. In the morning session Richard Baxter, a "venerable abolitionist from New Jersey," demonstrated the demoralizing effects of slavery on the slaveholder by telling the story of a young white man, bred and educated "amid all the sensibilities and refinements of New England" who, unfortunately for his moral health, made the decision to emigrate to Kentucky. Seven years there were sufficient for all his "finer feelings" to be destroyed, and he became the owner of slaves. By coincidence (and by way of revealing how much on the minds of the assembled listeners was the case of Delia Webster) he was "now the owner of 'Israel,' the slave who was so inhumanly flogged last year to extort a confession that should implicate Miss Webster in the crime of slave stealing."[13]

Kentucky slavery was indeed a major theme that Thursday. Earlier in the same morning session the audience had been treated to the spectacle of a slaveholder from the Bluegrass state trying to justify the "peculiar institution." Gerrit Smith had just delivered the major address of the convention, arguing vehemently against the annexation of Texas. His speech was about to be adopted as the official will of the convention, when a lone dissenting voice piped up. It belonged to a Mr. George Bryan, from Kentucky. In a spirit of magnanimity, and in order to show to the world that antislavery folk, unlike Southerners, believed in the American ideal of free speech, the crowd urged him to ascend to the stand to give his reasons. It was thus without preparation that Bryan spoke, and he readily confessed that he was not used to speaking in public. "It was unkind of the abolitionists," asserted the *Christian Freeman*, "to urge him upon the platform. He was confused and embarrassed."[14] But gathering his courage, Bryan told the crowd that he lived some twenty-five miles from Lexington, and claimed that his slaves were well treated. He permitted them to attend church on Sunday, and they would all be educated "were it not for the abolitionists." Slavery was an evil, Bryan admitted, but slaveholders did not wish to be deprived of their property. He personally favored a plan of emancipation that would declare all slaves free when they reached a certain age. Asked if he sympathized with Cassius Clay, whose Lexington, Kentucky, newspaper, the *True American*, had been forcibly, if temporarily, silenced in August, Bryan answered that the Clay he favored was Henry.

Just how well slaves were or were not treated in Kentucky was then addressed by an even more expert witness, Lewis Clarke, a fugitive slave from that state. Clarke, who had been held in bondage on a Madison County farm, escaped in August, 1841. He did so rather more easily than most, as his skin color allowed him to pass for white. With sixty-four dollars in his pocket, he rode a pony to Lexington, where he spent the night with his brother, rode the next day to Mays Lick, purchased lodging in a tavern, then bought a ticket on the Maysville ferry the next day.[15] He reported having attended the very church meetings Bryan had said slaves were free to attend, but said that the only message ever preached there was "slaves, be obedient to your masters."[16] As for education, he had once been whipped for trying to learn to spell.

From the account of the convention given in the *Green Mountain Freeman* it may be possible to conclude that Delia Webster was accorded the honor of gracing the platform on Friday as well, serving along with a score of fugitive slaves as evidence of the brutality of Southern bondage. Reporting on the final day's events, the paper recounted that while a number of slaveholders were present (hailing from Kentucky, South Carolina, and Alabama), except for Bryan they refused to communicate other than by "clenched hands and blank faces," having "left their chivalry all at home, except a branded hand [an allusion to Captain Jonathan Walker, who displayed his hand branded with "S.S." for "slave-stealer"], an imprisoned Green Mountain girl [Delia Webster], and some twenty others of their flayed and scarred victims of slavery, who sat upon the platform, looking them calmly in the face."[17] The latter, presumably, were escaped slaves like Lewis Clarke, for it was more common for fugitive bondsmen to bear the marks of whips and other instruments of torture than for such rescuers as Delia Webster, who in any case bore none.

Having just alluded to the other victims of slavery displayed on the platform in its account of the Friday afternoon session, the *Green Mountain Freeman* then recounts what must have been a truly dramatic moment in the proceedings. "Rev. Mr. Colver, of Boston [who had introduced Delia Webster to the audience the day before], here inquired for Lewis Hayden, the slave who was assisted by Miss Webster, and for which crime she was imprisoned in Kentucky." Colver reported to the convention that Hayden had not been seen since early that morning, and that it was known that his former owner "was prowling about the city," and had even been seen in the Convention the day and evening before. Thus Lewis Baxter or his colleague Thomas Grant may have been present on Thursday afternoon when Webster was on the speaker's platform and Reverend Day spoke in her defense. It would appear that Delia Webster's intent of saying one thing to the Kentuckians who had persecuted her and another to the abolitionists whose support she desired was thus contravened. Unless, that is, Baxter—or Grant—was too preoccupied in the search for Lewis Hayden to pay attention to what Day was saying.

It is possible, of course, that the news that Hayden's owner, or his agent, was present was false. Yet the conventioneers must have believed the threat to be real, for a Mr. Staunton then announced that he did not know where Hayden was but that "he knew well where the slave catcher was—his movements had all been noticed, and they were fully prepared for him." John Pierpont then said that if there was a slave catcher in the vicinity "with any design of interfering with the personal liberty of Mr. Hayden" he had better go take out a life insurance policy right away. Not that the Bostonians would murder anyone, but that they would throw so many obstacles in his way that "he might die of mere vexation of spirit before he got his slave out of Boston." If Lewis Hayden was in Boston, said Pierpont, his safety was assured. Word somehow got to Hayden of everyone's concern for his safety. He entered the hall, "made his appearance upon the platform, and thus relieved the anxiety of his friends."[18]

A year and a half later, Lewis Hayden described what it felt like to stand before the crowd. "On looking over the vast assembly, and hearing the expressions of sympathy and encouragement . . . I forgot myself, and felt for a time that I was in Paradise." He was moved by the sight of those "thousands of men and women assembled to see what could be done for my father, my brothers and my sisters, and millions of others who are still clanking their chains in this *Christian* land."[19] Hayden's disgust with the Christian hypocrisy of slaveholders was already evident in the letter he had written to his former owners stating "I thought if that was Religion I would be off" and that he was more of a mind to "fight than pray."[20] "The impression then made upon my mind," he says of the convention, "I shall never forget. The old and the young were there—everybody but slaveholders seemed to be there"—as if he had not taken the threat of his former owner's presence very seriously, or had missed the Thursday morning session when the Kentucky slaveholder Bryan took the stand.[21] If he missed the Thursday morning session, and was absent Friday afternoon until his sudden and dramatic arrival on stage, was he not present, either, to see Delia Webster displayed and hear Day's explanations? Evidence either way is lacking, though it seems likely he wasn't there, else he would have been called up to the platform to share the glory.

As to what precisely the Reverend Day said to the convention—a subject on which the newspaper accounts are disappointingly vague—there is the testimony of Amos Phelps, editor of the *Anti-Slavery Reporter*, who was present at the scene. According to Phelps, Day's

> statement averred that she was an abolitionist and not a colonizationist; that she was so before she went to Kentucky and while she was there; that while there she did aid in the escape of slaves—having on more than one occasion emptied her purse for the purpose; and that she aided the escape of the very slaves, on charge of which she was arrested. The object of [Day's] statement was to reconcile these facts with certain remarks in Miss Webster's letters and book—particularly, her denial, in Kentucky, that she was an abolitionist and had done the things alleged. The plain Saxon of the explanation was, that her letters were written for

her friends and not for the public, and that, as they knew her sentiments before she left, and certain equivocal passages were underscored, &c., and she assured them of "no change" in her views, they would understand them, though written so as naturally enough to deceive her keepers and mislead the public, and that she was obliged to write thus in order to get any word to her friends. And on the other point, the explanation was a play upon the word "seduce"—that she did not seduce slaves to run away, to be sure, but only counselled or aided such as were of themselves disposed to go.[22]

Phelps was "not a little annoyed" with this explanation, for he was offended by the prevarication. His article in the *Anti-Slavery Reporter* was in fact a serious attack on Delia Webster's character in light of the contradiction between what she said in her book and what she said, through her spokesman Reverend Day, at the convention. "We pass over all that might be said about the letters to friends. We fix only upon her denial of having aided the escape of slaves. She admits in Boston, by her friend, that she did it. In her book and in Kentucky, she denies it."

It is curious that despite Day's explanation some confusion should persist among abolitionist newspapers about her participation in the Hayden rescue. In December, 1845, two months after the convention, for example, the *National Anti-Slavery Standard* quotes the *Christian Freeman* quoting the *New York Tribune* as reporting having recently seen a fugitive slave, evidently Lewis Hayden, who had said that "he was assisted to escape by Delia Webster, and Mr. Fairbanks." The *Tribune* commented, "This would seem almost sufficient to settle the question of their participancy in the offence with which they were charged." But why—after Day's explanation to the convention—would the *Tribune* have reason to think it still was a question? What is more, the *Christian Freeman* responds with disbelief to the *Tribune*: "We have been surprised to see [the *Tribune's* story] quoted without an expression of doubt, in some of the Anti-Slavery papers."[23] But the editor of the *Christian Freeman*, the same William H. Burleigh who had taken such pains to defend Delia Webster in the columns of his papers (calling what other editors termed her untruthfulness an irony like the prophet Elijah's, and comparing it to the innocent stratagem of a man tricking a lion) attended the same convention as Amos Phelps. The official minutes list "W.H. Burleigh, Hartford" as appointed to the Connecticut committee, as well as serving on the standing committee "On the Address," while fellow conventioneer Amos Phelps was a member of the standing committee "On Resolutions."[24]

Burleigh goes on to say that "a friend of ours saw this very slave in Boston, when he positively denied that Fairbanks or Miss Webster had anything to do with his escape from Slavery. This we believe, and to represent the contrary will be to embarrass the case of poor Fairbanks, and Heaven knows, he has been oppressed enough, already."[25]

The "friend of ours" may be Ladd Haselton, of Haverhill, Massachusetts, who would write to the *Green Mountain Freeman* in January, 1846, to say that he had become acquainted with Lewis Hayden at the convention. Or it may be someone who overheard the conversation Haselton had with Hayden. "I asked him this plain question," writes Haselton. "Did Miss Webster do anything to seduce and entice you to leave your master? 'No,' was his reply, firmly—'neither Miss W. or Fairbank seduced me; it was Gov. Slade of Vermont seduced me, if any body did. . . . A friend gave me Governor Slade's message to read'"—alluding to some public statement from the governor about slavery—"'and after that I was "seduced" and determined to have my liberty if I could get it; and Fairbank came to me to get money to aid him to get off Berry's wife; and I told him I wanted to go too. So the plan was fixed.'" The plan was for Hayden to escape through Fairbank's (and Webster's) agency. Haselton makes clear in his letter that "the slave in question [was] helped away by Fairbank," curiously omitting Webster's role.[26] Burleigh, or the friend who may have reported this exchange to him, might have misunderstood, or was perhaps seizing on anything he could find to defend Delia Webster. In any case what the editor of the *National Anti-Slavery Standard*—Sydney Gay—makes of all this is that either the editor of the *Tribune* and the "friend" of the editor of the *Christian Freeman* "did not see the same person, or else somebody lies." Gay opts for the *Tribune* version, concluding that its editor "has no doubt told the truth, as he has probably seen the man Lewis, who, as hundreds of Abolitionists know, was assisted, with his wife and child, by Fairbanks and Miss Webster, to escape from Kentucky."

Webster wrote a lengthy reply to Phelps's attack and demanded that he print it in his *Anti-Slavery Reporter*. He refused, telling her it was too long and furthermore, "I do not see that its reasonings and statements help the case at all."[27] Writing for the *Green Mountain Freeman*, which did agree to print her reply, Webster counters with the argument that if it was too long for one issue of Phelps's paper he could have spread it out over two and that he should allow his readers to be the judge of whether its arguments were satisfactory or not. Phelps's philippic had come as a surprise, as "I had no reason to suppose that any candid mind, after hearing the explanation, as given by my friend at the great eastern convention, would still persist in condemning me. . . . I never did *seduce* a slave to leave his master, while I admit I have *counseled and aided* more than one in their flight to Canada. . . . I have not, at any time . . . denied that I *aided* slaves in their escape. For this

I often did before I went south; I did it while there, and have done the same since my return. . . . In every instance where I assisted slaves in securing their liberty, they had decided to leave, at all hazards, previous to any counselling or assisting them."[28]

Phelps had written, "We were not a little annoyed with the explanation, as given to the convention, and were on the point, more than once, of expressing our condemnation of it."[29] Why didn't you rise up and make your objection then? asks Webster. Perhaps, she insinuates, it was because Phelps wasn't up to debating with an equal—the Reverend Day, whom she describes here as "a friend, sent there by my father, whom I think you would have found abundantly qualified to defend his position." Rather, she complains, he finds it "easier to assail a weak, inexperienced female." What is worse, Phelps saves his objections for an audience—his readers—"which never heard the explanation" Day gave at the convention.[30]

Phelps wrote that he had not read *Kentucky Jurisprudence* until after the convention, in the train on his way home. His unfamiliarity with the book at the time of the convention would have justified his declining to contest Day's explanation at the time, though he doesn't say so, not deigning to answer her charge that he preferred to attack her when Day was not around. He certainly did read the book with care before he wrote his attack, eager to find discrepancies to her disadvantage. With regard to her letter to Judge Buckner, reproduced in *Kentucky Jurisprudence*, Phelps takes her to task for there claiming that "I have never, in any way, shape, or manner, seduced, or endeavored to seduce any servant whatever to leave his or her master or mistress." Webster responds by quoting Webster (Noah), as she had in her reply to Garrison: to "seduce" is "to entice from the path of rectitude and duty . . . by flattery, promises, bribes, or otherwise; to tempt and lead to iniquity; to corrupt; to deprave." By quoting the lexicographer at length, she suggests what is ridiculous about the notion of "seducing" slaves to free themselves from slavery, since the iniquity, corruption, and depravity are all on the side of those who keep them in slavery. She lets the dictionary quotation say this for her; she does not explicitly say it herself. But she does point out that "in every instance where I assisted slaves in securing their liberty, they had decided to leave, at all hazards, previous to any counselling or assisting them."

In his painstaking reading of *Kentucky Jurisprudence*, Amos Phelps had seized upon her declaration, in the letter to M.C. Johnson, that "I have done nothing . . . to merit the animosity or displeasure of this community." Would not assisting slaves to escape merit Lexington's displeasure? Webster wriggles out of that one by taking once more the dictionary tack: "The word *merit* means, to deserve. Now . . . the very act for which they imprisoned me deserved, instead of their disapprobation, their warmest approbation."

Phelps then turned to the testimony at her trial, in particular Thomas Grant's declaration that he spoke "with Miss Webster in relation to Lewis [Hayden] and the other negroes, and she denied that she had any thing to do with, and said she knew nothing about them."[31] Phelps had remarked that "others testify the same, and Miss Webster re-publishes the testimony without a word of contradiction." Webster replies that she certainly did contest the testimony, complaining of "the abominable mistakes of witnesses such as Keizer. . ., Mrs. Glass . . ., Mr. Fairbank"—the latter an interesting slip of the pen for *Franklin*, as it is in her book.[32] In replying to Phelps she does not make mention of the fact that she had not actually included Grant's name in this list of false witnesses on that page in *Kentucky Jurisprudence* (nor in her response). But she does point out that Grant was "the professed owner of one of the slaves in question" (still not mentioning Hayden's name) and therefore "his testimony should be received with no small degree of caution." How, she asks, could an abolitionist like Phelps take the word of a slaveholder? She gives her version of the misreported conversation with Grant: His affirmation "that I denied that I had any thing to do with the slaves, is not true. He asked me where the slaves were, and I answered that I did not know, &c., which was true; I did not know where they were." One wonders what lies (possibly in two senses) in the "&c."

Phelps pounced on her declaration, in a letter to one of her lawyers, that she "has never violated the laws of her country." The slave enactments of the south, she retorts, are not the laws of her country. To obey them, indeed, would be to violate the laws of her country. Phelps took issue with her statement in the same letter that she is "not guilty of the crime imputed to her." But citing the exact language of the indictment, Webster counters that it says nothing about aiding slaves, but that she "Did wilfully and feloniously ENTICE and SEDUCE. . . ." "I never did commit that offence," she declares.

Phelps took up her request for a new trial, also reproduced in her book, in which she swore under oath "that she knew no one could possibly be procured who would swear that any negroes went in the hack with her," and so forth. He charged her with lying under oath. Not at all, she responds. "Did I say that the negroes did not go in the hack with me, or that I did not aid them in their escape?—Nothing of the kind." Just that no witness could be produced who said they did. At this point Webster clearly affirms her participation in the escape. "I know that the thing was so managed that there was no one they could require to testify, who knew anything about the matter," except Fairbank, who could not be required to testify against himself.

In the "extract from the second affidavit of Calvin Fairbank," sworn to on December 23, after her trial was over, and reproduced on pages 67-68 of *Kentucky Jurisprudence*, Fairbank swore "I do know, to a positive certainty, that Miss Webster is innocent of aiding and assisting Lewis wife and child to escape." This time what is at issue is no longer seducing but aiding. Phelps charged that to include it in her book was a clear case of lying. Webster's response is to deny responsibility. "I am not responsible for anything Mr. Fairbank has done. *His* denial is not *my* denial." One incidentally learns more detail about Day's speech to the convention: "As to its appearing in the book, you knew full well . . . that it was forced there by my father against my will, and entirely without my consent; for an explanation of that fact was given at Boston, which you heard." She tears into Phelps for not sharing with his readers that fact, which amounts to a lack of "candor" on his own part.

On one point, and one point only, does she make any concession—with regard to the troublesome conclusion to *Kentucky Jurisprudence*, in which she almost appeared to become an apologist for slaveholders. She refers Phelps, and the readers of her reply, to her letter in the *Green Mountain Freeman* of August 28, 1845, where she had already begun to apologize for her apologetics. To Phelps she says that when she was approaching the end of her book a serious illness kept her prostrate for twenty days, but "as I was impatient to get the work before the public, and as it had already been delayed some time, I concluded it hastily without weighing my language as I ought." She makes the interesting admission that she had been somewhat swayed by Kentucky voices: "I had frequently listened to the strongest arguments that can be presented" on the question of sowing discontent in the mind of the slave "by some of the ablest minds in Kentucky"—among them, as subsequent evidence will reveal, Newton Craig's—"and I think it not at all surprising that my mind was somewhat in the dark upon that point." Now she has had time to reflect and—as if she were a weak reed bending to the breeze of the most recent display of logic—"to listen to the arguments presented on the other side of the subject by my anti-slavery friends at the north." Thus she no longer feels that it is "dishonorable" to sow discontent in the mind of the slave, though it may still be "inexpedient."

Webster closes with a veiled threat of a suit for slander, and with the complaint that by his unfounded accusations Phelps has done his worst not only to "prevent my getting employment as a teacher" but also to discourage sales of her book, on which she had hoped for some relief from the debt her trial had forced upon her (to which must now be added the expense of printing the book). Worst of all, his attack "upon my moral standing is calculated to prostrate my usefulness entirely" to the cause of the slave.

Amos Phelps was not silenced by Webster's response. He returned to the charge in the columns of the *Green Mountain Freeman*. First he makes the point that Webster was perfectly aware that Kentuckians made no such fine distinctions between seducing and aiding. "She knew well that denying that [that is, denying seducing], in the way she did, was understood as denying more." Then he comes up with three new pieces of evidence. The first two he had alluded to, he writes, in the letter to Webster in which he declined to publish her response; the third, which he considers something of a bombshell, lay hidden all along in *Kentucky Jurisprudence* but he had only just realized its significance.[33]

The first hitherto undisclosed proof is "the testimony of a gentleman who saw her in the Kentucky penitentiary." Phelps does not elaborate, but evidently Webster told the visitor she was not guilty of aiding the Haydens. That would substantiate Phelps's charge that she lied in Kentucky, but as a private conversation it would seem a less serious offence than publicly proclaiming her innocence.

The second is the testimony of the *Oberlin Evangelist*, which Phelps does not detail either, but is evidently the article in the December 3, 1845, issue that cites the *Exchange Paper*'s approving account of Phelps's attack in the *Anti-Slavery Reporter*: "Gov. Owsley [the Kentucky governor who pardoned her], upon reading her statements before the Boston Convention, will have just reason to consider himself imposed upon and insulted by her solemn and repeated protestations of innocence." Delia Webster's brief tenure as a student there in 1842 meant that whatever the college officially had to say about her would carry much weight. They knew her there: What would they say? After a self-imposed silence the *Oberlin Evangelist* finally made its judgment known: "For ourselves we felt peculiarly tried with this case from the first. While from our situation many were expecting us to speak out in behalf of Miss Webster, we were shut up completely, for we knew quite too much to speak approvingly, and too little to speak otherwise. So we held our peace, for time to do his work of development." As previously mentioned, in 1856 the treasurer of the college would recall that Webster "appeared to be a young lady of some energy and self-reliance, but for some reason she failed to secure the confidence of her teachers and many of her fellow pupils. Unfavorable reports were circulated with regard to her conduct in some respects. Her moral character was not impeached but there were circumstances which gave rise to apprehensions of her honesty."[34]

The third, and most telling, piece of evidence, which Phelps says he had only recently discovered, is the way Webster had worded her "remarkable petition for release" (his words)—the letter to Governor Owsley printed on page 59 of her book: "Your petitioner Delia A. Webster, would represent, that she has been indicted in the County of Fayette, for *aiding* negroes to escape . . ., an offense of which she is not guilty." On the same page of *Kentucky Jurisprudence* is reproduced the "Remonstrance" signed by 120 Lexington citizens against granting Webster's pardon. There too the charge is described as not seducing but aiding ("lately convicted on a charge of having aided slaves to escape"). It is not that she had misrepresented the charge as seducing when it was really aiding, but that the wording of the remonstrance proves Phelps's point that to Kentuckians there was no difference between the two, and that Webster was guilty in her letter to the governor of saying she was not guilty of aiding the Haydens in their escape.

Given the extreme importance she consistently placed on the difference between seducing and aiding, not only in her argument with Amos Phelps and in Day's defense at the convention, but from the time of her imprisonment and trial, it is remarkable that the discrepancy should have surfaced at such a late date. But surely Webster could be excused for not noticing it if Phelps himself, who had read her book with such a critical eye, had missed it too. "It may be a little surprising to some," she responds in the same issue of the *Green Mountain Freeman*, "when I say that I never before noticed that this phraseology differed from that in the indictment."[35] Never that is, until Phelps called her attention to it. Returning to the days immediately after her trial, she explains that it was only after much persuasion that she consented to apply for a pardon at all. "At length, when my father and counsel were about going to the Governor with the letters of the jury, Mr. Clay, and others, praying an immediate pardon, they came in and entreated me to enclose my petition also, lest my silence should have the appearance of indifference and displease the Governor."[36] Even then she refused. Finally, one of her friends stepped out of the room and quickly drafted a letter. He returned and begged her to sign it. "Exceedingly annoyed by the continued solicitations of my father and others, and in a state of high excitement, I cast a hasty glance over its note, and not discovering, at the time, that the word aiding was used in it, instead of the term seducing, which is given in the indictment, I gave it my signature; and had an individual said to me, two days ago, that the word aiding was there, I should have confidently denied it."

As for how she missed noticing the wording a second time, when she included the letter in *Kentucky Jurisprudence*, Webster explains that the letter, as well as other documents (including, presumably, the "remonstrance"), was "put into the hand of an amanuensis who copied for that purpose," and that when the sheets were returned for proof-reading "I was on a sick bed and unable to attend to it, so that it passed into the book without being discovered." The worst, she concludes, that Phelps can make of this is that it was "a mistake, or an unintentional denial," which "certainly does not amount to a falsehood."

The editor of the *Green Mountain Freeman* then appends a comment expressing hope that the controversy has been sufficiently aired, but not without the implication that Phelps was at fault for not allowing her to publish her initial response in his own journal, "so that those who read his article might have an opportunity of seeing her defence."[37]

Even William Lloyd Garrison, who had also attacked Webster—but then had enough of a sense of honor to allow her to respond in the columns of his paper—thought Phelps had gone too far. His refusal to print her reply "was neither magnanimous nor just . . . for he ought not to have made the attack, if he did not mean to give the assailed fair play, especially in a case vitally affecting her character for veracity." Garrison even goes so far as to say that her argument that she was not guilty of enticing and seducing is persuasive: "Technically, at least, she must stand acquitted of the charge of tergiversation. The indictment against her said nothing about her *aiding* any slave to escape. . . . She was bound to plead only to the indictment,—not to implicate herself by supplying the omission of any important word in that instrument."[38]

The editor of the *Voice of Freedom*, a paper in Brandon, Vermont, joined in Garrison's censure of Phelps, and hinted at what might have been the reasons he had refused to print her response.

> I can see no ground for this refusal, unless it be the *extending* of the principle he laid down in 1840, when he and others seceded from the American Antislavery Society, because females were allowed to *speak* and *vote* in their meetings; or because he thought the defence published would show the readers of the Reporter that Delia had the best of the argument; and was more than a match in talent, to his reverence. Probably a little of both;—for it would be a ludicrous sight to behold an opposer of the equality of woman with man, *prostrated on his own chosen field*, by the *superior* power of the *inferior* sex![39]

On February 4, 1846, the *Green Mountain Freeman* published the letter from Ladd Haselton already cited, in which he recalls Hayden having said that neither Webster nor Fairbank "seduced" him into running away. "Although Mr. Phelps and others may pick flaws in Miss Webster's book, owing to her peculiar situation and circumstances of its publication, yet in this one specific charge," writes Haselton, "I earnestly hope Mr. Phelps will be satisfied that he has labored under wrong impressions in his publication, and will be guided by a manly and frank acknowledgment of it to Miss

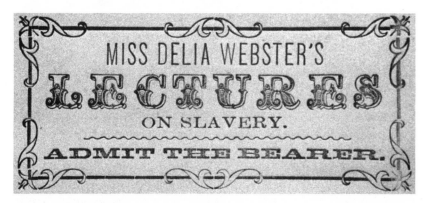

A ticket of admission to one of Delia Webster's lectures. Courtesy of Bard and Gina Prentiss

Webster, who already has suffered too much to have a wrong fixed upon her which she ought not in justice and charity to bear."

One might give the last word on this issue to Lewis Hayden himself, in a letter to Sydney Howard Gay. "At the Convention in Oct. I saw Miss Delia A. Webster—a lady whom I shall ever revere notwithstanding all that has been said against her. [It is the] strangest thing in the world that men of learning and talent cannot employ their time better than fighting against a feeble female who, when she was in the midst of enemies, happened to make one remark, which appears to have a *double meaning*. Strange world this. Oh consistency, thou art a jewel!"[40]

Who was the "Rev. N. Day, of Vt.," who so ably defended Delia Webster at the Boston convention? His name has already been seen alongside hers in the list of Ferrisburgh residents who had answered a call for a state convention of antislavery Christians: "*Ferrisburgh*: . . . Rev. N. Day, Miss Delia A. Webster, and some 30 more."[41] Ferrisburgh and Vergennes, just two miles apart, were considered for all intents and purposes the same community—as one can deduce from the following notice in the *Green Mountain Freeman*, earlier in 1845: "We are happy to be able to announce to Liberty [that is, Liberty Party] town and county committees, that the Rev. N. Day, of Ferrisburgh, may be obtained to lecture in the anti-slavery cause, by applying to him at Vergennes." It would appear that Day did not hold a pulpit at the time, but earned his living by going around the state making anti-slavery speeches. "Mr. Day," the notice continues, "will, if desired, give a course of lectures in a township, or go through a county. We earnestly hope that, as the State Committee have determined not to send out lecturers upon their own responsibility, the friends who feel interested will be prompt in securing the services of Mr. Day that he may be continually employed in the State for the year to come." Ferrisburgh and Vergennes lie in "Addison County, where Mr. Day is best known." All those who heard "his thrilling appeal" at the recent Randolph Convention, will no doubt want to book his services in their locality, the announcement averred.[42]

Day did get around. The *Green Mountain Freeman* of March 14, 1845 places him in East Bethel on March 15, at Royalton March 16-19, and at Norwich March 23. So peripatetic was the clergyman that it seems that sometimes he could only be reached by a notice placed in the paper. A personal message in the May 23 issue "To Rev. N. Day" from a Rev. S. Cummings of Corinth requests him "to visit them and deliver a series of Anti Slavery lectures early in June. You are requested to give notice through the *Freeman* or otherwise, as soon as convenient." Day was a key player in the Addison County Liberty Convention held at Weybridge on July 4, 1845, serving on a committee to prepare resolutions (one of which declared "That to imprison, or to punish in any other way, a person" for doing God's will by clothing the naked, feeding the hungry, or assisting the fugitive—as had Delia Webster—"is a high-handed sin against God, and a violation of true republicanism"), and giving the principal address, "which was listened to with deep interest."[43]

Clearly the Reverend Norris Day and Delia Webster knew each other. They came from the same town, moved in the same antislavery circles, and spoke to some extent with the same voice. Interestingly, it appears that at times they wrote with something like the same voice as well. Already noted is Webster's tendency, evident in her letter to Garrison and her reply to Phelps, of having recourse to another Webster (not Daniel but Noah). In his pamphlet *Bible Politics*, based on the antislavery speeches he had been giving in Vermont at this time, Day repeatedly makes the same gesture: "By turning to Mr. Webster we shall be furnished with the following definition: 'Politic'. . . . Mr. Webster defines 'Government' in the following manner. . . . 'Justice,' says Mr. Webster. . . .'"[44] Nor do the parallels stop there. A striking one is evident between the first page of Day's *Bible Politics* and the first page of Webster's *Kentucky Jurisprudence*: The "fact," wrote Webster, that "prejudice and interest cannot always be relied on to garrison the mind against the assaults of truth... animates me to take the *pen*, and . . . attempt what I *hoped* to have seen done by a much *abler hand*."[45] That that much abler hand was probably Norris Day's is suggested by his performance at the convention, where he would in fact be her abler mouth. Not only that, but *his* book's first page would bear the same apology, expressed through precisely the same vocabulary: "I very much regret that the defence of some of the positions I shall feel constrained to advocate, in the following pages, had not fallen into *abler hands. . . . Hoping* that the thoughts I shall present will wake up a much *abler pen* than my own. . . .”[46]

In the spring of 1845, when Webster had returned to Vermont (arriving home on March 14) and was writing *Kentucky Jurisprudence* (whose first page so curiously echoes the first page of the booklet Day was writing), the Reverend Norris Day, despite his growing success as an antislavery lecturer, was becoming a source of scandal. A letter from "A Witness" in East Poultney, Vermont, dated December, 1845, and published in the *Green Mountain Freeman* of January 1, 1846, recounts the circulation of "certain false reports," of efforts to "pull down the man" by those who could not pull down his antislavery arguments, of "many a slanderous lie"—and of the hope of his friends "that the slanders might cease," a hope frustrated when "they seemed to spread and increase with every passing day." In the winter of 1843, Day had preached a series of revival meetings at the East Poultney Congregational Church, converting some one hundred and fifty souls. He was such a success that they begged him to become their new pastor, as the present incumbent was leaving. He did not accept the post, but was asked back to that town two years later, in the spring of 1845, in a different capacity—not that of revival preacher but of antislavery lecturer. He would therefore have been solicited this time not by the church itself but by the local abolitionist society. One of the members of the church did ask that he be invited to present his address in their building, but evidently Reverend Myers, who had taken the post that Day had turned down, was too jealous of Day's oratorical ability to allow that to happen. He was also opposed to Day's antislavery politics. Day was not formally invited to speak in the church, but the report gained credence that he had been, and much excitement reigned in the community, especially among members of the church. The doors were locked and the keys hidden away, even the windows were securely fastened— all to prevent the event from taking place. "He whom, two short years ago, they had thought almost an angel of light, and whom they had well nigh worshipped, was now denied the privilege" of addressing them. It was because they knew all too well that "the miserable sophistry with which they were wont to prop up slavery . . . would wither before the irresistible power of his arguments, like mown grass beneath a scorching sun" and therefore they resorted to slander: "If you can't pull down his arguments, pull down the man."

Just how they did attempt to pull down the man is not said. The article is silent on the content of the slander that appears to have begun here, and continued to spread at least until the time the letter was written. No doubt the writer was of the opinion that to spell it out would only make things worse.

As it happened, some unrelated circumstance kept Day from coming to East Poultney on that occasion anyway. But not long after, he did show up, having made arrangements to visit Reverend Driver of the local Baptist church. Early that Sunday, a sympathetic member of the Congregational church came to ask Day if he would preach. "It seems that you have shut your doors against me," replied Day. He went on to say that even if he could not choose in which church he would speak, he did insist on "the liberty of choosing his own text and illustrating it in his own way." The man went to Myers, who reluctantly gave permission for Day to speak in his church. Myers did not go so far as to issue an invitation, but Day was misled by the go-between into thinking he had. That afternoon Day preached in the Congregational church on I Thessalonians 5: 21, "Prove all things; hold fast that which is good." It was a sermon he had preached before, "And the truth of its sentiments had never been called into question."

But this time it would be. At its conclusion, Reverend Myers rose and thanked Day, and announced that he planned to preach from the same text in the near future. Three weeks later he did. Day happened to be in the vicinity, and was therefore present when Myers spent an entire Sunday before the combined Congregational and Baptist congregations giving a highly negative "review" of Day's sermon. At the end of his discourse, a member rose to announce that Day would speak that evening in the Congregational church. Myers "immediately rose and said that he was sorry the notice had been given, and he felt it his duty to object to it, as he considered *Mr. Day an unfit man to preach in that desk*—and gave as his reason the sermon which Mr. Day had preached three weeks ago." Upon Day's whispered suggestion, the venue was changed to Reverend Driver's church. The Baptist church that evening was filled beyond capacity, everyone waiting to see if Day's "injured feelings might triumph over the spirit of a Christian." They did not. Day calmly rebutted each of Myers's objections, then made allusion to the affection in which he had once been held. "Many a bosom heaved with emotion and many a cheek was wet with tears as they listened to the flood of touching eloquence, which swelled some hearts almost to bursting. And then, with tears staring in his eyes, he prayed that God might forgive them their iniquity who would take from him his good name"—echoing that Shakespearean cadence Delia Webster was at about the same time choosing to decorate the title page of *Kentucky Jurisprudence*: "He that filches from me my good name . . ."

That both Day and Webster had reason to complain, and in the same language, of having been robbed of their good name invites speculation that the unspecified scandal attaching to each may in fact be the same scandal; that each, that is, was accused by word of mouth of a liaison with the other that went beyond their cooperation in the cause of the slave and their collaboration in the "endeavor to arrange the facts" of Delia's Kentucky experience.[47]

The "witness" who defends Day against the unspecified slander gives no particular date for its inception, but does place it in the spring of 1845, in conjunction with his difficulties in East Poultney, forty miles south of Vergennes. Webster returned to Vergennes, Day's home base, on March 14, and possibly worked with him on the drafting of her story, perhaps even under her father's urging—for she would describe Day's role in Boston as that of a "friend, sent there by my father." It was probably well known in East Poultney, and throughout the Champlain Valley, that Delia Webster had returned and was busily writing the book that would justify all, and that Norris Day of Vergennes was her associate in the antislavery cause.

Norris Day was not the only man who may have taken a personal interest in the the much-maligned Delia Webster. Among the books in Newton Craig's personal library, now in the possession of Mrs. Galey Coleman of Wichita, Kansas, may be found *The Poetical Works of Thomas Moore* (Philadelphia: J. Crissy, 1843), bearing the inscription "Newton Craigs Book Bought in Philadelphia *Oct. 20th 1845*." And among the lines pencil-marked with parentheses, evidently by Craig himself, are these:

> . . . that sigh
> We sometimes give to forms that pass us by
> In the world's crowd, too lovely to remain,
> Creatures of light we never see again![48]

Craig would see those eyes again. His desire to do so is apparent in the letter he wrote February 25, 1845, the day Delia Webster left his prison gates, addressed to "Miss Dehlia [sic] Webster": "This is my signature, and I will add my particular request, remember me. Newton Craig."[49]

7

"IT MIGHT NOT APPEAR
WHAT I SHALL BE"

Not only did Lewis Hayden sing the praises of Delia Webster in his January 21, 1846, letter to Sydney Howard Gay, but he also expressed sorrow for the fate of her partner in his rescue, the unfortunate Calvin Fairbank, still languishing in the Kentucky penitentiary. "Miss Webster is highly valued, doubtless in the sight of Heaven. But poor Fairbank—he has to suffer on & on, that long fifteen years. I have just seen a gentleman from Lexington, Ky., who said that there is not one particle of sympathy from the people in Ky. for him. My heart bleeds for him. Could I relieve him in any way I should be exceedingly gratified. God is just. He will revenge His enemies."[1] The unnamed Kentuckian's description of his fellow citizens' animosity toward their prisoner is borne out by what happened to the Reverend Isaac Wade when he dared to come to Frankfort in the spring of 1846 to call upon his imprisoned friend. Ruffians brandishing knives followed him about town when the object of his visit became known. He had no difficulty getting in to see Fairbank, and prison keeper Newton Craig permitted them to converse within the limits allowed by the penitentiary rules. But when Wade walked out of the prison gates he knew he had better leave Frankfort in a hurry. He took the first available train to "the next city," but was pursued even there. "My blood seemed to chill in my veins while a villainous man placed his dirk to my breast, looked up toward heaven, exclaiming by the power of God and his thrones, that he would pierce my heart" if Wade denied the charge of having spoken with the notorious prisoner. By "soft words and persuasive arguments," he somehow got away from a crowd of "hundreds" intending to "lynch me," fleeing on a train to Tennessee (which one might have thought the wrong direction). Not only was their anger directed toward him, but he was "informed that the people of Kentucky had agreed among themselves to assassinate Mr. Fairbank at the expiration of his term of prison."[2]

When the penitentiary gates swung shut behind him on February 18, 1845, Fairbank had been put to work sawing stone; but Newton Craig, who "was very considerate of me, treated me much better than I had expected he would," and subsequently let him choose his trade. He picked shoemaking, which he would work at for three years, though he would later becomes a steward in the prison hospital and occasionally labor in the cooper-shop making barrels and wooden tubs.[3] Prison labor, of course, was for the personal profit of the warden, who shared with the state in the proceeds. Yet it might have done the prisoner some small good to have something practical to occupy his time, as long as he was not worked past the point of human endurance.

Fairbank had yet another employment, however, and from it he did indeed, as he told Wade, take "some comfort"—that of "teaching a Bible class of about forty prisoners, every Sabbath." A "lively interest in religion" ensued. "I often preached to the prisoners, and others who came out of curiosity." Though a Yankee abolitionist and convicted slave stealer, Fairbank had a pulpit in the heart of a slave state—indeed, in its seat of government. It was a remarkable indulgence on the part of Newton Craig. At least one minister, a Baptist from Louisville, was "astonished."[4] Craig could no doubt remember that his grandfather and great-uncles had once been persecuted for their reading of the Gospel, and that, to their glory, prison walls had never stopped them from preaching it.

Some measure of the degree to which he won the confidence not only of the warden but the governor may be taken from his account of how Craig, "confiding in my integrity," committed a fifteen-year-old boy imprisoned for the theft of a horse-blanket to Fairbank's keeping, making the boy his "pupil, ward, and room-mate. I took him, taught and guided him for six months. One day Governor William Owsley came in the staveshop," and Fairbank told him the boy had been sufficiently punished. "He has had lesson enough; any longer imprisonment will spoil him." Owsley pardoned the lad the following week.[5]

From early on Craig took an apparently genuine interest in Fairbank's welfare, and even joined in efforts to procure him a pardon. "Captain" Craig, Fairbank later wrote, "was a man of large self-esteem, courted the regard of wise people, thought well of Yankee excellence, and therefore bent his energies to signalize his magnanimity in our case."[6] As early as June 20, 1846, Governor Owsley had been petitioned in his favor. On that date Henry Clay wrote a letter to the governor to accompany an unnamed correspondent's letter to that end: "I have not felt at liberty to withhold from your Excellency a view of the enclosed strong letter in behalf of Mr. Fairbanks. I am not acquainted with the writer of it, but I have informed him that I would transmit his letter to you, beyond which I should not interfere in the case."[7]

By the end of 1845 the slave Fairbank had helped to free had become something of a celebrity. Not only had Lewis Hayden made a dramatic, if silent, appearance at the Liberty Party convention in Boston in October, but on December 25 addressed the throng at the Twelfth Annual Anti-Slavery Bazaar held in Boston's Faneuil Hall. Maria Weston Chapman recalled hearing "the interesting personal narrative of Lewis Hayden," which "met the warmest reception in every heart."[8]

In his letter to Gay, Hayden wrote that "My heart was greatly delighted with the two great Anti Slavery turnouts. . . . To think that 18 months [actually it had been just short of sixteen] since I wore manacles & chains. But thank God that I saw a host of friends coming up to do battle against the . . . System which holds my father & all my relations in bondage this day. . . . As an evidence of the goodness of God, He has influenced a host of ladies to battle."[9] These were the women from Boston and surrounding towns who organized the bazaar, which ran from December 23 to January 1 and raised nearly four thousand dollars by offering items for sale as Christmas and New Year's gifts.

Since the fall of 1845 Hayden had been on a speaking tour with Reverend John M. Brown—the Brown who had encouraged Fairbank to go to Kentucky in the first place to try to rescue Gilson Berry's family, the same Brown who Delia Webster pretended to claim in the postscript to the Mason letter was not black but white. Their object was to solicit funds for the African Methodist Episcopal Church in Detroit. By January, as Hayden proudly told Sydney Gay, some $600 had been raised. In March they spoke at antislavery meetings in towns throughout Massachusetts including Westminster, Fitchburg, Westminster, Watertown, and New Bedford.[10]

The fundraising tour successfully concluded, Hayden left Boston to return to Detroit on March 31. Passing by way of New York, he brought a letter from Garrison to his colleague Sydney Gay. Presumably the letter he bore was sealed, for in it Garrison gave a frank appraisal of Hayden's abilities. He "has won the esteem and friendship of all with whom he has become acquainted, and is a rare young man. Should he conclude to return, and take up his abode in New Bedford, I think he can be made very serviceable to our cause." Apparently Hayden had not yet made up his mind whether to stay in Detroit or return to the East. "He needs to be more with us, fully to understand the position that we occupy, in regard to Church and State." Garrison advocated that New England secede from a federal system corrupted by slavery, and he was a forceful critic of organized religion's complicity in that corruption. "But he is an apt scholar, and has made very good progress in a very short time. I have not had a good opportunity to hear him speak in public; but I believe he has generally acquitted himself to good acceptance. His chief embarrassment seems to be, to find language to express the facts of his history, and the thoughts and emotions of his mind."[11]

New Bedford, where Hayden was thinking of relocating his family, was "the best city in America for an ambitious young black man," according to William McFeeley, or at least it had been when Frederick Douglass settled there in 1838. "The Quakers, committed staunchly both to eradicating slavery . . . and to building great earthly fortunes, had made New Bedford, with its flourishing whaling industry, particularly attractive to black families in the 1780s, when the abolition of slavery in Massachusetts made that state seem more hospitable than nearby Rhode Island."[12] It was also safer than Detroit, for the Haydens were still subject to abduction by agents from Kentucky. Of course, he had been aware of that danger when he had decided to leave the safety of Canada. The desire to be actively engaged in the cause outweighed the peril and led him south of the border. But his New England speaking tour and contacts with the abolitionists there had made him realize that he could fight for justice and be relatively safe, too, if he moved East. The citizens of New Bedford in particular had a history of protecting their fugitive slaves. "Black churchgoers, using the pretext of a special meeting, had once lured into their church a man they knew to be an informer, and once they had him safely inside, told him that if ever again he tried to ply his ugly trade in New Bedford, they would kill him."[13] Local whites showed an equal determination, on one occasion, when some Southerners tried to force the return of a former slave, the New Bedford Quakers hired the best lawyer they could find and temporarily abandoned their pacifist tenets to guard her house by force. They won the case, but were prepared to take her—illegally—to Canada if they lost.

From Detroit, Hayden wrote Maria Weston Chapman on May 14, 1846, to convey good news about the African Methodist Episcopal Church for which he and Brown had been soliciting funds. "Am surprised to see how God has worked in pulling down strong holds since the erection of our House of Worship. . . . All classes, rich, poor, all colors assemble together in our unfinished Church. Prejudice vanishes. The true gospel gains ground. Light is breaking on us. I yesterday met a Gentleman of wealth, of the highest rank, who confesses his views were altered & his heart was drawn by this truth. One would scarcely know the place by reason of the change from oppression to Liberty."[14] After asking Chapman to show his letter to "Friend Garrison," Hayden announces his imminent departure for the East, on May 25. "I should have been East, now, but for an invitation to visit & take up collections in some of the popular Churches of the City." By July, the Haydens had taken up residence at 8 Phillips (then Southac) Street, on Boston's Beacon Hill.[15]

On the last day of July, Lewis Hayden spoke again in public, this time at a Boston meeting that combined a fundraising effort for the erection of a monument to the Reverend Charles T. Torrey, who had died in a Baltimore jail where he had been imprisoned for trying to free slaves, and a celebration of the anniversary of West Indian emancipation. At a few minutes before midnight, the assembled knelt in silence to recreate that moment in Antigua when the the West Indian slaves knelt to await the tolling of the cathedral bell that would announce their emancipation. The bells of Boston's Park Street Church rang out at twelve, and as "peal upon peal died away in the stillness . . . many prayers ascended together that America might ere long be blessed with a similar morn."[16]

Though Hayden must have gone to bed rather late that night, he would have had to rise early the next day, for he was scheduled to speak at the First of August Celebration in Concord, an event that was to begin at 10 o'clock in the morning. The meeting would take place not in Concord itself but "in a fine grove about three quarters of a mile south-east."[17] It was a beautiful day. "The clouds in the morning, and the rain of the preceding day, made the air of the right temperature; the grove seemed the best of all groves."[18] This best of groves was in fact the woods at Walden Pond, where Henry David Thoreau had been living since July 4, 1845. According to Thoreau biographer William Howarth, the speakers actually stood "on Thoreau's doorstep. From there one could see the surface of the pond."[19] It had been less than a week before that Thoreau had served his brief imprisonment in the Concord jail for refusing to pay his poll tax by way of objecting to the Mexican War, which he believed was being fought to extend slavery. That night in jail led him to write his essay "Civil Disobedience," whose ideals of social justice and passive resistance would inspire the American civil rights struggle of the mid-twentieth century.

While he makes no discernible reference to the event to which he evidently played host, in the "Visitors" chapter of Walden Thoreau does remark that "It is surprising how many great men and women a small house will contain. I have had twenty-five or thirty souls, with their bodies, at once under my roof."[20] That might have been about the number who gathered at Walden that day—a half-price railway fare had been arranged if the number from Boston reached a hundred, but as it happened "the number present during the day was small; in the morning quite so."[21]

Not only was Thoreau (probably) there, but so too (for a certainty) was Ralph Waldo Emerson. George W. Stacy and William H. Channing were the first to address the gathering, which included "the daughter of a signer of the Declaration of Independence, . . . a very few farmers, . . . about as many mechanics, one merchant, one lawyer, two physicians, . . . ministers, . . . [and] a handsome sprinkling of women and children." The first two speakers were followed by "the calm, philosophical Emerson, closely scrutinizing, nicely adjusting the scales, so that there should not be a hair too much in the one scale or the other, telling us the need be of all things. Then Hayden, stammering out touchingly that which none has power fully to utter, what a glorious thing liberty is."[22] A greater contrast is difficult to imagine, nor a harder act to follow. Here was an unschooled, only recently literate former slave, who in the opinion of his patron William Lloyd Garrison was hindered by an inability to "find language to express the facts of his history, and the thoughts and emotions of his mind," sharing the platform with the pre-eminent intellectual of his age. On the other hand, here was a man who could write an essay on "Self-Reliance" confronting a man who embodied it.

Self-reliant though he was, Lewis Hayden did not want to miss out on a chance to get forty acres for free. In the fall of 1846, Gerrit Smith, the immensely wealthy backer of the Liberty Party from Peterboro, New York, was giving away some three thousand parcels of downstate New York land to "deserving"—that is, poor and teetotaling—blacks. Smith replied to Hayden's request for land by pointing out that recipients had to be natives of New York state.[23] This opportunity gone, between October 1846 and April 1847 Hayden was settling into Boston's black community, and probably making at least occasional appearances at antislavery meetings, as he had in previous months and would do in late 1847 and early 1848. In a letter to his wife in New Bedford on April 22, 1847, he writes from Boston: "I have not been so very well since I left New Bedford yet I have not been so that I were on able [unable] to go . . . . You may come to Boston next Wednesday if you will on the first opportunity you can git."[24] Hayden traveled frequently between the two cities, writing a letter to C.C. Nichols on May 7 from New Bedford, and one to Sydney Gay on the next day from Boston.

    The letter to Nichols was published in the *Emancipator*, of which he was the editor, with the comment "Most of our readers will remember that Miss Delia Webster aided him, and his wife and child in gaining their freedom—for which she was imprisoned in the Kentucky Penitentiary." Given the attacks on Webster's reputation and credibility in 1845, it is interesting that it is she who is credited with his rescue here, and not Calvin Fairbank; it had often been the other way around. Webster had gone into eclipse for the preceding two years, teaching school (she would later say) in Vermont. In his letter Hayden recounts the joy he felt at the Boston Liberty convention of October, 1845, when he beheld "thousands of men and women assembled to

Lewis Hayden. Courtesy Philip Fairbank

see what could be done for my father, my brothers and my sisters, and millions of others." Since then, he writes, "I have travelled through several of the New England States, and have generally met with a cordial reception."[25]

The letter to Gay conveys a different tone. Hayden was writing to say he would not be able to attend the annual convention of the American Anti-Slavery Society in New York because of a prior speaking engagement. "I were in hopes that I should be able to be with you . . . that I might gain strength so as to be the better prepared to make war, not with Mexico, but with a foe more terrible, more to be dreaded than all the armies and navies in the world, and that is a slaveholding religion." His thoughts then turn to a more personal distress:

> While sitting alone in my room . . . my mind has been led to the South, there gathering together my scattered and chattelized relations, but I cannot find them. . . . I dare to think or bring to mind one dreadful and terrifying fact, that the wife of my youth, and my first born child, is dragging out a life on some tyrant's plantation. I pray you just look at the condition of my wife, driven all day, under the lash, and then at night to be at the will of any demon or deacon that has a white face.[26]

He was not speaking of Harriet and Jo, but of an earlier chapter in his life. In November he would provide more details. Responding to a story in the *New York Tribune* praising Henry Clay for being a friend to the slave through his "ardent and efficient advocacy of emancipation," Hayden made an astounding revelation. "At an unexpected moment . . . my poor wife came to me informing me of her having been sold. Yes! sold by that friend of the coloured race, Henry Clay! Sold and gone! and from them I have never since heard a word. May God save us all from such a friend!"[27] Hayden made this charge in a letter to Sydney Howard Gay published in the *National Anti-Slavery Standard* on November 11. Gay sent a clipping to Clay, who angrily denied the accusation. "I assure you, most truly, that I never was the proprietor of the Wife and child of Lewis (or, as he calls himself, Lewis Hayden) or either of them. . . . I never therefore sold one or the other of them. He is a drunken, worthless person, wholly regardless of the truth. . . . I cannot condescend to appear in the public prints to contradict the falsehoods of such a worthless being as the fugitive Lewis, whether prompted by others or himself."[28]

But is Clay to be believed? A subsequent letter to Gay revealed that he had had no idea who Lewis Hayden even was. "I find on enquiry that Lewis Hayden is not the Lewis that I supposed. From the tenor of his (L H's) first publication, I understood him to convey the idea that he and his wife were both in my service. . . . I do not now even know Lewis Hayden. It is quite possible that I may have seen him in the streets of Lexington, but if I ever did,

I have no sort of recollection of him."[29] It is likely that the Lewis with whom Clay had at first confused Hayden was Lewis Richardson, who had recently escaped to Canada and claimed in the abolitionist press in 1846 that Clay had mistreated him. Robert V. Remini, in his biography of Clay, calls Richardson's account of his former master's alleged cruelty "distorted" and describes the fugitive as "really a violent, drunken, unmanageable, and disgruntled man, whom Clay was happy to lose."[30] Clay's characterization of the man he first took to be Hayden as "drunken" and "wholly regardless of truth," together with his having first thought that he had owned him (which in his first letter he does not deny), suggests that he had mistaken one Lewis for the other. Much is known about the character of Lewis Hayden, and of the many accounts extant none make any mention of drunkenness. Richardson, on the other hand, according to Remini's characterization, would have perfectly fit Clay's description. Clay would not, in any case, have recognized Hayden's surname, for in Lexington he was known as Lewis Grant.

In the second letter to Gay, Clay nevertheless maintained that he had never owned, much less sold, Hayden's wife and child, and furthermore that "I never sold, in my life, any woman and child to go down the river or to go South. . . . My invariable habit has been to bring together, if I could, rather than to separate man and wife."[31] When Gay wrote to him of Clay's denial of the accusation, Hayden wrote Gay a reply that provides so many details and is expressed in such forceful language that it proves quite compelling. "I perceive through you that my statements concerning Henry Clay selling my wife and child . . . are called in question by 'high authority'"—presumably Clay himself.

> Why it should be thought at all incredible that Mr. Clay should sell my wife and child . . . I can't see . . . . [I]f all the spirits of heart-broken husbands and wives, parents & children, which the accursed system has made should arise to testify—their testimony would be called in question by "high authority."
> . . . My wife's name was *Esther* Harvey, who was claimed by Joseph Harvey a merchant in Lexington who failed in business and his goods and chattels, Esther & my child among them, were sold at Auction—the year I am unable to specify. Henry Clay was the purchaser of my wife and child whom he sent to live with his son Thomas Clay then living on a farm three miles east of Lexington, with whom she lived about one year. She was then sent to Henry Clay's who hired her out to a man named Mentelle: a Frenchman living near the residence of Henry Clay & the father-in-law of Thomas Clay. After residing there a little season she returned to Henry Clay's where she was confined & gave birth to a child which died soon after. About three weeks after her confinement Mr. Clay sold her and my son to a slave trader by the name of Payne to

go down the river, and I have not seen her or heard from either since. When I humbly besought H. Clay for a reason for his selling my wife and child, he haughtily & indignantly replied "he had bought them and had sold them!"

. . . These statements can be confirmed if necessary by many persons now residing in the Northern States, but then residing in Lexington. A man who is not too good to buy stolen men women & children and to kidnap those born in his plantations with the same *inalienable* rights to life, liberty, and the avails of their labour as Henry Clay himself has, is none too good to sell my wife & child.[32]

Whom to believe? No record survives of Clay having owned Esther Harvey, or sold her, but that proves nothing, for complete records of his slave transactions do not exist, or have not yet been found. Clay's powers of recollection, as his second letter to Gay reveals, were imperfect. Even in the second letter his mind was still not clear, for he seemed to think that because when Hayden escaped from Lexington in 1844 "he carried away with him *his wife and her child*" (Clay's underlining), Hayden's charge must be false.[33] He does not realize, or pretends not to, that Hayden was referring to an *earlier* wife and child.

A political animal, Clay had every interest in fostering the belief that he never sold any slave south or broke up a family—though he does not actually claim here that he never separated a family, just that his "invariable habit" was to avoid doing so. In the unpublished letter to Gay, Hayden addressed this issue. "My family is not the only one that Henry Clay has destroyed. When he is called to render an account for his deeds—other broken hearts besides mine and my wife's will rise up in judgment against him. He will have to meet the old man Jonathan, and his wife. Tom Baltimore & wife. Buster Bill & wife, my father & mother-in-law." Some of these names do appear in the surviving record of Clay's transactions. On April 26, 1837, Clay wrote James Erwin in New Orleans recalling his intention "to sell Tom Balto. [for Baltimore] & his wife . . . I should prefer it to a cash sale, at the price that this would bring."[34] By Hayden's recollection, the sale resulted in the separation of husband and wife, whatever Clay's original intention may have been. Clay owned Bill Buster until 1852, when on April 30 he conveyed "in consideration of . . . love and affection" plus one dollar to John Morrison Clay "a young negro man called Bill Buster"—though if Hayden is correct, Clay no longer owned Buster's wife.[35]

Lewis Hayden's accusation that Clay sold his wife and child south has probably attracted little attention from scholars because of the discredit into which Lewis Richardson's claim of similar cruelties has fallen and because Hayden's more detailed letter to Gay has, until now, gone unpublished—and his May 8, 1847, letter, in which he laments his loss, unnoticed. Hayden's account squares with the facts in some important particulars, and would situate Esther's purchase and sale sometime between 1835 and 1837. According to a letter Henry Clay wrote his son, Henry, Jr., on April 11, 1836, "Thomas was busily at work on the Logan farm, and I trust is doing better."[36] Clay entered into an agreement to purchase the Logan farm on April 30, 1835.[37] Hayden writes that Thomas "was then living on a farm three miles east of Lexington" when his father sent Esther and her child to live there. This could have been the Logan farm—or possibly the Mansfield farm, which abutted Ashland and which Thomas was managing for his father in 1836. Hayden also writes that a year later Esther was hired out to a Frenchman named Mentelle who was living near Henry Clay's residence and who was Thomas's father-in-law. Waldemar and Charlotte Mentelle (great-great-great-great-great-grandparents of the author of this book) had settled in Lexington in the 1790s, having fled the French Revolution. Some time in the 1820s Charlotte established Madame Mentelle's School for Young Ladies, whose most distinguished alumna was Mary Todd Lincoln.[38] Thomas married Marie Mentelle, daughter of Waldemar and Charlotte Mentelle, on October 5, 1837.[39] Thomas Clay and Waldemar Mentelle (son of Waldemar and Charlotte) would become partners in a bagging and rope factory that failed in 1842, putting Thomas and his father Henry each about twenty thousand dollars into debt.[40]

Though he was unable to attend the American Anti-Slavery Society meeting in New York, as he told Gay in the May 8 letter, Hayden would be present at the New England Anti-Slavery Convention in Boston. In the afternoon session on May 25, a fugitive slave from Louisiana was introduced, who realized when he faced the crowd that he was too shy to speak. He "gave way to Lewis Hayden, another fugitive, who stated that he had gained his Liberty through the instrumentality of Calvin Fairbanks and Delia Webster. He made out very well, and his success emboldened the other to try his luck again, and he came up to the work bravely."[41]

Two facts stand out from this account: First, the same Hayden, who before Emerson and the Concord audience was "stammering out touchingly" what he had to say, and whom Garrison found barely able to find the words to convey "the thoughts and emotions of his mind," had become such an accomplished speaker that he was now an original to be imitated. As William Wells Brown would observe a quarter-century later, "While he does not attempt to be an orator, Mr. Hayden is, nevertheless, a very effective speaker."[42] Second, he did not neglect to hold Delia Webster's name (and Calvin Fairbank's) up to public acclaim and acknowledgment, despite her disappearance from the antislavery scene in the wake of the generally, if not universally, negative response to *Kentucky Jurisprudence.* It is clear that she was on his mind, for he was about to pay a visit to Vergennes.

On June 29, Hayden bought two first-class tickets for himself and his wife on the Providence and Stonington Railroad. Their ultimate destination was Vermont, but their route would initially be a southerly one. Departing Boston by rail, they intended to change trains at Providence for Stonington, Connecticut. From there they would take a steamer to New York, continuing up the Hudson River to the Champlain Canal that connected it to Lake Champlain. They left Boston that day at 5 p.m. and enjoyed a pleasant journey to Providence, thanks to the "uniform politeness," wrote Hayden, of the conductors on that line. But when they tried to enter the first-class car on the train from Providence, the conductor blocked the door, then asked another passenger if Harriet was his servant. Told she was not, he instructed the Haydens to go to the second-class car. Hayden decided to do so, but also to confront the conductor again when he passed through there to show him that the tickets he had purchased were indeed for the first-class car. When he reappeared, Hayden showed him the tickets but the conductor claimed they were second-class tickets. Hayden went to the ticket salesman, who admitted that they were for first class, "but remarked that coloured people could not purchase such tickets in Rhode Island, at the same time abruptly closing the office against me."[43]

His first inclination was to occupy the second-class seats despite the injustice, because he did not want to be late for the engagements he had scheduled in Vermont. But when they returned to the second-class car, they found it "literally crammed to overflowing with the lower grade of emigrants; and the stench arising from whiskey, ship-diseases, &c. &c. was almost insupportable." The odor too much to take, the Haydens got off the train, spent the night in Providence, and returned to Boston the next day. There, Hayden obtained a refund, free tickets for a second journey, and an official letter demanding "no further molestation" from railway employees.

They set out again. This time an extra car was added to the train in Providence, which the Haydens apparently had to themselves. On the steamer to New York, the captain had to intervene before they were granted overnight accommodations. On the boat from Whitehall, they were not allowed to take breakfast with the other travelers, though some of the passengers were outraged at "such unfounded prejudice against colour."[44]

At eleven that morning the Haydens reached Vergennes, "where we were well received, and invited to dine with one of the first families in the city." Hayden does not name his hosts. Given the antipathy to the antislavery cause attributed to Benajah Webster two years before, it cannot be assumed that the older Websters would have welcomed him into their home.

But surely the week between the fourth and eleventh of July 1847—when he dates the letter from Ferrisburgh in which all this is recounted—was a time of pleasant reunion between the Haydens and the woman who had been so instrumental in securing their freedom.

At this time, Delia Webster was strengthening her ties with the Kentucky friends she had made in 1843-45. After her release from the penitentiary in February, she would later write, she "remained at the east a period of four years, during the whole of which time I was constantly beset with entreaties and the most urgent solicitations to return to Kentucky, and resume my teaching."[45] Former enemies now "acknowledged their error," and thought she should receive reparation for injuries received. Some even offered "to build an academy and present me with a deed of the same, to guarantee me a handsome salary for teaching and to give me a city residence, or, if I preferred rural life, to present me with a fine farm, ready stocked." Just a few months before, "In the spring of 1847, they prevailed upon my brother-in-law to move with his family to Frankfort." Thus, at the same time the Haydens were visiting Vergennes, Delia Webster's sister Martha and her husband Simeon Goodrich were taking up residence in the same city where Calvin Fairbank still lay imprisoned, under the supervision of Newton Craig. In 1848, according to Webster, "my brother also was induced to accept certain propositions to move to Kentucky, and locate with his family near Georgetown."[46] Near Craig's hometown, that is, where the prison keeper lived—on a farm worked by slave and prison labor—when he wasn't in Frankfort, less than twenty miles away.

On November 11, the *National Anti-Slavery Standard* published Hayden's revelation that Henry Clay had broken up his family by selling his first wife and child. On the day the article appeared, Hayden was speaking in Oriskany, New York. His schedule between November and February called for him to give antislavery lectures twice a day in dozens of villages and towns in the region, sharing the platform a Dr. E.D. Hudson. Hudson presented Garrison's doctrinaire position on issues of church and state, while Hayden told his own story, "exhibit[ing] the miseries of . . . slavery, as illustrated in his own personal experience," according to a local eyewitness, the Reverend Edgar Buckingham. "He mentioned to me," wrote Buckingham, "that he felt himself unable to make such an exposition of the relationship of the Constitution and the Government of our country to that institution, as would be satisfactory to himself."[47]

Hayden was probably uncomfortable with William Lloyd Garrison's rigid insistence that the U.S. Constitution supported slavery, that the North should therefore secede from the South, and that to enter the political arena to fight slavery was to acquiesce in constitutional evil. Frederick Douglass was already moving toward a break with Garrison on this very issue. At a meeting of the American Anti-Slavery Society held in Syracuse in May 1851, Douglass would assert, in a debate chaired by Garrison himself, that the constitution "might be consistent with abolitionist aims."[48] Perhaps it occurred to Hayden, as it would to Douglass, that if the North seceded from the Union, abolitionists would have even less of a chance of changing the South's "peculiar institution."

Hayden, observed Buckingham, "treated, with the manner of a closely observing man, the effect of Slavery upon private life and given a satisfactory explanation of the alleged happiness of the slaves. . . . I have listened to his conversation and public addresses, as to those of a man of reflection, and have been astonished that, with so little early mental cultivation, he should have been able to become so accurate an observer of men and manners. . . . The story of his sufferings awakens sympathy: his industry, refinement, and the cheerfulness of his manners secures affection." The audiences he drew were as large as ever gather in the village, and would have been larger had it not been for the bad weather.[49] Not only did he recount the story of his life, but Hayden sometimes opened the meeting with "Singing and Prayer." Another observer reported that his "honesty, simplicity, and position commend him to every heart; while his pathetic appeals for his brethren in bonds, seem sufficient to move a world to the rescue."[50]

Despite these good reviews, however, Hayden's status as an agent of the American Anti-Slavery Society was unexpectedly terminated by Wendell Phillips, who conveyed the news to Hudson. From Fort Plain, New York, on February 21, 1848, Hayden wrote a response bristling with resentment. "The letter you wrote to the Dr was read to me yesterday informing me of my agency being stop[ped] and after the first of March you will I have no doubt consider where *I am* how far I am from home the season of year and that you will remember it cost me more than two month wedges to get here."[51] The "Dr" to whom Wendell Phillips had written to announce that Hayden had been let go was "Dr. Hudson"—thus named in Reverend Buckingham's account of Hayden's appearance in Trenton—the man who had been appearing with Hayden in all those joint speaking engagements. If it cost Hayden personally more than two months' wages to travel from Boston to the New York counties where he was to do the work, then it was indeed a shoestring venture. Unless what he really meant was that a two-month lecture tour, which from the newspaper advertisements it appears to have been, cost him two months in wages he could have made at home.

"I do not complain at all though it will place me in a poor situation for by the time I get home I hope to be as well off as I was when I left home. Do you not think I o[ugh]t to be well[?] I do not think I shall be and I have not spent no more than I could help. Now if I had known this I should have said to friend Hathaway when he call on me in Boston well sir will you send me home again he would have said yes for he did not know then what I was." The "friend Hathaway" who had called on Hayden in Boston to engage his services was evidently "J.C. Hathaway, General Agent of the State of New-York" (for the American Anti-Slavery Society), as advertisements for the lecture tour in the *National Anti-Slavery Standard* describe him.[52] At the same time that Hayden and Hudson were touring Oneida, Oswego, and Onondaga counties, Hathaway himself was making a lecture tour elsewhere in New York State that was probably more of a financial success than the Hudson-Hayden team, as it featured the nationally famous Frederick Douglass, together with Charles Lenox Remond. But Hayden might not have been sacked for reasons of money, even if one can detect in his assertion that he has spent no more than he could help a defensive reply to the complaint that he had. Rather, the reason might have been his inability to toe the Garrisonian line—to expound on the U.S. Constitution and its relation to slavery in a way that "would be satisfactory to himself"—as well as to Garrison and Phillips. Though Garrison had told Gay "I think he can be made very serviceable to our cause," and the American Anti-Slavery Society had indeed put him into service, Phillips had now decided to abandon him in the wilds of New York state, without enough change in his pocket to make his way home.

Hathaway, who had interviewed Hayden in Boston for the job, "did not know but what I was a second yourself. But he and you all know it is not so. You know it is me jest three years from slavery. Well let me say to you if I am not Wendell Phillips now: it mought not appear what I shall be for I shall not leave one stone onturn to obtain light. I shall do all I can to make myself a man, that is if nature has done her part." Hayden's self-image in relation to Wendell Phillips is intriguing. Born to rich parents, Boston blueblood Phillips had enjoyed every advantage (Boston Latin, Harvard College), and became a spellbinding orator for the abolition cause.[53] Apparently Hathaway thought that Hayden, too, had the makings of one. But Hayden, discouraged by his termination and perhaps by his experience, saw that he could not become a second Wendell Phillips in that way. Yet he had not lost hope. He would become, if not Wendell Phillips, something. And would leave no stone unturned to do so.

"All though I am not able to say my bread is shore I therefore would like to be sent from [here] to Detroit Mich. Will you make this known to committee and do what you can for me. If you will you may do something to aid me on my way upward and onward to manhood. . . . You me [may] not like my composition. It is as good as any of yours when you was but three years old which is my age." Frederick Douglass would make the same point in *My Bondage and My Freedom* in 1855: Douglass was "but nine years from slavery" when he decided to launch his own newspaper in 1847. "In point of mental experience, I was but nine years old."[54]

The reference to Detroit is puzzling. Why would Hayden want Phillips to pay his way there if his home was in Boston? Perhaps his discouragement at his apparent failure as an antislavery agent extended to his effort to make in his way in Boston as well. He still had friends in Detroit, where he had made a name as a community leader. The record does not reveal what Hayden did or where he went from Fort Plain.

No further trace of him surfaces until July 13, 1849, when an advertisement began to appear in the *Liberator* for a clothing store located at 107 Cambridge Street in Boston. "Lewis Hayden, who, it will be remembered, was formerly a slave in Kentucky, . . . keeps a good assortment of men's and boys' clothing, of superior quality. He trusts that all will lend him a helping hand, for it will be his constant endeavor to keep for sale a *good* and *cheap* article.... He has also a good assortment of little Knack Knacks, such as are generally kept in a variety store." The new business must have prospered, for within three years Hayden impressed his contemporary Martin Delany as someone who "by perseverance, may yet become a very wealthy man".[55] By 1855, Hayden was "probably the wealthiest black in Boston."[56] Delany recalled that "in 1848, he went to Boston, and having made acquaintance, and gained confidence with several business men . . . opened a fashionable Clothing House in Cambridge street, where he has within the last year [1851 or 1852], enlarged his establishment, being patronized by some of the most respectable citizens of that wealthy Metropolis." He adds that Hayden "has made considerable progress, considering his disadvantages, in his educational improvements. He has great energy of character, and . . . is generally esteemed by the Boston people."[57] Delany's assertion that it was in 1848 that Hayden went to Boston, rather than 1846, suggests that it was not until 1848 that he made the definitive decision to commit himself to living, and making his living, there.

By the summer of 1849, Lewis Hayden had accumulated a significant amount of money for a quite different purpose than his own enrichment. Earlier that year, "it was ascertained that a pardon could be obtained" for Calvin Fairbank "if the parties who formerly held Mr. Hayden as a slave, would join in a petition to that effect."[58] The amount required was $650. By raising that sum, Hayden could effectively buy both Fairbank's freedom and his own. In his letter to Sydney Gay in 1846 he had said of Fairbank, "Could I relieve him in any way I should be exceedingly gratified." He had at last found that opportunity.

"Mr. Hayden of Boston had been active in enlisting sympathy in my behalf, in and about Boston. Captain Newton Craig was in correspondence with gentlemen and ladies in Boston of such a nature as to conciliate his dissatisfied mind and temper, and promise some remuneration to the parties claiming redress for the loss of their slaves."[59] In a letter to the *Liberator* dated March 19, 1850, Fairbank wrote that the present "motion made in Kentucky for my release" had actually begun back in the fall of 1848.[60]

Craig was likewise in correspondence with Fairbank's father, who had been gathering petitions from Allegany and Wyoming Counties in New York. On April 5, 1849, Chester Fairbank arrived in Frankfort to deliver these petitions to Governor Crittenden, who promised to grant the pardon "as soon as a petition from Lexington with the names of Judge Buckner, Commonwealth-Attorney Robinson, the jury, the claimants of the slaves, and Hon. Henry Clay could be secured."[61]

In April, Hayden began to solicit donations in Boston. Within sixty days he reached his goal, thanks to a hundred and sixty contributors. Early in June, Fairbank's father had succeeded in getting the Lexington signatures the Governor required. "But now something else interfered," according to Fairbank. "The question of emancipation was to come before the people in the August election. The question was not, 'Shall the constitution be changed by convention?' but, whether anti-slavery or pro-slavery men should sit in the convention. The Governor made the plea that he feared my pardon at that time would prejudice the election, and decided to wait until after the election was over."[62] Governor Crittenden must have concluded that pardoning Fairbank would stir up trouble if it were done in the heat of the campaign. Things heated up anyway, as it happened, when a certain R. Runyon blundered by approaching a paranoid Cassius Clay with a dangerously irrelevant question, thereby provoking a violent encounter between Clay and a political opponent at a rally in Foxtown on June 15. Clay slew his rival in a fair fight, but Clay biographer David Smiley concludes that "the fight not only put Clay out of the campaign" for the new state constitution," but it also aroused much opposition to emancipationists in general." His opponent became a martyr "and 'respectable' emancipationists would not be associated with so distasteful an affair. The result was the complete defeat of the gradual emancipationists in the election for delegates, held August 9. Not a single emancipationist won a seat to the convention."[63] As Thomas Clark observed, "Adoption of the new constitution dealt the emancipation movement a staggering blow."[64] It strengthened the institution of slavery. It made provision to send every freed slave from the state, and it could not be amended for eight years.

Meanwhile, as the aged Chester Fairbank was waiting for the election to take place and the governor to pardon his son, cholera was raging throughout central Kentucky. "My father was unacclimated, and Captain Craig and I urged him to leave the state, to go home, and protect himself from the terrible epidemic. But no persuasions could induce him to leave me in my sore strait. He went to Lexington, enlarged the petition, was attacked by cholera . . . and died Saturday night, July 7th, 1849, and was buried by and among strangers."[65] The *Observer and Reporter* of July 11 reported the death of "Mr. Fairbank, an old man, (the father of the Fairbank who is in the State Prison for Negro-Stealing), at Mrs. Timberlake's, on Water Street."

Two weeks after the election, Calvin Fairbank received his pardon at 3:30 p.m. August 23, 1849.[66]

He was lucky it was not aborted by the public excitement surrounding Kentucky's only genuine slave insurrection, which took place just before the election, on August 5. Patrick Doyle, a student from Centre College in Danville, led a band of some seventy slaves, for the most part trusted house servants of Lexington's most socially prominent families, on a march to the Ohio River that culminated in a gun battle in a hemp field in Bracken County. Ironically perhaps, one of the slaves (by the name of Jackson) belonged to Cassius Clay—held in trust in his wife's inheritance, Clay was legally barred from freeing him as he had freed those he personally owned. Clay saved him from hanging, as did some other owners theirs. Three slaves who were not fortunate enough to have wealthy masters were hanged in Brooksville on October 28. Doyle was sentenced to twenty years in the penitentiary, where he died before finishing his term. The *Lexington Observer & Reporter* did not fail to drag Fairbank's name into it: "The example of the notorious Fairbank, who is now in our state prison . . . has not, it seems, had the effect of keeping our state clear of these detestable villains who, under the false pretext of philanthropy . . . are perpetrating their foul practices in our midst. It is time that a more severe example should be made."[67]

"Upon my father's death," Calvin Fairbank would write on August 31 in a letter to Sydney Gay, he fell into a fit of depression in which he nearly gave up the attempt to secure the pardon. "I felt to complain; I felt like Logan: I would not have turned on my heel to have saved my life; but upon reflection I became more reasonable, for every advisable measure had been taken to procure my pardon, and I was as you would readily suppose somewhat out of patience that the work went on so slowly. But it was a great undertaking to attempt to effect the release of one in a State like Kentucky."[68] On Friday, August 24, the day after "the worthy keeper and agent of the Kentucky Penitentiary" (in Fairbank's words) handed him his pardon, Fairbank boarded a steamboat at the Frankfort wharf. "On my way down the Kentucky River . . . I heard gentlemen and ladies both freely and fearlessly and warmly discussing the subject of Emancipation." Naturally, the recent vote for delegates to a state constitutional convention was still on everyone's mind. "As we waited at the mouth of the river at Carrollton, I met with one lady who was exceedingly indignant at the treatment received by Pres. Malcom of Georgetown College, for voting for an Emancipation candidate." He thought it amusing that the woman had no idea that she was speaking to the notorious Calvin Fairbank, freshly released from the penitentiary for the crime of spiriting away slaves.

Though he soon made his way to Cincinnati, which is east of the point where the Kentucky flows into the Ohio at Carrollton, his first destination upon leaving prison was west, and downstream: "On the 24th I left for Madison, Indiana, where I obtained lodgings with Wright Ray, the famous slavehunter of that section. It was the first comfortable night's rest for near five years."[69] His choice of hostelry is interesting—as is the near certainty that when in Madison he renewed his acquaintance with Delia Webster, who had been residing in that city since the spring of that year. Steamboats regularly plied the route between Frankfort and Louisville, in which case they also stopped at Madison, and between Frankfort and Cincinnati. Since he said he waited at Carrollton, he had apparently boarded a Cincinnati-bound boat at Frankfort, perhaps the first available, and got off at Carrollton to board a westbound steamer which would drop him off at Madison, just a few miles down the Ohio. In any event, the wording—"I left for Madison"— makes it clear what his destination was. He makes no mention of visiting Delia Webster, but it is difficult to imagine that he would not have. The coincidence—that these two, who had shared such an adventure in the fall of 1844, could have been in the same Indiana town at the same time, and not met—would have been too great.

Besides, he could hardly have been unaware of her presence in Madison, for his good friend "the worthy keeper" knew all about it. Craig would have had to: His children were living in her house.

8

"THE SINCERE DESIRE OF YOUR FOND FATHER"

After her release from the Kentucky state penitentiary in February, 1845, Delia Webster claimed to have spent the next three years teaching school in Vermont, and living with her parents in Vergennes. "The Green Mountain storms of wind and snow," however, which (so she said, leaving out for the moment any consideration of helping slaves to escape) had led to her decision to come to Kentucky in the first place, once more took their toll on her health. On the advice of her family physician, in the fall of 1848 she left Vermont for New York City, where she could thrive on "sea-breezes, sea-bathing, and a diet that the salt-water alone could furnish." She taught school there to a "select class of young ladies" from New York, Brooklyn and Jersey City. But a severe attack of bronchitis in the spring of 1849 forced her to think of moving even farther south.[1]

Ever since leaving Kentucky in 1845, Webster claimed, she had been "constantly beset with entreaties and the most urgent solicitations to return . . . and resume my teaching."[2] So eager were the Kentuckians to have her teach their children that some went so far as to "offer to build an academy and present me with a deed of the same, to guarantee me a handsome salary for teaching, and to give me a city residence, or, if I preferred rural life, to present me with a fine farm." In the spring of 1847, as indicated, "they prevailed upon my brother-in-law to move with his family to Frankfort . . . and in 1848 my brother also was induced to accept certain propositions to . . . locate with his family near Georgetown." It was surely no accident that both these towns were on Newton Craig's native grounds. The Craig home, "a Greek Revival house" that the penitentiary warden would eventually transform into "a noble Italianate villa" of elegantly symmetrical design, still stands on the north side of the Frankfort Pike a few miles west of Georgetown.[3] In what was by 1850 a farm of some thirty thousand acres (according to the 1850 census), Craig farmed not only the customary crops of the time, but developed extensive vineyards. A three-story windowless structure of stone and brick served as a winery, manned by prison labor; a smaller, though equally solid, building behind the house was a holding pen for his prisoners. Craig maintained a home in Frankfort as well, where his penitentiary responsibilities kept him much of the time.

By her account, Delia Webster left New York not for Kentucky but Indiana. Madison was a prosperous, growing city on the banks of the Ohio, halfway between Cincinnati and Louisville. Her arrival there in 1849 coincided with its period of greatest growth. The Madison and Indianapolis Railroad, the first in Indiana, had just been completed, in 1847; it turned the city into the gateway to the rest of the state. All northbound produce passed from the Ohio River through Madison before reaching the capital and surrounding areas—until the development of rival railroads in the mid-1850s, which led to Madison's eventual decline. Since before the dawn of white settlement, its site had always been a natural river crossing. Indians had come down from what is now Michigan, creating a long wilderness pathway, to pass over into Kentucky. When settlement began in 1806, "this Indian trail, to become known as the Old Michigan Road, served as a ready-made highway for settlers to leave the river and to travel northward in search of fertile farmlands."[4] The peculiarities of geography were such that Madison was closely linked by commercial and passenger riverboat traffic not only with Cincinnati and Louisville but also with Frankfort. The Kentucky River, which was navigable to the capital, flows into the Ohio just eight miles upstream of Madison, at Carrollton. Regular passenger service was assured by the *Blue Wing*, described by Kentucky historian Thomas D. Clark as having "cabins and decks . . . so elaborate that it looked like a birthday cake," its "scroll-work and gingerbread" so gaudy as to transform the boat into "a veritable floating valentine."[5]

"Early in 1849," Webster would recall, "the Ex-Lieutenant-Governor of Indiana was employed to visit me and lay before my mind inducements to return to that climate, and very soon thereafter some Kentucky friends (slaveholders) made a trip to Vermont, expressly to gain the consent of my parents to my returning with them, and I did return and located in Madison, Indiana."[6] Establishing her residence in Madison appears to have been a way of returning to Kentucky without actually living in a state where certain citizens still held it against her that she had stolen away slaves. From her new base in Indiana, she "frequently visited different portions of Kentucky, and was everywhere received with the utmost cordiality, and the same respect shown me as though I had never been an inmate of their state prison." The "Ex-Lieutenant-Governor of Indiana" who had issued the invitation to come to Madison was General Milton Stapp, who was well on his way to becoming the mayor of Madison, an office he would occupy from 1850 to 1853. He was born in Scott County, Kentucky, in 1793, fought under Colonel Richard Johnson at the Battle of the Thames in the War of 1812, and settled in Madison in 1816. He was elected lieutenant governor of Indiana in 1828; this proved to be the high-water mark of his political career, as he finished a distant third in the race for governor in 1831. William Wesley Woollen, a Madison contemporary, described him as a "public spirited man," and one of the best chief executives the city ever had. So imperious was Stapp that when mayor he "often arrested offenders on the street and, unaided, marched them to jail." He was a vain man, proud of his "talents and honors." Yet "in his credulity he was as simple as a child," Woollen also observes, which may have some relevance to his dealings with, and enthusiasm for, Delia Webster.[7] Relevant as well may be his Scott County origins, for subsequent events would indicate he was a longtime friend of fellow Scott countian Newton Craig, and it is evidently through some sort of collusion between the two that Webster was invited to come to Madison.

Craig no doubt had commercial interests in Madison, for the river traffic between there and Frankfort afforded him a ready market for the products of prison labor. It might not, though, have seemed an ideal place for a Yankee abolitionist schoolteacher to relocate, were it not that the schoolteacher in question never shrank from the challenge of inserting herself into a proslavery community. For Madison, though in a free state, was "a quasi Southern city," according to Woollen. "The opinions and sentiments of her inhabitants were molded, to a great extent, by the opinions and sentiments of their Kentucky neighbors. Runaway slaves were hunted over the hills and through the valleys of Jefferson [County]. The abolition settlement in Lancaster township [ten miles northwest] was considered a plague-spot on the body politic." The Eleutherian College in Lancaster, named after the Greek word for "freedom," was founded in 1848 as "one of the first integrated and coeducational colleges west of the Alleghenies."[8] The school, Woollen writes, "received the maledictions of the people, because in it the fountain of knowledge was as free to the negro as to the white man. Dwelling houses which had been erected near this college for the use of colored students were burned and destroyed."[9]

The Underground Railroad was well established, with a station every ten miles. At nearby Ryker's Ridge, some slaves in transit on a Sunday could not be hidden in a barn because all the churchgoers were going to put their horses there; instead, the fugitives were concealed in the organ loft of the church itself during the services.[10] Robert Elliott was a teamster for one of Madison's pork houses by day but a transporter of fugitives by night. He boarded with Sheriff Robert Right Rea, the "runaway slave detective" at whose house Calvin Fairbank spent his first night of freedom on August 24, 1849. Woollen says of Rea that he was "unlettered but . . . unusually shrewd and cunning, . . . a natural detective and a terror to absconding thieves and runaway cows. He was also feared by runaway slaves, for many a panting fugitive was arrested by him and returned to bondage."[11] When Rea suspected what Elliott was doing at night, he kept as "close to him as a brother." When Elliott was given word that he had to take a load of slaves to his barn ten miles north of town he knew he would be closely watched by his landlord. He bid Rea good night and took his candle to bed. After everyone in the house was asleep, he tied the bedclothes to the bed post and slid two stories to the ground, taking the precaution of tossing the linked sheets and quilts back into his room. He made his rendezvous, returning in time to be at the wash bench the next morning to greet Rea, who was never the wiser, thinking he had just come downstairs.[12]

No doubt without regard to either its public pro-Southernness or its intense underground activity, Madison had been highly recommended to Delia Webster "as a desirable location for a school, and for my fancy painting" and she apparently did set herself up as a teacher there, though no trace of her involvement in any particular institution of learning has yet surfaced.[13] A Madison newspaper thirty years later did recall that "Miss Webster, after her release from the Frankfort penitentiary, came to Madison and boarded for a time with Mrs. Crozier, on West Third street, and afterwards she occupied a part of the 'Kinney house.'"[14] Mrs. Mary C. Johnson, an African American interviewed in 1931 at the age of 95, recalled that "Delia Webster was an ordinary sized, good looking woman of medium complexion. She always dressed becomingly and labored among the colored people teaching them to read and write and also gave religious instructions. There was a small colored Baptist church on Fifth street, between West and Mulberry, where she gave her willing service."[15] St. Paul's Second Baptist Church, now a garage, still stands in Madison; above its doorway is carved the date 1849.

It was not until later, however, that Delia Webster began teaching in Madison's African-American community.[16] In 1849 she had a different clientele: "No sooner was I located, than Mrs. Craig, of Frankfort, Kentucky, came and brought her children to be my pupils, confiding them to my special care, and they have remained with me up to the present moment," she wrote in December, 1851.[17] The Craigs had been married nearly twenty-two years, Newton Craig having wed his first cousin Lucy Craig on September 27, 1827, when both were twenty years old.[18] In 1849, the Craigs had six children living: Mary, 17; Lucien, 15; Dillard, 11; William, 8; Florida, 7; and Charles, 2. All but one of these may have been given by Lucy Craig to Delia Webster's charge, Charles being surely too young to leave home.[19]

The Kentuckians' entreaties to return had not come as entirely out of the blue as Webster claimed. According to the prison doctor William C. Sneed, "Some time after her return to her home in Vermont" in 1845, she had written "a long letter addressed to Gov. Owsley, Lieut. Gov. Arch. Dixon, Rev. Jas. M. Bullock, Capt. Craig, and Wm. Todd. This letter was sent to Capt. Craig's lady, whose sympathies had been aroused in her behalf while in prison."[20] Sneed's description is the only account available of the letter.[21] In *Kentucky Jurisprudence* Webster had written that during her six-week stay in the penitentiary she had become "most ardently attached" to Lucy Craig. "She often visited me in my room, and sometimes invited me to walk out with her, thus doing all in her power to promote my happiness. She took care that my food was of the best and most delicious quality, and prepared with neatness and elegance." Mrs. Craig, Webster wrote, "is a lady of strong and well balanced mind and appeared perfectly regardless of the flying rumors assailing my moral standing."[22] The letter Webster addressed to Governor Owsley, Newton Craig, and the others "was written in a simple business-like manner," according to Sneed, and stated that the climate of Vermont was so injurious to her health that she would either have to move back South or die from lung disease. "With his usual kindness the Captain [Newton Craig] replied to her letter, and gave her such advice as he thought proper and best for her good." Sneed does not say what that advice was. "From this grew up a considerable correspondence which resulted in establishing a friendship between them of some duration."[23] "Capt. Craig," Webster wrote in 1851, "though once a bitter opponent and full of prejudice against me, has since become a most decided friend and I believe delights in doing me justice."[24] "Mr. Craig," a writer for the *Madison Star* would later recall, "visited Miss Webster under various pretexts while she resided there."[25] Such pretexts included, no doubt, prison business that brought him to Madison, and the desire to visit his children.

An article several years later in the *Louisville Democrat* reported that Delia Webster had lived with Craig and his family in Frankfort before coming to Madison: "She entered the habitation of the Keeper himself, became a member of his family, and received from him the soft and loving appellation of 'my child.' . . . Not content merely to take this open and convicted abolitionist, to say no worse of her, under his own roof, at his own fireside and in the midst of his own family," Craig "gallanted her in the streets of Frankfort, and flaunted with her in his carriage from place to place." This went on for "many months, until public sentiment, patient and enduring as it had been, began to give evident signs of indignant contempt, and it therefore seemed to be prudent, that the 'child' should find an abiding place elsewhere. Accordingly she settled in Madison, Ind., where, it is said, the faithful and loving father purchased her a house and set her up in grand style."[26] That Craig bought her a house in Madison is an evident exaggeration, contradicted by the account in the *Madison Star* in 1879 that she boarded with Madison residents.[27] But the rest must have some basis in reality, and is in fact hinted at in her declaration that her brother-in-law settled in Frankfort in the spring of 1847, and her brother in Georgetown in 1848. Another source, "The Petticoat Abolitionist," an unpublished manuscript written in the 1940s and 1950s by Henrietta Galey, Dillard Craig's daughter, and apparently based at least in part on family tradition, suggests that it was in the fall of 1846 that Delia Webster first came to visit the Craig family.[28] This is corroborated by Webster's statement that it was in the spring of 1847 that her brother-in-law moved to Frankfort, as her sojourn is likely to have been somewhat in advance of her brother-in-law's arrival. Her brother-in-law is not mentioned in the Galey manuscript. Though no year is given, the narrative has Delia Webster arriving in Frankfort in what appears to be the fall of 1846. The *Louisville Democrat* characterizes the duration of her stay with the Craigs not as years but months (though "many"); thus it is not a question of her having spent the entire period there between 1846—after which there is no record of her whereabouts, apart from her claim of having spent the time teaching school in Vermont—and the spring of 1849, when she says she came to Madison.

Calvin Fairbank's silence on whether he met Delia Webster when he went to Madison is matched by his reticence concerning questions raised by her conduct. In the letter he wrote from Cincinnati to the *National Anti-Slavery Standard* on August 31, 1849, less than a week after he would have had the opportunity of seeing her in Madison, he replies to the criticism leveled at him four years before by a Dr. Brisbane, who had said that "'Fairbank and Miss Webster are not worthy the sympathy of honest-hearted Abolitionists, and for no other reasons than that Fairbank was a hypocrite, for he went to Kentucky, to aid away a slave, pretending some other business; and that Miss Webster's conduct did not please him.' Now I should like to know," counters Fairbank, "what reason there is to be found in either of these objections? I could not have gotten the slaves by any other means, and I was not accountable for Miss Webster."[29] The declaration of nonaccountability falls somewhat short of a wholehearted endorsement of her actions. Their reunion in Madison, after his release, might likewise have been less than warm.

If not towards Delia Webster, then at any rate towards the abolitionists who "not only refused, or neglected to aid me, but actually turned against me," Fairbank was quite angry. "I have suffered too much . . . to let these things pass one day longer without making them public." He had to get it off his chest now, "lest after I shall have conferred with these gentlemen my ardor may cool." Among these gentlemen was Professor Walker of Oberlin, who had sent him on his way to Kentucky with money to free the Berry family, but had denied him in a manner worthy of Simon Peter, "most positively declar[ing] to Gen. McCaller [McCalla] in a letter . . . that he did not know me."

Fairbank was obliged as well to confront the dismay of many over his apparent recantation at his trial. He had not recanted his opposition to slavery, he responded, but had changed his mind, and said as much at the trial, "so far as unlawful interference was concerned"—that is, actually helping slaves to leave their masters. "If . . . they charge me with inconsistency, I have only to say to them *try it.*" In other words, try freeing some slaves yourself and see what you say when you get caught. "I have said, however, that I will never, under present circumstances"—a potentially important distinction—"interfere unlawfully with the subject again and think the same yet. But I shall always be found in lawful opposition to it."

When Sydney Howard Gay published Fairbank's letter in the *National Anti-Slavery Standard* he prefaced it with a comment in which the newly-pardoned prisoner could have taken little comfort. "He avows his continued interest in the Anti-Slavery Cause, but confesses his repentance of the particular act for which he suffered punishment. For this we do not see that he gives any better reason than that others, he thinks, were faithless to principles which both he and they once thought true. If he has no higher incentive to duty than the opinions of his fellow-men, he was doubly unfortunate in becoming the victim of the vengeance of the Slave-power." Printing with the letter a statement from Francis Jackson and Ellis Gray Loring about the role played in obtaining his ransom by "Lewis Hayden, now a respectable and industrious tradesman in Boston," Gay expressed the hope that this evidence of Hayden's gratitude "may serve to soften somewhat the bitterness of feeling which Mr. Fairbank seems to entertain—we hope without cause— towards some of his former friends."

Fairbank nevertheless enjoyed the warm welcome given him by the Cincinnati anti-slavery community, which included the "President of the Underground Railroad," Levi Coffin. He would later recall that "I found an addition to the 'Old Guard'—Laura S. Haviland. I had never met Mrs. Haviland before, though I had been familiar" with her benevolence toward the slave, her devotion to the cause, and her efforts toward educating the poor of all races.[30] He preached at the Cincinnati Wesleyan church, visited Oberlin College, related his experiences in Cleveland, and in Detroit was reunited with a family he had rescued from slavery in 1841. Turning down an invitation to speak in Chicago, he traveled to Sandusky, where he helped place six fugitives on a steamer bound for Canada, gleefully pointing them out in the distance to their pursuers who arrived at the shore of Lake Erie a few minutes too late. Buffalo was next, then a reunion with his mother and sisters in Little Genessee, New York, where his father had left them in his brother's care because of the premonition, unhappily fulfilled, that he might never return.

He headed for Boston, stopping along the way in Syracuse in January, 1850, to attend a convention that brought together two warring factions of the abolitionist movement, the Liberty Party and the American Anti-Slavery Society. "This was the most exciting and instructive convention of my life."[31] William Lloyd Garrison, Gerrit Smith, and Wendell Phillips were all there— as was Frederick Douglass, whose passionate eloquence was dazzling, "a tornado in a forest."[32] Fairbank himself briefly spoke in the morning session on January 17. He said he "did not believe the Constitution was a pro-slavery instrument; and he hoped all would unite without reference to their views on the Constitutional question."[33] Thus Fairbank clearly weighed in on the side of Gerrit Smith, against Garrison. Fairbank in fact spent several days afterward visiting Smith on his Peterboro estate, accompanying him to Albany to hear him address the New York legislature in response to Daniel Webster's March 7 speech in favor of Henry Clay's Compromise of 1850, with its infamous Fugitive Slave Bill requiring the return of all escaped bonds-men.

By March 19, 1850, Fairbank had arrived in Boston, where he "was the guest of the Haydens for the season." On that date he addressed a letter to the citizens of that city announcing that he would be "happy . . . to visit you with the anticipation that I shall be permitted to give you a public ex-pression of the gratitude I feel for your timely interference in my behalf." In the letter he recounts the events that led to his imprisonment, characterizing his effort to break out of the Lexington jail with Richard Moore as "an attempt to rescue a slave"—strangely, as if it would not have been his own escape too. To this audience he dwells on Moore's Boston connection: Mrs. Turner, the mistress whom he had killed in self-defense, had been a native of that city. Of Delia Webster, Fairbank says, on the one hand, that her convic-tion upon the basis of the "Frater" letter found on his person was "unlaw-ful"; on the other, that he had sacrificed himself for her, pleading guilty so that she might be pardoned. For having already succeeded in obtaining, by a special act of the state legislature, a change of venue to Paris, Kentucky, "I had expected to avail myself of all privileges to prolong the trial of my case for at least one year, upon the assurance of acquittal by explanation of the 'Frater' letter, by Sam Shy," his attorney. But to facilitate her pardon, he asked Governor Owsley "to omit to sign that bill which would make it a law."[34]

Had he spoken of this sacrifice when they met in Madison? In the letter to the citizens of Boston he complained that upon his release from the penitentiary "I found myself thrown out upon a cold, heartless world." Was the reception Webster gave him in Madison, enmeshed as she was in her ties to Newton Craig, part of that cold heartlessness?

Fairbank concluded his letter by advertising for speaking invitations in New England, giving as his address "in care of Lewis Hayden, 107 Cambridge street." He must have received at least a few offers, for he did visit "at times, different parts of the state, where I was invariably received with enthusiasm by all unbiased anti-slavery people."[35]

Yet not all were unbiased. On April 24, he would complain of "a doubt in the minds of some who are not the best abolitionists I ever saw, whether I am pursuing the best course to reach the object at which we aim." Some had intimated that he "did not stand up to the rack."[36] In the Cincinnati letter of August, 1849, he had tried to deal with that issue, explaining that when his case came to trial he had come to believe that going into Southern territory to induce slaves to escape was not a wise course of action. For all that, however, he had not abandoned his commitment to abolition. "In what, pray," he now asked, did he show cowardice? "'Why, what did Miss Webster say in her letters?' they ask. Now, the letters written by Miss Webster were entirely unknown to me, until after they were published; and I could not have written them myself." The letters in question are the one to Reverend Harvey Leavitt and the one to Mr. Mason of Oberlin, Ohio. In the latter she had indeed said of Fairbank that "I never viewed him as polluted with the foul blot of abolitionism. From my earliest acquaintance with him he never hinted to me that he entertained any such sentiments."[37] The Mason letter, of course, was an exercise in writing one thing and meaning another, complete with a postscript that should have alerted the intended recipient.

Fairbank had also to deal with other damage caused by the letter he had written from Cincinnati just after his release. His omission there of any reference to Lewis Hayden's role in purchasing his freedom, having limited his thanks to certain prominent Kentuckians, had been a source of irritation. He replied by maintaining that he had been "informed that it was not expected that the fact that a sum of money was raised in Boston to buy my pardon would be made public." An "anti-slavery friend at Cincinnati" had told him "that some things I was about to say ought not to be said." Obviously, Hayden had not been offended by the omission, since he had invited Fairbank to live in his house. Fairbank would later relate that the six hundred dollars Hayden had raised was to be paid "whenever my release should be certified to by myself in Ohio."[38] It would probably have been imprudent to hand over the money before he was out of prison. This circumstance might in fact explain why he went to Madison and lodged with the notorious slave catcher Right Rea. Newton Craig and Governor Crittenden wanted to keep him under guard—through the agency of Rea, who may therefore have even accompanied him from Madison to Cincinnati—until the money was paid. To publicize the ransom before it had actually changed hands would have upset a delicate situation.

In July, Fairbank was addressing audiences in small towns in central Massachusetts, or trying to. In Northampton he was stopped from putting up an announcement on a tree by a clerk of the local Congregational church. In Thorndike, he was to hold a meeting at the local school house at 8 p.m., but found it locked. A large crowd of ladies having already assembled on the spacious porch and the moon affording sufficient illumination, he assumed a position between the pillars and sang a song, then began his speech. Soon the custodian arrived, with apologies for being late. He urged Fairbank to move the meeting indoors, but seeing a way to save the money he had contracted to pay for renting the hall, he refused. Indeed, the collection taken up by "a lady walking among the crowd with a hat" was, at eighty-four cents, rather meagre. On July 22 and 23, he gave two talks in Spencer. The first was "a good meeting," but the second was marred by a gang of rowdies who stood in the back and continually talked, whistled and bleated. Fairbank was the target as well of "about four quarts of beans." He kept his courage up, though, and concluded the letter in which he recounted these adventures by declaring that "if I could command millions, I should like to take music and other help with me," but as it is "I hate slavery so intensely . . . that, with no other means than the ability to carry my valise from place to place—and be reviled for it—I will continue."[39]

While Calvin Fairbank was dodging beans in Massachusetts, Delia Webster was continuing to serve as governess to Lucy and Newton Craig's children, traveling that summer with their eldest son Dillard in neighboring New York as she headed toward Vermont to visit her parents. En route, she even carried out some penitentiary-related business for the warden. These facts are apparent from two letters Craig wrote her that summer.

> Frankfort, June 20, 1850
>
> My dear Dehlia: Nearly six years have passed away since we first became acquainted. Early in that acquaintance we promised each other that we should be true friends. How has it been with us? Does that friendship wear well? Have I been your friend? Or are you sorry that we

ever became acquainted? For myself, the time, I think, will never come that I shall feel less; for there has been a good deal increase of my friendship for you, as I have become more and better acquainted with you. Oh, let us strive to avoid doing anything which will wound the feelings of each other. Nothing shall be withheld on my part that will make you happy, and you can do much to advance my weal or woe. Oh, then, let us often advise together. Let us often counsel together as dear friends, and let us often pour out our whole hearts to each other; for here in this bottom, my dear child, you may pour out all your sorrows, and commit them to a faithful, *true friend*. Hasten, O hasten back to him, for he cannot bear your absence much longer. O how he longs to see your return, and make his home your home, and share with him whatever blessings he may enjoy. And now may kind Heaven bless your dear heart, and send you speedily to his arms, is the sincere desire of your fond father.

N. Craig.

To HIS Dehlia.[40]

Ten years her senior, Craig expressed his affection for Webster as a father's fond embrace. She is "my dear child." He is her "true friend." Perhaps nothing in this letter might have offended Lucy Craig. Nor in the one he wrote a fortnight later, on July 6, addressed "To His Dear Children, New York." The letter makes clear that Delia is one of the children, the other being his twelve-year-old son Dillard. Presumably Charles at age three was too young to leave home, and the letter speaks of Mary and Florida as being home with their parents. In Henrietta Galey's manuscript, her father, Dillard Craig, is fourteen instead of twelve—because she sets the scene in 1852, apparently forgetting that Benajah Webster had died the year before—and Benajah and Dillard have a fine time roaming the fields of the Webster family's Vermont farm.[41]

The July 6 letter begins with instructions that reveal that by this time Newton Craig had placed total trust in Delia Webster's probity and discretion, entrusting her with penitentiary business that blended the institution's finances with his own. "Be sure to do as I have directed, and be ready to explain the whole matter. Mark the manner in which the bills are to be made out. It is important. Make the Penitentiary the purchaser and received payment of me for the whole amount, then pay the bill, five per cent less."[42]

He speaks of his intention to come to Vermont to accompany her on the return to Kentucky.[43] "I will leave home on the 22nd, and will be at your father's on the Saturday following. So soon as I learn the true state of the case, I will write you to Ferrisburg. But be that as it may, be sure you start home on the 29th, for of course I will start home that day."

Then he catches her up on news from home. "This leaves us all well. Florida and Mary Morris are learning very little but mischief. Miss Randall writes from Madison that she wants to come back. I look for her. Mayor Stapp, of Madison, allowed the Holtzclaws bail, and the people are very much out with him; but he did what was his duty under the law." Milton Stapp became mayor in 1850. The Holtzclaws to whom he allowed bail were a father and three sons involved in a famous Madison murder case. When constable Joseph Howard attempted to arrest one of the sons for having made a disturbance, "he got into a personal difficulty with the father and the sons," according to Madison historian William Woollen. When Howard tried to collar the son he had come for and drag him out into the street another son shot and killed the constable. "The Holtzclaws were arrested and admitted to bail, and then fled the country."[44] Hence Craig's comment that Madisonians were angry at Stapp for having granted them bail.

Returning to his plans to accompany her on the return from Vermont, Craig wrote, "Be sure you are at your father's house from the 25th till you start home on the 29th, as I will be there if I come; and I will either be there or I will have a letter there in due time letting you know that I cannot come. Should I come, I hope not be annoyed again on the road home, as I once was." What kind of annoyance he was alluding to can only be the subject of conjecture: Was it parental interference, Benajah and Esther Webster showing their perplexity at such a close association between their daughter and her former jailor? Or perhaps an encounter on the journey back with one of her abolitionist friends, a meeting in which the slaveholding prison keeper would have felt distinctly uncomfortable?

His eldest son occupied Craig's thoughts. "I have but one letter from Dillard, notwithstanding he has been gone so long and notwithstanding my strict charge to him, as he was to write to me every Monday. You tell me he is learning very fast. I hope you will check him in his speed in learning to promise me to do one thing, and then doing another. I am displeased with his course. Poor encouragement to let him go again. . . . I shall continue to write to you, as I promised. I will direct all the letters to Simeon, at Ferrisburg." This promise to keep up his end of the correspondence suggests he had other things to say than this fairly dry recital of business instructions and gossip from home. If the information necessary to her acting as agent for the penitentiary in its purchases and for their effecting a rendezvous for the return trip has already been conveyed by this letter, what need had he to continue to write? And why direct the letters to her brother-in-law, instead of her parents?[45]

A third letter gives some idea of what else Craig wished to convey, and why his letters could not pass through her parents' hands. Gone is all talk of

Dillard Craig. Courtesy Mrs.Galey Coleman

filial affection. Though it bears no date, internal evidence indicates the late spring or early summer of 1849. "BRING THIS TO ME - CONFIDENTIAL. *My Dehlia:* —You know I told you that I would write you a long letter about this time, to which I would urge your *closest attention,* but I so fully explained myself that I know you are aware of the whole matter, and I therefore need not recapitulate in writing." As the instruction preceding the salutation suggests, this letter is of a substantially different nature than the other two. Meant for her eyes only, it must be returned to the writer so that he can either destroy it or put it where no other eyes can find it. She evidently did not obey that instruction.

"In short, I want you to come home to live with us."[46] He means home in Kentucky, and "us" means Lucy too, who would prove either remarkably tolerant or remarkably unaware. "I am constantly unhappy about you while in Madison, and in dread; I fear fire—I fear sickness and accidents." Cholera was raging in the area in the summer of 1849. Fairbank's father would die from it in Lexington on July 7, having ignored Craig's pleas to "leave the state, to go home, and protect himself from the terrible epidemic."[47] Madison, subject to continual river traffic, would have been an even more likely site for contagion than rural Scott County. As the *Louisville Democrat* reported in 1854, Webster evidently first lived with the Craigs, and then moved to Madison (in the spring of 1849, as she has written).[48]

Craig deeply regretted her having left Kentucky for Indiana. "I fear that it"—meaning her relocation to Madison—"will not advance our interests; indeed, I know that the best possible way for our mutual good is for you to come right into the bosom of my family and friends, and by a prudent, judicious and discreet course, you will prove a *tall white plume* in my cap." By appearing to be a Yankee abolitionist converted to the superiority of the Kentucky way of life, a former slave stealer saved from a life of crime by the ministrations of a prison warden who had always sought the spiritual regeneration of his charges, Delia Webster would indeed be a feather in Craig's cap.

"Look at the impressions made on the minds of my friends, already eulogising my course. See what Shotwell, my merchant at Louisville, where Dillard recites his lesson) that, with similar things is what I want us to be at, which cannot be done by us." The text of this last sentence is evidently corrupt; no manuscript version, alas, is available to correct it. Even the punctuation (the closing parenthesis after "lesson" missing its predecessor) suggests that something must have been left out in the transcription. Nevertheless from this garbled sentence it is clear that Dillard was in Louisville, which means that the letter could not have been written in 1850, for the letter of July 6 of that year shows him to be in the East with Delia Webster.

"My dear child, if you come to Kentucky and make good what I have said of you, it will crush my enemies who have sought to injure me for being your friend, but until you are better known here they may still charge us, and the public know not the truth." What he said of her is evidently that she had been reformed out of her abolitionist tendencies. "My Dehlia I see the way so plain I cannot doubt as to the proper course. I therefore urge you—yes, I URGE you most affectionately URGE you to remove *at all hazards* every obstacle in our way to your coming home at once."

Now comes the heart of the letter: "I might enlarge and give the reasons all over and *over*, but you know my mind, and remember this—I LOVE you, yes, I LOVE you most dearly, and can never prosper in your absence." Craig's words here appear to test the limits of paternal affection. "I would much rather (so far as I am concerned) that the time from now to the 15th of July was passed.—It is a vacuum that nothing can fill but my Dehlia. Let me urge you not to disappoint my hope in your starting home on that day. I expect to meet you on the way. Ah, I hail the auspicious time with delight. May kind heaven grant its speedy arrival." The language is almost identical to that of the July 6, 1850, letter, except that the dates are different. There, she was to start home from her parents' house on July 29. As he would in 1850, Craig planned to meet her on the way home. It is significant that he would not, in 1849, visit her at her parents; very possibly their relationship was still a secret from Esther and Benajah Webster—as in 1850 he would still take the precaution of sending letters to her sister rather than to them.

"Your little trees at the farm are all ladened with fruit. It is all yours. Strawberries are commencing to be very abundant here. This will be a wonderful fruit year." This would place the letter about the first week of June, when strawberries appear in Kentucky and apple trees begin to bear fruit for later harvest. "Try hard to bring mother and father with you; but above all things never leave mother with a promise that you'll stay away from Kentucky, *no! no!*—free yourself from all on that point, for it was that that made me so desirous for you to be off to see mother and friends." Benajah Webster died on January 30, 1851, thus the reference to her father in this letter means it must have been written before that year.[49] It could not have been 1850, either, as he was to start home July 29 that year, not July 15 as this letter indicates. Since she moved to Madison in the spring of 1849 and her residence in Madison is a topic of the letter, then the letter cannot have been written before 1849. The most likely date is therefore early June, 1849.

"I do think you have been trammeled unjustly, and greatly to my disadvantage, and *now* I urge you to *relieve yourself.* Yes, break down every obstacle and learn your right to set your own deliberate will, and then if you prefer not coming, I must yield." He must be referring to the pressure her parents had been applying to persuade her to remain in Vermont. "I charge you to bring your letter from the church with you. My dear, don't fail to do that if you can possibly get it. Manage a little and then wash your hands of them. I shall feel grieved if you come without it." Letters from a local church attesting to good character and religiosity were essential at the time if one wished to gain full acceptance in a new community, and Craig was careful to assure that she was going to have proper entree in Frankfort. That she might find it difficult to obtain such a letter, presumably from the Vergennes Congregational Church, is intriguing. She had no such difficulty in 1844, when Harvey Leavitt was its pastor and her epistolary correspondent, and when the public hearing held in Vergennes in November of that year determined that she "remained in full fellowship" with that church and was "regarded as one of more than ordinary piety."[50] What might have happened since to change that opinion is not clear, though her friend the Reverend Norris Day had seen his character come under fire in religious circles.

"Write to me every Monday," Craig closed, asking of her what he would ask the following year of Dillard, and allowing the conclusion that if several Mondays remained for her to do so before July 15, then the letter must have been written perhaps a month or more before that date. "I will write again soon. I shall continue to urge some of the same in this. —Farewell, farewell, till we meet. Your true friend, N. CRAIG."[51]

If this letter dates from early June, 1849, then it was written at the same time that Fairbank's father was in Kentucky collecting signatures for his pardon. If Webster left Vermont on July 15, she would have been in Madison in time for Fairbank's arrival there August 24. In the summer of 1850, when Webster was going about her adopted father's business in New York and Vermont, Fairbank was giving antislavery lectures in Massachusetts that focused on an alarming new development, the impending Fugitive Slave Act. Passed in September, the law denied jury trials to captured slaves and provided instead for special commissioners, who would be paid $5 if he decided the captive could stay in the North, $10 if sent back to slavery. Northern bystanders could be legally liable not only for helping a runaway escape but even for refusing to help in his arrest (on the model of Southern conscription of whites to serve in local "patrols").[52] "I had fought this," Fairbank wrote, referring to the pending legislation, "through the summer of 1850, and continued to resist it after its enactment as far as possible with any show of safety."[53]

Living as he was at Lewis Hayden's Boston home in 1850, Fairbank would have had ample opportunity to resist the law with more than words. For Hayden's Cambridge Street store provided clothing and the funds to feed runaways en route to Canada, while his Beacon Hill residence was the main

Boston depot of the Underground Railroad, harboring at least a quarter of all the fugitives who passed through the city. When Harriet Beecher Stowe dropped by for a visit she was amazed to see thirteen there at once.[54]

9

"I AM AFRAID THEY WILL NOT ALWAYS BE ON AS FRIENDLY TERMS"

In the fall of 1850, not long after passage of the Fugitive Slave Act, William and Ellen Craft learned that their former owners had sent an armed posse to bring them back to Georgia. They had escaped to Boston the year before, light-complected Ellen disguising herself as a young white master, bundled up with obscuring clothing because of illness, accompanied by his manservant, who was in reality her husband. They traveled, naturally, first class. In Boston, William Craft had pursued his trade as a cabinetmaker, undisturbed until then.[1] When warning came of their impending capture, Ellen was hidden in the home of Ellis Gray Loring in Brookline, while William took refuge in Lewis Hayden's Beacon Hill residence, which a contemporary witness described as being in a virtual state of siege. The windows were barricaded, the doors double-locked and barred, while around a table heaped high with loaded weapons sat Lewis Hayden, his son Jo, "and a band of brave colored men armed to the teeth and ready for the impending death struggle."[2] Forty-four years later, Craft would recall that he and Hayden had hidden a keg of gunpowder in the basement "with a fuse attached ready to light it should any attempt be made to capture us."[3]

On November 6, 1850, Ralph Waldo Emerson, William Lloyd Garrison, Wendell Phillips, and other great lights of the abolition movement met at the Haydens' Phillips Street house to decide how to prevent the Crafts' recapture. Hayden's houseguest, Calvin Fairbank, was an eyewitness to the meeting: "Lewis Hayden, unconscious of who were present, having in his mind only the rescue of his friends, rose and began to speak with his whole soul, and was just pouring out one of his most fervid strains of native eloquence, when, turning toward another portion of his audience, he saw those notable, noble men, embodying the lore and wisdom of the Bay State, and sank into his seat abashed and silent."[4] The confrontation of the man of practical action with the men of practiced rhetoric recalled that August afternoon four years before when, on Thoreau's doorstep at Walden Pond, Hayden stammered out his touching paean to liberty as the transcendental musings of the sage of Concord were still lingering in his listeners' ears. This time, the former waiter of the Phoenix Hotel was too aware of the disparity between himself and his distinguished guests to continue. Looking around the room, he suddenly fell into an embarrassed silence. For Fairbank, the eloquence of those who did speak made the occasion "one of the most extraordinary in my memory."

Money was raised to assure the Crafts' escape out of the country. But before they left it was determined that they must first be given a brilliant wedding. It was feared that the doubtful legality of their previous marriage under slave law would delay their entry into the British Isles.[5] Theodore Parker performed the ceremony on the following day at the Haydens' residence. At its conclusion, he placed a Bible in the bridegroom's left hand and a dagger "of fearful length" in the other. "Take this," he commanded, "and defend your wife."[6] The newlyweds departed by train for Halifax, and from there set sail for England.

At eleven in the morning on Saturday, February 15, 1851, acting U.S. marshal Patrick Riley and deputy marshal Frederick Warren went to the Cornhill Coffee House to arrest a fugitive slave. The restaurant was located in the neighborhood of the Boston Courthouse. Riley had nine men stationed in and about the place but could not act until the arrival of a witness who could identify the slave, a Frederick Wilkins, known also as "Shadrach." To avoid suspicion the marshals entered the dining room and ordered some coffee. They were waited on by a black man who turned out, by chance, to be the man they sought. Impatient with waiting for the witness who still had not arrived, they drank their coffee, paid the waiter and rose to leave. As Shadrach preceded them out of the dining room and in the direction of the bar, taking to the cashier the money with which they had paid the bill, his arms were suddenly seized by two other white men, one of them the tardy witness, who walked him out a back door, across the street and into the courthouse. He was still wearing his linen apron.

Word of the arrest spread rapidly among the black citizens of Boston and the abolitionist community. A former slave who knew the prisoner hurried to the courthouse to see for himself. Confronting his fellow blacks milling in the streets, he begged them to do something. No one would until he met Lewis Hayden, who had already assembled a group of friends, posted near the doorway to the Courthouse and ready to do battle. Hayden, Shadrach's friend recalled, seemed "quiet and calm and full of faith."[7]

Within thirty minutes of the arrest, a crowd of one hundred fifty blacks and some fifty whites had gathered in the courtroom. Antislavery lawyers Ellis Gray Loring and Richard Henry Dana had agreed to defend the prisoner, and when the U.S. commissioner finally appeared they successfully argued for a postponement until 10 a.m. Tuesday. By Massachusetts law, the city jail could not be used to house a fugitive, who was therefore to be confined in the courtroom itself. Marshals cleared the court of all spectators. Unknown to the officers remaining in the room, between sixty and a hundred men, under Hayden's direction, had taken possession of the stairways and corridors outside. By 2 p.m. all civilians except a lawyer and a reporter had left. When one of the officers opened a door so that the lawyer could leave, it was suddenly grabbed by a multitude of hands trying to pry it the rest of the way open. Cries of "Tear him out!" were heard as a fierce struggle ensued between the officers within and the rescuers without. The twenty inside were no match for Hayden's besiegers. The door was sprung open and "in poured an avalanche of muscular and excited" blacks, "capable of overturning everything before them." Shadrach started for another door, but was headed off by an officer who was ordered by a Marshal's deputy "to shoot the prisoner, which order he was probably unable to obey." Someone picked up the U.S. marshal's sword from the table where it lay and swung it around; the officers were "kicked, cuffed, and knocked about in every direction." Shaken by his brush with death, Shadrach cowered in a corner of the room, but was soon lifted and carried out by his rescuers into the street. A carriage drew up, as if by prearrangement, and whisked him away as fast as the horse would go.[8] As Hayden later recounted, "We safely lodged him in the attic of a widow. . . . He remained in this hiding place for only a few hours. From thence he was taken by myself in a carriage to Cambridge, where a horse and chaise was substituted, and we drove to Watertown, where we spent the afternoon, returning to the home of Rev. Joseph C. Lovejoy in Cambridge." Hayden left him there, returning to Boston for a light wagon and two horses. Concealing the fugitive in the wagon, Hayden and a friend drove him to Concord; from there he followed the underground route to Leominster, then Vermont, and ultimately Canada.[9]

Hayden was subsequently brought to the bar of justice for his role in the affair. The testimony against him seemed unassailable, yet the case resulted, on June 16, 1851, in a hung jury.[10] He had expected to go to jail, and his lawyers were mystified by the outcome. Two years later, Richard Henry Dana met a blacksmith from northern Massachusetts from whom he learned that the jury had voted eleven to one to convict. The blacksmith had been the lone holdout. He had also been, as it happened, the underground agent who drove Shadrach from Concord to Leominster.[11]

On the floor of the U.S. Senate on February 18, 1851, Henry Clay expressed his outrage that the Fugitive Slave Act could be so easily contravened by a lawless mob. "Who committed this flagrant outrage? Was it our own race? No! But a band who are not of our people; it was by Africans and the descendants of Africans." He asked "whether the government of white men is to be yielded to a government by blacks."[12] Clay seems to have been aware of, though unwilling to accept, the historic reversal that had taken place: Boston, America's "Cradle of Liberty," had seen its revolutionary tradition renewed by the despised race, the stone the builders—the Republic's founding fathers—had rejected. Ironically, he was not aware that the leader of the band in fact was practically, in the peculiar Southern turn of phrase for referring to one's own slaves, one "of our people," for Hayden was "the son-in-law of one of his own slaves."[13] Hayden had certainly claimed a family connection in 1847 when he publicly complained of Clay's having sold his wife and son south.

It was impossible to repeat the success of the Shadrach rescue when the next occasion arose, with the seizure of Thomas Sims two months later, in April 1851. The civil authorities were now aware of how easily they could lose their prey, and the threat of legal prosecution had dampened the zeal of many who might have attempted to save him. Thomas Wentworth Higginson, a participant in these events, characterized the effectiveness of the Boston Vigilance Committee, the union of abolitionists formed to defend fugitives from recapture and which Hayden had joined early on, as vitiated by the non-resistance principles of many of its members, including William Lloyd Garrison. Such qualms did not "apply to the Negroes," Higginson recalled. "They had just proved their mettle" in the Shadrach affair, "and would doubtless do it again. On my saying this in the meeting, Lewis Hayden, the leading Negro in Boston, nodded cordially and said, 'Of course they will.' Soon after, drawing me aside, he startled me by adding, 'I said that for bluff, you know. We do not wish any one to know how really weak we are. Practically there are no colored men in Boston; the Shadrach prosecutions have scattered them all. What is to be done must be done without them.'"[14]

While intended as a precaution, the immense iron chain wrapped around the Boston Courthouse on April 4 served as well as a powerful symbol of the repressive authority of the state. Yet Higginson devised an ingenious plan, which he confided to a small group of fellow conspirators, including Leonard Grimes, an African-American clergyman, and (as Henrietta Buckminster recounts) "Hayden, the most daring man in Boston." Higginson had noticed that the third-floor cell in which Sims was confined had no bars on the window. Grimes, who as a cleric was permitted to see Sims in his cell, was to tell the prisoner to be at his window the next evening at a certain hour. "Not looking back, not hesitating, he was to climb quickly onto the sill of the window and leap" onto mattresses brought from across the street just the moment before.[15] To his dismay, Higginson discovered the next day that workmen were busily installing bars over the window. Either they had been betrayed or the police, for once, had been too smart for them.

On April 13, three hundred police and volunteers arrived at the Courthouse at four in the morning to escort Sims to the ship that would return him to slavery. Henry Ingerscoll Bowditch witnessed the event: "It was still quite dark and I could not see, but friends who were near told me that tears were streaming over his face, though he walked without faltering on his course toward his Georgia home, the land of whips and of servitude." Despite the early hour, a hundred abolitionists had gathered to watch the procession. As the escort marched past "the spot where fell [Crispus] Attucks, the colored man shot down by the king's troops on March 5, 1770, we pointed out to those minions of slavery the holy spot over which they were treading . . . desecrating by their act this martyr stand of the Revolution."[16] In later years, Lewis Hayden would be instrumental in preserving this holy ground for official remembrance.

In Savannah, Thomas Sims was dragged to the town square and publicly whipped.

By the time of the Sims rendition, Calvin Fairbank had left Boston to return to the anti-slavery field. That spring (1851) in the southwestern New York town of Bolivar, he held a week-long meeting at the local Methodist church, having brought the minister over to his view of the need to combat the Fugitive Slave Law. He rented the church for six nights and days, and on the fourth night began to encounter some opposition. A church official insisted on hearing his opinion of President Fillmore, hoping to provoke him into making some politically unpopular statement. Fairbank at first resisted the invitation, but finally, egged on by the pastor whispering encouragement in his ear, he said what he thought: "Well, if you are anxious to hear my sentiments on President Fillmore and his Cabinet, they are a brotherhood of thieves."

"Give it to them!" whispered the pastor.

"This church endorses Fillmore and his cabinet," declared the church official.

"Well, this church is a den of thieves."

"I am an officer of this church, and I endorse Fillmore and his Cabinet."

"Well, then, you are one of the thieves. How do you like that?"

Irate parishioners called for eggs to throw at Fairbank. Those who had been won over to his side mounted the altar to shield him from the barrage.

"Two or three gentlewomen and girls who could not get out from their pews soon enough, being obstructed by roughs on the other side, sprang right over the tops of the seats in front of them, and even over the heads of their occupants" to join the circle of defense. "Now throw your eggs if you dare!" shouted one of the ladies.[17]

The eggs never came, and Fairbank finished out the week with "little more molestation." In June, he took part in a convention at nearby Friendship to choose delegates to a Liberty Party convention in Buffalo in September.

That summer Fairbank made the acquaintance of a young woman from Williamsburg, Massachusetts, named Mandana Tileston. By the fall, they would become engaged to marry.[18]

On September 13, he addressed a meeting in Corning, where a Kentucky native who was visiting relatives in the vicinity and attended out of curiosity later described him as speaking "very harshly [and] eloquently" of the Fugitive Slave Law, Daniel Webster, and President Fillmore, saying "many hard things of Kentuckians [yet] many good things" too. He made the claim of having liberated forty-four slaves in his career. "People thought him a lion; the church admired him. . . . I thought him sincere."[19]

Soon after the Buffalo assembly in September, 1851, Fairbank returned to Cincinnati. His mother had been pleading with him to rescue "our father's body, which lay among strangers, far from any one who cared for him, or revered and loved his memory." Chester Fairbank had died trying to free his son in the summer of 1849. When Calvin was released in late August of that year his father's body could not be removed from the state "for hygienic reasons; but now it could be safely done, and I went South for that purpose."[20] But when he arrived in Cincinnati, he found that it was too hot to move the corpse. Waiting for cooler weather, he traveled throughout southern Indiana giving anti-slavery speeches. Although he "took the river tier of counties," which would undoubtedly have included Madison, he would not have found Delia Webster there, for she had not yet returned from her summer in Vermont.

When Benajah Webster had died on January 30, 1851, at the age of 72, that event so grieved his daughter, Delia would tell the *Louisville Courier* (on December 17, 1851), "that I was thrown upon a sick bed and obliged to discontinue my school."[21] This statement is corroborated by what she wrote her mother from Madison on March 18, her first communication since Benajah's death. "My Dearest, My Beloved Mother," she wrote, "You may think it singular that, amid our deep affliction I should maintain such a long silence. But I have two reasons to offer for it which, I doubt not will be satisfactory. When I heard, through Gen. Stapp"—Milton Stapp, the Madison mayor and friend of Newton Craig who had come East to entreat Webster to relocate in his city—"the unexpected & distressing intelligence of the death of my Father . . . I was so overwhelmed with grief that I was thrown prostrate upon a sick bed . . . for some ten days. Since I have been able to sit up, walk about my house & attend in some measure to the duties of my little school I have not considered it prudent to suffer my mind to dwell upon that heart-rending Providence long enough to write any of my friends"—or her mother. "Had I followed the impulses of my own sensitive nature, long ere this I should have hastened to your arms. . . . But my friends here will not listen a word to my leaving until my health is a little more firm." Those friends must have included Newton Craig, whom we have seen declare that he could never prosper in her absence.

"Their judgment doubtless, is better than mine in this matter, consequently, for the time being I yield to its control. But O how I long to be with you, my dear Mother, & mingle my tears with yours!" Whatever may have been the degree of her piety, Delia displays in the letter an impressive command of religious rhetoric with which to comfort her mother and atone for her silence.

> I know your heart is wrung with anguish & your load is too heavy for you to bear. But I thank Heaven you know where to look for help in this hour of distress. You are not a stranger to that grace which the Gospel proffers. How unutterably sweet that promise, that precious promise, in this hour of afflction! . . . We have not lost that dear Father & Husband: he is ours still, & we should bow with calm submission, & kiss the rod. . . . If we are God's dear ones, & faithful for a few, few short days, we shall soon meet that loved one again."[22]

Our departed friends now "live in the skies. May they draw our thoughts thitherward—wean us from the dross of earth—elevate our standards of piety, & warm our desires to meet them. Five of your loved children are there," alluding to Richard and Ruth, dead at birth in 1808 and 1816; William, who had died in 1814 one month shy of his first birthday; Esther, dead at ten years in 1830; and Charles, who died at age 28 in 1835.[23] They are in heaven now,

> helping to make up the celestial throng, & mingling their voices with the patriarchs & prophets in praises to the Redeemer. When I think what transports of joy filled those five angel spirits as they sped their flight on seraph's wing to Heaven's portals, there to meet a beloved Father— When I contemplate the joyous greetings & warm embraces of that happy band—the long separated but never-forgotten Parent & children, & his cordial welcome to their bright abode, to the society of good men

made perfect, to the smiles of a risen Savior; when I think what sincere rejoicings echoed through the courts of Heaven that another Saint was added to their choir, it seems almost wrong to grieve, & selfish to wish them back in this vale of tears.

But did Delia Webster, so unconventional in other respects, believe these comforting words? What she writes next seems more in harmony with what we know of her life, for her religous impulse was wedded to action in *this* world: "It is my daily prayer that God will sanctify this afflictive stroke" so that we might "be in constant readiness for the approaching hour of our own dissolution. May it stimulate us to do with our might what our hands find to do for the benefit of the human family, that when called to pronounce this our earthly history we may hear from the lips of our judge: 'Well done good & faithful servant, enter thou into the joy of thy Lord.'" For Webster, as her past actions had shown, the human family included the slave.

Yet though she had suffered imprisonment a half dozen years before on behalf of the oppressed, why—one might ask—was she now ingratiating herself into the society of their oppressors? In particular into that of Newton Craig, whose presence in her life becomes apparent even here, at the close of this elaborate expression of condolence: "P.S. Capt. Craig & Lady would be glad to continue their little son & daughter under my tuition; &, *if agreeable to your feelings*, that I should take them home with me. Please let me know, by return mail, your wishes." In the left margin she adds: "I will bring my servant girl."

In the letter she wrote that she hoped to arrive in April, but it was not until May, as she told the *Louisville Courier*, "that I was sufficiently recovered from the effects of grief to endure the fatigues of a journey. I then took Capt. Craig's children and my waiting maid and went to comfort my poor, bereaved and stricken mother."[24]

Contrary to her practice in preceding years, by October she had still not returned to Madison. This caused much anxiety to Newton Craig, as may seen from the letter he wrote her on October 1, 1851.

> *My Dear Child:* I have just finished several letters, one to Simeon, one to Warren, and one to *your children,* and it has so completely overcome my hand that I can hardly hold my pen; but now I must write a few lines to you. I wrote you a letter fourth September, another in a few days thereafter, and a third in a few days more. I urged you to write me at once what you had determined to do, whether you were going to *again* make New England your home, or whether I might claim you as my Dehlia, to hang upon my arm for a father's protection. I *again* MOST FONDLY *offer you that ARM.* I you promise me to come home in the

spring and bring the children, I will come for you. If you will not promise, then let me know, and they MUST return home NOW.

I hope you will take a firm stand, and let me know what to depend on. There is no less than a half-dozen important things now hanging on me, and which I must soon act in reference to, and I can't till I know what your course will be. One important point is in regard to how far I ought to go to induce Warren to come West. I might give other reasons, but you must suffice it to say, that I am in no little suspense to know your determination. I will name one other item. I am on the look-out to ship hemp to Boston. I have forty bales now ready. If you intend to make New England your home, I will ship no more hemp there. If you are willing to make my home your home, I will ship hemp for an excuse to come for you about the 1st May. I have directed Warren to show you the letters. I told them of the two openings for them to something here for a while. I ASK YOU, I BEG YOU, I CHARGE YOU, to answer me promptly. I am much hurried, and have to leave home a few days on business. I am the same true and unchanged friend.

N. CRAIG[25]

Her slowness to respond to his flood of correspondence may be explained by her absence from Vergennes, as she travelled with her mother and brother to consult various physicians about her health. She took the waters at Saratoga Springs, New York. "After spending some time at the Springs, Dr. Chapin advised me to visit Albany, and there consult the eminent Dr. Hun." Hun told her she could not survive another northern winter.[26] This would justify a return to Craig, and she probably needed it to persuade her mother to let her go.

Meanwhile, Fairbank was not only confronting pro-slavery hecklers in southern Indiana, but even daring to venture into Kentucky. On October 22, 1851, he addressed a letter to William Lloyd Garrison from Louisville. "Let not my friends be anxious for me," he boasts. "I will keep out of the lion's jaws." From his tour of the city he reports that there are four slave markets, and that all bondsmen must be home by 10 p.m. under pain of whipping. He feels a particular sympathy for one "woman, as white and fair . . . as most ladies," a slave to a "most unfeeling" Louisville mistress, who whips her, kicks her, and tears off her clothes. She almost broke for freedom when her owner took her to Boston, but was stayed by the thought of her children left behind in Kentucky. Upon her return to Louisville, she asked to see her youngest child, only to be told it had died. "I came back for my babe," she told Fairbank. "God has it. It is better off than I am. Now I want freedom."

In an addendum to the letter, written from Jeffersonville, Indiana, across the river from Louisville, he appeals for antislavery speakers like Charles C.

Burleigh and Lucy Stone to come to Indiana and join the fight. Public opinion there was even more pro-slavery than in Kentucky, where "many of the people are beginning to see the advantage of freedom over slavery, and . . . are convicted of their former sins." Racial prejudice is more pronounced among the Hoosiers, he adds, because there are fewer blacks. In Charlestown, thirteen miles northeast of Jeffersonville, he caused much astonishment by tearing down four posted bills offering rewards for runaways and putting them in his pocket.

In closing, Fairbank promises "I shall soon be in Massachusetts."[27]

At 8 in the evening on Sunday, November 2, 1851, Fairbank was seen in Louisville at the "Centre Street Church for colored persons . . . where Bird Parker preaches." He was shaking hands with a Wash Spradley.[28] An hour later the slave Tamar, "very confident in her demeanor, rather impudent, aged 27," according to her owner A.L. Shotwell, was discovered missing.[29] She had been hired out to Judge Purtle, who would testify that he "heard some noise below in the basement story about 8 o'clock in the evening [that] sounded like raising windows." Upon cross-examination, he said that it might have been closer to 9 o'clock. It was in any event after supper. Tamar had already "cleared off the supper table."

Though he boarded most of the time in Jeffersonville, when in Louisville Calvin lodged with a Mrs. Jane Webster (no relation, apparently), giving his name as Joseph Fairbank. That evening, he had gone out at sundown—apparently to the Centre Street Church. Between 8 and 9 o'clock Tamar came to ask for him and the landlady told her to go to the Union Hotel, as Fairbank had requested. There they met, and went down to the riverbank to a leaky skiff, old and in danger of sinking. Fairbank paddled them across with a four-foot plank, while Tamar "with a cup taken for the purpose," continually scooped out the water that crept around their shoes. At 4 or 5 that morning Fairbank was pounding on the door of a livery stable in Jeffersonville, while Tamar hid, shivering, in a field. A groggy Charles McDowell at last arrived, and Calvin told him he boarded at Mr. Rose's in town and would like to rent a buggy for a two-day trip to Vienna. He already had a sack of oats for the horse. He took the precaution of telling McDowell that he would pick up a woman in Charlestown, in case he should later be seen on the road with his passenger. His actual destination was Salem.[30]

At 8 in the morning, as Fairbank was driving "quite fast" still thirty miles short of their goal, the horse was spooked by barking dogs and bolted, and the carriage broke against a stump. Had this untoward event not occurred, all would have been well—as likewise the rescue of the Haydens might have been effected with no suspicion falling on Fairbank had Parker Craig's horse not taken sick at Millersburg. Joseph Gibson, the owner of the dogs, was walking toward the accident to see if he could help when he saw a handkerchief lying on the ground. It had evidently slipped from Tamar's hand and out of the window of the carriage at the moment the horse panicked. He picked it up and saw that it bore the name of a Mary Bullock. Fairbank met him on the way, retrieved the handkerchief, and asked him if he could repair the damage to the buggy. Gibson said he could; Fairbank said he would return for it in two days.[31]

At the nearest town, about a mile away, Fairbank and Tamar were able to board the next passing train, even though it did not normally accommodate passengers. Two brakemen helped her up into their car; Fairbank was asked to wait for the passenger train but refused, and climbed aboard too. Fairbank "appeared to pay as much attention to her as if she was his newly married wife, and was extremely jealous of whoever even looked at her." Some of the railroad men "made use of obscene language—smutty words. Mr. F[airbank] interfered, and said the girl is a decent girl, and should not be abused; talk then stopped."[32]

When the train arrived in Salem, Calvin accompanied Tamar up the street from the depot. He called a small boy over to him and asked where a black barber named Jackson could be found. He located the barber, and Tamar was on her way.

Fairbank returned to Jeffersonville and on Sunday, November 9, was planning to go to Lexington the next day to recover his father's body, take it home to New York state, and "then return to Williamsburg, Massachusetts, and consummate my marriage engagement with Miss Mandana Tileston."[33] But A.L. Shotwell was moving heaven and earth to recover his slave and apprehend her kidnapper. U.S. Marshal Ronald sent a Mr. Hamlet to bring the ostler who had rented Fairbank the horse and buggy over to Louisville for a detailed description. Hamlet was also to keep close watch on the Indiana side. That Sunday, as Fairbank was on his way to church, he made the mistake of walking past the stable where he had hired the horse and buggy. Someone called out to him from the livery stable. Three or four men then came up and asked McDowell if he was the man who had rented the buggy. They were told that he was.

"I asked, 'What do you want of me?' 'I want you to Louisville,' said he; 'you have been aiding off some niggers.'" Fairbank refused. A man named Ragan "then seized me by the cravat, putting his hand inside, and twisting it so as to confine me . . . rendering it uncomfortable for me to speak or even to breathe." The marshal took hold of him. "I resisted with all my might, throwing Ragan in a position of about forty-five degrees, when he recovered, throwing me in the same way" by the help of the marshal. "The struggle continued, I cried aloud for the citizens of Indiana to preserve the honor of the law of the State." None stepped forward. Finally the sheriff intervened and said he would take Fairbank into custody, which would have been a more fortunate outcome. But Marshal Ronald talked him out of it, and Fairbank was put on a skiff to be rowed back to Kentucky.[34]

As Ronald and Hamlet were taking Fairbank into custody, they noticed that he was chewing on something, evidently trying to destroy evidence. It was paper, he said. They discovered a receipt, so torn up they could not make out its contents. The lawmen took him to his lodgings and searched his trunk: they "found a map of Niagara Falls," Marshal Ronald later testified. "Found a list of towns also, beginning with Cincinnati, naming Columbus, Akron, Nebo, Cuyahoga Falls, Cleveland, and Oberlin, Ohio; [I] suppose this was his abolition tour." At the river's edge, Ronald asked him his name. Fairbank replied that it "might be John Doe." Ronald tried again. "I had given him my name," he later testified, "and it would be but fair to give me his. He said, 'then you can call me S.S. King.'"[35] In further conversation with his captors as they were crossing the river, he was told that "Mr. Shotwell will carry it on against you to the utmost, he's got the money." Indeed, Fairbank would later write that "a large reward had been offered for the escaped slave and her assistant."[36] The prisoner replied that Shotwell looked like a gentleman to him and furthermore that he did not particularly blame him.

Fairbank just happened to have stolen away a slave that belonged to one of Craig's closest friends. Alfred Lawrence Shotwell (1809-93) was a Georgetown native, referred to in Craig's June 1849 letter as "Shotwell, my merchant in Louisville, where Dillard recites his lesson" and who was "eulogising" Craig's "course" with regard to his apparent reformation of Delia Webster.[37] Shotwell may well have spent more money to retrieve Tamar than she was worth. He paid a thousand dollars bail, plus two hundred dollars in spending money, so that a prisoner in the Louisville jail named Forsyth could go to Indiana to find her. In doing so, Shotwell fell into a trap Fairbank had set, for it had been he who had first suggested the idea to Forsyth, intending to send him—and Shotwell—on a wild goose chase. He told him to go to Indianapolis, which was one place Tamar would not be; Forsyth talked Shotwell into it, was released, went to Indianapolis, and was arrested for drunkenness, but never returned to Kentucky.[38]

All this time in the Louisville jail, Fairbank had been careful not to reveal his identity, afraid that his reputation—his 1849 pardon from the Kentucky penitentiary being fresh on everyone's mind—would convict him. Unfortunately, when news reached him of what had befallen Forsyth, he rejoiced so visibly over Tamar's now certain freedom that the jailor was convinced he had aided her escape.

At the hearing on November 17, Fairbank gave up all attempt at disguise. He denied helping Tamar across the river, but did admit to assisting her in Indiana. During the proceedings he took copious notes, and when it was over handed them to the reporter for the *Louisville Courier* with the request that they be published. The paper found his record of what the witnesses said to be "in the main correct, and shows that the Reverend gentleman is a good hand at taking notes as well as taking negroes." The details of Tamar's escape narrated above come from this "Prisoner's Report of his own Trial" as well as from the *Courier*'s own account, both printed in the edition of November 18, 1851. Any further attempt at concealing his identity would have been pointless in the face of the testimony of one George W. Morris, a Kentucky native who recognized him as the Calvin Fairbank who gave an abolitionist speech, and even boasted of having freed many slaves, at Corning, New York. Newton Craig had been sent for as well to identify him at the hearing.[39] A.L. Shotwell told the court, with regard to the handkerchief Joseph Gibson had picked up outside the wrecked carriage, that that summer a Miss Bullock had visited his house and lost a handkerchief.

The judge summarily disposed of the case, holding Fairbank to $5,000 bail. Unable to pay, he was lodged in the local city jail to await his trial in circuit court.[40]

Back in October, Fairbank had called at Levi Coffin's in Cincinnati and told Laura Haviland of a letter he had received that told the plight of "an interesting slave woman" in Louisville who could be rescued if someone would volunteer to meet her in Jeffersonville. This was probably Tamar, though as it turned out Fairbank did considerably more than just meet her on the other side. Haviland strongly advised against his going so near to Kentucky. Tensions in the area were rising, for about this time an underground agent named Conklin had been captured with four slaves, bound with ropes and thrown into the river, where he was found a few days later. Calvin told Haviland he had thought Coffin and his associates would oppose his plans. Coffin being out of town, she asked him to consult with Dr. Brisbane. "But [Calvin] chose to keep the matter quiet," according to Haviland, "and went on his dangerous mission."[41]

Three weeks later, a letter arrived in Cincinnati with a mysterious signature, dated from the Louisville jail: "The signature is of stars, that he says is the number of letters in the name," Coffin told Haviland, "but we can make nothing of it." When she counted six stars in the first name, Laura Haviland knew it was from Calvin. The number in the last confirmed it. All were astonished that "Laura has found our riddle," but that was because she was the only one in whom he had confided his mission.

In the letter, Fairbank appealed for blankets, warm clothing, and money. After a few days of prayerful meditation, Laura Haviland decided, despite the urgings of Coffin and Brisbane, who were sure she would be thrown into prison herself, to go to Louisville with a trunk containing bed clothes, a thick pillow, under flannels, and some fourteen dollars. Levi Coffin was able to persuade his friend Captain Barker to offer passage at half fare on a steamship line in which he held an interest; Barker also contributed a letter of introduction to Colonel Buckner, the jailor. Haviland left on the *Ben Franklin No. 2* at 2 p.m., arriving at Louisville at dawn the next day, November 21.

Meanwhile, whether yielding to Newton Craig's insistence or for reasons of her own, Delia Webster had left Vermont on November 10, 1851. Accompanied by Craig's children, and "in the care of my brother and his lady"—Warren and Betsey Webster—she traveled by train to Philadelphia, and from there to Pittsburgh, where the entourage boarded the *Buckeye State* to Cincinnati. While descending the Ohio, they were "favored with the company of Hon. Thomas Hart Benton" (longtime senator from Missouri who had just suffered electoral defeat for his opposition to slavery and to Henry Clay's Compromise of 1850), Amos Kendall (Kentucky journalist who was once tutor to Clay's children, later turned against him, served in President Jackson's "kitchen cabinet," and had in recent years become wealthy by his association with Samuel F. B. Morse, inventor of the telegraph), among "other distinguished persons."[42] From Cincinnati they took the *General Pike*, arriving in Louisville on November 20. And thus by pure coincidence Delia Webster and Laura Haviland arrived in Louisville just a day apart, each on the morning mail boat from Cincinnati, Delia on the 20th, Laura on the 21st. Their paths did not cross. Nor may they have ever met. But each was soon to be come acquainted with the other's existence.

Webster's arrival did not pass unnoticed. Her notoriety had preceded her, but it was only by a fortuitous chain of events that her coming to Louisville became known. Apparently with no knowledge at all of her arrival but motivated solely by Fairbank's arrest, the *Georgetown Herald* had editorialized, in a colloquial tone, "Whar is Miss Delia Webster? as they hunted in couples, she ought to be somewhar in this vicinity." The *Madison Daily Banner* helpfully replied that Miss Webster was at that time in Louisville, having just arrived on the mail boat *General Pike*.[43] The Madison paper no doubt learned that fact from "Mr. Farnsworth and lady, who were among my patrons at Madison," and who according to Webster were fellow passengers on the boat from Cincinnati. They evidently continued on to Madison, where they spread news of her return.[44]

Laura Haviland. Courtesy of Philip Fairbank

Thus the *Louisville Courier* of November 21 was able to report that "Miss Delia Webster arrived here yesterday morning on the mail-boat Gen. Pike. Where she is from, where she is going, and what is her business West at this particular time, has not yet been made public." On November 22 the paper added a further, though inaccurate, detail: "Miss Delia Webster visited the Rev. Calvin Fairbank at his lodgings in jail yesterday." Actually, of course, it was Laura Haviland who had gone to the jail. Delia Webster had taken the first train for Frankfort: When the *General Pike* reached Louisville at 5 a.m., she was awakened and told that "we had not a moment to spare if we wished to take the cars at 6 o'clock. We were as expeditious as possible in looking up our baggage, a drayman and carriage, and making the best of our way through darkness, rain and mud to the depot, where we got our baggage checked, and secured seats as soon as possible; but no sooner was this accomplished than the cars were flying apace toward Frankfort."[45]

Webster had learned, however, of Fairbank's arrest. At about 8 p.m. the night before, on the way from Cincinnati, Amos Kendall "placed in my hands" a copy of that day's *Louisville Courier*, with its account "of the arrest, examination and commitment of a man in your city, supposed to be Calvin Fairbank. This was the first intelligence I had received concerning the unhappy affair."[46]

As for Laura Haviland, she arrived at the Louisville docks "about daydawn," climbed into a hack, and ordered the driver to take her to the jailor's house. She rang the doorbell, asked for Colonel Buckner, and presented her letter of introduction. The jailor treated her "genteelly," but delayed allowing a visit to Fairbank until he had the sheriff's permission, for fear of angering Shotwell, who he said "is very much enraged, and . . . a man of wealth and influence here." Buckner, who was trying to find a way both to further incriminate Fairbank and find out where Tamar had gone, persuaded Haviland to stay at his house for several nights instead of returning to Cincinnati the next day. He set a trap, introducing her to a just-released prisoner who claimed to be anxious to convey a secret message from Fairbank. The idea was to get Haviland to agree to take care of forwarding Tamar's trunk, which would disclose the slave's whereabouts. Haviland wisely declined, not knowing in any case where to send it. On a second attempt, the man returned with a note supposedly from Calvin to which she was asked to respond, "but I refused, becoming satisfied that he was more of a dispatch-bearer for the colonel than for Calvin Fairbanks. I learned afterwards that this was true, and that he was released for the purpose of getting hold of additional evidence with which to convict him, and perhaps convict myself also."[47]

That evening a friend of the colonel's came calling. Buckner had invited him over to check on the identity of his guest, for the report in the Louisville papers about Webster's visiting Fairbank had made him uneasy, and his friend claimed a personal acquaintance with the notorious Yankee schoolteacher. Haviland was not yet aware of the rumors concerning herself that were racing through the city, and which were confusedly based on her having been seen approaching the jailor's house and the publication of Webster's arrival at the wharf. Buckner's visitor was able to reassure him that the lady in his house was not Webster, and promised to "set the editors right." The following retraction, of sorts, appeared in the *Louisville Courier* on November 24: "We noticed a few days since the arrival in this city, on the Cincinnati mail boat, of Miss Delia Webster. We learned yesterday that the person alluded to is a Miss or Mrs. Sarah [*sic*] S. Haviland, of Cincinnati, and not Miss Webster, although she represented herself as that person—for what object we of course are unable to determine." Beyond getting her first name wrong, the paper went on make the accusation, surely false, that Laura had pretended to be the person she was accused of being. Perhaps the paper was covering for its earlier mistake, which had caused "much excitement" in Louisville.[48] Delia Webster was being eagerly sought. Thanks to what the paper went on to say, Laura Haviland would now be just as zealously pursued; concerned for her safety, jailor Buckner had been careful to keep her presence in his house a secret. "This Miss or Mrs. Haviland's mission here was to see Mr. Fairbank," commented the *Courier*, "and we presume to aid in the release or escape of this reverend villain, with whom she has been permitted to have an interview. She is a suspicious character, and as . . . she has been engaged in the business of running off negroes, it may be well for her to keep a sharp look out, or apartments may also be provided for her in Col. Buckner's castle!"[49]

A radical about-face concerning the personal morality of Delia Webster was then in order, as the article continued: "From the information we have obtained, we deeply regret that we were led into the error of calling this woman Miss Webster, who, since her pardon, has been leading an exemplary and unexceptionable life." The paper speaks of her residence in Madison, her father's death and her return "to visit her afflicted mother, with whom she remained until the approach of winter, when her poor health compelled her to seek a climate not so cold as that. She is now and has been for some weeks at Frankfort, and in such a condition that she cannot probably survive long." Apart from the inaccuracy concerning the length of her stay in Frankfort, where she had only just arrived, the paper's allusion to her illness gives evidence of having been nearly dictated by Delia Webster herself, perhaps through Newton Craig; for on December 17 she would write to the *Courier* that on the rail journey from Louisville on November 20 "I was too feeble to sit up, but reclined in the arms of my waiting-maid, till we reached the Capitol; and since my arrival until the last few days, have been confined to my bed; spitting blood, and thought by my friends to be in rather a critical state."[50]

What is most interesting is what Webster then says about why she would never have visited Fairbank in the first place: "I had *no disposition* to do so, even had there been time. Nor have I seen the man, or known any thing of his life since about the time of his pardon, some two years and a half ago"—possibly alluding to their reunion in Madison in August, 1849. "I will here take occasion to remark that I have no sympathy for the course he is charged with pursuing. No Kentuckian could be more disgusted with it. And though I would not seem *severe* upon an unfortunate fellow-being, yet I must be allowed to express my utter detestation of such an illiberal and ungrateful transaction. I was surprised and grieved that a man of his profession should condescend to lay himself liable to censure from those who had befriended him. But I regret most of all his seeming want of honor and moral obligation."[51] This is strong language, even if she didn't mean it.

Ensuing developments would suggest that these words were for public consumption only, and not indicative of her true feelings concerning Calvin's course of action. She had to maintain Newton Craig's esteem for at least a little while longer, for her brother Warren Webster and his wife had come with her to Kentucky to take up a position that Craig had arranged. In Newton's letter to her of October 1, 1851, he had wondered "how far I ought to go to induce Warren to come West" and wrote that he had "told them" (Warren and his wife) "of the two openings . . . here."

In a letter to his brother-in-law, Warren Bard, who was married to Delia's sister, Mary Jane, Warren Webster wrote from Frankfort on February 15, 1852, to tell of his arrival and his new job. He began working for a Mr. Blanton on February 4 at the salary of $350 per year, plus "a house, garden, fine wood, and pasturage for a cow."[52] Not only did Newton line up the job, but he agreed to contribute to Warren's income: "Mr. Craig says he will make it up to full four hundred Dollars a year in provisions &c." It is hard work, Warren writes, for he has to be on his feet all day, but it beats "being out of business as I have been for two or three months past." In fact, he evidently still owes a considerable debt back in Vermont, for he asks his brother-in-law to let him know "how the matter stands between Wm. Taylor & me, and whether I shall have to fork over the money to him if I should be so lucky as to get it." One can appreciate Delia Webster's willingness to enlist Newton Craig in her effort to help out her brother and his wife. Life in Vermont was hard, and many of its inhabitants were, like Warren, seeking better luck in the West.

"It has cost us so much to get here it seems to me we ought to make something to defray our expenses, and have a little something left." He has hopes of staying "one year if not longer," even though their immediate location "is by no means desirable, our being remote from town, and white neighbours living not very near to us, but Betsey is willing to put up with, and make the best of it, and so am I until we can do better." Ironically perhaps, Delia Webster's brother appears to have been hired as an overseer of slaves: "I have the charge of four men & some of the time six or seven. They are all black but very well disposed and do what I tell them and no grumbling at that."

As for his sister, Warren reports that "Delia has moved to Madison, Ia., and when I left there about three weeks ago she was well as usual. Mr. Craig has been there since and returned home a week ago today. He said she was rather poorly but I do not think much of that for he always thinks so." Delia had given the impression, reported in the *Louisville Courier* on December 27, of being at death's door, "in such a condition that she cannot probably survive long." Sickness, real or feigned, was a nearly constant theme in her life, from the illness in the fall of 1844 that prevented her from making an adequate legal defense to the one in the summer of 1845 that made her too weak to resist her father's insistence that she write *Kentucky Jurisprudence* as he wished. And it had been, she maintained, her inability to survive New England winters that drove her South in the first place.

Warren not only writes that her health was fine, but that she was well *as usual* (says it twice, actually: "she was well as usual. Mr. Craig . . . always thinks" she is poorly "even when I should not notice but she was well as usual"). It was Newton who was sick, so despondent at her absence that he seemed to be wasting away. "Mr. Craig's health is quite poor, and has been so for some four weeks." Those four weeks probably mark her departure for Madison; she had been gone for at least the three weeks that had elapsed since Warren saw her there. Craig "called on us," Warren continues, "the other evening, and staid half an hour or so. He looked as if [he] had better be in bed. His mind has been very much agitated on account of Delia's refusing to remain in Frankfort and make his house her home. I think that is the principle [*sic*] cause of his illness."

Warren Webster was in a position to be a better judge than Newton Craig not only of his sister's real state of health, but what was likely to be the future of their relationship: Craig "says he means to treat her as a friend, and Christian. He says he thinks she is a Christian & a lady &c. I hope he will always think so but I am afraid they will not always be on as friendly terms." What did Warren Webster know?

Delia Webster had been living in Madison before she left in May of

1851 for the extended visit to her mother in Vermont. It was perhaps natural that she would eventually leave Frankfort, despite her brother and sister-in-law's presence there, to resume her life in Madison. But why now? Because it may have been even more natural, despite what she said about Calvin Fairbank in the December 17 letter, that she find untenable the prospect of living in Newton Craig's Frankfort house at the same time that Fairbank was going to be his prisoner just a few blocks away, in the Kentucky State Penitentiary.

Fairbank's trial would come in March. While he awaited the disposition of his case in late 1851, Laura Haviland was at last permitted to visit Calvin Fairbank in the Louisville jail. Incarcerated with him were the "forty sad faces" of slaves held for safekeeping before being shipped south. "With this scene before me, I could not restrain tears, neither were Calvin's eyes dry." She thought he had no chance, given "the bitter prejudices against him." But he had bright hopes of securing a good lawyer. A Mr. Thruston would take his case for six hundred dollars, but that was more than he could afford. He asked her to see Thruston and get him to reduce the fee. She would do so, and he agreed to take the case for whatever the defendant could afford. After her ten minutes with Fairbank, she was passing through the prison yard when a slave whispered to her, asking if she had seen Calvin Fairbank. When she said she had, "'Glory!' he cried, just loud enough for me to hear." Likewise, the Buckners' kitchen slave Mary, when told she had seen the prisoner, clapped her hands for joy. An "electric current" seemed to have passed as well through the forty slaves housed with him; four policemen had seen it, and took it as evidence that Haviland had come with the intention of rescuing them all. Buckner told her they were about to arrest her, that he was afraid he could no longer protect her, and that "Shotwell has had his officers out hunting in every hotel." He advised her to cross over immediately to Jeffersonville, and not dare return to the Kentucky side. As she passed unrecognized through knots of Kentuckians eagerly discussing what they would do when they caught her, she smiled to herself and thought, "Little do you think this is the little old woman you are troubling yourselves over."[53] Haviland may have thought herself old, but she was not yet forty-three. And she must have looked young enough for someone to mistake her for Delia Webster, who at thirty-four was still able to turn at least one man's eye.

Fairbank's aspirations for a decent lawyer came to nothing. Thruston must have changed his mind, for Fairbank had to settle for an incompetent named Lovell Rousseau. His only hope now was, as he put it, "bail or break jail." Working toward both goals at once, he paid the attorney's fee for a recaptured slave named Baker who together with a just-released fugitive named Marshall would go north to raise money for his bail, and at the same time conspired with a convicted murderer, who with the help of his wife and brother planned to evade the hangman's noose by having keys made and saws smuggled in. If five thousand dollars could be raised for bail, Fairbank planned to interview witnesses in Indiana, "buy them off, then go into trial and beat Kentucky." Unless he escaped in the meantime. The keys and saws arrived, plus strychnine for the guard dogs, while Baker stood on the wall ready to let down a rope. Even better, Buckner had somehow neglected to shove the bolt in the loop, so the door was actually unlocked. The poison was tossed out into the yard, killing all the dogs but one. Everything was going well until turnkey Casenbine unexpectedly came in at 11 p.m. with a man under arrest for public intoxication and found the door open and the dogs dead. "So ended that plan."[54]

Casenbine flew into a rage, tearing about the cell, lifting first one end of the bed and the other, looking for the tools of escape. He never found them, even though the key and the saws were indeed hidden under the bed, but in the middle, where he never looked. As soon as he left, Fairbank threw them down the sewer. But for trying to escape he was put in irons.[55]

Marshall raised "an immense amount of money" for Fairbank's bail, but absconded with it all, fleeing to Liberia. He later wrote from Africa to Lewis Hayden asking permission to return. But Hayden had in the meantime made inquiries to Cincinnati and found out the truth. He threatened Marshall with prosecution if he ever set foot in the States.[56]

Fairbank on February 4 wrote a despairing letter to Frederick Douglass. He complained of feeling forgotten by his friends in the antislavery cause. "I know the many outlets for their money, and the calls upon their time. I have felt much discouragement; three months in jail, and rolling the ball alone." Looking at the certainty of a long prison term, and having an intimate knowledge of the penitentiary where he would have to serve it, he seems to have thought of taking his own life. "I am not afraid to die. It does not take long. . . . Let me die, but I do not wish to be ruled over by a master." That master was Newton Craig, who still ran the state prison. "If the friends do not feel like helping me, like caring for me, truth is no less precious, though his standard-bearers should desert me. However, I am not worth troubling any man's mind with."[57]

At the trial, Rousseau was so inadequate that his client felt the case was lost "by default—without even an ordinary effort of an advocate."[58] He was sentenced on March 7, 1852, to a term of fifteen years; on the 9th he was taken, in irons, to Frankfort.

He was locked into his cell until Newton Craig returned on March 11. On that day, Fairbank was summoned to the prison chapel. Before the governor and an audience of invited dignitaries, Craig gave a speech in which he berated Fairbank for his crimes, "cursed [and] misrepresented" him. Fairbank was allowed to respond. The proceedings concluded, Newton Craig gave the order: "Mr. Davis, take Fairbank to the hackling house and kill him."[59]

The killing would take place by overwork. In one week alone, six men perished from the labors in the hackling house, so named from the steel-toothed hackles on which the hemp was dressed "after being broken from the stalk, filling the room so full of dust—poison dust—that on a still dry day it was impossible to distinguish a man from a block of wood."[60] Hemp, a cousin of modern day marijuana, was as widely grown in Kentucky then as tobacco is today, and converted into rope for sailing ships and bagging for southern cotton.

The contrast between Newton Craig's attitude during Fairbank's first imprisonment and that during his second was striking. In 1845, "I was treated with more consideration than Northern people were expecting," wrote the prisoner. Craig "was proud to be called magnanimous." But this time, "I found him inexorable."[61]

10

"THE VERY MADNESS
OF THE MOON"

Although Delia Webster had chosen Madison, Indiana, as her new home in the spring of 1849, she already had her eyes on a much more interesting site. In fact, she had it constantly in view from the window of her Madison residence, as it was the plateau dominating the high cliffs on the opposite shore, in Kentucky. She would embroider the location with the legend of a sacred arbor in its northeast section, where, upon the rock "Jehovah Shalom," beneath "the loved branches of an ancient Oak, oft knelt a maiden form to mark the fading of the stars, and watch alone, in silent awe, the earliest streak of dawn—signal for daily prayer" she wrote. "Morning's first ray and night's last star were witness to the worship from that altar; and hence the oft consecrated hill bears the appropriate name—MT. ORISON."[1]

Among the lines marked in the book of Thomas Moore's poems that Newton Craig bought in Philadelphia in October 1845, after Delia's departure from his penal care, are the following, where orisons are made on bended knee at dawn's first light: "Oh, live to pray for her—to bend the knee . . . / So shall thy orisons like dew that flies / To Heaven upon the morning's sunshine rise / With all love's earliest ardor to the skies!" They are the dying words of the maiden Zelica in "The Veiled Prophet of Khorassan," an embedded tale in Moore's *Lalla Rookh*. Mistakenly thinking her lover Azim dead, she is lured by the hope of seeing him again in heaven into becoming the beloved "child" and consort of the false prophet. The prophet, whose veil is said to hide a radiance too strong for human sight but in fact conceals a hideous deformity, commits suicide when his fortress is besieged by the true followers of Mohammed, Azim among them. In despair at her sin, Zelica arranges for her death by assuming the prophet's veil and standing on the ramparts of his fortress. Pierced by Azim's lance, she reveals her identity to her lover, rejoicing that death comes by his hand. ". . . oh! believe me, yes," the pencil-marked passage begins, "I would not change this sad, but dear caress, / This death

164

within thy arms. . . ." The light in Azim's eyes is "Like the first dawn of mercy from above." She begs him not to kill himself in his grief, but to pray for her salvation instead, to daily kneel and make orisons that will ascend to heaven like dew before the morning sun. If Azim's prayers are heard, Zelica may one day descend from the bliss of pardoned souls and "come to thee— in some sweet dream—and tell . . .". Years pass, and a now aged Azim, having prayed at her grave all his life, is at last granted the promised vision of his beloved: "A gleam of rapture on his eye and cheek, / That brightened even Death—like the last streak / Of intense glory on the horizon's brim"—a "last streak" that becomes (together with the poem's "earliest ardor") the "earliest streak of dawn" in Delia Webster's retelling, as she resituates these elements of Oriental legend on the Trimble County shore.[2]

Who penciled the parentheses that surround these lines? Newton Craig? Delia Webster? Did they read Moore's poems to each other on long evenings in Scott County after Lucy and the children were asleep, or in Madison alone? Did she include *Lalla Rookh* with Shakespeare in her teaching syllabus for the children (Dillard, perhaps, might have been old enough to understand such texts)? In any case, the words therein marked were prophetic, for Newton Craig would come more and more to resemble less a fond father than the hideous prophet, and Delia Webster the maiden he sought to imprison.

As for Mt. Orison, on November 16, 1852, she bought it. "In 1851 the firm owning these valuable possessions failed, and Miss Webster, viewing it as an opening of Providence, availed herself of the earliest opportunity to bargain for the whole tract."[3] She did not, however, buy it alone. According to records in the Trimble County Courthouse, it was sold on that November 16 by Willis and Elizabeth Hodges of Louisville for some nine thousand dollars to Delia Webster, Parmenas M. Collins, Norris Day, and John Preston. Webster, Day and Collins shared two-thirds of the property, while Preston held an undivided one-third share. Preston, a native of Lexington, Virginia, was doubtless a descendant of the Thomas Lewis Preston who first purchased the land in 1782 and surely not an active participant in the activities Day and Webster envisioned for the property. On November 18, an undivided third of the Webster-Collins-Day two-thirds was conveyed to Oliver Pitcher, a Madison lawyer, on the condition that if a series of promissory notes dating up to five years from November 10, 1852, were paid off to Pitcher, his share would revert to them. This was evidently a mortgage on an interest in the farm.[4]

Where did Delia Webster get the money to buy her share in the property? She may have obtained some eleven hundred dollars of it from Newton Craig. For the Trimble County records also disclose that as early as April 6, 1853, he had already begun a suit against her to recover that amount. By that date, Craig had already placed an attachment on some of her property. On June 21, in the case of "Newton Craig vs. Delia Webster" leave is given the defendant to file her answer; on November 29, on the plaintiff's motion the case is continued at his cost; likewise in June 1854, but on the defendant's costs. On June 16, 1856, the suit would finally come before a jury, which on the following day found for the plaintiff in the sum of $1150 plus costs.[5]

But much else will have taken place between 1852 and 1856 to immensely complicate the relation between the prison warden and his "dear child."

The Norris Day who bought a share of the farm was the same Reverend Day who signed his name next to Delia Webster's in a call for a Vermont convention of antislavery Christians in the spring of 1845, who made antislavery lectures from his base in her native Vergennes, who spoke in her defense before the Liberty Party convention in Boston, whose 1846 pamphlet *Bible Politics* shares certain stylistic similarities with *Kentucky Jurisprudence* and other of her writings, and who was described in the January 1, 1846, *Green Mountain Freeman* as the victim of certain false reports and slanderous lies.

A reporter for the *Philadelphia Register* interviewed Norris Day in Cincinnati on February 27, 1854, and found him to be "a man of gentlemanly appearance and of very intelligent countenance." Though a native of New England, Day "had spent some time in the vicinity of Madison, Indiana; and finding that he could purchase a farm on the Kentucky side of the river, at low rates, he did so."[6] According to the Madison correspondent for the *Louisville Democrat*, a year or two before these events, Reverend Day "left his family in the East and came here [to Madison] and lived under the same roof with Miss Webster, until about eight months ago"—June 1853— "when they bought a piece of land" across the river in Trimble County.[7] Although the sale took place November 16, 1852, the deed was not delivered until June 6, 1853, which corresponds to the time the Madison reporter says the purchase was completed.

Though their "ostensible purpose" was farming, "their manner of living and their conduct in general soon became mysterious to their neighbors, and they were regarded with a great deal of suspicion. They had a great many mysterious visitors. Steamboats have frequently stopped at their farm and put off curious and suspicious-looking people." The *Democrat*'s correspondent describes the enterprise as a "Webster-and-Day farm and partnership," indicating that Pitcher, Collins, and Preston were silent partners at most. Not only did mysterious steamboats come calling, but in the previous eight months "no less than twenty or thirty thousand dollars worth of slaves have run away from that immediate neighborhood. Immediately after they moved over there six or eight negroes on one of the adjoining farms ran off," and others have continued to disappear "every week since these abolitionists have occupied this tract of land."[8] In his interview with the Philadelphia reporter, Day seems to place the blame for their neighbors' suspicions on his colleague, saying that he had spent some time on the farm by himself "without any apparent uneasiness on the part of his neighbours; but when Miss Delia Webster, an old acquaintance, came to live upon the same place, the people conjectured that their farm might be a depot of the Underground Railroad."[9]

For her part, in an account she gave three years later of events connected to the farm, Delia Webster left Norris Day out of the story entirely. "In 1852, I purchased a valuable farm consisting of six hundred acres of superior upland on the fertile banks of the beautiful Ohio (south side,) directly opposite and overlooking the city of Madison."[10] The prospectus for the Webster Kentucky Farm Association, published with her participation in 1858, would recount that "having long entertained a desire to establish . . . a school . . . which would be to that region what Oberlin is to Ohio . . . she spent some time in travelling to select a location, and was inspired with the belief that such a school might be located in Kentucky. . . . In the spring of 1849, while passing down the Ohio River, her eye fell upon a charming site, precisely suited for such an institution. She at once endeavored to purchase it, but was unable to complete a trade and gain possession until 1852."[11] No mention of Norris Day is made in that document, either, though surely he was involved at an early stage in the enterprise. J. Winston Coleman, Jr. wrote that the farm was purchased "with funds supplied by Northern abolitionists."[12]

The Webster Kentucky Farm Association prospectus describes Webster's purpose in obtaining the property as not only to establish a school, but also to "afford an opportunity to try the experiment of Free Labor on Slave territory," showing by its efficient production of crops that hiring workers was more profitable than enslaving them. This had been in large measure the substance of Cassius Clay's speeches against slavery, that it was less profitable than free agricultural labor. Clay continually pointed to Ohio's greater prosperity compared to Kentucky's. Evidently it became the conviction of Delia Webster and whoever was backing the Day-Webster enterprise that the argument could be more convincingly presented if the experiment took place on Kentucky soil.

Yet it is difficult to determine how much of their purpose was to conduct such an experiment, and how much was to pretend to do so in order to take possession of a large parcel of Southern land that ran right down to the river, from which fugitive slaves could be more easily ferried to freedom.

Certainly that is how Day and Webster's neighbors came to view the venture. The prospectus declares that "in 1852 several individuals joined Miss Webster in her Free Labor enterprise. Some took an interest in the Farm, and others in the crops and improvements; but in less than six months the whole atmosphere was rife with threats and predictions that they would all be driven off on account of their anti-slavery." Six months after the date of purchase would be about the time of Craig's lawsuit, although it is not at all evident that he was moved by the plight of local slaveowners who were losing their property. The break that was inevitably to come between him and Webster is more likely to have been the impetus, together with his having lent her a considerable sum of money or material property (she would later allude to some pieces of furniture) or both. "Scarce a year had elapsed after they moved upon the place, before some became intimidated by the threats of violence, and left, while the others were literally driven off the Farm and out of the State by lawless officials or soulless mobs. More than twenty persons were thus expelled. Miss Webster alone stood her ground and faced the enemy, declaring her constitutional rights and her intention to maintain them."[13]

By late February 1854, Norris Day had adventures of his own to relate. At about the time Delia Webster joined him on the farm, he told the reporter from Philadelphia, two valuable slaves were discovered missing. Despite his protests of innocence, Day was sued by their owner for $1,500. On November 29, 1853, the trial began in Bedford, the county seat. Day claimed to the reporter that the "testimony was manufactured to suit the owner." He was fortunate therefore to see the case eventuate in a hung jury, though the vote was eleven to one against him. The case was dismissed.[14] Reporting on the trial and subsequent difficulties, the *Madison Courier* recalled that Day "owned a portion of the tract of land immediately opposite to the city [of Madison], upon which the saw mill and village of Hodgesville is situated." The name of the settlement likely bears some relation to the Hodges family, from whom it was purchased. "The celebrated Miss Webster owns or did own land adjoining. It is well known that both Miss Webster and Mr. Day have been objects of suspicion for some time among their Kentucky neighbors." Alluding to the trial in Bedford, the paper recounts that afterward, "to avoid similar prosecution, Day sold out his farm and removed to this city."[15]

Day did not sell out until February 10, but had apparently been planning to do so before that date. He did return to the farm after the Bedford trial, according to his interview with the Philadelphia reporter. One evening he was sitting in his parlor when he heard voices outside. Either some more slaves had been lost or his fellow Trimble countians were not happy with the outcome of the trial. Day took refuge in an adjoining room and gave his daughter charge of the key. Someone started pounding on the front door, threatening to break it down if he was not let in. The daughter stood firm, as did Day's nephew. Elizabeth Day, his wife, was possibly not in residence on the farm; some indication of this comes from the fact that she is described as living in Saybrook, Ohio, on February 10, 1854, when the Days' share of the farm would be conveyed to Delia Webster for the sum of $3,056.[16]

At length, realizing that whatever case they had against him might be jeopardized if they made an illegal entry, the posse sent one of their number to obtain a warrant, meanwhile stationing themselves around the house to prevent his escape. By two o'clock in the morning, Day had thought of a stratagem that recalls the fable of the lion and the cloak that the editor of the *Christian Freeman* had once told to excuse Delia Webster's behavior at the time of her trial a decade before. Day's nephew resembled him in size and build. Day took his own hat and cloak, which his neighbors had often seen him wear, and put them on the nephew, instructing him to go out for a brisk walk in the night air. When the posse began to give chase he was to give them "an opportunity to try their legs." The nephew had not gotten far before he was spotted. "Here he is!" someone called out, and the whole party took off in pursuit. With no one left to guard the house, Day was able to slip out unnoticed by the opposite door, reach the Ohio River, find a canoe, and paddle across to Madison. He soon paid a visit to Joseph G. Marshall, the city's most eminent lawyer, and told him his plight. Marshall sent a letter detailing his client's claim of total innocence to the secretary of state of Indiana, hoping it would reach the governor. But a few days later, responding to a Kentucky indictment against him, the Indiana chief executive issued an order for Day's arrest, which took place on February 1, 1854.[17] Marshall succeeded, however, in obtaining a writ of habeas corpus, with the opportunity of arguing in Madison before Judge C.E. Walker that the Indiana governor's requisition for Day's arrest was illegal.[18] The hearing was scheduled for February 7. Sheriff Right Rea would recall a few months later, in a letter to the public explaining his official conduct in the year 1854, that "whilst Mr. Day was in my custody I allowed Miss Webster to visit him in jail, and she spent most of her time in jail with him, saying she was copying his writings." Rea adds a fascinating detail, which may explain why Newton Craig complained in his July 6, 1850, letter about being "annoyed . . . on the road home" the last time he had gone to New England to fetch her back: "Miss Webster told me that Craig and Day had had a serious difficulty at the East."[19]

Meanwhile, on February 6, a mass meeting was being held in the Bedford Courthouse in Trimble County. Its object was to do something about Delia Webster and her incessant slave stealing. "Flaming and exciting speeches were made," Webster recalled, "and plans concocted to drive me from the State." Among the resolutions adopted was the following: "Whereas it is known that Miss Delia A. Webster has recently run off numerous slaves from Trimble county, therefore resolved that it is the will and determination of the citizens of said county that Miss Delia A. Webster leave the State." The next day, February 7, "while quietly seated at my cheerful fireside, enjoying the peaceful retirement of my own little paradise, I was suddenly surprised by the arrival of a large force who had come to carry their plans into execution." It was a committee of fifty men, including "the most respectable and wealthy" of the county. The day was "dark and dismal," the rain pouring down in torrents. Seeing that her visitors were drenched and shivering, she invited them in to warm themselves by the fire. Grateful for the warmth and no doubt somewhat intimidated by her commanding presence, the committeemen sat for forty-five minutes before they got around to the reason for their visit. "At length the president introduced the secretary, who reluctantly drew forth a paper, and with a trembling voice read the mighty resolves."[20]

When they had finished, she answered with defiance, charging them with illegality of procedure and cowardice for doing as a mob what they would not dare as individuals. "I told them that I had chosen Kentucky for my home, and . . . that I expected to live and die there, notwithstanding their 'determination.'" They required a written reply, which she subsequently sent to the court. In it she told them "in very decided terms that I should exercise my right as a 'free white citizen of the United States' . . . to live where I choose; that I was not intimidated by their threats, and should stand my ground defenseless and alone." She did not hear from them again for a month.

On the same day in Madison, Day's hearing before Judge Walker began. In the week since his arrest, according to Day, the people of Madison had become "greatly aroused" in his favor, "determined that he should not be taken across the river on any terms." The Madison correspondent for the *Louisville Democrat* alludes to Day's having curried favor there when he "harbored himself under the same roof with Miss Webster, in this city for a long time. He traveled through the adjacent country, preaching, and being a genuine Yankee, soon got the denizens hereabouts very much prepossessed and infatuated with him."[21] The reporter attended the hearing, where he thought Day had "decidedly the worst looking countenance of any man I ever saw. . . . His two daughters sat in court with him, but he could not excite much sympathy in this community." The latter statement contrasts with Day's assertion of Madisonians being "greatly aroused" in his favor, but then, so does the reporter's impression of his countenance with that of the Philadelphia journalist, who thought he had a "very intelligent" one. No doubt the difference between being in the prisoner's dock in Madison, in imminent peril of being locked away in the Kentucky penitentiary, and reflecting upon it at leisure from the safety of Cincinnati, had something to do with the discrepancy. "Strange as it may appear," remarked the *Madison Courier*, on the first day of the hearing, "the question of the stability of the Union some how got mixed up in the proceedings." This no doubt alludes to the issue of how Indiana should respond to Kentucky's demand to hand over the defendant. "Judge Walker remanded the prisoner to the custody of the Sheriff until his decision should be made up." Walker had found an error in the prosecution's documents, namely that no actual copy of an indictment had been presented to the governor of Indiana, as required by federal law.[22] Walker was disposed to grant the prosecution time to correct this problem, Day told the interviewer, "but he could not withstand the outcry of public sentiment" on Day's side, and therefore when the hearing resumed on February 9, he set him free.[23]

But Day was not out of the woods yet. Another, and this time enforceable, indictment was on its way from Indianapolis that morning by the eleven o'clock train. As he left the court house he immediately mounted a swift horse his friends had hired and, in the company of a guide who would show him the way, "left the city at a rapid gait. . . . We understand the crowd assembled around the court house cheered him as he started on the *upper* [as opposed to under] ground railroad to get out of the reach of a second warrant," reported the *Madison Courier*, contradicting the *Louisville Democrat*'s assertion that he had but few supporters.[24] Day and his companion had not traveled more than a city block when they were overtaken by Joseph Rea, the livery stable owner, who had found out to what use his horse was being put and run to catch up with them. Day's friends urged him not to delay his departure by paying any attention to Rea. With whip and spurs, Day and his guide were soon out of town. Enraged, Rea returned to the livery stable, saddled his fastest horse and took off after them. He found them in the next village. This time, Day gave up the horse, accepting his companion's offer of his mount. Even though he had already recovered his property, Rea took out his whip and gave Day two or three lashes "by way of showing that he lived in a free country." Back in Madison, he boasted of having given the slave stealer a good flogging. "Thereupon the friends of Day turned the tables and had him arrested for assault and battery, and expected to convict him on his own confessions." As for Day, realizing that officers with the new warrant would soon arrive, he disguised himself in woman's clothes and hid in a stack of cornstalks. The next day he was placed on the Underground Railroad to Ohio.[25]

On February 10, probably through legal representation, Norris Day

Street scene, Madison,Indiana. Photo taken in the 1850s by Joseph P. Gorgas. Courtesy Madison-Jefferson County Public Library

relinquished his share in the Trimble County farm. On the same day, the *Louisville Democrat* printed an attack on Newton Craig's fitness to serve as warden of the state penitentiary. His contract was up for renewal by the state legislature, then in session at Frankfort. In addition to criticizing his financial administration of the prison, the writer found fault with the longstanding and "remarkable" kindness he had shown Delia Webster. "A woman of intellect and intelligence, but who had prostituted both" to the dishonest end of seducing slaves from their masters, Miss Webster did not stay in the North where she belonged, after her pardon in 1845, but "entered the habitation of the Keeper himself, became a member of his family, and received from him the soft and loving appellation of 'my child.'" Not content to take this convicted abolitionist under his roof, Craig "galanted her in the streets of Frankfort, and flaunted with her in his carriage from place to place." Public opinion, however, made Craig desist, so he placed her in Madison, "where, it is said, the faithful and loving father purchased her a house and set her up in grand style." But as a consequence of having to leave one adopted father, "who could only visit her occasionally, child like, she affiliated one or two other fathers, who it seems, poor child, stole her affections, and thenceforth she has refused to acknowledge the tender relations she once bore toward the Keeper of the Kentucky Penitentiary." Craig's response to this was, "in a fit of indignant rage," to bring suit against Delia Webster to recover "a few of the thousands he had lavished upon her." Commenting on the article, which was signed "W," the *Democrat's* editor asserted that these "facts" came "from a responsible source. They are not new to us. Rumor has told the story for some time."[26]

If Craig bore the enmity of the *Democrat*, he had a friend in its rival the *Louisville Courier*, which was as active in the campaign for his re-election as the other was against. On February 11 and 12, 1854, the *Courier's* Frankfort correspondent visited the state penitentiary for the purpose of finding good things to say about Craig's wardenship. He spent two hours there between supper and lock-up on Saturday, the 11th, and returned for Sunday morning service. He therefore did not see the prisoners performing the exhausting forced labor that consumed the rest of the week. He did not see the "filling walk," where hemp was spun into rope, and which required the prisoner to walk backwards thirteen miles a day at a good trot. "I have often seen the new spinner with his ankles so swollen that he was just able to hobble to his cell at night," wrote Calvin Fairbank, "sore, tired, hungry; lungs filled with hemp dust . . . hands gashed by the thread, and flesh gashed with the rawhide for some trifling mishap." Nor did the reporter see them weaving "one hundred and fifty yards of coarse hemp sacking with two to two and a half threads or shots to the inch." That was what Craig required of every man; Fairbank could manage two hundred and twenty-five yards a day, and "counted the overplus as over-work on Saturday night" at the rate of seventy-five cents for every additional fifty yards. With this "overwork" he could buy sugar and flour and other articles.[27]

What the *Louisville Courier* reporter did see was the Saturday evening meal, where the "fare is plain, but ample and wholesome." Whether it was nutritious is another matter, for supper was nothing more than a second breakfast, consisting of cornbread, meat and coffee. Only at the noon-day meal did the prisoners have the "occasional soup and vegetables." Calvin Fairbank, who had a deeper acquaintance with this "wholesome fare," recalled: "Our food was, in the main, bacon, and cornbread mixed with hot water. At times we had beef soup, beef, potatoes, green corn, etc., when they did not cost too much." As for the plentiful coffee, it "was made from burnt rye, in the same forty-pail kettle, with the same old grounds cooked over and over for weeks, until sour."[28]

Craig believed in the virtue of order. Each of the one hundred and eighty-five seats in the refectory was numbered. The inmates filed in by twos, presumably in silence. After Saturday supper their one weekly hour of leisure was spent on this occasion in observing with interest "the gambols of a dog in a pool of water. . . . Some even enjoyed the scene, if quiet smiles upon their countenances were true indices of their feelings." At twilight the bell signaled the end of the day and the men formed another double procession, entering their cells two by two as their names were read off the roll. The *Courier's* reporter examined the cells and found most of them "lighted by small lamps, that twinkled brightly in the surrounding darkness. I noticed that the arrangement of beds was different in the various cells, according to the taste or fancy of those confined." Though this one small liberty was allowed the prisoners, the cells, measuring "four and a half feet by seven from back wall to door, and seven feet high," recalled Fairbank, were made less than comfortable by "our bed-fellows, swarms of fleas and bedbugs."[29]

At nine o'clock the next morning, the correspondent saw Craig deliver a Sunday lecture, "as is his custom, upon certain points of moral honesty. This excellent gentleman is forcible in the presentation of truth, and it is to be hoped that his labors for the immortal welfare of the prisoners will not prove unavailing."[30] Craig, who Fairbank found to be "very pious" but at the same time "vain, prejudiced" and "revengeful," made his invariable appearance in the pulpit of the chapel every Sunday, whether there was a chaplain appointed for the day or not. It was his church. His sermons rambled on for two to four hours, and were "dissertations on law, gospel, theology, philosophy, race and the 'Institution.'" The institution, that is, of slavery, which in Craig's estimation not only had a biblical basis but was evidently an essential pillar of his faith. Not that Craig was entirely insensible to the degree to which his exploitation of a truly captive audience at times bordered on the ridiculous, for "one time as he was dealing out peculiar lessons to the prisoners, and aiming at one of the distinguished prisoners who dared to say what he wished, the prisoner said: 'Captain, you are too tedious.' 'Well, Thompson, I don't know but I am,' and closed at the end of three hours."[31] The *Louisville Courier* had earlier reported that Craig's efforts had led to a "Revival of Religion in the Kentucky Penitentiary." On Sunday, December 16, 1853, a clergyman from Scott County saw Craig give a sermon after which "several came up and made a public profession of their faith, while many were discovered weeping in the congregation. That same afternoon at 3 o'clock seven persons were baptized in a pool within the prison walls"— perhaps the same pool in which a dog was seen to splash about on a Saturday night some two months later.[32]

A correspondent for the *Democrat* reported on February 13 that the February 10 issue of the paper with its searing attack on Craig was just then very much in demand in Frankfort. At the same time, other candidates for the post of warden, seeing their sudden opportunity, were "swarming" about and Craig, now "on the alert," was taking counter measures. "He had another levee on Friday night, and a stag-dance. His walking-canes are plentifully scattered about the burgh, and his friends are warm in his behalf. Unfortunately divers letters of the Keeper to Miss Webster have found their

way to Frankfort, and are shown about to the members of the Legislature."
The correspondent writes that he had "a sight of them" but will make no
further comment, as he expects they will be sent to the *Democrat* for publication.[33]

Over ten thousand valentines passed through the Louisville Post Office
on St. Valentine's Day, 1854.[34] Appropriately, on that date readers of the
Louisville Democrat were treated to convincing evidence of the state penitentiary warden's loving nature when the newspaper printed five of the letters he had written to his children's governess between 1845 and 1851. They
were apparently the same ones being circulated among the legislators. Reproduced in these pages in chapters 6, 8, and 9, they date from February 25,
1845; June 1849 (though undated); June 20, 1850; July 6, 1850; and October 1, 1851. The *Democrat* leeringly remarked upon "the beauties of this
correspondence. It is rare and rich. . . . The last"—the undated one, where
Craig declared "I LOVE you, yes, I LOVE you most dearly, and can never
prosper in your absence"—"is a model for those affectionately and amorously inclined."[35]

As for their authenticity, the *Democrat* affirmed that they were copies
furnished by "a responsible man" who attests that the originals are in Craig's
handwriting and "can be seen at any time in Frankfort." As for their prov-
enance, "We don't know how these letters were procured, except that Miss
Webster and her friend have fallen out. He had sued her, and she has doubtless sent these documents to Frankfort." Coming to Craig's defense, the *Courier* decried "the meanness of an attack on his private character" on the eve
of the election. It alleged that the letters were obtained "through a scoundrel
recently liberated from the prison named Wolfe, an inmate of other prisons
before this, and often punished for stealing the flour, sugar, and other little
articles bought by the overwork of his fellow convicts." Wolfe had such a
"passion for stealing that he would pilfer one man's tobacco, to give another,
he not using it himself"—which may have been what he did with the letters,
conveying them from their addressee to whoever among Craig's rivals most
wanted them, for the pure joy of the thing. The prisonkeeper had been warned
two months before that "application had been made for these letters," most
likely from one of the rivals for his post, who had offered "a large amount"
of money to get them. The *Courier* went on to accuse Webster of selling "her
reputation for money, for certain it is, that these letters have caused the purchaser a round sum."[36] Craig had profited enough from his wardenship that
the sum required may well have appeared a worthwhile investment to, for
example, Zebulon Ward, to name his chief rival and thus a likely perpetrator.
Though a convicted thief, Moses Wolfe apparently did not have to steal the
letters in order to act as the go-between. Yet he certainly had the credentials

to do so, having served two years in the Tennessee State Prison for passing counterfeit money, and then two in the Kentucky Penitentiary for larceny, from which he was released on August 5, 1853. Aged 33 and of German birth (a number of German families lived on Webster's Trimble County farm) and "intemperate" habits, he bore a four-inch scar on his left jaw and one of equal length on his forehead, was a butcher by profession, lacked one front tooth, and displayed tattooes of buffaloes and crossflags on one arm, a bull's head with implements of the butcher's trade on the other.[37]

That Wolfe did indeed have the full cooperation of Delia Webster in their delivery to Frankfort is evident from the fact that she herself accompanied their arrival. A correspondent reported in the *Courier* that "the quiet of Frankfort was disturbed this morning by the advent in town of Miss Delia Webster, just now *the* topic of conversation." Another correspondent in the February 20 issue writes that "Miss Delia herself has been imported to the Capitol, and habitates at the Mansion House, as an ex-cathedra expositor of the correspondence. . . . She is a woman of extraordinary art, aside from her personal hideousness of uncommon intellectual attractions."[38] It is not clear if he means that she is personally hideous or if her uncommon intellectual attractions make her so, though the latter is more likely. "She had woven her toils completely around Newt and made him believe" that she "was an injured, persecuted woman" and "that it was his mission to defend her." She could have "persuaded him to believe anything else she desired. Let any one who doubts this, attend the levees of the sybil, while she gives audience to those who may disgrace themselves by listening to her orgies." Anyone who beholds her as she casts her spell on her listeners "will realise how he was surrounded by her meshes."

Damning as the letters were both to Craig's reputation and to his chances for re-election, the *Courier* nevertheless sought to defend him. Craig had been infatuated, to be sure, suffering from "the 'very madness of the moon,' but it is nothing more."[39] In a letter from Frankfort dated February 16, 1854, a correspondent for the *Courier* put the best face possible on Craig's letters, stressing the fatherly terms of his affection. The writer alluded to Craig's wish in the undated letter that Webster come to Kentucky "and make good what I have said of you" (by which he may have meant that she show the Kentuckians that she does not harbor abolitionist sentiments, but on the contrary admires the Kentucky way of life), for "until you are better known here, they may still charge us and the public not know the truth." Could such a confidential letter, the correspondent asks, "have ever been written to a guilty paramour?" In other words, far from wishing to conceal their friendship, Craig is here asking that she help him bring it out into the open. He must therefore have felt no guilt. And he evidently believed that her mere presence in Frankfort would suffice to put all doubts to rest. Of course her presence in Frankfort now was raising all kinds of doubts.[40]

"Much commentary," the correspondent continues, "is made upon that part of the letter" of July 6, 1850, in which Craig instructed Webster to "make the Penitentiary the purchase and receive payment from me for the whole amount; then pay the bill, five per cent less." Some construed this to mean that Craig was getting credit for paying five percent more than in fact he paid for penitentiary purchases. For some reason, the correspondent seems perfectly certain of what really happened with that five percent: "What it was, is most clearly true. The creditor sold the bill to the penitentiary—5 per cent was deducted from the face for the cash—Miss Webster paid it, and Craig allowed her the benefit of the 5 percent deduction for the cash, on the settlement."

The correspondent writes with such assuredness that he gives the impression of having obtained this explanation from Craig himself. Perhaps he did, but if so Craig must have decided to change his story. For when Craig published his own "vindication" in the *Louisville Democrat* on February 18, he gives an entirely different version of the five percent deduction. Craig dates his letter to the *Democrat* February 16, 1854, the same as the *Courier*'s correspondent—while the latter's differing version of the rationale for the deduction, would not appear until the 20th, two days *after* the publication of Craig's vindication on the 18th. Though every word the correspondent wrote was meant to support Craig's cause, his saying that the deduction went to Webster was hardly helpful, since it contradicted what Craig had just published, and besides made Webster appear to profit from the penitentiary (and from the excruciating labor of, among others, her former associate Calvin Fairbank).

In his defense, which took the form of a long letter "To the Members of the Kentucky Legislature and the Public" published in the *Democrat* on February 18, Craig reproduces the July 6, 1850 letter to his "Dear Children" telling them to request that the "Messrs. Howard" (not the "Misses," as the *Democrat*'s February 14th version erroneously had it) grant a five percent discount. Then he presents a letter dated July 4, 1850 from himself to Messrs. Howard in which he had already asked for the deduction "for cash," and including as well some interesting detail with regard to Dillard—and even more interestingly, to Delia: "Gentlemen: Enclosed you will find a check on the Bank of America drawn in my favor and transferred to the order of my little son who is in his eleventh year. . . . If you can spare the time please see my son and daughter on board some vessel and question him closely. I dote on him as a dear boy, tell him I am displeased at his not writing me oftener." Elsewhere in the same letter, he had written of what daughters Florida and

Mary were up to at home in Kentucky; thus the only "daughter" this could refer to is Delia Webster. Craig was thus pretending to Joseph Howard and sons that Dillard's governess was his older sister.[41]

He further produces a letter from the Howards in response, informing him that they showed his letter of July 4 to Dillard "when he called on us, and regret we could not further your wishes in regard to your son." They could not, that is, place his son and "daughter" on a vessel and take the former to task for not writing his father more often. No doubt his "daughter" was quite capable of taking charge of the embarkation all by herself, as well as of transmitting the paternal displeasure at Dillard's slowness to write. Craig had in fact asked her to do so in the July 6, 1850 letter: "I have but one letter from Dillard, notwithstanding . . . my strict charge to him . . . to write me every Monday. . . . I hope you will check him in his speed in learning to promise me to do one thing, and then doing another."[42]

Craig attaches an affidavit from the clerk of the penitentiary (appointed by the governor, not the warden, he is careful to say) attesting that the five per cent was deducted for cash, "which sum was saved by the Penitentiary, and not by him individually." Nor, of course, by Miss Webster.

As for the charge of fraternising, or worse, with an inmate of his own prison, Craig turns the charge upon his accusers. It is they who are conspiring with a former inmate of both the Kentucky and Tennessee penitentiaries (meaning Moses Wolfe), and indeed conspiring with Webster herself. "While they endeavor to destroy me for befriending an abolitionist who deceived me, they have her now here and are in communication with her, again availing themselves of the services of the convict mentioned; for he came with her and, at the moment I write this, is, with others, perhaps engaged in some other plan to strike again."

To prove his innocence of any improper feelings toward Delia Webster, Craig cites the letter in which he had urged her to come to Kentucky, "into the bosom of my family and friends," so that "by a prudent, judicious and discreet course you will prove a *tall white plume* in my cap." Then he explains what he meant by this. "Honestly and conscientiously believing her to be a good but persecuted woman, I was resolved to satisfy the public of that fact, and if possible to restore her in public estimation, if I could do so without too great a sacrifice; and in order to effect this object, I thought it best that she should come and remain here in Kentucky, where she had brought all her dishonor upon herself, and was willing to bring her to my house for that purpose, if I could do so without giving additional cause for prattle. . . . If the whole correspondence were exposed, it would show that my object was to make her a good woman, to induce her to join the church and become useful, and so I thought her capable of being." The passage in the undated letter in which Craig demanded that Webster bring her letter from the church with her thus finds its explanation. She would need it to obtain membership in Craig's church, though the transition from (Northern, antislavery) Congregational to (Southern, pro-slavery) Baptist might not have been easy.

Craig found he had to give some explanation for having written Webster about shipping hemp "for an excuse to come for you" in the letter of October 1, 1851. With the view of persuading her to return to Kentucky, he explains, "I was willing to make another shipment of hemp to Boston to cover my expenses there and back, and at the same time afford me business which would justify my going there without giving adequate cause for talk and censure." For "I knew that my motives of friendship for the woman . . . were censured, misunderstood, and greatly misrepresented by persons claiming to be my friends" back in 1851. "I could go nowhere and upon no kind of business, that my enemies were not circulating reports prejudicial to my character in connection with her." As for the hemp, "the prison profited by preparing and I by shipping" it.

Elsewhere in his letter of vindication, Craig sheds interesting light on the history of their relationship. He speaks of the letter which William C. Sneed in his history of the penitentiary would say Webster addressed to Governor Owsley, Craig, and others, but of which she never speaks. According to Craig, it arrived "six months after" her pardon, which would place it around August 1845. Sneed said Craig answered the letter and "gave her such advice as he thought proper and best for her good," but does not say whether he thought she should come to Kentucky, as she had requested.[43] Craig says that in the letter she had "asked our advice as to the propriety of her return, and declaring her innocence, but many of us thought it best that she should not return." Sneed wrote that a correspondence began between Craig and Webster at this point. For his part, Craig here writes that "She was after this [that is, after the letter of August 1845] invited to Madison, In., where she located under the control of and association with many of the best families of the city, among them that of Gen. Stapp, then Mayor of the city and former Lieut. Governor of the State." This fits exactly with what Webster said in her letter to the *Louisville Courier* of December 17, 1851 (shortly after Fairbank's arrest, and while she was recuperating from an illness at the Craigs'). So too does Craig's next sentence: "I sent two of my children to her school, under Gen. Stapp's care" (except that Webster had not specified how many of his children he had sent).

What Craig next says, however, reveals something entirely new: "I at this time owned a small lot in Madison, which she proposed to buy as a home for her brother, and advising with my friends there, I let her have it on condition that it should be paid for in the tuition of my children. My wife provided them some articles of furniture, but she was insatiable, still wanting more. This I denied giving her, and seeing that I had been sadly deceived, I took my children home and instituted suit against her for my property." The *Louisville Democrat* had charged that Craig "purchased her a house," but must have been confused or exaggerating; though by Craig's own admission he gave her the lot.[44] According to the *Madison Star* a quarter-century after the fact, Delia Webster lived in boarding houses at least some of the time she spent in Madison.[45] More contemporaneous is the statement by the *Madison Courier* on July 22, 1854, that Craig "rented a house for her and placed his children with her to board and be instructed by her." That account provides some interesting new information of its own, saying of her year in New York (1848-49), during which according to her she taught school, that she "established herself as a daguerreotypist and manufacturer of window shades." There was, in fact, in the 1840s a large window shade factory in Webster's native Vergennes.[46] "She was then induced to abandon that business and to remove to this city by Craig, who promised to assist her in establishing a manufactory of window shades here. That business not proving profitable," he rented her the house and sent her his children to populate her school. One thing that is clear is that Newton Craig took the extraordinary step of paying his children's tuition in advance, years in advance surely, by giving her the lot.

This was going too far, as he admits: "I candidly confess that one of the greatest weaknesses of my nature is to go, very often, too far for those whom I respect and believe to be injured, and under this feeling I would have gone any reasonable length for this woman." Until this point in his letter of self-defense, Craig had sounded reasonable enough, if not in his past behavior, at least in his explanation of it. But from here on a note of bad faith begins to emerge: "I intended to retain her as a teacher to my children, and to have rewarded her well"—as if giving her a piece of real estate was not enough reward already—"until she overreached herself by avarice, and began again, as her neighbors suspected, her old trade of negro stealing." Southerners liked to accuse abolitionists of stealing slaves in order to resell them, and some unscrupulous individuals may well have described themselves to slaves as antislavery agents in order to do exactly that, but Craig and his readers were perfectly aware that this was not what motivated such people as Calvin Fairbank and Delia Webster. It was a myth Kentuckians told Northerners though they knew it was false. There was no money to be made in the Underground Railroad, yet Craig persisted in claiming that the lust for lucre is what drove Delia to steal her neighbors' property. "The instant I knew this, I promptly discarded her, and did all a man could to expose her as a woman not to be trusted, a bundle of deceit, who knew not where to stop when avarice goaded her on, a fanatic on the subject of slavery, that would embrace every opportunity to steal such property."

Stressing Craig's assertion that Lucy Craig "read every letter he had ever written" (though one may doubt whether she read the one marked "CONFIDENTIAL," with its insistent declarations of love), the *Courier* editorializes on February 20, the day of the election, that the letters show "no criminal conduct." The most they show is "weakness and folly in the writer, . . . the weakness that springs from gratitude for benefits conferred—the folly that grows out of misplaced and misunderstood affection." The "benefits conferred" were doubtless, as yet another Frankfort correspondent wrote in the same issue of the paper, that of "teaching his children, two of whom were scarcely above imbeciles."[47]

According to the *Louisville Courier*'s correspondent, Delia Webster's "remarkable ability to instruct, soon developed itself by the children's learning to spell and read handsomely"—including, apparently, the two victims of their parents' consanguinity—"and hence the fond attachment of the parents." Interestingly, the reporter mentions that Webster had begun to teach the children "while in the penitentiary"—that is, back in January-February 1845. "What father and mother," he continues, "who themselves being own cousins, and feeling the deep parental interest natural on such occasions, looking at the weak and uncultivated intellect of part of their offspring, would not have been tempted to defend one to whom it was natural they should feel obligations the most sacred of all others?" It is curious that this defender of Craig's reputation, who gave perhaps the most satisfying explanation of the warden's affection for his children's governess, should then come the closest to admitting what many at least would imagine to be the worst one could say about the affair: "Even if it were true that an improper intimacy existed between Capt. Craig and Miss Webster. . . ."—even if it were true, that is, such conduct would be much less objectionable than that of the enemies who stooped so low to defeat him.[48]

In his vindication, Craig had declared, "that I erred and have been sadly deceived, I candidly confess, but that I have acted criminally, I deny, with the fear of God before me; for every letter I wrote this woman was read by my wife." By acting "criminally," Craig did not mean embezzlement, a charge against which Lucy's reading the letters would not have protected him, but sexual impropriety. "I again most solemnly aver, in the sight of God... that the charge of criminal connection with this woman is false— false!"[49] The *Oxford English Dictionary* defines "connexion" itself as "sexual relation or intercourse," and cites the phrase "criminal connexion," which Craig uses here, from Boswell's *Life of Johnson* in this sense.[50] In response to his defense the *Louisville Democrat* commented, "Mr. C. complains that he is charged with having had 'criminal connection' with Miss Webster. Too fast, Mr. C. We are not aware that any such charge has been made by any one—certainly not by us." The gentleman doth protest too much, behavior which tends to suggest an inner sense of guilt with regard to his relation with "this naughty abolitionist. . . . Well, Mr. C. may not have come it over the wily miss; but . . . if we were to tell a young lady . . . that we loved her dearly, . . . that we could not endure her absence, &c, &c, we should not wonder if people . . . would think we were after something else than to 'make her a good woman.'"[51]

Craig was defeated in his quest for re-election, though it took several votes to do so, as no candidate on the earlier ballots received a majority. One by one the other candidates were winnowed away, leaving only Craig and Zebulon Ward, who finally triumphed, 75 votes to 60, late in the afternoon of February 20, in a joint session of both houses of the legislature.

Craig still had a year left in his term, which would not expire until March 1855. He could take out his anger on his prisoners (and Fairbank would prove a particular target of his wrath)—or his slaves: According to local legend, Craig had two fifteen-feet high posts four feet square at the base, tapering to two feet square at the top, placed across the road from his Scott County home. The warden, "whip in hand, is reputed to have ordered slaves who had violated his rigid code of obedience to straddle the posts. Then, with his whip cracking dangerously near the ankles of the terrified victim, Newton told him to 'reach for the moon.'"[52] But, as events unfolded that spring and summer, the real target of his revenge would be Delia Webster.

Craig had overextended himself not just amorously but financially, as his diarist cousin would record on February 21, 1854. "This morning I heard that Newton Craig had lost the place of keeper of the Penitentiary. . . . This will be a great mortification to Newton, and perhaps a serious injury to him, and perhaps to his securities, of whom I am one. . . . It is to be feared that he is not in condition to wind up his business, that is, not able to pay his debts." Concerning the letters themselves, Jefferson Craig recorded his reaction on February 15 to their publication: "This is mortifying to him and his friends, though the letters show nothing criminal." Evidence of Newton Craig's new financial difficulties can be garnered from the entry of January 20, 1855, when Jefferson would contract to accept, with a General Johnson, a mortgage on Newton Craig's farm so that Newton could deal with a $5,000 claim against him. "It is with great reluctance that I incur such responsibilities, but by taking this mortgage I get a lien on his land and negroes to secure me against loss when I am already bound for him." On January 21, it was agreed that Jefferson and the General would get a mortgage "on all his negroes—15 in number." On June 26, 1855, Jefferson Craig "applied to Dr.

Keene to lend Cousin Newton some money, but without success." In the entry for September 2, he recalls that he had "gone security . . . for $5000 to help Newton out of a bad scrape . . . but I am resolved not to do so again. Yesterday Dr. Keene lent him $5000 to pay that debt, and I feel relieved of that liability. He gave Dr. Keene a mortgage on his farm."[53] Newton Craig's financial distress can be traced to the loss of his post at the prison, a significant, if not indeed his principal source of income. All of which was due, of course, to Delia Webster's decision to release his letters and become the sybil of the Mansion House in order to personally guarantee their authenticity.

Having been the toast of Frankfort, or at least of Craig's enemies, she had to return to face the wrath of her Trimble County neighbors, for the issues raised in their confrontation of February 7 had not been laid to rest. Besides that, an enraged Newton Craig would soon join their ranks to take an active role in her persecution.

11

"A VERY BOLD AND DEFIANT KIND OF WOMAN"

On March 7, 1854, a month after their first visit, the committee of Trimble countians returned to Delia Webster's farm to issue an ultimatum: "Unless you consent forthwith to sell us your plantation, and speedily leave the State no more to return, you will be mobbed at a dead hour of the night, and the threats of the mass executed." The "threats of the mass" had already been delivered. They were: "Your fences will all be torn down, your fine orchard ruined, your valuable timber destroyed, your cattle and horses slain before your eyes, your barns and out-houses burned, your dwelling houses blown up, and yourself assassinated at the midnight hour."[1]

As in the earlier encounter, here again it proved easier to draw up a list of bloodthirsty threats than to actually say such things to her face. Remarkably, accommodation was still possible, at least for a while. In the course of the committee's conversation with Webster, it appeared that there had been a misunderstanding. They had been under the impression that she had made no reply to their demands of a month before and "that I had treated their resolutions with silent contempt." It was almost as if all they had wanted was to be listened to with respect. They wanted dialogue, and were relieved to discover that she had in fact made a proper response—its propriety residing in the fact of her having made it, not in its actual content, which was, of course, utter defiance. "Thus saying, they apologized, assured me of their respect and kind feeling, and tendering their good wishes, bade me adieu; and I was once more left in quiet."[2] Kentucky gentility, despite the financial distress of the continual loss of their slaves, was still highly valued by the gentlemen of the committee. Yet they could not withstand indefinitely the pressures exerted by others who were less enamored of the ideals of community.

Six days later, the farm was invaded by a "gang of ruffians" brandishing pistols and clubs, determined to lay hands on Delia Webster. As it happened, she was away from the farm, having gone to Cincinnati for reasons of business and health. That is what her domestics told them, though only after long and industrious searching did they believe it. The next day she returned, but had not been in the house an hour before the sheriff and his men arrived and demanded of her servants that she appear. Drawing upon her feminine resources, she sent down word that "I was in my dressing-room attending to the duties of the toilet" and that they should take a seat in the parlor. Unhappy with that answer, the sheriff and his band were rushing up the stairs, axe in hand (for purposes of breaking and entering), when Delia Webster emerged from her bedroom. "I approached and requested them to return to the parlor and await my convenience. They apologized and withdrew to the parlor." She kept them waiting a few minutes more, then descended and "was formally introduced to the sheriff," who produced a warrant for her arrest: "Whereas John W. Coleman states under oath that he suspects Delia A. Webster has made an attempt to entice away Daniel McCarty Payne's slave Tom, and divers other slaves from Trimble county, therefore I command that said Delia A. Webster be forthwith apprehended, and brought before me to be dealt with according to law. (Signed) [Judge] Robert Gray."[3] It was hardly a valid warrant, as suspicion alone does not constitute grounds for arrest. Its illegality was doubtless a tribute to the skill with which Webster and Day had been spiriting the slaves away—undetected but, unfortunately, not unsuspicioned.

The sheriff pretended that this had been done "only to appease the excitement of a few individuals" and that if she would only consent to appear before the judge she would be discharged. Webster knew better, telling him she was convinced the case was already decided and that she was going to jail. She asked permission to pack some clothes for her stay. He assured her there was no need of that, and hustled her off to the courthouse in Bedford. Allowed neither attorney nor witness nor jury, she faced "a score of witnesses and three attorneys [who] were introduced against me, and I had a mock trial."[4]

The *Madison Courier* took issue with these proceedings, finding fault in particular with the notion of convicting someone of being "*suspected* of enticing away slaves. . . . There was no pretence of any evidence . . . but it was shown that since her residence in that county some twenty slaves had escaped." It was also alleged against her that Norris Day had been indicted (though not convicted) for the same offense and that he resided on the same farm and was her friend and associate. Her previous conviction (in Lexington in 1844) was held against her. The suspicions of her neighbors were introduced as evidence. The judge ruled that she could post ten thousand dollars bond under promise to leave the state and never return or face imprisonment in the county jail. Having neither the money nor the desire to make such a promise, she was committed to jail. "This is indubitably the land of liberty," concluded the *Courier*.[5]

Everything was done to make her confinement as painful as possible. She was placed in a "log hut of rude construction, foul and filthy," normally used to house slaves awaiting shipment south. "The weather was cold," she recalled, a declaration to which the diary of Jefferson Craig, who made daily meteorological observations in nearby Georgetown (fifty miles to the southeast), can attest. An icy cold snap reigned between March 18 and April 3, bringing a peach-killing frost on March 25, snow on the 29th, and as late as April 2 a temperature of 29 degrees Fahrenheit.[6] "When persons in the vicinity remonstrated at the cruelty" of keeping her in an unheated cell, her jailor consented to light the unvented stove which for several days "filled the cabin with smoke, and when this reached to the point of suffocation they dashed water upon it, and then it was confidently said that I had enjoyed a fire in my prison."[7] When she tried to write by the light of an opening high up in the wall, standing up to do so, the jailor boarded it up. She had no change of clothing and very little in the way of blankets.

The jailor justified these conditions by declaring that "my spirit had got to be subdued by hardships till I would be willing to give up and leave the State." The wife of a prominent slaveholder took pity on her, and arrived at the jail in her carriage, accompanied by her servant and bringing clothing and other necessities. The jailor refused to let her in. Undaunted, the woman ordered her servant to tear the boarding off the window, "resolutely stood by while he passed to me the contents of the basket, and when the jailor undertook to interfere, she told him he would be made to feel her husband's influence on his position if he did not desist."[8]

Thanks to this intervention, Webster was at last able to communicate with the outside world, in particular with her lawyers. Through their efforts, she was removed on a writ of habeas corpus and tried before the circuit judge of another county, who found the charges against her groundless. Released on April 8, she returned to her farm, oversaw the plowing and planting of a hundred acres of corn and ten of potatoes, and the harvesting of her winter oats. That accomplished, she left the farm in the care of her tenants and took up residence in Madison.

While Delia Webster was engaged in rural pursuits, so too was her former foster father. On April 22, Jefferson Craig recorded in his diary paying a visit to his cousin Newton's farm. "Found him at the pond with four negroes catching gold fish, which he sends to Louisville and sells at $9 a dozen." Two weeks later, Newton gave Jefferson a dozen seedling strawberry plants to take home. It had been with strawberries that Newton had tried to entice Delia to come back from Vermont back in the spring of 1849.[9] He was just as proud of his grapes. "We drank some of Newton's Catawba wine, and brought a bottle home."[10]

On the evening of Friday, May 26, Jefferson Craig and his family were making plans for a strawberry party the following day to enjoy the fruits of the seedlings cousin Newton had given them three weeks before.[11] That same evening in Boston, Lewis Hayden was about to spearhead an event that would result in what Thomas Wentworth Higginson would later call "the first drop of blood actually shed" in the escalating violence that precipitated the Civil War. "It was, like the firing on Fort Sumter, a proof that war had really begun."[12] Another fugitive slave had been captured, and another attempt would be made to set him free. The plot called for the crowd already assembled at Faneuil Hall to hear a slate of antislavery speakers and thereby be galvanized into action. A voice from the back of the hall would announce that the rescue of Anthony Burns from the Federal Courthouse had at that moment begun but that for it to succeed all those who valued freedom must immediately run out to lend a hand. Confusion reigned when the announcement was made, however, since the platform speakers who were supposed to encourage the crowd to respond to the appeal faltered; but at least a few men rushed out to join the melee at the courthouse. Seeing the reinforcements arrive, Hayden and Higginson brought out their axes, broke open a door, and forced their way in. They were met by half a dozen policemen wielding clubs. In the ensuing struggle, a shot rang out, and Deputy Marshal Batchelder fell to the ground.

For years Higginson thought Hayden had fired the shot, even though the deputy's last words were "I've been stabbed," and the police concluded he had died from a knife coming through the door. Since no autopsy was performed, they were confirmed in their error. According to Kenneth Wiggins Porter, Hayden had fired a shot, though not the fatal one.[13] In 1888, Higginson learned that a Martin Stowell, whose idea the rescue had been and who was to die in the Civil War before the truth came out, had actually shot and killed Batchelder. Higginson also found out, from talking to the United States marshal, that the plot very nearly succeeded. But not enough men of firm determination had materialized from the Faneuil Hall assembly, and the death of Batchelder shocked the besiegers into retreating.[14] As for Anthony Burns, he was marched by armed escort to Boston harbor to await shipment south as hundreds of abolitionists shouted "Shame!" The Marine Band answered with a rendition of "Carry Me Back to Ole Virginny."

Delia Webster's experiences in Trimble County in March, 1854, had apparently convinced her that the days of her farm's usefulness were over. Once her fields were planted and she had removed to Madison, she "determined to, if I could sell my farm without too much sacrifice, henceforth make [Madison] my home, and publicly offered my place on the Ky. hill for sale."[15] She sent a notice to one of the Louisville newspapers, but it was delayed in the mail, "and remained upon the boat some time." On June 16, she went over to the farm to bring some medicine to a woman among her tenants who was bedridden with illness. "The walk was too much for me," the day being "excessively hot."[16] She collapsed with fatigue and had to be carried to the house, where she herself was confined to bed under a doctor's care.

On June 19, men arrived on a warrant from Lexington to arrest her for the escape of Harriet, Lewis Hayden's wife, ten years before. Webster had spent much time in Kentucky in the preceding decade, in the company of Newton Craig in Georgetown and Frankfort, and on her Trimble County farm. Why had the authorities waited until now? The indictment for which she was tried in December 1844 concerned Lewis alone; she had been indicted for his wife and son, but these had been stricken from the docket in 1845. But someone had dug them up and brought them back to life. "My pursuers had among them a man who, from certain reasons of his own, was my personal enemy. By his agency . . . through his intrigues three old indictments which the commonwealth attorney had stricken from the docket ten years ago, by order of the court, were re-docketed, and warrants issued for my arrest."[17] That man, of course, was Newton Craig. "The motives of his malice," she wrote that summer,

> as near as I can account for it in a few words, are, first, that he experienced a decided repulse and totally failed to have his ungentlemanly and uncivilized desires accommodated, and next, that I was unwilling to have him visit my house even under the pretence of seeing his children, whom he had, by previous contract, engaged to keep under my tuition for a certain time. Then, after finding that his entreaties and letters he had written to me availed nothing, he, in his rough, Kentucky manner, swore with an oath that, if I would not agree to marry in case his wife should die—which he expected would take place before long, as she was then sick—he would get somebody to swear to enough on that old indictment to send me to the penitentiary, where his will should be my law, and where resistance would be vain![18]

She might also have mentioned, but didn't, that the resurrection of the indictments seems to have taken place just after she made Craig lose the election.

When the officers came to arrest her, they found she was too sick to be moved. So they stationed three armed men at the house to prevent any escape, and placed several others at some distance, "to prevent the possibility of my being rescued by the Indianians."[19] But early the next morning, when the guards inside the house were asleep, a messenger did manage to sneak through to tell her that Craig was on his way—"that the fatal hour had arrived when she was to be delivered up to the merciless 'Legree,' who had sworn violence. That he had arrived from the interior of the State with his posse of bloody hirelings, to receive her, and that they were rapidly approaching the house. Knowing there was not a moment to be lost, she was nerved to effort, and made an almost miraculous escape to Indiana."[20] In letter to the *Madison Banner* written just days after the event, she wrote that "recollection of his former violence in trying to break into my house, and my narrow escape, rushed upon my mind with such terrific force that the excitement nerved me with more than natural strength, and I determined to leave the house and secreted myself in the woods."[21] The *Madison Courier* reported that "the guard slept at their posts or were careless, or were seduced, as the keeper of the penitentiary, Craig, it is said was; anyhow, Miss Webster escaped on the 'underground railroad,' vanished, vamoused, left her disconsolate guard to watch the empty house."[22]

When Craig arrived, she was gone. Brandishing two pistols and a Bowie knife, he "ordered the Germans in my employ to leave the premises with their wives and children, threatening them if they refused to obey." Terrified, they fled to Madison, except for one who "remained and, with tears and entreaties, begged him to spare his poor sick wife, but the inhuman being ordered her out of bed and out of the house, with her infant child!" Craig was convinced Webster was still hiding somewhere in the house, "and I suppose wanted no witness to his dark and monstrous designs." When in the end he had to conclude she had escaped him, "he tore around like a mad man" and began to complain about the furniture she had that was his. Its value, according to Webster, was only $250. But he proceeded to remove from the farm "cattle and other property to the amount of more than a thousand dollars, leaving not even my articles of dress."[23] The booty included her "furniture, library, and wardrobe, fifteen hundred bushels of corn, twenty head of cattle, forty swine, [and] all her farming utensils."[24]

Though this is Webster's version of what happened, it is corroborated by the Madison correspondent of the *Louisville Democrat*, who reported that Trimble countians "are very anxious for Miss Webster to leave their midst, but they do not desire to see her cast in prison." Perhaps they knew she had planned to sell out, after her stay in the Bedford jail; they were willing to let her go without further ado. So that the persecution that began in June had nothing to do with them, but was instigated entirely by Newton Craig. "I verily believe," writes the *Democrat's* correspondent, "they [the Trimble countians] had no agency in her late arrest. As Miss Webster has juggled him out of considerable of his money, and unceremoniously cast him off, I think it would have been far the better policy in Craig, being a married man, to have hushed the matter up, instead of parading it before the public." The correspondent alludes to "several thousands of his money" that passed into her hands, and to her then having "suddenly cut the meshes of the net with which she had caught him," telling him "that thenceforth he must keep aloof from her." Thus, Craig moved "to make her the special object of a most malignant revenge." As for the character of Miss Webster herself, "she is a very bold and defiant kind of woman, without a spark of feminine modesty, and, withal, very shrewd and cunning."[25]

For twelve days, between June 20 and July 1, Delia Webster hid out in Indiana, Craig in the meantime having managed to obtain a writ from the governor of Indiana requiring that she be arrested and delivered to an agent of the governor of Kentucky. With the help of sympathetic Hoosiers, she was concealed at times in Madison and at times in the countryside, "in a hay mow, in the woods, under brush heaps, in the rye fields, in clefts of rocks."[26] But Sheriff Robert Right Rea, notorious for nearly always getting his man, and a specialist in ferreting out the hiding places of runaway slaves, finally located her in the house of a friend, a Mr. Lee of Shelby township. According to Webster, at the time of her capture she was "prostrate with sickness" and while she "lay sick and nearly helpless," Rea and his deputies "took me from a sick bed, in spite of the remonstrances of myself and the family who had been taking the tenderest care of me."[27] According to Rea's version of events, however, he had "found Miss Webster sitting up, and apparently in good health." Shortly after the warrant for her arrest was read, she did complain "of being unwell, but attributed her sickness to excitement." It was only "after having delayed one and a quarter hours to allow her time to arrange her toilet" that Rea and his men were able to escort their prisoner away. He was anxious to get started, having been warned of the imminent probability of being "molested by a mob" of Webster sympathizers.[28] Indeed, a New Albany, Indiana, paper reported that when the arrest "was made in Canaan or its vicinity [it] caused very great excitement in that quarter."[29]

Webster later claimed that Rea was motivated by the hope of reward to try to deliver her directly to her Kentucky pursuers, and therefore made her "to ride in an open buggy under the hot scorching sun in a round-about way twelve or fifteen miles to avoid passing through the city of Madison, and went to a point on the river above town, where they expected to find Kentucky gallants waiting to smuggle me over the Ohio in a skiff." But not finding the Kentuckians they were counting on, Rea then took her to the Madison jail, and word was sent to Craig's agents to come and get her there. "The bloodhounds arrived about two o'clock at night, but a writ of *habeas*

Madison viewed from the Kentucky side. Lithograph from Gleason's Pictorial Drawing-Room Companion, *July 8, 1854. Courtesy Madison-Jefferson County Public Library*

corpus arrived a little before them, and for once despoiled them of their prey."[30] Rea later vehemently denied all she said about the scorching sun and the rendezvous at the river.[31] The correspondent of the *Louisville Democrat*, however, repeated her version of events: Craig "did have her arrested near Canaan, in this county, under the cover of night, and endeavored to force her across the river about two o'clock at night, but could not find any conveyance for getting her across."[32] The *Democrat* was motivated by continuing hostility toward Craig, against whom the paper had vigorously campaigned that February; this is evident in the central role it assigns him in her arrest, even though Webster herself did not go so far as to say, as the paper implies, that he went with Rea to capture her. Rea, on the other hand, at the time he published his defense in the Madison newspapers, was running for re-election and thus had plenty of reason to deny her charges.

It was attorney Abram W. Hendricks who had managed to obtain the writ of habeas corpus from Judge Walker, which meant that Webster would be granted a hearing in Madison to determine whether she could be delivered up to Kentucky. The proceedings were first scheduled for July 4, then postponed until the 20th. By that time, Webster had enlisted a brilliant advocate in the person of Joseph Glass Marshall. Born in 1800, Marshall was in the prime of his career in midsummer 1854. Standing over six feet tall, he had "a great big head, thickly covered with sandy hair . . . and his uncouth form and careless dress served to show" his features "to the best advantage." Wasting no time "in dallying with the graces of oratory," in his court appearances he "at once hurled the javelins of his logic at the weakest points in his adversary's armor. He had the element of pathos," able to sway a jury to tears or mirth as best suited the interests of his client. Known as the "Sleeping Lion," he was "indolent" by nature, but "it was almost impossible to get a verdict against him when he was thoroughly aroused and 'shook his mane.'"[33]

John Lyle King, another local attorney, was an eyewitness to the event, and recorded his impressions in his diary. July 20, 1854, he wrote, was the hottest day of the year, the temperature outside standing at 105 degrees. Inside the courtroom, packed to the rafters, it was hotter. All "available spaces are filled, with an outside fringe of Negroes to the crowd. . . . And then they patiently stand and sit sweltering . . . fusing with one evaporating mass listening" to the respective attorneys' "effusions, to most avid technicalities and details of cases from the books, panting for air enough to keep their lungs in low vitality and every brow a fount of perspiration. . . . Wonderful what sympathy there is for Miss Webster."[34]

King felt that the ten year old indictments had been "revived by private malice" and found fault with the Indiana governor for being so accommodating to the Kentuckians as to have "afforded her pursuers two different warrants." But he was shocked by the extremes to which Marshall would go in his client's defense. A man from Milton, the Trimble County town immediately opposite Madison, was present on the first day of the hearing and would no doubt have agreed with King on that point. He reported that Hendricks began by appealing to sectional feeling, calling all those engaged in trying to catch Miss Webster "cowards" and "blood-hounds," and that Marshall continued in the same vein, telling the crowd that "Hoosiers had submitted too long to the arrogance of Kentuckians, and now was the time for them to show that they were men and freemen. His whole speech was assumption and invective."[35]

Prominent among the Kentuckians hoping to get their hands on Webster had been John W. Coleman, the sheriff of Trimble County, the same who had sworn under oath in March that she had been seducing away slaves. It happened that Coleman died from cholera the day before the hearing began. Marshall, wrote the Milton correspondent, alleged that "God had shown his displeasure at this unrighteous persecution" by killing "one of this lady's most inveterate enemies with the cholera. This was the judgment of God."[36] King likewise recorded that Marshall had alluded to Coleman "as one having been shortly summoned to his long account," as if his demise had been the result of divine intervention, and was shocked at the attorney's words as well as their effect on the spectators. "The crowd in the Court House applauded! Horrible!"[37] Marshall's defense and the support of the crowd must have been cheering to Delia Webster, who "sat with as much confidence as if she knew that she would not be given up."[38]

The hearing continued into the next day. King again beheld "a dense crowd" that was "deeply interested" in the spectacle. Marshall, he noted, actually spoke more to them than to the judge. King "turned frequently towards" the crowd "and deflected from the line of law argument frequently to launch off into political haranguements. These inevitably brought cheers." He was chagrined at Marshall's antics. "The most unseemly and improper demonstrations I ever saw in a Court. Judge Walker heard them quietly and was silent."[39] The *Madison Courier*, while reporting that the attorney's speeches "elicited frequent bursts of applause," did note that "the Judge and bailliffs vainly attempted to suppress" them.[40]

Marshall's principal argument hinged on a technicality: that the papers which were before the governor of Indiana when he issued the warrant were a necessary part of the authority for a fugitive's arrest, subject to the inspection of the court, but that these documents were not included in the warrant. He also contended that the crime with which his client was charged is not specified in the U.S. Constitution, that the warrant did not state that the indictment is pending in the Fayette County (Kentucky) court, and that "it does not appear, from the recital in the warrant, that the petitioner is a fugitive from justice."[41]

By noon on the second day of the hearing, the arguments for both sides had been completed. Judge Walker recessed for the noonday meal, after which he returned with his decision, which caught both parties by surprise. He overruled all of Marshall's objections to the warrant, but came up with one of his own. A state does not have the right under the constitution to inquire into the guilt of a fugitive it is asked to give up to another state, nor into the issue of whether the indictment is pending, yet it does retain "the right of looking into the charge" in order to decide "whether a charge of crime appears upon the papers." Walker had looked into the Kentucky statutes and found that the relevant law included language that said "If any free person not having lawful, or in good faith, a color of claim thereto, shall steal, or seduce, or entice a slave to leave his owner. . . ." He focused on the phrase "a color of claim" and ruled that, because the warrant for Webster's arrest did not specify that she did not have color of claim to the slave she was accused of enticing, the charge was not a good one.[42] John W. Chapman, one of the prosecuting attorneys, wrote King, "admitted to me that it took him by surprise and said he was not certain but what 'twas a good point."[43]

There had actually been two warrants for Webster's arrest, the first being, as she correctly described in her July 4 letter from the Madison jail, for seducing away Harriet, Lewis Hayden's wife. Having always (except perhaps within the safety of New England) denied ever having enticed any slaves to escape, she denied the truth of this indictment as well, though without actually saying she did not help Harriet escape. The indictment stated that the enticing was committed on September 20, 1844. "A baser falsehood never was uttered. I had never seen that woman before her escape."[44] All this denies, of course, is having seen her before her escape. Having consulted Harriet's husband at length before the rescue, there was no need to. As for the other warrant, it was for having, on August 1, 1844, "seduced and enticed Gibson, a slave the property of Lewis Berry, to leave his owner and escape to parts unknown."[45] This is the Gilson Berry (to respect Fairbank's spelling of his name) who had accosted Fairbank in Oberlin to go to Kentucky to bring out his wife and children. Webster never spoke of her role, if any, in his rescue.

Judge Walker devoted nearly all his opinion to a consideration of the second—Gilson Berry—warrant. He concluded his remarks by dismissing the one for Harriet Hayden on the grounds that it did not show that its indictment was certified as authentic by the governor of Kentucky. When he discharged her the courtroom resounded with "cheers and congratulations."[46] She emerged from the courthouse, "got into a buggy and drove off amidst the cheers of the populace."[47]

Chapman, an attorney for the prosecution, told King "he had good reason to know that had she been surrendered to the agent of Kentucky there was an organized arrangement to rescue her at all hazards and prevent her delivery into Kentucky. There is little doubt of this."[48] Now that Delia Webster was no longer in danger of being returned to Kentucky, the citizens of Madison focused their attention on Newton Craig. Craig had been in the city since July 19 and stayed for the duration of the hearing, claiming he had been requested to do so by the agent of the governor of Kentucky in order to identity the defendant as the former inmate of the penitentiary, "should that question be raised by her counsel."[49] Upon the advice of Chapman's colleague, M.G. Bright, he did not show his face at the hearing, but kept in his room at the Madison Hotel as much as possible, "and entirely avoided all irritating remarks or actions." Craig would later claim that Marshall had so excited the crowd against him that at the conclusion the spectators all ran out shouting, "Now let us give Craig hell!"[50]

Craig was told immediately after the hearing that he had only two hours left to leave town, or he would be killed. Friends urged him to cross over to the safety of the Kentucky shore. He replied that he intended to take the mail boat home, which was not due in Madison for four or five hours, and would not be deflected from his course.[51] King recorded that when the crowd heard that Craig was at the hotel, they "went down there to do him some indignity. But did not then see him."[52] According to Craig, they did see him: "After a while the rabble, thirsting for blood, had filled the bar-room. His only weapon was in his carpet bag in that room. He walked deliberately in among them, picked up his carpet bag, took it up stairs, and put on his knife."[53] He was soon joined by a half-dozen fellow Kentuckians who promised their assistance, and the crowd dispersed.

At 7 o'clock that evening, Craig and his friends were at the wharf awaiting the boat when a fight broke out between them and a large number of Indianians. Tensions had been high since the proceedings began, for the Kentuckians had been strutting about the streets of the city for several days, showing their Bowie knives and spoiling for a fight. One of them had gone into a barber shop opposite the hotel, where several locals began talking to him "about Miss Webster. He got up from the chair and cursed them for every thing mean and dishonorable, and said he could whip all of them." According to a correspondent from Trimble County, and thus displaying a Kentucky bias, "They did not dare to say a word."[54] At the wharf, a Madison citizen fell into an argument with a Kentuckian named Yeager, who thought he had been insulted and called him a liar. "The valiant Hoosier then crawfished into the crowd, when two or three struck Yeager with rocks and colts." Slingshots were also employed. Craig's men, according to this version of the encounter, were outnumbered about thirty to one, with four or five Hoosiers holding down each of the Kentuckians, who were getting the worst of it. They "beat the men most horribly and barbarously."[55] Craig opened his carpet bag and threatened to shoot the first man who took a step closer.

The steamboat was in sight. As Craig stood on the gangway, the crowd was still "cursing him and threatening his life in the most outrageous and blasphemous manner." He answered defiantly that they could kill him but could not drive him away. Some friends came out of the crowd to shake his hand; as the *High Flyer* was approaching, passengers streamed into the wharf boat but none made any threatening gestures toward Craig. When the steamboat pulled up, it happened to bump the wharf boat, jarring everyone, and producing "a momentary commotion." It was at this moment that Newton Craig was shot in the back. "He turned and saw the pistol lowered and the assassin dodge through the crowd."[56] Craig was rushed to the home of Milton Stapp, who had been so instrumental in persuading Delia Webster to locate in Madison, where a Dr. Robinson attended his wound.

The shot was fired by William Randall, a tenant on Webster's farm, who had been complaining "of much abuse received from Craig and his sympathisers, having been by them driven away from his employer's premises, as he alleges," commented the *Madison Courier*. "If he committed the act with which he is charged, the provocations may be found in these former transactions."[57] Randall apparently charged that when Craig invaded the Webster farm he "had treated said Randall's wife or his mother amiss." This charge was rebutted in a notice inserted in the *Madison Banner* signed July 31 by I.C. Yeager (possibly the same who was involved in the fight at the wharf) and five other individuals denying Randall's assertion. The six signatees had been summoned to attach Webster's property on behalf of Craig back in June, and claimed to have been with Craig the whole time he was there.[58] Randall served three years in the Indiana Penitentiary for shooting Craig. Prison records show he was twenty-eight at the time of the crime, 5 feet 8 inches in height, a native of New York, a moderate drinker, and capable of reading and writing "poorly." He was generously tattooed with moon, stars, anchors, and figures of "women and flags."[59] It is not known whether he was thinking of his mother or of Delia Webster when he fired at Newton Craig.

Three days later, Craig dictated a letter to Dr. Robinson in which he informed his Kentucky friends that his wound was still critical, "the ball having entered on the right side of my backbone, and lodged somewhere above the right nipple, passing the right lobe of my lungs. I have thrown up some blood, but not a great deal, and I think a few days will determine my case."[60] When he "thought he was about to die," the *Madison Courier* reported, "he insisted on 'seeing that girl once more.'"[61] "That girl" tried to comply: "Miss Webster, at Craig's earnest request, went to General Stapp's . . . to see him, but was properly denied admission by Mrs. Craig."[62] Denied Delia's company, Craig was brought out of danger by the ministrations of Lucy and his doctor. He was well enough to board the *Wheeling City* on the evening of July 24, 1854, headed home.

On July 28, diarist Jefferson Craig recorded having "heard today that Newton had come and is getting well." By August 4, he was sufficiently recovered to address a packed house in the Frankfort Courthouse. He castigated Delia Webster for being "false and wicked," and Joseph G. Marshall for having inflamed the spectators against Kentuckians in general and himself in particular, thereby contributing to the charged atmosphere that led to the attempted assassination. His recital of complaints "produced in the large audience a universal and intense loathing and indignation at the cowardly malice of the mob, and of those who set them on; and a high appreciation of the courageous conduct and upright intentions of Capt. Craig."[63]

He repeated his speech in Georgetown on August 21. "I was engaged," wrote Jefferson Craig, "and heard little of it." But on August 7, Jefferson

Lucy Craig. Courtesy Mrs. Galey Coleman

had already heard the story directly from his cousin: "Newton and his wife came to town today . . . He looks pretty well and seems almost recovered from his wound." The bullet had not been found, but was thought to have exited through his lung. "He seems to think of nothing but the ill treatment he and other Kentuckians received at Madison, and talks seriously of going with a party and battering down two or three houses in Madison, with cannon, from this side of the river." On the 17th, Jefferson "met Newton Craig in town and he came home with me to dinner. He is still weak and has some pain in his breast, but thinks he is improving."[64]

Though he had lost re-election for warden, his term of office did not expire until the following year. When news came to the penitentiary of the attempt on his life, Calvin Fairbank was closely watched by the foreman of the cooper shop where he worked, "who by fear or flattery suborned others in the shop to testify against me." His actual response to the news was prudent: "I bowed my head upon my breast, faint with fear of what might come of it to me, sighed, and raising my head, said: 'I'm sorry; sorry for his family. He ought to have staid away.'" When Craig returned to Frankfort, Fairbank was locked in solitary confinement to await a "trial" in the prison yard. All the prisoners in the cooper shop but one were brought to testify that he had said "I'm glad of it! I wish they had killed him!" The one man who told the truth "was soon removed to the hemp," which constituted severe punishment, as the working conditions there were often fatal.[65]

Craig had set up his own rules of evidence. Fairbank was not allowed to cross-examine witnesses. When he tried to point out a contradiction in the testimony against him, Craig laid him low with his heavy hickory cane, which "shivered into tooth-picks" on the prisoner. He was found guilty of rejoicing at the news of his warden's misfortune, and sentenced to thirty-nine cuts of wet raw-hide on his bare back. Ephraim Whiteside, the assistant keeper and a friend of Fairbank's, tried to deal them leniently, for he "knew well the inside of the whole question and its animus," and "despised Craig for his vanity, pride, tyranny, dishonesty and silliness." But after the first two blows Craig grew suspicious. "Stop! Mr. Whiteside, those shan't count. They are too light. Begin again. Strike harder!" The prisoner felt them "clear through to the lungs as if they were beaten with a cudgel."[66]

Fairbank was well aware that "all this injustice grew out of the spleen he entertained toward me for my sentiments and my partiality toward Miss Webster."[67] Newton Craig may have taken some additional satisfaction in imagining the punishment to be vicarious.

12

AFTERMATH:

"THIS REMARKABLE HISTORY"

The happy outcome of her hearing before Judge Walker on the writ of habeas corpus did not mean that Delia Webster's legal troubles with Newton Craig were entirely over. He continued his lawsuit against her, although at times the history of their relations tended to conform to Karl Marx's observation that in history events tend to happen twice, the first time as tragedy, the second as farce.[1] On March 27, 1855, she appeared as a witness for Madison attorney Oliver Pitcher, who held a substantial interest in the Trimble County farm, in *Pitcher v. Craig*, and diarist John Lyle King was there to record his impressions. According to King it was a "suit on a note assigned by Delia Webster made by her suspected former paramour Newton Craig to Oliver Pitcher."[2] Dunn and Hendricks, who with Marshall had defended Webster at her habeas corpus trial, represented Pitcher; Chapman, who had prosecuted her then, would have represented Craig, but due to illness he was replaced by Daniel Kelso, who had been elected Madison's prosecuting attorney in the fall of 1854.[3] "Kelso's buffoonery," wrote King, "and *brusqueries* and the presence and tendency of Miss Webster as witness enhanced the interest of the trial." Webster "detailed the whole history of her connection and quarrel with Craig which was savory autobiography to the ears of the multitude."[4] King did not stay for the verdict, nor did the *Madison Courier* record it.

A fortnight later, Delia Webster called on John Lyle King to see if he would represent her in a suit of her own. Joseph G. Marshall, her champion of the previous summer, may have been her first choice; but he died on April 8, having contracted a bad cold over the winter from which he never recovered. On Saturday, April 14, 1855, King recorded, "Miss Webster came in with a little girl for company"—perhaps one of the students in her school, if the school was still a going concern, or the daughter of the family where Webster lodged. She wanted "to bring suits at Milton to dispossess tenants from her farm." King needed to know more about the relevant Kentucky

199

statutes, so he suggested she return at six that evening. He went to a fellow lawyer's office, but found his edition was incomplete, lacking in particular the provisions concerning "Forcible Entry and Detainer." So he had to cross the ferry over to Milton to confer with some colleagues there and borrow a copy of the Kentucky Code. He got back just in time for Webster's return visit. They had a long conversation, in the course of which "she tried to drive a sharp bargain with me for my fee." It was difficult to come to terms because King was doubtful of success. "Though I might be ever so certain of the law and testimony," he wrote, "I was not so sure of public feeling in Trimble County doing and suffering justice to be done her." No conclusion was reached, except to meet once more "at Mr. Stiver's," where she was boarding.[5]

The next day was a Sunday, a day on which King did not normally do business, but Webster had to leave on the train for Louisville on Monday, so it was unavoidable. After attending morning services, he arrived at Mr. Stiver's at two o'clock. "The little girl who received me at the door went off to Sunday School, and we were alone together in a back room, a bedchamber at that. At the moment, all I had ever heard of scandal against Miss Webster recurred to me and I wondered if *I* should have the opportunity of playing the Joseph to a suspected Mrs. Potiphar." Genesis 39 recounts how Joseph, whom Potiphar, an officer of Pharaoh's guard, had made overseer of all his house, got into grievous difficulties when Potiphar's wife took a fancy to him. On a day when there was no one else in the house (as there was no one else in Delia Webster's bedroom that Sunday afternoon), "she caught him by his garment, saying, Lie with me: and he left his garment in her hand, and fled."[6] Joseph was thrown into prison. As for King, "my virtue rallied itself to an unshakeable stability... and we proceeded to business." Webster's reputation as a seductress, whether justified or not, was well known. Back when Craig's letters to her were published in February 1854, the *Madison Courier* commented that they "may serve as a warning to Miss Webster's Attorneys; for if she by her charms could soften the stony heart of a turnkey of a prison, the said charms might be dangerous to lawyers of every age."[7] King's interview with her "was nearly an hour protracted," and in the end she accepted his terms.[8]

However, on April 30, 1855, King learned that Webster, having left that morning on the train for New England, had discontinued her two law-suits without consulting him, "she requiring the funds left as security for costs to help her in her Eastern trip." He was greatly perturbed, and though she wrote him letters from Indianapolis and later from Vermont giving in-structions about beginning the suits again, "I informed Mr. Stiver, who boards her, that I couldn't attend to her business any longer. And there's an 'end to it' for me."[9]

Not quite the end. On July 2, he found a note sticking in his keyhole asking if he would be kind enough to come to the Kirchener Hotel to call on a Mr. Wayland, who "wishes to consult Mr. King in reference to some business of Miss D.A. Webster whose agent Mr. W. is." He found Wayland to be "a fine looking fellow" from Worcester, Massachusetts. "When I had told him what I knew about Miss Webster's business we talked about professional matters generally in the States, the Courts, the Bar, and the Bench. He is intelligent, affable and I should hope a promising young man."[10] Best of all, he would relieve King of any further need for tête-à-têtes with Delia Webster.

It was from Worcester on October 19, 1855, that Webster wrote the autobiographical letter that was published in the *New York Independent* on November 29, previously cited in these pages. She says there that after the trial in Madison in July 1854, she traveled to visit her "aged mother" in Vermont, and that during her absence her enemies "steal and sell all my crops, pocket the money; and when I return to make a payment of $2000 on my place, lo! I have nothing with which to make it." In the spring of 1855, "to prevent my sending on tenants to take care of the place, they broke open and demolished six of my dwelling houses, and burnt the seventh." No less a personage than Harriet Beecher Stowe appended a note to the letter for its publication in the *Independent*, attesting that "This remarkable history is authenticated by the most perfect documentary evidence, which Miss Webster is able at any time to produce, and which has been seen by many persons of distinction in different parts of our State."[11]

Two years pass, for which no record has come to light of Webster's activities, apart from evidence that in the spring of 1857, with the prospect looming of the expiration of the mortgage in November, she tried to persuade John G. Fee to take over the Trimble County land for a new college he was seeking to found. A fearless antislavery activist working within the heart of Kentucky on land southeast of Lexington that Cassius Clay had provided, Fee had placed notices in the *American Missionary*, the national journal of the American Missionary Association, asking for assistance. In a letter to his superiors, Jocelyn Whipple and Lewis Tappan, on April 4, 1857, he wrote, "Among others I have an offer from Delia A. Webster of grounds for building—pleasure grounds—stone for building college, buildings, chapel & boarding house—convenient quarry—on her farm opposite Madison, Indiana. [It is located] just before mouth of Kentucky River—land high—view beautiful—on river bank—easy of access to East, West & North and soon I

202 / DELIA WEBSTER AND THE UNDERGROUND RAILROAD

think we might build up a very flourishing college. . . . Delia Webster promises two thousand dollars in addition to lots for building."[12]

It was in December 1855 that Fee had first announced his plans in the *American Missionary*. The college "would be to Kentucky what Oberlin is to Ohio, Anti-slavery, Anti-caste, Anti-rum, Anti-secret societies, Anti-sin."[13] Strikingly similar language appeared in *South Western Seminary: Description of Its Site*, an undated prospectus Delia Webster evidently published some time before 1858: "In 1842 Miss Delia A. Webster went from New England into the very heart of Kentucky and founded the Lexington Academy, being at the same time known as an open advocate of anti-caste, anti-slavery, anti-rum, and anti-tobacco principles. . . . Miss Webster had long entertained a desire to establish somewhere in the south-west [as Kentucky was known at the time] a school . . . which shall be to that region what Oberlin is to Ohio, or the Mt. Holyoke school to New England."[14] Both the anti-caste, -slavery, and -rum principles and the phrasing of the comparison to Oberlin show a decided influence, either of Webster on Fee or Fee on Webster. Perhaps the latter, as Delia tried to make her project even more appealing to Fee. Her prospectus concludes, "Miss Webster donates the grounds for the seminary and also the main portion of the building materials, and now wishes to go forward and establish an anti-slavery colony there, so as to continue the example of free labor. Funds are being raised to erect the masonry buildings so as to prosecute her original plan."

But the offer to Fee fell through. He wanted a college closer to the "interior" of Kentucky, particularly the mountains, so that the students could "return home or into the surrounding counties to teach during the long vacations." Besides, an association with Delia Webster would only bring trouble: "She was arrested under charge of aiding away slaves. This would make our college buildings obnoxious to the mob."[15] Yet Fee's "own reputation was almost as bad as hers," his biographer Richard Sears comments, "but that seems not to have occurred to him."[16]

Delia Webster apparently continued to raise crops on the Trimble County farm, but most likely did so from the safety of Madison and through the agency of tenants. Her slaveholding neighbors continued to give her trouble. "Repeatedly have her large crops been seized, and virtually confiscated by the Slave Power, to defeat her meeting her yearly payments. Last Fall [1857], in the worst of the crisis, an installment became due, and she applied for an extension. Encouragement was given that it would be cheerfully granted."[17] But then came notice of foreclosure and imminent auction. The creditor in question was John Preston of Lexington, Virginia, who might have been willing to give her an extension had he not received letters from her Kentucky neighbors warning him that it "was dangerous to the interests of Slavery for Miss Webster to remain the owner of her Farm in Kentucky."[18] In the nick of time, she staved off foreclosure by paying him a certain sum, and conceived a solution to her continual financial difficulties.

The solution was to form the Webster Kentucky Farm Association. A letter Webster wrote from Boston on March 24, 1858, to Lewis Tappan, the prominent New York abolitionist and president of the American Missionary Association (and to whom Fee had addressed his letter of April 4, 1857), shows her hard at work on this project.

> I am succeeding well in my business matters, & meet with much sympathy from men of influence. Gov. Banks and Lady [Nathaniel P. Banks was elected governor of Massachusetts in the fall of 1857] express a decided interest in my behalf & think the plan of an Association not only feasible, & for my pecuniary advantage, but that it must result in good to the cause.
>
> I had an interview with the Gov. yesterday, after he had taken time carefully to examine the constitution and by-laws, & find he is much pleased with them.
>
> The *State Treasurer*, Hon. Moses Tenney takes an interest, & has consented to officiate as one of the Board of Directors. One or two of the Governor's Council are also on the board. Lee Claflin (formerly Pres. of the Hopkinton Bank, now Pres. of one of the Boston Banks,) is chairman of the Board. Samuel B. Sewell Esq. is Atty. & Secretary; & now, Mr. Tappan, the object of this hasty note is to apprise you that they are about electing you as *President* of this Association (which, as yet, has no *name* but the Governor is to-day thinking up a name appropriate.) There will be no duties devolving upon you except the signing of the Certificates of Stock, of which there will be one hundred.
>
> Should your business call you this way within a few days they would like to have you present at the meeting of the Stockholders. Otherwise they will forward the Certificates for your signature.
>
> I will send you a copy of the by-laws, in pamphlet-form, as soon as they are printed. —Our officers are all leading men, & men of considerable wealth. Mr. Tenney has just informed me that Mr. Claflin is worth half a million. He has increased his Subscription to $1,500. Mr. Randall also invests fifteen hundred.
>
> Would Judge Jay allow us to use his name as one of the Directors provided no duties were required of him?
>
> Very Gratefully
>
> > Yours,
> > Delia A. Webster.[19]

The pamphlet prospectus was printed some time before June 1858, with some changes in personnel. Lewis Tappan did not consent to become president, as that office was filled by Lawrence Brainard, of St. Alban's, Vermont, though Tappan and Moses Tenney did serve on the board of directors. Nor did Judge Jay. Governor Banks's name does not appear on the list of officers, nor Samuel B. Sewell's; the latter's post of secretary is filled by John A. Andrew, a Boston lawyer who in 1858 served in the lower house of the Massachusetts legislature, and two years later would be elected governor of the state. Nearly all the officers and board members are from New England; two exceptions are McKee Dunn of Madison, Indiana, and, intriguingly, a "Judge John L. Winn, Oasis Farm, Kentucky." The purpose of the association was to raise $10,000 (100 shares at $100 each) to apply to the mortgages, the remainder going to Delia Webster. In turn, she would convey the deed to the Association, though continue to manage the farm. She could redeem the deed within ten years. The philosophical purpose of the Association was that of "saving a valuable estate from the grasp of the Slave Power, for the benefit of Freedom" through "the practical demonstration of Free Labor on Slave territory."[20]

The money was raised, the shares sold, and the financial difficulties overcome. "This put Miss Webster on her feet again, and, though still harassed by the slave holders and their satellites, she went on with her improvements on the farm."[21] In April 1859, she arrived in Madison accompanied by some thirty Massachusetts families, and "a handsome lot of farming implements, ox-yokes, patent plows, drills, planters, hoes, shovels, spades"—and a steam engine. Not only would it be a working farm again, but there would be established "a large manufacturing town on her six hundred acres farm."[22] The steam engine and other industrial machinery were for a projected shoe peg factory. In June it was reported that she had bought "the Magnolia Mill lot" in Madison for $1,000, on which she "designs erecting, at once, a flour mill and buildings for other manufacturing purposes."[23] The thirty families settled "among the hills and clefts around Mount Airy, which is the name of Miss Webster's Kentucky property," the name of Mt. Orison having evidently been abandoned.[24] Webster herself, for the time being, remained in Madison. The steam engine and other machinery for the projected Kentucky factory, however, "lay at the Madison depot for a long time, she not daring to cross the same to the Kentucky side. The machinery disappeared, being either sold for charges or reclaimed by the parties from whom it was purchased."[25]

A letter dated February 6, 1861, to her sister and brother-in-law Mary Jane and Warren Bard reveals that Delia Webster was at that time still running the farm, but doing so from a considerable distance, as she was living in a Cincinnati boarding house. A tornado on May 21, 1860, had wreaked havoc along the Ohio River from Louisville to Portsmouth, downing thousands of trees on her Trimble County farm.[26] Anxious to convert the fallen timber to firewood before rot set in, she proposed to Warren Bard that he invest a thousand dollars in the purchase of a portable steam engine attached to a sawing and splitting machine and the cost of labor and transport, and that he come out to supervise the work. The following excerpt illustrates the thoroughness with which she entered into the management of the business: "My plan is to hire coal barges in Madison (which I can get for a trifling sum) & which will hold from 250 to 300 cords of wood. Load two of these barges at a time & have them towed up to the city at an expense of $100. . . . The wood can at *all times* be sold quick sale for *ready cash* & it will only cost from 15 to 25 cts. pr. cord to send it to Cincinnati where it will bring from $1.50 to $2.00 more pr. cord than in Madison where there is no demand for large quantities."

On a more personal note, she writes that "I keep thinking I shall come home *sometime*. And shall, as soon as I can. Politics are lively & prosperous in the West," she wrote on the eve of the Civil War. "We are opposed to any kind of a compromise. Government is right side up, & like[ly?] to be."[27] Lincoln had been elected in November, but had not yet taken office.

In 1859, the story of Webster and Fairbank's rescue of Lewis Hayden was retold in "Little Lewis," the lead story in *The Child's Anti-Slavery Book*, first published that year. The narrative is attributed to Julia Colman, who was also the author of numerous temperance works intended for a Sunday School audience; two other slaves' stories were written by a Matilda G. Thompson; a fourth is uncredited. In the preface, the editor, identified only as "D.W.," says of the stories that "The characters in them are all real, though their true names are not always given."[28] The coincidence between these initials and those of Hayden's female rescuer is intriguing.

Hayden's autobiographical sketch in Stowe's *Key to Uncle Tom's Cabin* (1853) was available as source material for Colman's story of his Kentucky childhood and escape from slavery, which repeats the Stowe account of how his mother was driven insane by a Mason's lust and tried to kill her son. But other elements in Colman's narrative cannot be found there. She might have interviewed him in Boston, and probably did; she might also have spoken with Delia Webster (or have collaborated with her more closely, if she is the D.W. who provided the preface). The events of Hayden's rescue are retold for a juvenile audience, the narrative departing in many ways from the facts. But it displays a surprising connection to another part of Delia Webster's past. Webster is present in Colman's narrative as "Miss Ford . . . , the governess of the children" of the last of Hayden's various masters, an Englishman named Mr. Johns.[29] To nineteenth-century educators like Webster (and possibly Colman) the substitution of Ford for Webster would be an obvious literary allusion to two Johns who were Englishmen, the contemporaneous Jacobean playwrights John Ford (c. 1586-c. 1640), author of 'Tis Pity She's a Whore, and John Webster (c. 1580-c. 1634), famous for The White Devil and The Duchess of Malfi; both collaborated at one time or another with a third dramatist, Thomas Dekker. Colman's Mr. Johns is an avid horticulturist, and hires a "free white man named Spencer" to supervise his garden, as well as take charge of young Lewis, who found that "Spencer's kindness made the heaviest work seem light."[30]

Where would Colman have found the name Spencer? Not in Hayden's letter to Harriet Beecher Stowe. But it was a name prominent in Webster's life prior to the time she said she became acquainted with Hayden. In Kentucky Jurisprudence she wrote of visiting Kentucky early in 1843 in the company of "a Mr. and Mrs. Spencer, teachers and friends of mine. We taught several painting classes in the vicinity of Lexington, and in July of the same year opened a class in that city."[31] In the spring of 1844, both Spencers fell ill and left her alone with the school. In Colman's version, "Miss Ford," who like Miss Webster "was from the free states," takes a hand in teaching "Little Lewis" to read, giving him lessons at sunrise every morning.[32]

Mr. Johns discovers this, but being British is not as unalterably opposed to his slaves learning to read as a native Southerner would have been. He tries to take Miss Ford to task, but "There was evidently no such thing as pinning her fast to serious reasoning on the subject," so he let her do as she liked. "She had been a long time in the family, and as they had seen no ultra-abolition traits, they thought her 'sound at heart'"[33] So, too, had Webster appeared—when a governess in the Craig household, long after the Hayden rescue—to be "sound at heart" in some Kentuckians' eyes, and no ultra-abolitionist.

Fairbank appears in the story as "Mr. Dean, of whom she [Miss Ford] had heard as the worst abolitionist in the neighborhood." Mr. Dean hands little Lewis a note to transmit to Miss Ford in which he asks if she "would be willing to do anything to advance his freedom. She unhesitatingly replied that she would be very glad to do so." Arrangements are made for "running off the boy," but they are quite different from what took place in Lexington in September 1844. This time, Webster (a.k.a. Ford) will not accompany Hayden on the trip north but will try to secure Mr. Johns's permission to send Lewis on an evening errand on which he would not be missed until morning. Lewis is to go to Mr. Dean's house, and with a change of clothes and his "face and hands dyed" (for what purpose is not clear) will accompany Mr. Dean to Cincinnati as a servant.[34]

The plan works, but Miss Ford is immediately suspected. Dean and

Lewis were spotted in Cincinnati by one of the neighbors (as Fairbank, Webster, and Lewis were recognized in Millersburg by some Lexington slaves). Worse (and even more strikingly like the real thing), tangible evidence of Miss Ford's participation "was soon afforded by the imprudence of Dean." Two days after the escape, he casually tosses a note over the garden fence by the arbor where she customarily passes her mornings. It reads: "All right, and no suspicion." It proves as incriminating as the "Frater" letter Fairbank stupidly left unmailed in his pocket to be discovered upon his arrest. From her window Miss Ford sees Mr. Johns pick up the note. Dean would have been arrested immediately upon his return, but they were waiting to catch Miss Ford. The letter sealing both their fates, Dean and Ford are sent to jail. "Many months passed before they were brought to trial," at which Dean is sentenced to ten years and Ford to five, "but the governor finally granted a reprieve of the last two years," as the governor reprieved Delia Webster after considerably less time.[35]

"After many adventures Lewis reached Boston, where he still lives, for aught I know, with a nice little woman of his own color for a wife, and three smart little boys."[36] The real Lewis was indeed prospering in Boston at that time, though by 1859 he had suffered some financial reverses. A financial panic in 1857-58 led to his relocating his clothing establishment in a smaller store. Soon afterwards, a fire destroyed the store and his stock, and he "took to pedling jewelry."[37] Fortunately, income was assured when he was appointed to the office of messenger to the Massachusetts secretary of state on July 1, 1858.

At the same time, Hayden was conspiring with John Brown to capture the federal arsenal at Harper's Ferry. Brown paid seven visits to Boston between 1857 and 1859 to drum up support for his project, staying at least some of the time at 66 Phillips Street.[38] In early October 1859, Hayden received the message from Brown that he was in dire need of money and could not launch the raid until he found it. The same day he received the letter, Hayden chanced to run into Francis Meriam, wealthy grandson of abolitionist Francis Jackson, and asked him for a substantial contribution, showing him the letter. Bearing $600 gathered from a covert group of Brown supporters (whose activities Edward J. Renehan Jr. recounts in his fascinating *The Secret Six: The True Tale of the Men Who Conspired with John Brown*), Meriam left the next day for Chambersburg, Pennsylvania, to join the Harpers Ferry adventure.[39] His frail physique was "not cut out for the work in hand," Robert Penn Warren wrote, "but the money was welcome; it removed the last delay."[40] Brown's band soldiered arms and marched out of camp on October 16, the day after Meriam's arrival—thanks to Hayden's timely intervention.[41]

A letter Hayden had written in September to John Brown, Jr., in Ohio, who forwarded it on to his father, is extant. It breathes of conspiracy. "I have sent a note to Harriet," he wrote, referring to Harriet Tubman, "requesting her to come to Boston, saying . . . that she must come right on . . . & when she does come I think we will find some way to send her on. I have seen our friend in Concord, he is a true man. I have not as yet said anything to anybody except him. I do not think it is wise for me to do so. . . . Have you all the hands you wish?"[42] Harriet Tubman's role had been to recruit for the raiders among the fugitives living in Canada; it was now, Brown intended, to guide north the multitude of slaves he expected to free in the neighborhood of Harper's Ferry.[43] Hayden's remark about "hands" suggests he had been recruiting for Brown's impending venture. Years later, it was said that in Hayden's Phillips Street house "the John Brown raid was discussed and means of aid devised. In the front parlor under the carpet were secret the telegrams sent from time to time giving an account of the progress of the raid."[44]

Hayden's friend—and Delia Webster's—John A. Andrew was elected governor of Massachusetts in 1860. According to Benjamin Quarles, "Hayden had been the first to suggest to John A. Andrew," then a first-term legislator, "that he run for governor."[45] Kenneth Wiggins Porter writes that "After the outbreak of war Hayden, according to Andrew himself, suggested that slaves should be considered 'contraband of war,' sometime before Gen. Benjamin E. Butler made the expression well known. And Hayden always claimed credit for having urged the governor to organize a regiment of colored volunteers."[46] This became the Fifty-Fourth Massachusetts Regiment that, under the command of Robert Shaw, fought with such distinction in the suicidal charge on Fort Wagner, South Carolina, on July 18, 1863, an event depicted in the motion picture *Glory*. The creation of an African-American regiment had doubtless been a major topic of conversation when the governor came to celebrate Thanksgiving Day 1862 at the Haydens' home.[47] Hayden was a principal recruiter for the Fifty-Fourth among Boston African Americans in early 1863. In addition, he "began travelling in Canada, New York, Pennsylvania and other states, securing recruits for the Fifty-fifth Infantry and Fifth Cavalry, Massachusetts Volunteers."[48] Henry Ingersoll Bowditch recalled that "Lewis was of infinite service in going West to gain recruits among the fugitive slaves in the Western states and Canada."[49] Hayden's son Jo, who as a child had escaped with the family from slavery in 1844, was a casualty of the war. He died at Fort Morgan, Alabama, on June 27, 1865, at the age of twenty-eight, perhaps (as the *New York Age* claimed) from wounds received "in a naval engagement under Admiral Farragut."[50]

Ever since his arrival in Boston in the late 1840s Hayden had been interested in the black Masonic movement. After the war he intensified his

Masonic activity, publishing pamphlet after pamphlet (including *Caste Among Masons* [1866], and *Grand Lodge Jurisdictional Claim; or, War of Races* [1868]) denouncing the white Masons for not admitting the black lodge, and providing learned arguments, distinguished by a high degree of rhetorical polish, for the validity of the claim of the Prince Hall African Lodge, founded in 1775, to Masonic authenticity. Ultimately, he would go so far as to argue, in *Masonry Among Colored Men in Massachusetts* (1871), that the white Massachusetts Grand Lodge that kept denying the African Lodge's claim was itself illegally constituted, and that only the Prince Hall Lodge was truly Masonic. "The illegitimate has endeavored to attach bastardy to the lawful born, and audaciously assumed the title and estate which in law are the property of the legal heir."[51]

Apart from the coincidence that it had been a white Mason who had driven his mother insane, as he recounted the story in his letter to Harriet Beecher Stowe, Hayden embraced Masonry because the Prince Hall Lodge provided the framework for the accomplishment of certain goals in the African-American community. It promoted the middle class values of thrift and industry; it gave help to widows and orphans; it promoted solidarity. Since its founding in 1775, writes William A. Muraskin, "the Prince Hall Order has served as one of the bulwarks of the black middle class. It has worked to separate its members, both socially and psychologically, from the black masses. ... Members of the Order have felt that only by the use of rigid, exclusionary admission system—which screens initiates on the basis of public adherence to conventional bourgeois morality—can this exceptional status be maintained."[52]

Hayden chose the Masonic movement also because it was a worthy substitute for a Christianity corrupted by its tolerance for slavery. Hayden's feelings on this score were evident as early as his letter to his former master just weeks after his escape from Kentucky: "I thought if that was Religion I would be off."[53] In the same vein, he observed in the letter to Stowe that "I never saw anything in Kentucky which made me suppose that ministers or professors of religion considered it any more wrong to separate the families of slaves by sale than to separate any domestic animals."[54] In a speech given before the Prince Hall Lodge on December 27, 1865, he said of Masons that "they have never been guilty of the wrongs which the Church has committed. Churches in their associate capacity have bought and sold their own members; but never yet has a Lodge of Freemasons bought or sold a member; never yet has a Mason so treated a brother. It is in view of these facts that I say we have ground for hope."[55]

As grand master of the Prince Hall Lodge and national deputy grand master of the National Grand Lodge, Hayden traveled to Virginia and the

Carolinas in the months after the war's end, visiting the new lodges springing up there. He reported that the freedmen at Richmond "did not present so hopeful an aspect, so intellectual nor so dignified a character, as I found among the people of Petersburg and Charleston." There was bickering in Richmond, while at Petersburg former slaves were forming land associations and building companies. In Charleston, where he was honored by the naming of "Hayden Lodge, No. 8," he found "a still higher class of people, even, than at Petersburg, as regards general education, the mechanical arts, and all the elements which tend to make a first-class society." He observed a significant difference between urban and rural residents. "Away from the cities and the seaboard, the condition of the colored man is deplorable. . . . Lacking the intelligence and opportunities of the freemen of the city,—never having enjoyed the same advantages,—he is still almost completely at the mercy of his old master." As for the former slaveholding class, "in each of the places I visited, there is evidently a deep and unalterable purpose in the hearts of the old oppressors to blast, or at least to crush out, the rising hopes and dawning prospects of their late bondmen."[56]

A more hopeful note was sounded by the symbolism of the gift Governor Andrew had conveyed to Lewis Hayden in late 1864 for presentation to the Prince Hall Grand Lodge. It was a gavel made from a piece of the whipping post at Hampton, Virginia. "I know of no place more fitting," Andrew wrote, "for the preservation of [this memorial] of the barbarous institution that is now tottering to its rapidly approaching fall, than the association of free colored citizens of Massachusetts over which you preside."[57]

Calvin Fairbank was no stranger to whipping, receiving by his count 35,105 stripes in the course of his imprisonment in the Kentucky State Penitentiary. Though he had received occasional cuts from the rawhide strap under Newton Craig's tenure, when Zebulon Ward took over as prison keeper in 1855 they became a regular feature of his life. Ward demanded more weaving of hemp sacking than was humanly possible and lashed those who did not produce it. Fairbank was one of the better workers but for him "It was the first thing in the morning, then before noon, then after noon, and the last thing in the evening. Sometimes Jack and 'Salty' Sam . . ., both well whiskied, would strip for the work, and one dealt on until tired; then, puffing, would hand the strap over to the other, until a hundred and eight stripes seemed to appease their wrath, the walls ten feet away being splattered with particles of flesh and blood." Yet the punishment was general: "The smack of that strap, and frequently two were in full play at the same time, and the howling of the victims could be heard every minute of the day. Men cut off their hands, cut their throats, drank poison, and in various other ways rushed eagerly upon the gates of death." As a result of such hard driving, Ward made one hundred thousand dollars in his four year term (a lot of money in those days), and caused the deaths of two hundred and forty men (out of an average population of three hundred and ninety).[58]

Ward was succeeded in 1858 by Jeremiah W. South, who showed somewhat "more humanity." His daughter Eliza would visit Calvin in secret when he was locked up on a Sunday for not weaving enough bagging, "her face adorned with the jewels of her sorrow." Having demanded the key, she would let him out of his solitary confinement; at other times, she would intervene to prevent or lessen his corporal punishment.[59]

Though Eliza South, like Clelia Conti in Stendhal's *Charter-House of Parma*, evokes the classic topos of the jailor's daughter who forms a romantic attachment with a political prisoner, Fairbank's true love lived in Oxford, Ohio, forty miles northwest of Cincinnati. Mandana Tileston had come there from Massachusetts, having found a teaching position in that college town in order to be near her fiancé, and visit him in prison when she could. On October 8, 1855, she recorded that she had "again been permitted to see my beloved C. and am very happy to find his condition so much improved. . . . His kind keeper permitted us to have an interview in his own house so that I was spared the painful necessity of seeing him in his gloomy prison." The "kind keeper" was Zebulon Ward, of whom Fairbank had a different opinion. "Now the Keeper," she wrote on July 23, 1855, "has assured us that we shall be permitted to write regularly," but months passed with no letter from Fairbank. "I am deeply troubled by the long silence of my Friend," she wrote on January 2, 1856. "I sometimes fear I may never hear from him again." Two years later, she exclaimed "Would that he could be permitted to write often."[60] Ward had evidently rescinded his promise.

In the late summer of 1859 the possibility arose that Fairbank might again be pardoned. Mandana received a letter on August 23 that showed him to be in "excellent spirits"; a few weeks later he had taken to writing poetry to express his happiness. Upon Laura Haviland's urging, Mandana went to Frankfort on October 15 to pay a personal call on the governor, finding him "more favorably disposed toward Calvin than I expected." She visited Fairbank that day and the next, and received "much kindness from his Keepers." On the 17th she met with Lovell Rousseau, the lawyer whom Fairbank had found so ineffectual seven years before, but who had nevertheless been engaged to work towards a pardon. Hopes were high: "I most earnestly pray for his speedy release," she wrote, "if it is God's will."[61]

Unfortunately, a few days earlier Lewis Hayden had happened upon Francis Meriam in a Boston street, and on Saturday, October 15, the very day Mandana Tileston was arriving in Frankfort, Meriam was arriving at

John Brown's encampment. On Sunday, as she was bidding Calvin "a sad farewell," though with the hope of an imminent pardon, Brown and his men were on the road to Harper's Ferry, where they struck in the early morning hours of October 17. As a result, Mandana was compelled to write in her diary on November 9 that "the late insurrectionary movements have destroyed the hopes that were raised in regard to a pardon for Calvin." It was a small world indeed.

Despite his ill treatment, Fairbank had been something of a celebrity in the penitentiary. So much so that on February 14, 1858, it was arranged that he would address an audience in the prison yard composed of the governor, many of the members of the legislature, and a capacity crowd of ladies and gentlemen drawn there by notices in the Frankfort, Lexington, and Louisville newspapers. Speaking from an elevated platform, Fairbank spoke for an hour, prophesying the conflict to come. Three years before Fort Sumter, he was sure that "The war is inevitable, and let it come! . . . and slavery will melt away like a hoar-frost." His listeners, Fairbank recalled (perhaps unconsciously comparing himself to Frederick Douglass, who in January 1850 had impressed him as "a tornado in a forest"), "were electrified—swayed like a mighty forest in a wind." Governor Morehead congratulated him on his speech, but thought him crazy to predict a war, for "the Yankees won't fight."[62]

The events at Harper's Ferry, Fairbank recalled, made "my neck ache; for Kentucky saw clumps of imaginary men under arms in many a nook," including the state penitentiary. The danger only increased once the war began. Three times he was threatened by Confederate soldiers who arrived with a rope, ready to hang him. "Once I stood in the kitchen door with axe in hand" and dared them to try. On the two other occasions he found a hiding place, once with the help of assistant keeper Whiteside.[63]

He was granted regular access to newspaper accounts of the progress of the war. Remarkably, "during the battle of Bull Run I was allowed to leave my work in the shoe-shop and sit in the chapel, where, in company with my friend Eliza South, I received the printed dispatches of the work of slaughter."[64] While Fairbank was sitting in the chapel with the jailor's maiden daughter, his fiancée in Ohio was recording in her diary on the day after the battle: "Heard most deplorable news from our brave army. Trust reports are greatly exaggerated."[65]

Fortunately for Fairbank, a new warden took over on March 1, 1863— Harry Todd, "a square, just, honorable man—loyal to the core." And the election in August of a new governor—and, more importantly, lieutenant governor—was the best news imaginable. Lieutenant Governor Richard T. Jacob, brother-in-law of John Frémont, Republican (and hence antislavery)

Calvin and Mandana Fairbank. Courtesy Philip Fairbank

presidential candidate in 1856, and son-in-law of Thomas Hart Benton, the Missouri antislavery senator who became acquainted with Delia Webster on her trip down the Ohio in November 1851, had been a good friend to Fairbank for some time. "I well knew . . . that the first time [Governor] Bramlette should be called away . . . Jacob would pardon me as lieutenant and acting governor of the state."[66]

And so, on April 15, 1864, he did. Because Bramlette had tried to interfere with Lincoln's order that Kentucky ex-slaves be enlisted in the Union Army—a policy Lewis Hayden had been instrumental in bringing about a year before—the president ordered the governor to Tennessee for consultations, and Jacob made his move. Fairbank received the pardon. On the 16th, armed with a pair of Colt revolvers and escorted by "a Kentucky lady, who had volunteered to accompany me to Cincinnati for my protection," he boarded the train in Frankfort.[67]

The guns came in handy. He overheard some passengers discussing the news of his release. He recognized one of them, who didn't recognize him— Benjamin Gratz, a prominent Lexington landowner. Gratz told his companion that if Fairbank was indeed on the loose he would just like "one pop at him. I'd shoot him as soon as I would a wolf." Seated behind them, Fairbank asked Gratz if he thought he would recognize his prey on sight. He hesitated. "Yes, I think I should." "Well," said Fairbank, "here I am," flashing his revolver. "But you'll have to be mighty sharp; for I think I have the first pop." There was general applause, and Gratz extended his hand and said, "Let us make friends and call this a joke."[68]

After a brief stay with Levi Coffin in Cincinnati, Fairbank headed for Oxford, where he hoped to surprise Mandana Tileston with the news. She knew, but kept the secret. On June 9 they were married. Then began an extended speaking tour to Cincinnati, Chicago, Detroit, Toronto, Philadelphia, Baltimore—and Washington, where he addressed an audience in a black church that included Abraham Lincoln and most of his cabinet. On March 4, 1865, the Fairbanks stood in the rain for three hours to get a good view of Lincoln's Second Inaugural. That night they were among the guests at the White House witness to Lincoln's embrace of Frederick Douglass, who had had a little trouble getting past the doorkeeper, and of Sojourner Truth.[69] Five weeks later the president was dead.

Within ten days of the assassination, Delia Webster had written a letter to a Reverend Dr. Cushman outlining a proposal to establish a "Lincoln Memorial University" on one hundred acres of her Trimble County farm. "As she had received signal favors from President Lincoln, she would like to have the ground sacred to his memory, and the school a living monument of his excellence." Cushman read her letter to a meeting held on May 5, 1865, at the Old South Chapel in Boston, with Webster in attendance. If $100,000 could be raised, she would donate $30,000 (though it seems unlikely she would have had command of so much money), together with the proceeds of her other acres. Webster took the floor, vaunting the farm's profitability and the material advantages of its location. A committee was appointed to study the matter further. "During the winter Delia has been lecturing in Boston upon the wrongs she has received at the hands of the people of Kentucky," commented a correspondent of the *Madison Courier*, who had forwarded the report of the meeting, "and of her sufferings and losses during the war. By that means she succeeded in raising quite an amount of sympathy, for you know the Yankees are very sympathetic where the negro is concerned, and taking that as a basis she is now endeavoring to get her hands into their pockets."[70]

Though the Civil War was over and slavery abolished, Webster still encountered serious difficulties in Trimble County. The *Madison Courier* reported on August 8, 1866, that she had been ordered once more to leave the state. "We should suppose that Miss Delia would not desire to live in such an antagonistic community." Just how antagonistic became apparent on October 22, when the *Courier* reported that "another unjustifiable raid was made" on her premises. Taking advantage of her temporary absence, some "evil disposed persons" piled up her goods and set them on fire, carried off bedclothes, emptied her cupboards on the floor, wrung the necks of her chickens, turned the cow in, and hung two ganders from the ceiling. When she returned "she expressed a strong determination to stand her ground at all hazards." Two weeks later, the city of Madison "was again illuminated last night by a large fire over the river upon the premises of Miss Delia A. Webster." Flames were first visible at eleven p.m., and continued until four in the morning; at three o'clock the next afternoon the smoke was still rising. Plans for the Lincoln school may have been going ahead, for the *Courier* of November 2, 1866, reported that not only were a large barn and several other outbuildings consumed, but "also several piles of seasoned lumber which she had got ready for some school buildings."

This must have been the final blow, together with the approaching end of the ten-year period dating from May 9, 1858, during which Delia Webster could regain the deed she had given to the Webster Kentucky Farm Association for $10,000. On November 12, ten days after the disastrous fire, the property (or some of it) was transferred to Lee Claflin, a member of the Association's board of trustees, pursuant to a suit entitled *Claflin v. Webster*. Some indication of her financial straits may be gathered from another quarter as well, the records of the Clerk of Addison County, Vermont, which state that Delia's brother-in-law Simeon Goodrich recovered judgment against her on March 20, 1868 for $146.60. Webster being out of the state, and neglecting to respond to the summons, Goodrich took possession of four acres of land in Ferrisburgh, including a dwelling house and outbuildings, being her share of her father's estate, in payment of the claim.

In Trimble County, on June 15, 1868, Claflin "convey[ed] and quit claim[ed] the same property conveyed to him by the Trimble County Court" to William Washburn, another Association trustee, for $1300. Yet Webster was not entirely out of the picture, for on March 19, 1869, John Preston of Virginia sold her his 191 acres for $4086.45.[71] It is not clear if she was able to hold on to this property or was obliged to hand it over to the Association. The record does show, however, that on November 28, 1868, a Daniel Murdock bought what Washburn owned, taking possession October 8, 1869. Shortly after, Delia Webster "called at his farm and personally served a notice on him to vacate the place and give her possession," which he declined to do. Murdock was interviewed by the *Madison Star* in 1879, at which time he was still living on the farm. "He still has the notice in his possession" that Webster served him. "It bears date at Louisville, Ky., Oct. 11th, 1869. Mr. Murdock also informs us that Miss Webster died at Jeffersonville, Ind., about three years ago."[72]

That would put the date of her death around 1876. Thus the most recent publication on her career, the article "Delia Ann Webster" in *The Kentucky Encyclopedia*, has it that after losing her farm in October 1869, she "later taught school in Madison [and] died in 1876 in Jeffersonville, Indiana."

The year 1879 witnessed a revival of interest in what was by then considered a romantic past. Not only did the *Madison Star* publish a long two-part article on Webster (October 8 and 15), but in January and February as well the events involving Webster and Craig between 1844 and 1854 had been recalled in the Louisville press. It was all prompted by an article in a Newport, Rhode Island, newspaper, picked up in the *New York Tribune* that recounted Fairbank's Underground Railroad career and recalled the horrors of his imprisonment, concluding with an appeal for funds to support him in his old age.

A son, Calvin Cornelius, had been born to Calvin and Mandana Fairbank on April 17, 1868. The Fairbanks had operated a bakery for a while in Northampton, Massachusetts; in August 1874, they abandoned the bakery for a 15 acre farm near Chicopee.[73] Less than a year later, the family moved to Hartford, Connecticut, where Fairbank had been offered a salaried position at an orphanage.[74] In September 1875, Mandana developed a serious cold; it grew worse, and by November Fairbank began to fear the worst. She died on September 29 of the following year.

The post at the orphanage was not renewed. Unable to provide for his son, Fairbank left him with Mandana's sister in Williamsburg and looked for work. "No money—no business," he wrote in his journal. "It seems that I can't take care of my boy. It nearly kills me."[75] He never did find a position that would bring in enough income to provide a home for the child, and Callie was obliged to spend the rest of his childhood with his aunt and uncle in Massachusetts, while his father settled in distant Angelica, New York. Communicating for years almost entirely by letter, with only rare visits, Fairbank suffered prolonged separation from his son as he had from Callie's mother those many years in the Kentucky penitentiary.

The *Tribune* article appealing for funds for Calvin Fairbank in January 1879, prompted the editor of the *Breckinridge (Ky.) News* to recount his childhood experiences with Fairbank and Webster; his article was picked up on January 27 in the *Louisville Courier-Journal*, a paper read throughout the state. The Breckinridge editor, however, was somewhat muddled in his recollection, and confused Fairbank with the Reverend Spencer, with whom Delia Webster had taught school in various places in Kentucky before 1844, and Patrick Doyle, the Centre College student who organized a slave exodus in August 1849 that resulted in gun battles being fought in Harrison and Bracken Counties and with which neither Webster nor Fairbank had had anything to do. The recollections are valuable nevertheless for the light they shed on what Webster was doing before she helped rescue the Haydens, particularly because the Breckinridge editor revealed that he had been one of her students. "Fairbanks [i.e., Spencer], his wife, and Miss Webster"—whom the editor remembered as the wife's "sister" (which she may indeed have pretended to be)—"organized a school at Cynthiana, and the writer of this was one of their scholars. . . . Miss Webster appeared to be the only one of three possessed of masculinity in nature and disposition." (Spencer, by contrast, was "gentle as a woman.") Delia Webster "possessed one accomplishment to perfection. She was master of the pencil, and could draw exquisitely. They left Cynthiana, sojourned a while in Bourbon [County], from whence Mrs. [Spencer] returned East, and finally brought up in Woodford [County], where [Spencer] and Miss Webster took charge of a school.[76] The editor of the *News* goes on to recount the Doyle insurrection, but erroneously attributes its instigation to Fairbank, who was in the penitentiary at the time.

The publication of this recollection in the *Courier-Journal* prompted a Georgetown resident, identified only as "L.A.S.," who recognized many of its errors, to go to an unimpeachable source. "Captain Newton Craig," he wrote, "to whom I am indebted for the facts herein narrated, is a prominent citizen of Scott County and candidate for State Senator from this district. He was keeper of the State prison during most of the time of Fairbank's incarceration, and perfectly recollects the circumstances of the exciting period preceding his trial and imprisonment." The result of his conversations with the former warden appeared as an article in the *Covington* (Ky.) *Daily Commonwealth* on February 21, 1879, and is fascinating in that it represents Craig's perspective a quarter-century and more after the event, recollected in the tranquillity of old age and at a time when he thought Delia Webster dead.

The writer is at pains to exonerate Craig from any charge of cruelty towards his prisoner. He points out that Fairbank never taught school in Cynthiana (not realizing that Delia Webster *had* done so with the Spencers) and that the leader of the 1849 slave revolt was Patrick Doyle. More interestingly, he (and therefore Newton Craig) was of the opinion that "the evidence upon which [Fairbank] was tried and convicted" in the Hayden case "was purely circumstantial, but such was the condition of the public mind" that a guilty verdict was reached. Fairbank's "first offense had not been clearly proven," he goes on to say (and Craig, evidently, to believe), and about his guilt "there was considerable doubt." As for Delia Webster in December 1844, "There was no positive evidence against her. . . . It was no secret that her conviction and removal to Frankfort was for the purpose of placing her beyond the reach of the mob who thirsted for her blood." Thus, by Craig's 1879 recollection at least, the pardon must have been part of the plan from the beginning. "The odium of having shown humanity to a helpless woman, instead of allowing her to be torn to pieces by the frenzied mob, has hung over the Judge and others [including, of course, Craig] who sympathized with and assisted Delia Webster, believing she was innocent, for many years."

As for her former pupil's recollection of her "masculine" qualities, Newton Craig must have been anxious to set the record straight. "She was anything but masculine," reported his interlocutor, "either in appearance or intellect, and the fervid imagination of the editor of the *Breckinridge News* furnishes all the other endowments with which nature had failed to adorn her." Newton Craig's granddaughter imagined something like that which Craig, through his interviewer, here ascribes to the fervid imagination of Delia Webster's former student. In her manuscript detailing the great love of her grandfather's life for this "Jezebel" (her appellation), Henrietta Galey has Benajah Webster make the supposed discovery, as he stumbles across his daughter bathing naked in a forest pond, that she was hermaphroditic.[77] Newton Craig, as the *Louisville Democrat* hinted with regard to the "criminal connection" he denied when he had never been accused of it, perhaps doth protest too much. The editor of the *News* said nothing of any particular "endowments" nature might have given her, just that she was the most masculine of the three "by nature and disposition." Unless Newton was taking issue with the word "nature."

In any case, Craig was equally eager to deny what the editor had said about a "shameful liaison" between him and Delia Webster. It "has not a scintilla of truth."

"Delia Webster has most probably passed from the scenes of the earth," the interviewer concludes. "She has not been seen in Kentucky for twelve or fifteen years."[78]

Craig certainly suffered no lasting disgrace from his association with Webster. In 1873, he was elected to represent Scott County in the state legislature. A man of considerable culture, his personal library comprised—besides the Irish poet Thomas Moore—the complete works of Shakespeare, Robert Burns, Lord Byron, and William Cowper. His taste in reading extended as well to ancient history (Oliver Goldsmith, *The Grecian History, The Roman History*; Flavius Josephus), the American Founding Fathers (Benjamin Franklin's *Autobiography*, Parson Weems's *Life of George Washington*, J. T. Headley's *Washington and His Generals*), the more recent conflict (Alexander Stephens's *A Constitutional View of the Late War Between the States*), and inspirational literature (Charles Reade's *It Is Never Too Late to Mend*). From the numbering system on his bookplates, it appears that his library must have included at least seven hundred other titles.[79]

Slow to the altar, Delia's former student Dillard Craig (1838-1902) was fifty-two when he married Emilie Brashear (1869-1958), thirty-one years his junior. Though Newton had been averse to slaves' escaping to Canada, he felt differently about his son, whom he had sent there for the duration of the Civil War to avoid both military service and incarceration by occupying Union forces. As Emilie Brashear Craig later told her granddaughter (whose words are quoted here), "since they were close cousins, the family shuddered at their intentions." Newton and Lucy, it will be recalled, had themselves sinned in this regard, being first cousins. Dillard and Emilie "sneaked off to the Phoenix Hotel in Lexington"—where Lewis Hayden had once been employed—and found a preacher who would perform the ceremony, on August 28, 1890. "Newton, of course, was made aware of the happening, was not pleased, but was mellowed by age and the death of his wife Lucy four years earlier. He was even relieved that his old-maid daughter Florida"—Delia's other principal charge—"had a place to live . . . with them." When the wedded pair passed in their carriage, "people stopped and gazed—she, so young and adoring and he, his white hair shining. . . . And she did adore him until, after their two daughters were born, he continued to be the country squire, not the responsible provider."[80]

On September 6, 1890, less than two weeks after his son's wedding, Newton Craig died "at his home on the Frankfort Pike, on Saturday morning last, in the 83d year of his age," reported the *Georgetown Times*. "His death was not unexpected, as he had been gradually growing feebler."[81]

The young bride was present to hear her father-in-law's last conversation. His good friend Judge James Kelly had come to bid farewell. "'Well, Newton, you will soon be going over the Great Divide. You will be seeing my father and my mother and all my loved ones who have gone over and I want you to tell them for me that I have lived a good life and will be coming along soon.' Newton Craig seriously promised to convey the messages."[82]

As for Calvin Fairbank, "like many idealists," John P. Herrick recalled, he "came to believe in his later years that the sacrifices he had made were without reward." This was especially true after the publication of his autobiography in 1890, "which the newly freed colored citizens would have none of."[83] Actually, though sales may have been disappointing, Fairbank's name was not forgotten among African Americans. In fact, an article in a black New Orleans newspaper in 1891 aligned him in a veritable Mount Rushmore of heroic martyrs to the cause of liberation. Alluding to a young black musical group called the Texarkana Minstrels, who had performed for a reunion of a local Confederate Veterans' Association where the proceeds were said to go for a projected monument to Jefferson Davis, the editor of the *Southwestern Christian Advocate* complained that "their action dishonors their race and curses the memories of John Brown, Abraham Lincoln, Wm. Lloyd Garrison, Calvin Fairbank, and the host of abolitionists that fought and bled that they might enjoy the privilege of organizing such a troupe."[84] The episode is of historic interest for another reason: It is one of the first appearances in print of the name of the Texarkana Minstrel who would go on to achieve the most prominence, ragtime composer Scott Joplin.

After the disappointing reception to his book, Fairbank "often said that there would not be an ex-slave or child of an ex-slave at his funeral," wrote Herrick. His death on October 12, 1898, certainly did not attract national attention, and perhaps no ex-slaves came from out of town to attend his funeral, but he was not unmourned by two friends in Angelica who were the children of an ex-slave. "They were Dr. James Jordan and his sister, Ada Jordan, who wept as though their hearts would break. . . . When the gravel rattled on the coffin lid, rain began to fall gently, and the minister, as he walked away, involuntarily repeated, 'Blessed are the dead that the rain rains on.'" The grave remained unmarked for many years.[85]

By contrast, when Lewis Hayden died in Boston on April 7, 1889, he was mourned by thousands. Every one of the twelve hundred seats in the Charles Street A.M.E. Church was taken. Outside, "a great crowd of people patiently surged to and fro, waiting for an opportunity to cast one more look of tender affection upon the face of him whose ... crowning triumph was deservingly won."[86] The son of William Lloyd Garrison, Thomas Higginson, Lucy Stone, and a former mayor of Boston delivered eulogies. Hayden was praised not only for his activities on behalf of fugitives and his leadership in Boston's African American community in the years leading up to the Civil War, but for being "foremost in the struggle for the abolition of the color line in the schools of Boston, in agitating the temperance case, and the woman's suffrage question." He was one of the founders of the Boston Museum of Fine Arts. His last achievement was the erection of a monument honoring Crispus Attucks, a black patriot who fell in the Boston Massacre on March 5, 1770. At the monument's dedication Hayden had addressed an assembly at Faneuil Hall with these words: "I am happy and ready to die now. They cannot take from us this record of history showing that we participated in the revolution to secure American liberty, as we have participated in every great movement in the best interests of the country since."[87]

Daniel Murdock, the *Madison Star*, and Newton Craig were mistaken about Delia Webster's demise. She did not die, as the first two thought, in Jeffersonville, Indiana, in 1876. In fact, she had evidently left Indiana long before then, for on June 1, 1874, she wrote her sister Mary Jane Bard from Dexter, Iowa. The letter is full of good cheer and family gossip: "How I would like to see you & that darling pet of a grandchild! ... Jane, darling, this is the ever welcome anniversary of our dear, youngest Sister's birthday"— alluding to Martha, who was living in La Porte, Iowa. "I sent her a picture of a Mezzo rosebud in a letter to show the day did not pass unnoticed."[88] Delia, who had taught painting thirty years before to Kentucky children, was still engaged in her art.

The letter gives some indication of her travels. "I staid in Des Moines much longer than anticipated. Like it so well it was hard leaving. Left on the 6th ult. still westward bound. Am now about 170 miles from Martha[,] 60 South[,] 110 West"—coordinates that correspond to the distances between La Porte, in northeast Iowa, and Dexter, west of Des Moines. Was she, as these words suggest, "still westward bound"? Would she, at age fifty-six, push on beyond Iowa?

The landscape afforded her great delight. "Think I have found the summit of the beauty & excellence of Iowa. The farms & improvements are the best I have seen since I left Ky. & the scenery is certainly fine, beyond description." The next sentence gives some glimpse of what might have been the nature of her religious feelings: "The very vastness of the extent of these broad, rich prairie landscapes begets sublimity of thought & feeling, & el-

"The Webster Girls." Back: Martha Webster Goodrich (left) and Betsey Wilson Webster; front: Delia Webster (left) and Mary Jane Webster Bard. The only known likeness of Delia Webster. Courtesy Bard and Gina Prentiss

evates the mind to a more hallowed contemplation of the glorious attributes which constitute the Grand Architect of the Universe, if not the very Essence of Deity."

Delia Webster had so successfully escaped from the troubled scenes of her past life that her Kentucky and Indiana neighbors would soon think her dead. But she was very much alive: "My health is excellent. Do write me here. Regards to all from your loving Delia."

Other traces of her passage include a note in the Oberlin College records from an M.R. Webster of Rochester, New York, saying he received a letter from her in 1894, written from Oconomowoc, Wisconsin.[89] In 1932, B. L. Wick wrote in the *Annals of Iowa* that Webster spent her later years near the family of her sister Martha, wife of Simeon Goodrich, in Wisconsin (evidently Oconomowoc), and later in Le Grand and La Porte, Iowa. In Le Grand she "was well known, and had a number of friends" yet was "set in her ways, bitter and penniless, having spent a considerable fortune in unprofitable litigation. . . . During the last few years of her life she was, undoubtedly, considered by her relatives a burden and a misfortune." Those whom Wick interviewed in Le Grand and La Porte "alleged that she was more or less of a trouble maker, who lived too ardently in the past. She would write letters to prominent people, who had been connected before the war with the antislavery movement, and frequently these letters were never mailed." In the Goodrich household in Le Grand she "generally lived in part of the house alone. She was called Aunt Tippy. She loved chickens, and was old and queer."[90]

Wick, who had spent some time in Le Grand in his youth (he was born in 1864), later contributed a further recollection to the *Le Grand* (Iowa) *Reporter* in which he recalled having seen "the old woman a time or two, although I don't think I ever talked to her, looking after her chickens and known as Aunt Tibby [*sic*]." Though he had not spoken with her himself, Wick did hear from Le Grand contemporaries who "told many interesting stories of what [they] had heard from Delia Webster when she was in a good mood." It was on such testimony that he based his description of the bitterness of her last years. "All of her near relatives and friends had passed away. She felt that she belonged to an age that was passing. In her earlier years she had faced and defied danger; now with old age coming on, she was not so sure." Corwin O'Neal, editor of the *Reporter*, added this note: "Names we remember of her most illustrious Buff Cochin chickens: Pompey, Julius Caesar, Mark Antony, Cleopatra. Remnant of a piece of French poetry 'Aunt Delia' taught the writer when quite youthful . . .: 'Le fils don la brach, dis aux pere!'"[91]

A T.E. Mann wrote the following recollection of his own in the *Le*

Grand Reporter: "In the southeast corner of the dooryard there stood a small out-building which for some time housed the eccentric, though talented, Adelia [*sic*] Webster. Housed with her were a few chickens and a very especially bred dog. . . . Miss Webster was artistic—did creditable paintings, writings and lectures. She was, shall we say, an aristocratic spinster, giving lessons in the fine arts for a livelihood, not being able to realize her claim on the government for anti-slavery services." Mann recounts her eviction from this house, or another:

> Occupying a small house near the Christian church, Miss Webster was urged to vacate the place for some good reason. An official, big Thornton Hayes, and his deputies went to the place to discharge the unpleasant duty of evicting the obdurate tenant. After kindly insisting that she quit the place peacefully, it was found necessary to carry her belongings out into the yard, the final piece being her trunk on which she "sat tight" while it was being carried out. What this performance lacked in dignity on her part, was offset in courtesy and efficiency on the part of the officers.[92]

What was going through her mind—was she reliving her forcible evictions from her Trimble County farm? Could it have been the same trunk so zealously searched in Mrs. Glass's boarding house in October 1844?

She may have gained some measure of independence towards the end. The 1900 Census recorded Delia Webster as living in Oconomowoc, Wisconsin, in a house which she owned, free of mortgage.[93]

Wick, however, recounts that "after the death of her sister" (Martha Goodrich died on August 17, 1902) "she made her home with her niece, Alice Goodrich . . . a prominent doctor in Des Moines." Alice Goodrich (1852-1916) was the first female graduate of the medical school of the University of Iowa. Never married, she emulated her mother's sister as a pioneering woman; it is fitting that Delia should end her days in her company.

Delia Webster, reported the *Des Moines Register and Leader*, died on January 18, 1904, "aged 86 years, at the home of her niece, Dr. Alice A. Goodrich."[94]

NOTES

1
"DECEIVED IN THE DISTANCE"

1. J. Winston Coleman Jr., *Slavery Times in Kentucky* (Chapel Hill: University of North Carolina Press, 1940), 196.

2. "Case of Miss Webster," *Western Law Journal* 2 (1845): 233. Hereafter abbreviated as *WLJ*.

3. Delia A. Webster, *Kentucky Jurisprudence: A History of the Trial of Miss Delia A. Webster* (Vergennes, Vt.: E.W. Blaisdell, 1845), 45. Hereafter abbreviated as *KJ*.

4. In her account of her trial, Webster does not mention her travels with the Spencers before their arrival in Lexington: "Early in 1843, I visited Kentucky, in company with a Mr. and Mrs. Spencer, teachers and friends of mine. We taught several painting classes in the vicinity of Lexington, and in July of the same year opened a class in that city" (*KJ*, 5). She does speak of them in 1855, however: "In the year 1842 [*sic*], by the advice of physicians, I first went to Kentucky for the improvement of my health, in company with a clergyman and his wife from Oberlin, O., and visited different portions of the State, and at length went to Lexington" (*New York Independent*, November 29, 1855; hereafter abbreviated as *Ind*). The *Covington (Ky.) Intelligencer*, March 5, 1845, according to the *Emancipator*, March 19, 1845, paints a different picture, charging "Miss W. with having come to Kentucky in company with one Spencer and his wife, and being driven from place to place with him, on account of lascivious conduct, until she settled in Lexington, where her conduct was lewd enough." The *Intelligencer* article (which has not been located), to judge from the account of it in the *Emancipator*, evidently names some of the localities the three visited as Fleming County, Georgetown, and Cynthiana.

5. *Ind*, November 19, 1855.

6. Ibid.

7. Margaret K. Nelson, "Vermont Female Schoolteachers in the Nineteenth Century," *Vermont History* 49 (1981): 5-30. It is not clear whether the $800 Webster claimed her Lexington academy made was its gross income or her personal take.

8. Thomas D. Clark, *A History of Kentucky* (New York: Prentice-Hall, 1937), 306-7.

9. Cited by Jean H. Baker in *Mary Todd Lincoln: A Biography* (New York: W.W. Norton, 1987), 56-57.

10. Description taken from *South Western Seminary: Description of Its Site*, a prospectus that bears no date but was probably printed shortly before 1858.

11. KJ, 4.

12. Calvin Fairbank, *Rev. Calvin Fairbank During Slavery Times* (Chicago: Patriotic Publishing Co., 1890. Reprint. New York: Negro Universities Press, 1969), 5, 7. Hereafter abbreviated as *CF.*

13. *CF*, 12-13.

14. *CF*, 13-16.

15. *CF*, 6-7, 19.

16. Coleman, *Slavery Times*, 131, 158-59; *CF*, 26-33.

17. *KJ*, 83.

18. Arthur Schomburg, Foreword to *Out of Bondage and Other Stories* by Rowland E. Robinson (Rutland, Vt.: Charles Tuttle, 1936), 5; see also Rowland E. Robinson, *Vermont: A Study of Independence* (Boston: Houghton, Mifflin, 1892), 333-34.

19. Schomburg, 5-6; see also Wilbur H. Siebert, *Vermont's Anti-Slavery and Underground Railroad Record* (Columbus, Oh.: Spahr and Glenn, 1937), 5.

20. Frederick Douglass, *The Life and Times of Frederick Douglass* (New York: Library of America, 1994), 671-72.

21. Douglass, *Life and Times*, 672.

22. Siebert, *Vermont's Anti-Slavery Record*, map facing p. 66.

23. Siebert, *Vermont's Anti-Slavery Record*, 74.

24. Robinson, *Out of Bondage and Other Stories*, 21-48.

25. *KJ*, 4.

26. Letter from Hamilton Hill to Joseph A. Howland, February 22, 1856, Oberlin College Archives.

27. *KJ*, 8.

28. *KJ*, 6.

29. *CF*, 46-47.

30. *CF*, 47-48; *KJ*, 54.

31. *KJ*, 52-53.

32. Calvin Fairbank, "Memoir of Calvin Fairbank," in *Reminiscences of Levi Coffin* by Levi Coffin (Cincinnati: Robert Clarke, 1898. Reprint. New York: Arno Press, 1968), 719.

33. Letter from Lewis Hayden to Sydney Howard Gay (undated but probably late 1847 or early 1848), Sydney Howard Gay Papers, Columbia University Library.

34. John D. Wright Jr., *Lexington: Heart of the Bluegrass* (Lexington: Lexington-Fayette County Historic Commission, 1982), 49.

35. Marion B. Lucas, *A History of Blacks in Kentucky*, vol. 1. *From Slavery to Segregation, 1760-1891* (Frankfort, Ky.: Kentucky Historical Society, 1992), 103-5.

36. "Two gentlemen in Lexington purchased him, at his instance, with the view of his ultimate emancipation; . . . his hire or earnings were to be applied to that object" (Henry Clay to Sydney Howard Gay, December 22, 1847. *The Papers of Henry Clay*, ed. Melba Porter Hay [Lexington: University Press of Kentucky, 1991], 10: 391).

37. *CF*, 46.

38. Lewis Hayden to Harriet Beecher Stowe. In Stowe, *A Key to Uncle Tom's Cabin* (Boston: John P. Jewett and Co., 1853): 154-55.

39. Both were descended from William Rankin, who was Adam's great-grandfather and John's great-great-grandfather. A Scotch Presbyterian, William emigrated to Ireland in 1688. Flossie Cloyd, "Rankin Genealogy," typescript in the Tennessee State Library.

40. George W. Ranck, *History of Lexington Kentucky: Its Early Annals and Recent Progress* (Cincinnati: Robert Clarke, 1872. Reprint. Lexington: Henry Clay Press, 1970), 109.

41. Charles R. Staples, *The History of Pioneer Lexington (Kentucky) 1779-1806* (Lexington: n.p., 1939. Reprint. Lexington: Lexington-Fayette County Historic Commission, 1973), 272. The *U.S. Gazette*, in Philadelphia, reported Rankin's death in its November 27, 1827, issue.

42. Stowe, *A Key to Uncle Tom's Cabin,* 155.

43. Stanley J. Robboy and Anita W. Robboy, "Lewis Hayden: From Fugitive Slave to Statesman," *New England Quarterly* 46.4 (December 1973): 594.

44. *KJ*, 46-47.

45. *KJ*, 7-9.

46. *Emancipator*, March 19, 1845 (hereafter abbreviated as *Em*); Fairbank, "Memoir of Calvin Fairbank," 719.

47. *KJ*, 52, 54.

48. *KJ*, 48.

49. Fairbank, "Memoir of Calvin Fairbank," 718. Cassius Clay, a native of Kentucky and a distant cousin of Henry Clay, attended Yale College, where he came under the spell of abolitionist William Lloyd Garrison. By 1844, he was well known for his opposition to slavery, which he vociferously argued in newspapers and pamphlets. Fairbank's assertion that Clay's Lexington residence served as a rendezvous point for the Hayden rescue might not necessarily imply his participation, for Clay always made a point of staying within the letter of the law. His broadsides against slavery and other political stands were nevertheless capable of inciting violence in his enemies, to which he responded in kind, claiming the legitimate right of self-defense. At a political rally in the summer of 1843 he challenged a statement made by Robert Wickliffe (son of the slave owner who escorted young Liza to receive her manumission papers after Fairbank purchased her freedom), whom he had already fought—to a draw—in a duel two years before. Clay found himself knocked down by Samuel Brown, a fierce and bullying defender of slavery just arrived from New Orleans, who by some accounts had been hired to assassinate him ("Cassius Marcellus Clay," in *The Kentucky Encyclopedia*; the best account of Clay's life is *Lion of White Hall: the Life of Cassius M. Clay*, by David L. Smiley [Madison: University of Wisconsin Press, 1962]). Clay drew his bowie knife and leapt at Brown, who drew his pistol and fired pointblank when Clay was almost upon him. The wound, just over the heart, would have been fatal had the bullet not struck the silver-lined scabbard in which Clay kept his bowie knife. Before Brown could fire again, Clay cut open his skull, gouged out an eye and removed an ear, then tossed the body over a bluff into the stream below. Brown survived. Henry Clay successfully defended his distant cousin at the ensuing trial. The repercussions of this incident in the life of Delia Webster will be recounted in chapter 2.

50. *CF*, 48.

51. *KJ*, 48.

52. J. Winston Coleman Jr., *Stage-Coach Days in the Bluegrass* (Louisville: The Standard Press, 1935), 233, 235-36.

53. *KJ*, 8.
54. *KJ*, 69.
55. *KJ*, 8.
56. Fairbank, "Memoir of Calvin Fairbank," 720; *CF*, 48.
57. Fairbank, "Memoir of Calvin Fairbank," 720.
58. *KJ*, 67.
59. *CF*, 2.
60. *CF*, 8. J. Winston Coleman thought that Fairbank and Webster had "delivered the three slaves to the Reverend John Rankin" (*Slavery Times*, 198), but this goes counter to what Fairbank says about his rebuff from Rankin and his explicit statement (twice, on pp. 48 and 49 of his book) that he took them to "Hopkins.'" Wilbur H. Siebert, in *The Mysteries of Ohio's Underground Railroads* (Columbus, Oh.: Long's College Book Company, 1951), 78, names a Gordon Hopkins among the operators at Red Oak.
61. *Green Mountain Freeman*, January 31, 1845. Hereafter abbreviated as *GMF*.
62. *KJ*, 45.
63. *KJ*, 61.
64. In her affidavit claiming grounds for a new trial, Webster expressed the wish "to examine a toll-gate keeper this side of Washington, who stated on her return the facts of the negroes having made their escape, and he also had a handbill, as well as she can recollect; and he said the negroes took to the dirt road that led to the Ohio River left of Washington" (*KJ*, 64). Fairbank, in a letter to Herman Safford dated October 1, 1844, apparently alludes to the same conversation when he writes that, having "crossed over into Ohio to Aberdeen, and having started on my return, I was informed of some runaway negroes viz. Lewis, his wife and his child." Cited in Coleman, "Delia Webster and Calvin Fairbank—Underground Railroad Agents" (*Filson Club History Quarterly* 17.3 [1943], 133. The keeper's assertion that "the negroes took to the dirt road . . . left of Washington" would make it appear, however that he was alluding to a party other than the Haydens, as would as well the fact that he does not associate Webster and Fairbank with the escape (unless he heard it at second hand). A road to the river "left of Washington" would have made possible a crossing directly opposite Ripley, but was evidently not the route Fairbank took, for he crossed at Maysville to Aberdeen, proceeding to Ripley on the Ohio side.
65. *GMF*, January 31, 1845.
66. *KJ*, 10-11.
67. *KJ*, 11.
68. *KJ*, 11-12.
69. *KJ*, 13-14.
70. *KJ*, 11-15.

2
"PERHAPS YOU CAN DECIPHER ITS CONTENTS"

1. Clay Lancaster, *Vestiges of the Venerable City: A Chronicle of Lexington, Kentucky: Its Architectural Development and Survey of Its Early Streets and Antiquities* (Lexington: Lexington-Fayette County Historic Commission, 1978), 48; see also John D. Wright Jr., *Lexington: Heart of the Bluegrass*, 56.

2. *KJ*, 56; 33, 16. Prison reformer Dorothea Dix visited the Megowan
Hotel, also known as the Fayette County Jail, exactly a year after Delia Webster's
sojourn there, in November 1845. The county jail, she writes, "is connected with
a large Hotel, of which, indeed, it seems to make a part. The prison consists of
two cells on the ground floor, and one apartment above these, called the debtor's
room." Of the latter, she writes: "Over the cells, and entirely disconnected there-
with, is a large and comfortable apartment, called the debtors' room. This is
entered from the passage common to the Hotel, and is little distinguishable from
the apartments in that wing of the same"—that is, from the hotel rooms—"except
by the guarded windows, and a strong lock to secure the door. The room was well
furnished, decently arranged, and seemed to be in common use. A fire may be
supplied, and such accommodations as are required." D.L. Dix, *A Review of the
Present Condition of the State Penitentiary of Kentucky, with Brief Notices and
Remarks upon the Jails and Poor-Houses in Some of the Most Populous Counties*
(Frankfort: A.G. Hodges, State Printer, 1846), 19.
   3. *KJ*, 16, 34.
   4. *KJ*, 34; 16, 17.
   5. Did she mean Henry or Cassius? From Mrs. Megowan's response, it
would appear to be the latter. So thought J. Winston Coleman, Jr. (*Slavery Times*,
199). Yet it is possible that she meant Henry, the only Clay elsewhere mentioned
in her account of her arrest, trial, and imprisonment. She certainly asks for Henry
Clay later, when she needs a lawyer.
   6. *KJ*, 18.
   7. *KJ*, 18.
   8. *CF*, 51.
   9. *KJ*, 19-21.
   10. *KJ*, 22-23.
   11. *KJ*, 22-23.
   12. *KJ*, 23-24.
   13. *KJ*, 24.
   14. Coleman, *Slavery Times*, 250.
   15. Ibid., 250-51; reward notice, *Observer and Reporter*, late August 1844.
Coleman mistakenly thought Moore was included among Turner's husband's slaves,
but the reward notice specifies that he had been purchased from a James Jones of
Fleming County, "who this year brought him to Lexington and sold him." Charlotte Turner's husband had died in 1843.
   16. Letter from Calvin Fairbank to the *Boston Republican*, March 19, 1850,
reprinted in the *Liberator*, April 5, 1850. Hereafter abbreviated as *Lib.*
   17. *CF*, 51, 52.
   18. Original in the University of Kentucky Library. In publishing the letter
in his 1943 article "Delia Webster and Calvin Fairbank—Underground Railroad
Agents," Coleman did not indicate that he had omitted the first paragraph, a few
words in the second, and the first half of the third paragraph.
   19. Quoted in Coleman, "Delia Webster and Calvin Fairbank," 134.
   20. Quoted from the *Ohio Statesman*, November 13, 1844. There, the
salutation is given as "Mr. ——." In Delia Webster's letter to William Garrison
published in the September 12, 1845, issue of the *Liberator*, however, it is apparent that in speaking of a letter to a "Mr. Mason of Ohio" she is alluding to this
letter. The Mason letter has never been reprinted since, and was evidently not
known to Coleman. The Mason in question has not been identified. Oberlin
College records indicate that no one by that name was on the faculty in 1845.

21. *Lib*, September 12, 1845.
22. Laura S. Haviland, *A Woman's Life-Work* (Cincinnati: Walden and Stowe, 1882), 70-71.
23. Ibid., 77-78.
24. *CF*, 45.
25. "John Mifflin Brown," in *The Dictionary of American Negro Biography*, ed. Rayford W. Logan and Michael R. Winston (New York: W.W. Norton, 1982).
26. Nat Brandt, *The Town That Started the Civil War* (Syracuse: Syracuse University Press, 1990), 40-41.
27. Joan D. Hedrick, *Harriet Beecher Stowe: A Life* (New York: Oxford University Press, 1994), 104.
28. Robboy and Robboy, "Lewis Hayden," 595-96.
29. *Lib*, September 12, 1845.
30. Cassius Marcellus Clay, *The Life of Cassius Marcellus Clay* (J. Fletcher Brennan & Co., 1886. Reprint. New York: Negro Universities Press, 1969), 85.
31. Pictured on p. 59 of Wright, *Lexington: Heart of the Bluegrass*; both the Wickliffe and the Glass residences are visible in the 1857 bird's-eye view of Lexington reproduced on the end-papers of Lancaster, *Vestiges of the Venerable City*.
32. Quoted in the *National Anti-Slavery Standard*, April 3, 1845. Hereafter abbreviated as *NASS*.
33. *KJ*, 47-48.
34. Lewis Hayden to Lewis Baxter, October 27, 1844. University of Kentucky Library.
35. Betty Fladeland, *James Gillespie Birney: Slaveholder to Abolitionist* (Ithaca, N.Y.: Cornell University Press, 1955), 113ff.
36. Robboy and Robboy, "Lewis Hayden," 594.

3
"PARTNER OF HIS GUILT"

1. Robert V. Remini, *Henry Clay: Statesman for the Union* (New York: W.W. Norton, 1991), 182.
2. Ranck, *History of Lexington*, 249. On October 23, McCalla appeared at a "Mass Meeting and Barbecue for Bath and Montgomery counties" that attracted a crowd of six thousand, and "addressed the vast assemblage for upwards of an hour" (*Lexington Gazette*, October 26, 1844). Hereafter abbreviated as *Gaz*.
3. Remini, *Henry Clay*, 653.
4. *KJ*, 26.
5. *Gaz*, October 5, 1844.
6. *Observer and Reporter*, October 2, 1844. Hereafter abbreviated as *O&R*.
7. *Em*, December 19, 1844.
8. *O&R*, October 5, 1844.
9. *O&R*, November 2, 1844.
10. *Gaz*, October 5, 1844.
11. *Gaz*, November 9, 1844

12. *O&R*, November 2, 1844.

13. *Gaz*, November 9, 1844.

14. *The Papers of Henry Clay*, 10: 172.

15. *Em*, December 19, 1844.

16. Ranck, *History of Lexington*, 290-92; "Leslie Combs," *The Kentucky Encyclopedia*.

17. *Em*, December 19, 1844.

18. Copied in *Lib*, January 3, 1845.

19. *Em*, December 19, 1844.

20. Ibid.

21. *Em*, November 22, 1844.

22. *Lib*, December 6, 1844.

23. *KJ*, 39.

24. Coleman, *Slavery Times*, 201.

25. *KJ*, 29-30.

26. *KJ*, 41.

27. Strangely, he would continue to claim that it was not in his handwriting, long after his release from prison: "I had, in my trepidation, retained on my person a letter signed 'Frater,' addressed to parties in Oberlin, *not in my writing*, which was the only testimony that could be brought against either Miss Webster, or myself" (*CF*, 49; emphasis added).

28. *WLJ*, 234.

29. *WLJ*, 232.

30. *KJ*, 42, 44, 45.

31. *KJ*, 46.

32. *KJ*, 46-47.

33. *WLJ*, 234 (emphasis in the original).

34. *KJ*, 43.

35. *KJ*, 48-50.

36. *KJ*, 3.

37. *WLJ*, 234-35.

38. *KJ*, 54-55.

39. *Frankfort Commonwealth*, December 31, 1844. Hereafter abbreviated as *FC*.

40. *Ind*, November 29, 1855.

41. *KJ*, 62.

42. *KJ*, 63.

43. *KJ*, 59.

44. *KJ*, 59.

45. *KJ*, 72-73.

46. *KJ*, 74.

47. *KJ*, 74-75.

4
"ON ACCOUNT OF HER SEX"

1. Frank M. Masters, *A History of Baptists in Kentucky* (Louisville: Kentucky Baptist Historical Society, 1953), 17-19. See also Lewis Peyton Little, *Imprisoned Preachers and Religious Liberty in Virginia* (Lynchburg, Va.: J. P. Bell,

1938), especially 54-55; and Joseph Craig, *The History of Rev. Joseph Craig* (Lexington: n.p., 1813), especially 6-8.

2. "Traveling Church," *Kentucky Encyclopedia.*

3. Masters, *History of Baptists in Kentucky*, 19. Yet the other brothers likewise did more than preach. Lewis Craig took up milling and distilling. Elijah Craig laid out the city of Georgetown, and was credited for many years with the invention of bourbon whiskey—though local historian Ann Bevins has discovered that the long-running legend (accepted by noted historian Thomas Clark in 1937 [*A History of Kentucky*, 243], and still perpetuated in Kentucky tourist brochures) was "none other than Newton Craig," Elijah's great-nephew. The attribution to Elijah first surfaced when Newton contributed material on Scott County to the 1874 edition of Lewis and Richard Collins's *History of Kentucky* (Covington: Collins and Co., 1874), 2: x; 1: 516). See Ann Bevins, *A History of Scott County as Told by Selected Buildings* (Georgetown, Ky.: n.p., 1981), 218. For a refutation of the myth, see Henry G. Crowgey, *Kentucky Bourbon: The Early Years of Whiskeymaking* (Lexington: University Press of Kentucky, 1971), 135-36.

4. From "A record of the Craig family left by Lewis Mason, written from personal knowledge of the members of the family," in the possession of Mrs. Galey Coleman (Newton Craig's great-granddaughter), of Wichita, Kansas, consulted by the author March, 1983.

5. *Annual Report of the Keeper of the Ky. Penitentiary* (Frankfort: 1848), 1-2.

6. *CF*, 114-15.

7. Bevins, *History of Scott County*, 217; "Documents Accompanying the Governor's Message, October 12, 1844," in *Legislative Documents* (Frankfort: n.p., 1845), 339-42.

8. William C. Sneed, *A Report on the History and Mode of Management of the Kentucky Penitentiary from Its Origin, in 1798, to March 1, 1860* (Frankfort: n.p., 1860), 521.

9. Bevins, *History of Scott County*, 217.

10. *Em*, February 12, 1845.

11. *Legislative Documents*, 369.

12. *KJ*, 76; her italics.

13. Ibid.

14. *Em*, February 12, 1845.

15. Copied in *Em*, February 12, 1845.

16. *Christian Freeman*, January 16, 1845. Hereafter abbreviated as *ChF*.

17. *Em*, January 8, 1845.

18. *Broadway Journal*, January 11, 1845.

19. *ChF*, January 30, 1845.

20. *ChF*, December 19, 1844.

21. *Lib*, April 5, 1850.

22. "But Governor Owsley, being well disposed towards Miss Webster's release, and desiring to guard against the possibility of bringing her testimony into court for my defense, decided that whenever I would go into trial and the case should have passed the verdict of a jury, whatever might be its result he would pardon her" (Fairbank, "Memoir of Calvin Fairbank," 720).

23. Ibid.

24. *Em*, March 12, 1845.

25. *CF*, 53.

26. Fairbank, "Memoir of Calvin Fairbank," 721.
27. Quoted in *GMF*, March 14, 1845.
28. *FC*, February 18, 1845.
29. *Lib*, March 7, 1845.
30. Lucas, *History of Blacks in Kentucky*, 59.
31. *GMF*, March 14, 1845.
32. *Em*, March 12, 1845.
33. *CF*, 54.
34. *KJ*, 79.
35. *Em*, March 12, 1845.
36. *KJ*, 78; her italics.
37. *KJ*, 79.
38. *KJ*, 81.
39. *FC*, February 25, 1845.
40. *KJ*, 81.
41. *Em*, March 12, 1845.
42. *KJ*, 80.
43. *Em*, March 12, 1845.
44. Ibid.
45. Ibid.
46. Ibid.
47. *KJ*, 83-84.
48. *KJ*, 84.
49. *Cincinnati Atlas*, March 1, 1845, copied in *Lib*, March 21, 1845.
50. Copied in *Em*, March 19, 1845.
51. James Lane Allen, *Aftermath* (New York: Macmillan, 1926), 202-3.

5
"THE ERROR OF A WOMAN'S HEART"

1. *KJ*, 82.
2. Copied in *FC*, April 8, 1845.
3. *KJ*, 2.
4. *Lib*, May 3, 1850.
5. *GMF*, January 8, 1846.
6. Ibid.
7. *KJ*, 3.
8. *KJ*, 5.
9. *By-laws of the Webster Kentucky Farm Association* (Boston: Rand and Avery, 1858), 9. Hereafter abbreviated as *WFA*.
10. Letter from Hamilton Hill to Joseph A. Howland, February 22, 1856. Oberlin College Archives.
11. *KJ*, 5-6.
12. *KJ*, 30.
13. *KJ*, 43-44.
14. *KJ*, 68.
15. *KJ*, 70.
16. *KJ*, 71.
17. *KJ*, 76.

234 / *Notes to Pages 77-89*

18. *KJ*, 84.

19. Robboy and Robboy, "Lewis Hayden," 596.

20. J. Winston Coleman Jr., *Sketches of Kentucky's Past* (Lexington: Winburn Press, 1979), 11-18; "Cassius Clay," *Kentucky Encyclopedia*; Clark, *History of Kentucky*, 298-99; Clay, *Papers of Henry Clay* 10: 212.

21. *GMF*, July 17, 1845.

22. *Em*, July 30, 1845.

23. Ibid.

24. *ChF*, February 27, 1845.

25. *GMF*, January 17, 1845.

26. *Lib*, August 1, 1845.

27. I Kings 18: 27.

28. *ChF*, April 10, 1845.

29. *ChF*, April 24, 1845.

30. *NASS*, April 3, 1845.

31. *ChF*, May 8, 1845.

32. *Lib*, August 1, 1845.

33. Ibid.

34. *GMF*, August 28, 1845.

35. *Lib*, September 12, 1845.

36. *Em*, December 25, 1844.

37. The body of Christ, in Paul's context. Webster shifts the context to that of the Union of states, which is not exactly what the apostle had in mind.

38. The rest of I Corinthians 12: 23, which Webster does not cite, must have caused some consternation in the Victorian age: "and our uncomely parts have more abundant comeliness." Evidently the second sense (in the *Oxford English Dictionary*, for example, to cite a slightly later source) of "comely" is what is meant—that is, not "pleasing to the eye" (the first sense) but "seemly." This is the sense of the Greek *euskémòn*.

6
"DID ENTICE . . . AND SEDUCE"

1. *GMF*, October 9, 1845.

2. *Boston Courier*, October 2, 1845.

3. *GMF*, October 9, 1845.

4. Dorothy Sterling, *Ahead of Her Time: Abby Kelley and the Politics of Antislavery* (New York: W.W. Norton, 1991), 174.

5. *GMF*, October 9, 1845.

6. *Em*, October 8, 1845.

7. *Lib*, May 3, 1850.

8. Merrill D. Peterson, *The Great Triumvirate: Webster, Clay, and Calhoun* (New York: Oxford University Press, 1987), 462ff.

9. *ChF*, October 9, 1845.

10. *GMF*, October 9, 1845.

11. *Lib*, March 6, 1846.

12. *Fourteenth Annual Report Presented to the Massachusetts Anti-Slavery Society* (1846. Reprint. Westport, Conn.: Negro Universities Press, 1970), 71-72.

13. *GMF*, October 9, 1845.
14. *ChF*, October 16, 1845.
15. Lucas, *History of Blacks in Kentucky*, 77.
16. Ephesians 6: 5.
17. *ChF*, October 16, 1845.
18. *GMF*, October 16, 1845.
19. Lewis Hayden to Sydney Howard Gay, January 21, 1846. Sydney Howard Gay Papers, Columbia University Library.
20. Lewis Hayden to Lewis Baxter, October 27, 1844.
21. *Em*, May 12, 1847.
22. *Anti-Slavery Reporter*, November 1845. Hereafter abbreviated as *ASR*.
23. *NASS*, December 4, 1845; *ChF*, November 20, 1845.
24. *Proceedings of the Great Convention of the Friends of Freedom of the Eastern and Middle States* (Lowell, Mass.: Pillsbury and Knapp, 1845), 11, 3, 4.
25. *ChF*, November 20, 1845.
26. *GMF*, February 4, 1846.
27. *GMF*, January 8, 1846.
28. Ibid.
29. *ASR*, November 1845.
30. *GMF*, January 8, 1846.
31. *KJ*, 71.
32. *GMF*, January 8, 1846; *KJ*, 71.
33. *GMF*, January 22, 1846.
34. Letter from Hamilton Hill to Joseph A. Howland, February 22, 1856, Oberlin College Archives.
35. *GMF*, January 22, 1846.
36. No such letter from Henry Clay to Owsley seems to be extant, yet it is possible that he did write such a letter, for on June 20, 1846, he would convey to the governor a letter written by a third party requesting that Fairbank be pardoned. *Papers of Henry Clay* 10: 273.
37. *GMF*, January 22, 1846.
38. *Lib*, February 27, 1846.
39. *Voice of Freedom*, March 5, 1846.
40. Lewis Hayden to Sydney Howard Gay, January 21, 1846 (emphasis is Hayden's), Sydney Howard Gay Papers, Columbia University Library.
41. *GMF*, July 4, 1845.
42. *GMF*, February 7, 1845.
43. *GMF*, July 11, 1845.
44. Norris Day, *Bible Politics* (Montpelier, Vt.: Poland and Briggs, 1846), 4, 5, 7.
45. *KJ*, 3.
46. Day, *Bible Politics*, 3 (emphasis Day's).
47. *KJ*, 3.
48. On page 38 of Newton Craig's edition. Another line thus marked is "And lost their Heaven for woman's eyes!" (58). The following passage appears on a dog-eared page: "But here alone I'll tête-à-tête you, / Over a little attic feast, / As full of cordial soul at least, / As those where Delia met Tibullus . . ." (285).
49. *Louisville Daily Democrat*, February 14, 1854. Hereafter abbreviated as *LD*.

7
"IT MIGHT NOT APPEAR WHAT I SHALL BE"

1. Lewis Hayden to Sydney Howard Gay, January 21, 1846. Sydney Howard Gay Papers, Columbia University Library.
2. *GMF*, November 19, 1846.
3. *CF*, 53-54.
4. *CF*, 57.
5. *CF*, 58.
6. *CF*, 54.
7. *Papers of Henry Clay* 10: 273.
8. *Lib*, January 23, 1846.
9. Hayden to Gay, January 21, 1846.
10. *Lib*, March 27, April 3, and May 8, 1846.
11. William Lloyd Garrison to Sydney Howard Gay, March 31, 1846. In Garrison, *Letters*, ed. by Walter Merrill (Cambridge: Belknap Press of Harvard, 1971-1981), 3: 334-35.
12. William McFeeley, *Frederick Douglass* (New York: Simon and Schuster, 1991), 76-77. However, not until 1847 did segregation end at the New Bedford Lyceum (*Lib*, April 30, 1847).
13. McFeeley, *Frederick Douglass*, 78.
14. Lewis Hayden to Maria Weston Chapman, May 14, 1846. In George E. Carter and C. Peter Ripley, eds., *Black Abolitionist Papers, 1830-1865* (Sanford, N.C.: Microfilming Corporation of America, 1981), 05: 0220.
15. Robboy and Robboy, "Lewis Hayden," 597.
16. *Lib*, August 7, 1846.
17. *Lib*, July 31, 1846.
18. *Lib*, August 7, 1846.
19. William Howarth, *The Book of Concord* (New York: Penguin, 1983), 39. The *Concord Freeman* (August 7, 1846) likewise specified that the event "was celebrated in a grove near Walden Pond."
20. Henry David Thoreau, *Walden* (New York: Library of America, 1985), 434.
21. *Lib*, July 31 and August 7, 1846.
22. *Lib*, August 7, 1846. The *Lowell Journal*, by contrast, reported that Hayden "spoke with a good deal of fluency and vigor" (*Lowell Journal*, August 8, 1846). The meeting lasted until six in the evening, the *Journal* added, and included "some most delightful singing by Miss Bacon of Lowell."
23. "Dear Lewis," came the reply from a busy Gerrit Smith, "I can give but a moment to each of the multitude of letters I receive every day. The 3000 parcels of land I give away are given to colored men of *this* state—& staying put. Therefore, it is unfortunate for you that you live out of this state. Mrs. Smith & I are pleased to hear from you. She joins me in affectionate regards." Gerrit Smith to Lewis Hayden, October 8, 1846. In Carter and Ripley, *Black Abolitionist Papers* 05: 0281. I am grateful to William McFeeley for his help in deciphering this letter.
24. Lewis Hayden to Harriet Hayden, April 22, 1847. In Carter and Ripley, *Black Abolitionist Papers* 5: 0414.
25. *Em*, May 12, 1847.
26. Lewis Hayden to Sydney Howard Gay, May 8, 1847, *NASS*, May 20, 1847.

27. *NASS*, November 11, 1847. In his letter to Harriet Beecher Stowe published in *A Key to Uncle Tom's Cabin*, Hayden must have been alluding to the child Clay sold when he wrote, "I've got another [child] that is sold nobody knows where, and that I never can bear to think of" (155).

28. Henry Clay to Sydney Howard Gay, December 1, 1847. *Papers of Henry Clay* 10: 383-84.

29. Henry Clay to Sydney Howard Gay, December 22, 1847, ibid., 10: 391.

30. Remini, *Henry Clay*, 670n.

31. Clay to Gay, December 22, 1847. *Papers of Henry Clay* 10: 391.

32. Lewis Hayden to Sydney Howard Gay, undated, Sydney Howard Gay Papers, Columbia University Library.

33. Clay to Gay, December 22, 1847.

34. *Papers of Henry Clay* 9: 42.

35. Ibid., 10: 966n.

36. Ibid., 8: 841.

37. Ibid., 8: 763n.

38. Baker, *Mary Todd Lincoln*, 42-44.

39. Remini, *Henry Clay*, 499.

40. Ibid., 621.

41. *Lib*, June 4, 1847.

42. William Wells Brown, *The Rising Son: or, the Antecedents and Advancement of the Colored Race* (Boston: A.G. Brown, 1876), 548.

43. *NASS*, July 22, 1847.

44. Ibid.

45. *Ind*, November 29, 1855.

46. Ibid. Genealogical records show that Simeon and Martha Goodrich were indeed living in Frankfort in 1847, for their daughter Jennie was born there on December 15 of that year. Delia Webster's only living brother was Warren (1809-1866), who married a Betsy Wilson in 1834; no children were listed from this marriage. Henry Anthon Bostwick, *Genealogy of the Bostwick Family in America* (New York: n.p., 1901. Reprint. Bowie, Md.: Heritage Books, 1987), 561, 880, 315; see also William Holcomb Webster, *History and Genealogy of the Gov. John Webster Family of Connecticut* (Rochester, N.Y.: E.R. Andrews, 1915).

47. *NASS*, November 18, 1847.

48. McFeeley, *Frederick Douglass*, 169.

49. *NASS*, November 11, 1847.

50. *NASS*, February 3, 1848.

51. Lewis Hayden to Wendell Phillips, February 21, 1848. In Carter and Ripley, *Black Abolitionist Papers* 05: 0441.

52. *NASS*, December 23, 1847.

53. James Brewer Steward, *Wendell Phillips: Liberty's Hero* (Baton Rouge: Louisiana State University Press, 1986), 1.

54. Douglass, *Life and Times*, 704.

55. Martin Robison Delany, *The Condition, Elevation, Emigration, and Destiny of the Colored People of the United States. Politically Considered* (Philadelphia: published by the author, 1852), 106.

56. Dorothy Porter Wesley, "Integration versus Separatism: William Cooper Nell's Role in the Struggle for Equality," in Donald M. Jacobs, ed., *Courage and Conscience: Black & White Abolitionists in Boston* (Bloomington: Indiana University Press, 1993), 211.

57. Delany, *The Condition*, 106.
58. *Lib*, September 7, 1849.
59. *CF*, 54-55.
60. *Lib*, May 5, 1850.
61. *CF*, 55-56.
62. *CF*, 56.
63. David L. Smiley, *The Lion of Whitehall: The Life of Cassius M. Clay* (Madison: University of Wisconsin Press, 1962), 142; "R. Runyon's Statement," in *NASS*, July 26, 1849.
64. Clark, *History of Kentucky*, 301.
65. *CF*, 56.
66. *NASS*, September 13, 1849.
67. *O&R*, August 9, 1848, cited in Coleman, *Slavery Times*, 89.
68. *NASS*, September 13, 1849. Fairbank's allusion is to Mingo chief John Logan's speech to Lord Dunmore in 1774, often cited as an example of Native American eloquence, and of courage in the face of grief. Logan's wife and children were murdered in cold blood by whites, toward whom he had long behaved as a friend. He erupted in vengeance, a war was fought, the Indians were at last defeated and forced to sue for peace. "For my country," said Logan, "I rejoice at the beams of peace. But do not harbour a thought that mine is the joy of fear. Logan never felt fear. He will not turn on his heel to save his life." Logan's speech is reproduced in Thomas Jefferson's *Notes on the State of Virginia* (in Jefferson, *Writings* [New York: Library of America, 1984] 188-89).
69. *CF*, 57.

8
"THE SINCERE DESIRE OF YOUR FOND FATHER"

1. Letter from Delia Webster, December 17, 1851, to the *Louisville Daily Courier*, published December 27, 1851. Hereafter abbreviated as *LC*.
2. *Ind*, November 29, 1855.
3. Bevins, *History of Scott County*, 216.
4. John T. Windle and Robert M. Taylor, Jr., *The Early Architecture of Madison, Indiana* (Madison and Indianapolis: Historic Madison / Indiana Historical Society, 1986) xv, 3.
5. Clark, *The Kentucky: Revised Edition* (Lexington: University Press of Kentucky, 1992), 80-81.
6. *Ind*, November 29, 1855.
7. William Wesley Woollen, *Biographical and Historical Sketches of Early Indiana* (Indianapolis: Hammond and Co., 1883) 526, 172.
8. Windle and Taylor, *Early Architecture*, 111.
9. Woollen, *Biographical and Historical Sketches*, 534.
10. "Appendix F: Underground Railroad Incidents," in the Drusilla Cravens Collection at the Madison-Jefferson County Public Library, Madison, Indiana, 158, 159.
11. Woollen, *Biographical and Historical Sketches*, 524.
12. "Appendix F," 159-60.
13. *LC*, December 27, 1851.
14. *Madison Dollar Weekly Star*, October 16, 1879. Hereafter abbreviated as *MS*.

15. "Appendix F," 159-60

16. According to an article in the *Madison Star* thirty years later, it was not during her first residence there in 1849 but "at another time" (probably after 1854) that "she appeared as a teacher of colored children in Madison township outside the city" (*MS*, October 16, 1879).

17. *LC*, December 27, 1851.

18. Lucy Craig was also the sister of Parker Craig, from whom Calvin Fairbank had rented the hack and driver with which they freed the Haydens (*KJ*, 74).

19. Dillard Craig's granddaughter, however, asserted that only Mary, Dillard, and Florida were lodged in Madison (letter from Mrs. Galey Coleman to William Albert Davis, December 17, 1982). She was, however, probably basing this assertion on the notes among her mother's manuscripts, which list William and Lucien as "died young before 1850 census" when in fact "William Craig, 11, male" does appear on the 1850 census and Lucien, while his name does not appear in the census, lived until August 25, 1855, as Newton Craig's cousin Jefferson Craig records in his diary for that date (Jefferson Craig Diary, 80).

20. Sneed, *History of the Kentucky Penitentiary*, 524.

21. That is, it is the only account apart from what Newton Craig himself would say in a letter to the *Louisville Democrat* in February, 1854, to be quoted at length in chapter 11.

22. *KJ*, 79.

23. Sneed, *History of the Kentucky Penitentiary*, 524.

24. *LC*, December 27, 1851.

25. *MS*, October 16, 1879.

26. *LD*, February 14, 1854.

27. *MS*, October 16, 1879.

28. The manuscript is a projected novel, its author evidently inspired by the desire to celebrate the virility of her grandfather but at the same time to portray Delia Webster as a freak of nature (in fact, a hermaphrodite). Dillard Craig, born March 10, 1838, married Emilie Brashear (born January 10, 1869) on August 28, 1890. Henrietta Craig Galey, the author of the manuscript, was born September 1, 1894. Though she was only eight years old when her father died on November 13, 1902, her mother lived until 1958, and was a rich source of family lore.

29. *NASS*, September 13, 1849.

30. *CF*, 60.

31. *CF*, 68.

32. *CF*, 70.

33. *NASS*, January 31, 1850.

34. *Lib*, April 5, 1850.

35. *CF*, 71.

36. *Lib*, May 3, 1850.

37. Webster to Mason, October 7, 1844.

38. *CF*, 55.

39. *Lib*, August 9, 1850.

40. *LD*, February 14, 1854.

41. In Henrietta Galey's manuscript, Delia Webster "persuaded Captain Craig to let the boy go, saying that she could tutor him while he enjoyed the cool Vermont weather. The trip would certainly contribute much to the boy's education. She did not add, of course, how much freedom Dillard's presence would assure her. . . . The boy was an apt pupil, far advanced in Latin and Greek, and in

higher mathematics he showed marks of genius. . . . Like his father he could do almost anything with his hands. Newton's fame had spread even to neighboring states for his inventions and paintings and experiments in architecture and construction. Dillard had a father he could well look up to and he unconsciously imitated the man's talents. Delia, as his governess, was proud of his accomplishments. She accepted full credit for them though, in her heart, she knew it was not due her. . . . The life on the Vermont farm was new to Dillard. It held his interest from dawn until dusk. . . . He followed his friend Benajah Webster from the table each morning and stayed by his side until Miss Delia summoned him to his lessons. . . . The boy felt free to ask questions of the old man, who always took time to answer in detail. Mr. Webster had no sense of humor. . . . During the long cold winters, he had read good books, from which he had gather a valuable fund of knowledge. It came as a relief to him, to let some of it escape like steam, and he loved the boy who opened the valve, with his curiosity and interest.

"Lessons took up several hours each morning. Of afternoons, Delia and her pupil took turns reading aloud, after their naps. Even when they were in the wee boat fishing, the tutor did not relax from her teaching" (214-15; 221-22).

42. *LC*, February 14, 1854.

43. The announcement of his probable arrival in Vermont is preceded by a puzzling reference: "I have not yet learned the true condition of those scamps at Albany, and of course I cannot tell whether I will come for them or not. If I do, I will leave home on the 22nd. . . ." The "scamps" may be William and Lucien. "Lucien was one of the two boys that were foolish," commented Jefferson Craig (Jefferson Craig Diary, 80). This confirms the assertion in the *Louisville Courier* that of the Craig children "two . . . were scarcely imbeciles" (*LC*, February 20, 1854). The other retarded child may have been William (who, with Lucien, is never mentioned in the extant correspondence), and both may have been in Albany by reason of their common condition, possibly in an institution.

44. Woollen, *Biographical and Historical Sketches*, 532-33.

45. Simeon and Martha Goodrich had settled in Frankfort, on Craig's invitation, in 1847, but returned to Vermont some time before June 1, 1849, when their son George was born in Ferrisburgh (Bostwick, *Genealogy*, 880).

46. *LD*, February 14, 1854.

47. *CF*, 56.

48. *LD*, February 14, 1854.

49. *Vergennes Vermonter*, January 30, 1851.

50. *Lib*, December 6, 1844.

51. *LD*, February 14, 1854.

52. The higher fee was allegedly justified by the extra paperwork extradition necessitated. See William W. Freehling, *The Road to Disunion: Secessionists at Bay, 1776-1854* (New York: Oxford University Press, 1990), 501-2.

53. *CF*, 78.

54. Robboy and Robboy, "Lewis Hayden," 598-99.

9

"I AM AFRAID THEY WILL NOT ALWAYS BE ON AS FRIENDLY TERMS"

1. John Daniels, *In Freedom's Birthplace: A Study of the Boston Negroes* (Boston: Houghton, Mifflin, 1914), 61n.

2. Robboy and Robboy, "Lewis Hayden," 601.
3. Vincent Y. Bowditch, *Life and Correspondence of Henry Ingersoll Bowditch* (Boston: Houghton, Mifflin, 1902), 2:373.
4. *CF,* 79.
5. Henrietta Buckminster, *Let My People Go: The Story of the Underground Railroad and the Growth of the Abolition Movement* (New York: Harper, 1941), 189.
6. *CF,* 80.
7. Bowditch, *Life,* 1: 213.
8. Buckminster, *Let My People Go,* 202.
9. *Boston Globe,* April 7, 1889; Robboy and Robboy, "Lewis Hayden," 601-3.
10. Benjamin Quarles, *Black Abolitionists* (New York: Oxford University Press, 1969), 206.
11. Buckminster, *Let My People Go,* 203.
12. *Lib,* February 28, 1851.
13. Robboy and Robboy, "Lewis Hayden," 604. It is not clear whether this refers to the father of Hayden's first or second wife.
14. Thomas Wentworth Higginson, "Cheerful Yesterdays, v. The Fugitive Slave Period," *Atlantic Monthly* 79 (1897): 346.
15. Buckminster, *Let My People Go,* 205.
16. Bowditch, *Life,* 1: 221.
17. *CF,* 81-83.
18. They must have first met on July 5, 1851, to judge by the entry in her diary for that date in 1855: "Is it possible that four years have rolled their round since I first saw him who has become to me a second self. Time has wrought its changes, but I am still the same. Though my sky is oft o're cast, I look with hope to the future. We shall meet again if God wills." Mandana Tileston Diary, July 5, 1855.
19. *LC,* November 18, 1851. The *Courier* quotes George W. Morris as having said Fairbank boasted in Corning of freeing fourteen slaves, but this is undoubtedly a misprint for *forty*-four. In his autobiography, Fairbank gives that figure: "Up to [and including] the liberation of Mr. Hayden and family, I had liberated forty-four slaves." Tamar was the forty-seventh; numbers forty-five and forty-six were "Julia with her babe," whom "during the short time I spent in Southern Indiana in 1851, I liberated, before undertaking the case of Tamar" (*CF,* 149-50).
20. *CF,* 85.
21. *LC,* December 27, 1851.
22. Delia Webster to Esther Webster, March 18, 1851.
23. Jennie Bard Martin, "Family Register."
24. *LC,* December 27, 1851.
25. *LD,* February 14, 1854.
26. *LC,* December 27, 1851.
27. *Lib,* November 7, 1851.
28. *CF,* 100.
29. *LC,* November 18, 1851.
30. *CF,* 85-86, 158.
31. *CF,* 99; *LC,* November 18, 1851.
32. *LC,* November 18, 1851.
33. Fairbank, "Memoir of Calvin Fairbank," 722.

34. Letter from Calvin Fairbank, November 13, 1851, in *Frederick Douglass' Paper*, November 21, 1851. Hereafter abbreviated as *FDP*.

35. This might have been an inside joke along the underground railroad, though no doubt beyond the marshal's comprehension: Back in 1844, Jonathan Walker, convicted in Pensacola, Florida, of the crime of freeing slaves, was punished by having his hand branded with the letters "S.S"—for "slave-stealer" (*NASS*, December 12, 1844). Fairbank, who in September had boasted in Corning, New York, of rescuing forty-four slaves, was perhaps with a touch of bravado calling himself the Slave Stealing King.

36. Fairbank, "Memoir of Calvin Fairbank," 722.

37. Shotwell surname file, Filson Club, Louisville, Kentucky.

38. *CF*, 90-91.

39. *FDP*, November 21, 1851.

40. *LC*, November 18, 1851.

41. Haviland, *A Woman's Life-Work*, 140-41.

42. *LC*, December 27, 1851; "Amos Kendall," *Kentucky Encyclopedia*.

43. Cited by Charles H. Money, "The Fugitive Slave Law," *Indiana Magazine of History*, 17 (1921): 283.

44. *LC*, December 27, 1851 (editor's note accompanying Webster's letter of December 17, 1851).

45. Ibid.

46. Ibid.

47. Haviland, *Woman's Life-Work*, 143, 145.

48. Ibid., 145-46.

49. *LC*, November 24, 1851.

50. *LC*, December 27, 1851.

51. Ibid.

52. Warren Webster to Warren Bard, February 15, 1852.

53. Haviland, *Woman's Life-Work*, 154-58.

54. *CF*, 95.

55. *CF*, 97.

56. *CF*, 95-96.

57. *Lib*, March 5, 1852.

58. *CF*, 103.

59. *CF*, 104.

60. *CF*, 107.

61. *CF*, 109.

10
"THE VERY MADNESS OF THE MOON"

1. *WFA*, 11.

2. *The Poetical Works of Thomas Moore* (Philadelphia: J. Crissy, 1843), 47. Cf. *Thomas Moore's Complete Poetical Works* (New York: Crowell, 1895), 415-16.

3. *South Western Seminary: Description of Its Site*.

4. Trimble County Deed Books.

5. Trimble County Circuit Court Order Books.

6. *NASS*, March 25, 1854.

7. *LD*, February 15, 1854.

8. Ibid.

9. *NASS*, March 25, 1854.

10. *Ind*, November 29, 1855.

11. *WFA*, 10.

12. Coleman, *Slavery Times*, 239.

13. *WFA*, 12.

14. *NASS*, March 25, 1855.

15. *Madison Courier*, February 8, 1854. Hereafter abbreviated as *MC*.

16. Trimble County Deed Books.

17. *MC*, February 2, 1854.

18. *NASS*, March 25, 1854.

19. *MC*, September 6, 1854.

20. *Ind*, November 29, 1855.

21. *LD*, February 15, 1854.

22. *MC*, February 15, 1854.

23. *NASS*, March 25, 1854.

24. *MC*, February 15, 1854.

25. *NASS*, March 25, 1854.

26. *LD*, February 10, 1854.

27. *CF*, 110, 118.

28. *CF*, 113.

29. Ibid.

30. *LC*, February 15, 1854.

31. *CF*, 114.

32. *LC*, January 7, 1854.

33. *LD*, February 14, 1854.

34. *Covington Journal*, February 25, 1854.

35. *LD*, February 14, 1854.

36. *LC*, February 16, 1854.

37. Tennessee State Prison and Kentucky Penitentiary records.

38. *LC*, February 16, 1854.

39. *LC*, February 20, 1854.

40. Ibid.

41. *LD*, February 18, 1854.

42. Ibid.

43. Sneed, *History of the Kentucky Penitentiary*, 524.

44. *LD*, February 19, 1854.

45. *MS*, October 15, 1879.

46. Nevius and Haviland, on Canal and Main Streets: "Self Acting Shade Rollers. A word to the wise is 'efficient.'" The company had a New York office as well, at 406 Broadway (poster on display in the Addison County Public Library, Vergennes, Vt.).

47. These two were probably William and Lucien (see chapter 8, note 43). Newton's cousin Jefferson Craig wrote in his diary on August 25, 1855: "I recd. a message from Newton to go out there—his son Lucien died this morning. Lucien was one of the two boys that were foolish. . . . After dinner we went out to Newton's. . . . The coffin did not come in time and we came home before the burial" (Jefferson Craig Diary).

48. *LC*, February 20, 1854.

49. *LD*, February 14, 1854.

50. "The Earl Rivers, on account of a criminal connexion with whom, Lady Macclesfield is said to have divorced from her husband." *Oxford English Dictionary*, 2d ed. (Oxford: Clarendon, 1989).

51. *LD*, February 21, 1854.

52. Richard Weisenberger, "Century Old House Harbors Legend of 'Slave Driving Simon Legree,'" unidentified newspaper clipping (though apparently from a Georgetown, Kentucky paper) in the Kentucky State Historical Society.

53. Jefferson Craig diary.

11
"A VERY BOLD AND DEFIANT KIND OF WOMAN"

1. *Ind*, November 29, 1855.

2. Ibid.

3. Ibid.

4. Ibid.

5. *MC*, March 22, 1854; *Ind*, November 29, 1855.

6. Jefferson Craig Diary, March 18-April 3, 1854.

7. *Ind*, November 29, 1855.

8. Ibid.

9. Craig to Webster, undated (probably June 1849). in *LD*, February 14, 1854.

10. Jefferson Craig Diary, April 22, 1854.

11. Jefferson Craig Diary, May 26, 1854.

12. Higginson, "Cheerful Yesterdays," 352.

13. "Lewis Hayden," *The Dictionary of American Negro Biography*, ed. Rayford W. Logan and Michael R. Winston (New York: W.W. Norton, 1982).

14. Higginson, "Cheerful Yesterdays," 349-52; *NASS*, June 3, 1854.

15. *Madison Daily Banner*, July 4, 1854; copied in *FDP*, August 11, 1854.

16. *FDP*, August 11, 1854.

17. *Ind*, November 29, 1855.

18. *FDP*, August 11, 1854.

19. *Ind*, November 29, 1855.

20. *WFA*, 14.

21. Copied in *FDP*, August 11, 1854.

22. *MC*, June 28, 1854.

23. *FDP*, August 11, 1854.

24. *WFA*, 15.

25. Copied in the *New York Times*, July 24, 1854.

26. *Ind*, November 29, 1855.

27. Ibid. and *FDP*, August 11, 1854.

28. *MC*, September 6, 1854.

29. *New Albany Daily Ledger*, July 6, 1854.

30. *FDP*, August 11, 1854.

31. *MC*, September 6, 1854.

32. Copied in the *New York Times*, July 24, 1854.

33. Woolen, *Biographical and Historical Sketches*, 447-48.

34. John Lyle King Diary, July 20, 1854. Indiana Historical Society, Indianapolis.

35. *Frankfort Commonwealth*, copied in *LC*, July 29, 1854.

36. Ibid.

37. King Diary, July 20, 1854.

38. *LC*, July 29, 1854.

39. King Diary, July 20, 1854.

40. *MC*, July 22, 1854.

41. *MC*, July 26, 1854.

42. Ibid.

43. King Diary, July 20, 1854.

44. *FDP*, August 11, 1854.

45. *MC*, July 26, 1854.

46. King Diary, July 20, 1854.

47. *LC*, July 29, 1854.

48. King Diary, July 20, 1854.

49. *MC*, July 26, 1854.

50. *FC*, August 7, 1854.

51. Ibid.

52. King Diary, July 20, 1854.

53. *FC*, August 7, 1854.

54. *MC*, July 29, 1854.

55. *LC*, July 29, 1854.

56. *FC*, August 7, 1854.

57. *MC*, July 22, 1854.

58. *Madison Banner*, copied in the *Frankfort Yeoman*, August 3, 1854.

59. Indiana State Prison (South) Records. In his July 6, 1850 letter to Delia Webster, Craig writes of a "Miss Randall" who "writes from Madison that she wants to come back. I look for her." It may only be a coincidence, or she may be related to William. Equally intriguing is a notation in the Indiana State Prison Records that (in 1857, at the time of his release) William Randall had "a married sister" who "lives in Frankford." While this could be Frankfort, Indiana, it could be Frankfort, Kentucky, and there may have been some connection to Newton Craig.

60. *MC*, July 26, 1854.

61. *MC*, August 16, 1854.

62. *MC*, July 25, 1854.

63. *FC*, August 7, 1854.

64. Jefferson Craig Diary, August 21, 7, and 17, 1854.

65. *CF*, 111, 107.

66. *CF*, 111-12.

67. *CF*, 113.

12
Aftermath: "This remarkable history."

1. Karl Marx, *The Eighteenth Brumaire of Louis Bonaparte* (New York: International Publishers, 1963), 15.

2. King Diary, March 27, 1855.

3. *MC*, March 27, 1855.
4. King Diary, March 27, 1855.
5. King Diary, April 14, 1855.
6. Genesis 39:12.
7. *MC*, February 22, 1854.
8. King Diary, April 15, 1855.
9. King Diary, April 30, 1855.
10. King Diary, July 2, 1855.
11. *Ind*, November 29, 1855.
12. John G. Fee to Lewis Tappan and Jocelyn Whipple, April 4, 1857, *American Missionary Association Archives*. Microfilm. Item no. 43458.
13. *American Missionary*, December 1855; cited in Richard Sears, *The Kentucky Abolitionists in the Midst of Slavery, 1854-1864* (Lewiston, N.Y.: Edwin Mellen Press, 1993), 170.
14. *South Western Seminary: Description of Its Site.*
15. Fee to Whipple, April 4, 1857.
16. Sears, *The Kentucky Abolitionists in the Midst of Slavery, 1854-1864*, 172.
17. *WFA*, 15.
18. *WFA*, 16.
19. Delia Webster to Lewis Tappan, March 24, 1858, *American Missionary Association Archives* (New Orleans: Amistad Research Center, 1983). Microfilm. Item no. 53848.
20. *WFA*, 3, 8.
21. *MS*, October 15, 1879.
22. *MC*, April 29, 1859.
23. *MC*, June 13, 1859.
24. *MC*, April 29, 1859.
25. *MS*, October 15, 1879.
26. Richard Collins, *History of Kentucky* (Covington: Collins and Co., 1874), I: 83.
27. Delia Webster to Warren and Mary Jane Bard, February 7, 1861.
28. Julia Colman, *The Child's Anti-Slavery Book* (New York: Carlton and Porter, 1859), 16. Hereafter abbreviated as *CASB*.
29. *CASB*, 52, 53.
30. *CASB*, 53.
31. *KJ*, 5.
32. *CASB*, 53-54.
33. *CASB*, 56-57.
34. *CASB*, 59.
35. *CASB*, 60.
36. *CASB*, 61.
37. *Boston Globe*, April 7, 1889. Hereafter abbreviated as *BG*.
38. Robboy and Robboy, "Lewis Hayden," 607.
39. Ibid., 608; Oswald Garrison Villard, *John Brown* (Boston: Houghton Mifflin, 1910), 421; Edward J. Renehan Jr., *The Secret Six: The True Tale of the Men who Conspired with John Brown* (New York: Crown, 1995).
40. Robert Penn Warren, *John Brown: The Making of a Martyr* (New York: Payson and Clarke, 1929. Reprint. Nashville: J.S. Sanders, 1993), 346.
41. Renehan, however, disputes Hayden's claim to have recruited Meriam, awarding that honor to James Redpath. *Secret Six*, 194.
42. Lewis Hayden to John Brown, Jr., September 16, 1859. In Carter and Ripley, *Black Abolitionist Papers*, 12:421.

43. Villard, *John Brown*, 327, 396.

44. *New York Age*, April 13, 1889. Hereafter abbreviated as *NYA*.

45. Benjamin Quarles, *The Negro in the Civil War* (Boston: Little, Brown, 1953. Reprint. New York: Da Capo Press, 1989), 101.

46. "Lewis Hayden," in Logan and Winston, *The Dictionary of Negro American Biography*.

47. Quarles, *Negro*, 101; Porter, "Lewis, Hayden," in Logan and Winston, *The Dictionary of Negro American Biography*.

48. *BG*, April 7, 1889.

49. Bowditch, *Life*, 2: 350.

50. *NYA*, April 13, 1889.

51. Lewis Hayden, *Masonry Among Colored Men in Massachusetts* (Boston: Published by the author, 1871), 31.

52. William A. Muraskin, *Middle-Class Blacks in a White Society: Prince Hall Freemasonry in America* (Berkeley: University of California Press, 1975), 26.

53. Lewis Hayden to Lewis Baxter, October 27, 1844.

54. Stowe, *A Key*, 154.

55. Lewis Hayden, *Caste Among Masons* (Boston: Coombs, 1866), 28.

56. Ibid., 7-8.

57. *Lib*, January 20, 1865.

58. *CF*, 149, 122, 121, 119.

59. *CF*, 129-30.

60. Tileston Diary, February 19, 1858.

61. Tileston Diary, October 16, 1859.

62. *CF*, 70, 131.

63. *CF*, 133.

64. *CF*, 135.

65. Tileston Diary, July 22, 1861.

66. *CF*, 139.

67. *CF*, 148.

68. *CF*, 148-49.

69. *CF*, 174, 176-78.

70. *MC*, May 16, 1865.

71. Trimble County Deed Books.

72. *MS*, October 15, 1879.

73. Fairbank Diary, August 17, 1874.

74. Fairbank Diary, June 17, 1875.

75. Fairbank Diary, July 17, 1876.

76. *Louisville Courier-Journal*, January 27, 1879.

77. Henrietta Galey, "The Petticoat Abolitionist." Galey Coleman believes this a pure invention of her mother's, who "may have manufactured that to prove her grandpa had never seen the girl intimately." Galey Coleman to Randolph Paul Runyon, July 21, 1995.

78. *Covington (Ky.) Daily Commonwealth*, February 21, 1879.

79. From remnants of Newton Craig's library in the possession of Galey Coleman.

80. Galey Coleman to Randolph Paul Runyon, July 21, 1995.

81. *Georgetown Times*, September 10, 1890.

82. Notes by Henrietta Galey.

83. John Herrick, "Calvin Fairbanks Freed 47 Slaves," *Olean (N.Y.) Times Herald*, February 19, 1953.

84. *Southwestern Christian Advocate*, August 13, 1891, cited in Edward A. Berlin, *King of Ragtime: Scott Joplin and His Era* (New York: Oxford University Press, 1994), 10.

85. Herrick, "Calvin Fairbanks."

86. *BG*, April 11, 1889.

87. *NYA*, April 13, 1889.

88. Delia Webster to Mary Jane Bard, June 1, 1874.

89. Oberlin College Archives. The note appears to date from 1908.

90. B.L. Wick, "Delia Webster," *Annals of Iowa* 18.3 (January 1932): 228-31.

91. *Le Grand Reporter*, May 12, 1939. I am by trade a professor of French, but have not yet been able to trace the source of this line, whose orthography should be corrected to "Le fils dans la branche dit au père" ("The son in the branch says to the father"). It may have something to do with Absalom. I might add that when visiting Le Grand, Iowa, in 1981 I located an elderly resident who could remember her mother talking about Delia Webster. Unfortunately, she could not remember what she said.

92. *Le Grand Reporter*, April 29, 1939.

93. United States Census Records, Cincinnati Public Library.

94. *Des Moines Register and Leader*, January 19, 1904.

BIBLIOGRAPHY

PRIMARY SOURCES

Allen, James Lane. *Aftermath*. New York: Macmillan, 1926.

American Missionary Association Archives 1839-1882. New Orleans: Amistad Research Center, 1983. 261 microfilm reels.

Annual Report of the Keeper of the Ky. Penitentiary. Frankfort: 1848.

Brown, William Wells. *The Rising Son: or, the Antecedents and Advancement of the Colored Race*. Boston: A.G. Brown, 1876.

By-laws of the Webster Kentucky Farm Association. Boston: Rand and Avery, 1858. Abbreviated as *WFA*.

Carter, George E., and C. Peter Ripley, eds. *Black Abolitionist Papers, 1830-1865*. Sanford, N.C.: Microfilming Corporation of America, 1981. 17 microfilm reels.

"Case of Miss Webster." *Western Law Journal*, 2 (1845): 232-35. Abbreviated as *WLJ*.

Clay, Cassius Marcellus. *The Life of Cassius Marcellus Clay*. J. Fletcher Brennan & Co., 1886. Reprint. New York: Negro Universities Press, 1969.

Clay, Henry. *The Papers of Henry Clay*, ed. Melba Porter Hay. Lexington: University Press of Kentucky, 1991.

Colman, Julia. *The Child's Anti-Slavery Book*. New York: Carlton & Porter, 1859. Abbreviated as *CASB*.

Craig, Joseph. *The History of Rev. Joseph Craig*. Lexington: n.p., 1813.

Daniels, John. *In Freedom's Birthplace: A Study of the Boston Negroes*. Boston: Houghton, Mifflin, 1914.

Day, Norris. *Bible Politics*. Montpelier, Vt.: Poland and Briggs, 1846.

Delany, Martin Robison. *The Condition, Elevation, Emigration, and Destiny of the Colored People of the United States, Politically Considered*. Philadelphia: published by the author, 1852.

Dix, D.L. *A Review of the Present Condition of the State Penitentiary of Kentucky, with Brief Notices and Remarks upon the Jails and Poor-Houses in Some of the Most Populous Counties*. Frankfort: A. G. Hodges, State Printer, 1846.

Douglass, Frederick. The Life and Times of Frederick Douglass. In Autobiographies, ed. Henry Louis Gates, Jr. New York: Library of America, 1994.

Fairbank, Calvin. "Memoir of Calvin Fairbank." *In Reminiscences of Levi Cof-*

fin by Levi Coffin. Cincinnati: Robert Clarke, 1898. Reprint. New York: Arno Press, 1968: 719-26.

———. *Rev. Calvin Fairbank During Slavery Times.* Chicago: Patriotic Publishing Co., 1890. Reprint. New York: Negro Universities Press, 1969. Abbreviated as CF.

Fourteenth Annual Report Presented to the Massachusetts Anti-Slavery Society. 1846. Reprint. Westport, Conn.: Negro Universities Press, 1970.

Garrison, William Lloyd. *Letters.* 6 vols., ed. by Walter Merrill. Cambridge: Belknap Press of Harvard, 1971-1981.

Haviland, Laura S. *A Woman's Life-Work.* Cincinnati: Walden and Stowe, 1882.

Hayden, Lewis. Caste Among Masons. Boston: Coombs, 1866.

———. Letter to Harriet Beecher Stowe. In Stowe, *Key to Uncle Tom's Cabin,* 154-55.

———. *Masonry Among Colored Men in Massachusetts.* Boston: Published by the author, 1871.

Higginson, Thomas Wentworth. "Cheerful Yesterdays, V. The Fugitive Slave Period." *Atlantic Monthly* 79 (1897): 344-55.

Jefferson, Thomas. *Writings,* ed. Merril D. Peterson. New York: Library of America, 1984.

Legislative Documents. Frankfort, Ky.: n.p., 1845.

Moore, Thomas. *The Poetical Works of Thomas Moore.* Philadelphia: J. Crissy, 1843.

———. *Thomas Moore's Complete Poetical Works.* New York: Crowell, 1895.

Proceedings of the Great Convention of the Friends of Freedom of the Eastern and Middle States. Lowell, Mass.: Pillsbury and Knapp, 1845.

Sneed, William C. *A Report on the History and Mode of Management of the Kentucky Penitentiary from Its Origin, in 1798, to March 1, 1860.* Frankfort: 1860.

South Western Seminary. Description of Its Site. No author, publisher, or date, but as an earlier version of what became the Webster Kentucky Farm Association, it probably dates from shortly before 1858. Only known copy in the possession of Bard Prentiss, Dryden, New York.

Stowe, Harriet Beecher. *A Key to Uncle Tom's Cabin.* Boston: John P. Jewett and Co., 1853.

Thoreau, Henry David. *Walden.* New York: Library of America, 1985.

Webster, Delia A. *Kentucky Jurisprudence. A History of the Trial of Miss Delia A. Webster.* Vergennes, Vt.: E.W. Blaisdell, 1845. Abbreviated as *KJ.*

SECONDARY SOURCES

Baker, Jean H. *Mary Todd Lincoln: A Biography.* New York: W.W. Norton, 1987.

Berlin, Edward A. *King of Ragtime: Scott Joplin and His Era.* New York: Oxford University Press, 1994.

Bevins, Ann. *A History of Scott County as Told by Selected Buildings.* Georgetown, Ky.: n.p., 1981.

Bostwick, Henry Anthon. *Genealogy of the Bostwick Family in America.* New York: n.p., 1901. Reprint. Bowie, Md.: Heritage Books, 1987.

Bowditch, Vincent Y. *Life and Correspondence of Henry Ingersoll Bowditch.* 2 vols. Boston: Houghton, Mifflin, 1902.

Buckminster, Henrietta. *Let My People Go: The Story of the Underground Railroad and the Growth of the Abolition Movement.* New York: Harper, 1941.

Brandt, Nat. *The Town That Started the Civil War.* Syracuse: Syracuse University Press, 1990.

Clark, Thomas D. *A History of Kentucky.* New York: Prentice-Hall, 1937.

———. *The Kentucky: Revised Edition.* Lexington: University Press of Kentucky, 1992.

Cloyd, Flossie. "Rankin Genealogy." Typescript in the Tennessee State Library, Nashville.

Coleman, J. Winston, Jr. "Delia Webster and Calvin Fairbank—Underground Railroad Agents." *Filson Club History Quarterly* 17.3 (1943): 129-42.

———. *Sketches of Kentucky's Past.* Lexington: Winburn Press, 1979.

———. *Slavery Times in Kentucky.* Chapel Hill: University of North Carolina Press, 1940.

———. *Stage-Coach Days in the Bluegrass.* Louisville: The Standard Press, 1935.

Collins, Lewis and Richard Collins. *History of Kentucky.* 2 vols. Covington: Collins and Co., 1874.

Crowgey, Henry G. *Kentucky Bourbon: The Early Years of Whiskeymaking.* Lexington: University Press of Kentucky, 1971.

Fladeland, Betty. *James Gillespie Birney: Slaveholder to Abolitioist.* Ithaca, N.Y.: Cornell University Press, 1955.

Freehling, William W. *The Road to Disunion: Secessionists at Bay. 1776-1854.* New York: Oxford University Press, 1990.

Hedrick, Joan D. *Harriet Beecher Stowe: A Life.* New York: Oxford University Press, 1994.

Herrick, John. "Calvin Fairbanks Freed 47 Slaves." *Olean (N.Y.) Times Herald,* February 19, 1953.

Howarth, William. *The Book of Concord.* New York: Penguin, 1983.

The Kentucky Encyclopedia. Ed. John Kleber. Lexington: University Press of Kentucky, 1992.

Lancaster, Clay. *Vestiges of the Venerable City: A Chronicle of Lexington, Kentucky: Its Architectural Development and Survey of Its Early Streets and Antiquities.* Lexington: Lexington-Fayette County Historic Commission, 1978.

Little, Lewis Peyton. *Imprisoned Preachers and Religious Liberty in Virginia.* Lynchburg, Va.: J.P. Bell, 1938.

Logan, Rayford W., and Michael R. Winston. *The Dictionary of American Negro Biography.* New York: W.W. Norton, 1982.

Lucas, Marion B. *A History of Blacks in Kentucky.* Vol. 1, *From Slavery to Segregation, 1760-1891.* Frankfort, Ky.: Kentucky Historical Society, 1992.

Marx, Karl. *The Eighteenth Brumaire of Louis Bonaparte.* New York: International Publishers, 1963.

Masters, Frank M. *A History of Baptists in Kentucky.* Louisville: Kentucky Baptist Historical Society, 1953.

McFeeley, William. *Frederick Douglass.* New York: Simon and Schuster, 1991.

McPherson, James M. *Battle Cry of Freedom: The Civil War Era.* New York: Oxford University Press, 1988.

Money, Charles H. "The Fugitive Slave Law." *Indiana Magazine of History* 17 (1921): 257-97.

Muraskin, William A. *Middle-Class Blacks in a White Society: Prince Hall Free-masonry in America.* Berkeley: University of California Press, 1975.

Nelson, Margaret K. "Vermont Female Schoolteachers in the Nineteenth Century." *Vermont History* 49 (1981): 5-30.

Peterson, Merrill D. *The Great Triumvirate: Webster, Clay, and Calhoun.* New York: Oxford University Press, 1987.

Porter, Kenneth Wiggins. "Lewis Hayden," in Logan and Winston, *The Dictionary of American Negro Biography.*

Quarles, Benjamin. *Black Abolitionists.* New York: Oxford University Press, 1969.

———. *The Negro in the Civil War.* Boston: Little, Brown, 1953. Reprint. New York: Da Capo Press, 1989.

Ranck, George W. *History of Lexington Kentucky. Its Early Annals and Recent Progress.* Cincinnati: Robert Clarke, 1872. Reprint. Lexington: Henry Clay Press, 1970.

Remini, Robert V. *Henry Clay: Statesman for the Union.* New York: W.W. Norton, 1991.

Renehan, Edward J., Jr. *The Secret Six: The True Tale of the Men who Conspired with John Brown.* New York: Crown, 1995.

Robboy, Stanley J. and Anita W. Robboy. "Lewis Hayden: From Fugitive Slave to Statesman." *New England Quarterly* 46.4 (December 1973): 591-613.

Robinson, Rowland E. *Out of Bondage and Other Stories.* Rutland, Vt.: Charles Tuttle, 1936.

———. *Vermont: A Study of Independence.* Boston: Houghton, Mifflin, 1892.

Schomburg, Arthur. Foreward to *Out of Bondage and Other Stories* by Rowland E. Robinson: 5-9.

Sears, Richard. *The Kentucky Abolitionists in the Midst of Slavery, 1854-1864.* Lewiston, N.Y.: Edwin Mellen Press, 1993.

Siebert, Wilbur H. *The Mysteries of Ohio's Underground Railroads.* Columbus, Oh.: Long's College Book Company, 1951.

———. *Vermont's Anti-Slavery and Underground Railroad Record.* Columbus, Oh.: Spahr and Glenn, 1937.

Smiley, David L. *The Lion of Whitehall: The Life of Cassius M. Clay.* Madison: University of Wisconsin Press, 1962.

Staples, Charles R. *The History of Pioneer Lexington (Kentucky), 1779-1806.* Lexington: n.p., 1939. Reprint. Lexington: Lexington-Fayette County Historic Commission, 1973.

Sterling, Dorothy. *Ahead of Her Time: Abby Kelley and the Politics of Antislavery.* New York: W.W. Norton, 1991.

Steward, James Brewer. *Wendell Phillips: Liberty's Hero.* Baton Rouge: Louisiana State University Press, 1986.

Villard, Osward Garrison. *John Brown.* Boston: Houghton, Mifflin, 1910.

Warren, Robert Penn. *John Brown: The Making of a Martyr.* New York: Payson and Clarke, 1929. Reprint. Nashville: J.S. Sanders, 1993.

Webster, William Holcomb. *History and Genealogy of the Gov. John Webster Family of Connecticut.* Rochester, N.Y.: E. R. Andrews, 1915.

Weisenberger, Richard. "Century Old House Harbors Legend of 'Slave Driving Simon Legree.'" Unidentified newspaper clipping. Kentucky State Historical Society.

Wesley, Dorothy Porter. "Integration versus Separatism: William Cooper Nell's Role in the Struggle for Equality." In *Courage and Conscience: Black & White Abolitionists in Boston*, ed. Donald M. Jacobs. Bloomington: Indiana University Press, 1993: 207-24.

Wick, B.L. "Delia Webster." *Annals of Iowa* 18.3 (January 1932): 228-31.

Windle, John T., and Robert M. Taylor, Jr. *The Early Architecture of Madison, Indiana*. Madison and Indianapolis: Historic Madison / Indiana Historical Society, 1986.

Woollen, William Wesley. *Biographical and Historical Sketches of Early Indiana*. Indianapolis: Hammond and Co., 1883.

Wright, John D., Jr. *Lexington: Heart of the Bluegrass*. Lexington: Lexington-Fayette County Historic Commission, 1982.

NEWSPAPERS

Anti-Slavery Reporter, 1845. Abbreviated as *ASR*.

Boston Courier, 1845.

Boston Globe, 1889. Abbreviated as *BG*.

Broadway Journal, 1845.

Christian Freeman (Hartford, Ct.), 1844-45. Abbreviated as *ChF*.

Concord (Mass.) Freeman, 1846.

Covington (Ky.) Daily Commonwealth, 1879.

Covington (Ky.) Journal, 1854.

Des Moines Register and Leader, 1904.

Emancipator, 1844-45. Abbreviated as *Em*.

Frankfort (Ky.) Commonwealth, 1844-54. Abbreviated as *FC*.

Frankfort (Ky.) Yeoman, 1854.

Frederick Douglass' Paper, 1851-54. Abbreviated as *FDP*.

Georgetown (Ky.) Times, 1890.

Green Mountain Freeman (Burlington, Vt.), 1845-46. Abbreviated as *GMF*.

Le Grand (Iowa) Reporter, 1939.

Lexington (Ky.) Gazette, 1844. Abbreviated as *Gaz*.

Lexington (Ky.) Observer and Reporter, 1844. Abbreviated as *O&R*.

Liberator, 1844-65. Abbreviated as *Lib*.

Louisville Courier, 1851-59. Abbreviated as *LC*.

Louisville Courier-Journal, 1879.

Louisville Democrat, 1854. Abbreviated as *LD*.

Lowell (Mass.) Journal, 1846.

Madison (Ind.) Courier, 1854-66. Abbreviated as *MC*.

Madison Star, 1879. Abbreviated as *MS*.

National Anti-Slavery Standard, 1844-55. Abbreviated as *NASS*.

New Albany (Ind.) Daily Ledger, 1854.

New York Age, 1889. Abbreviated as *NYA*.

New York Independent, 1855. Abbreviated as *Ind*.

New York Times, 1854.

Oberlin Evangelist, 1845.

Ohio Statesman (Columbus), 1844.

U. S. Gazette (Philadelphia), 1827.

Vergennes (Vt.) Vermonter, 1838-45.

Voice of Freedom (Brandon Vt.), 1846.

UNPUBLISHED LETTERS

Galey Coleman to William Albert Davis, December 17, 1982.
Galey Coleman to Randolph Paul Runyon, July 21, 1995.
Calvin Fairbank to Herman Safford, John Brown, et al., October 1, 1844. University of Kentucky Library.
Lewis Hayden to Lewis Baxter, October 27, 1844. University of Kentucky Library.
Lewis Hayden to Sydney Howard Gay, January 21, 1846. Sydney Howard Gay Papers, Columbia University Library.
— Undated (probably between late 1847 and early 1848). Sydney Howard Gay Papers, Columbia University Library.
Delia Webster to Esther Webster, March 18, 1851. In the possession of Bard and Gina Prentiss, Dryden, N.Y.
Delia Webster to Warren and Mary Jane Bard, February 7, 1861. In the possession of Bard and Gina Prentiss, Dryden, N.Y.
Delia Webster to Mary Jane Bard, June 1, 1874. In the possession of Bard and Gina Prentiss, Dryden, N.Y.
Warren Webster to Warren Bard, February 15, 1862. In the possession of Bard and Gina Prentiss, Dryden, N.Y.

MANUSCRIPTS

"Appendix F: Underground Railroad Incidents." Drusilla Cravens Collection. Madison-Jefferson County Public Library, Madison, Indiana.
Jefferson Craig Diary. Typescript. Scott County Public Library, Georgetown, Ky.
Calvin Fairbank Diary. In the possession of Mrs. Hazel Young Winter, Williston, Vt.
Galey, Henrietta. "The Petticoat Abolitionist." Manuscript of an unpublished novel. In the possession of Mrs. Galey Coleman, Wichita, Kans.
——. Miscellaneous notes. In the possession of Mrs. Galey Coleman, Wichita, Kans.
John Lyle King Diary. Indiana Historical Society, Indianapolis.
Martin, Jennie Bard (granddaughter of Mary Jane Webster Bard, sister of Delia Webster). "Family Register." In the possession of Bard and Gina Prentiss, Dryden, N.Y.
"A record of the Craig family left by Lewis Mason, written from personal knowledge of the members of the family." In the possession of Mrs. Galey Coleman, Wichita, Kans.
"Shotwell Surname File." Filson Club, Louisville, Ky.
Mandana Tileston Diary. Typescript. In the possession of Mrs. Hazel Young Winter, Williston, Vt.

INDEX

Note: Page numbers in italics refer to illustrations.

Allen, James Lane, 69
Andrew, John A., 204, 208, 210
Anti-Slavery Reporter, 72, 92-93, 94.
  See also Phelps, Amos
Attucks, Crispus, 146, 221

Bard, Mary Jane Webster (sister),
  159, 204, 221, 222
Bard, Warren, 159, 205
Baxter, Lewis, 11, 12, 37, 49, 91
Beecher, Lyman, 33-34
Berry, Gilson, 1-2, 10-11, 30, 31, 33,
  35-36, 48. 75, 94, 131, 194
Bevins, Ann, 232 n 3
Birney, James G., 38, 40, 87
Boston Chronicle, 81, 82
Boston Courier, 70
Brandt, Nat, 33
Breckinridge (Ky.) News, 217, 218
Broadway Journal, 59-60
Brown, John. *See* Hayden, Lewis: and
  John Brown
Brown, John Mifflin, 28, 33, 36, 75,
  108
Brown, William Wells, 116
Buckminster, Henrietta, 145
Bunyan, John, 62
Burleigh, William H. *See Christian
  Freeman*

Christian Freeman, 59, 79, 81-82,
  88, 89, 93, 94
Cincinnati Atlas, 67, 68
Cincinnati Herald, 49, 68
Clark, Thomas, 2-3, 122, 126

Clarke, Lewis, 90-91
Clay, Cassius M., 16, 24, 34, 40-41,
  77-78, 90, 122, 201, 227 n 49,
  229 n 5
Clay, Henry, 13, 16, 31, 38, 40-41,
  43-44, 45-46, 54, 66, 87, 99, 122,
  132, 144-45, 229 n 5, 235 n 36;
  transmits a letter petitioning CF's
  pardon, 107-8; denies Hayden's
  accusations, 113-16.
Coffin, Levi, 6, 131, 154-55, 214
Coleman, Galey, 219, 239 n 19, 247
  n 77
Coleman, J. Winston, Jr., ix, 48, 228
  n 60, 229 nn 5, 15, 18
Colman, Julia, 205-6
colonization, 40, 45, 66
Colver, Nathaniel, 87, 88, 89, 91
*Covington (Ky.) Daily
  Commonwealth,* 218
Combs, Leslie, 44-45, 52, 53
Craft, William and Ellen. *See*
  Hayden, Lewis: and William and
  Ellen Craft
Craig, Dillard (son of NC), 128, 130,
  134, 135, 136, *137,* 138, 153,
  177-78, 219, 239 n 41
Craig, Elijah, 56, 232 n 3
Craig, Joseph, 56
Craig, Jefferson, 182-83, 186-87,
  196, 198, 243 n 47
Craig, Lewis, 56, 232 n 3
Craig, Lucy (wife of NC), 55, 64,
  128, 129, 135, 138, 179, 181,
  196, *197,* 219, 239 n 18

Craig, Newton, *60,* 97, 105, 123,
127, 164, 165, 186-87; meets DW,
55; family background, 56, as
keeper of Ky. Penitentiary, 56-58,
173-74; treatment of CF, 57, 64,
106-7, 198; lodges his children
with DW, 124, 128; as farmer,
125-26; letters to DW, 129, 134-
36, 138-40, 149-50, 175-81;
regrets her leaving for Madison,
138, 160; helps Warren Webster
settle in Ky., 159-60; sues DW,
165-66, 199; object of controversy
involving DW, 172-73, 174-82,
189-90; loses re-election, 182;
attempts to capture DW, 188-89;
attacked in Madison, 194-96;
returns to Ky., 196, 198; on the
origin of bourbon whiskey, 232 n
3; interviewed in 1879, 217-19;
his library, 219; death, 219-20.
Craig, Parker, 1, 14, 15, 16, 19-20,
50, 51, 55, 239 n 18
Craig, Reuben (father of NC), 56

Day, Norris, 78, 101-5, 165; defends
DW at Liberty Convention, 87,
88, 92-93, 95; in Trimble Co., Ky.,
165, 166-72, 185
Delany, Martin, 121
Des Moines Register and Leader, 224
Dix, Dorothea, 229 n 2
Douglass, Frederick, 7-8, 109, 118-
19, 120, 121, 132, 214
Doyle, Patrick, 123, 217, 218

"Eliza," 5-7, 24, 34
Emancipator, 41, 45-46, 49, 62, 63-
64, 65, 66, 78-79, 82, 88, 111
Emerson, Ralph Waldo, 110-11, 142

Fairbank, Calvin, 42, 48-49, 50, 67-
68, *213;* family background, 4,
18; education, 5; as clergyman, 9;
Hayden rescue, 1, 9, 11, 12, 14-
21; attempted Berry rescue, 1-2, 9-
11, 33; previous Underground
Railroad activity, 4-7; "frater"
letter, 10-11, 15, 48, 50, 52, 53,
61, 75, 207, 231 n 27; imprisoned
in Lexington, 23-24, 26-29; letter
to Herman Safford, 28; letter to
John Rent, 28-29; and John
Mifflin Brown, 33; tried for
Hayden rescue, 61-63; imprisoned
in penitentiary, 63-64; 106-8; on
KJ, 71, 72; on DW, 76, 130;
teaches religion in penitentiary,
107; pardoned (1849), 122-23;
replies to critics, 130-31, 133-34;
welcomed in Cincinnati, 131;
1849-50 speaking tour, 131-32,
134; lodges with Haydens, 132,
142-43; 1851 speaking tour, 146-
47; engaged to Mandana Tileston,
147; returns to Cincinnati, 147;
arrested in Jeffersonville, Ind.,
152-53; imprisoned in Louisville,
153-58, 161-62; trial in Louisville,
162; in penitentiary a second time,
162-63; 210-12; "tried" by NC,
198; pardoned (1864); marries
Mandana Tileston, 214; financial
and family difficulties, 216-17;
death, 220. *See also* Craig,
Newton: treatment of CF
Fairbank, Calvin Cornelius (son of
CF), 216
Fairbank, Chester (father of CF),
122-23, 140, 147
Fairbank, Mandana Tileston (wife of
CF), 147, 211-12, *213,* 216
Fee, John G., 201-2
Frankfort (Ky.) Commonwealth, 53,
62, 65, 67

Galey, Henrietta Craig (granddaugh-
ter of NC), 130, 135, 218, 239 n
28, 239-40 n 41
Garrison, William Lloyd, 31, 81, 82-
86, 87, 89, 100, 118, 120, 132,
142, 145, 220. *See also Liberator*
Gay, Sydney Howard, 94, 101, 108,
113, 131. *See also National Anti-
Slavery Standard*
Georgetown (Ky.) Herald, 155
Georgetown (Ky.) Times, 220
Glass, Mrs. David, 1, 9, 14-15, 21, 48, 50

Goodrich, Martha Webster (sister of DW), 118, *222*, 237 n 46
Goodrich, Simeon, 118, 124, 215-16, 237 n 46
Grant, Thomas, 11, 12, 37, 49, 91
Gratz, Benjamin, 214
Green Mountain Freeman, 72, 78, 82, 83, 84, 88, 89, 91, 94, 97, 98, 99, 100, 101, 102, 166

Haviland, Laura, *156;* writes a deceptive letter, 32-33; meets CF, 131; deciphers CF's signature, 154-55; visits CF in Louisville jail, 155, 157-58, 161; mistaken for DW, 157-58
Hayden, Esther (first wife of LH), 114-16
Hayden, Harriet Bell (second wife of LH), 14, 16, 30
Hayden, Jo (son of LH), 15, 16, 30, 142, 208
Hayden, Lewis, *112;* introduced to CF by DW, 11, owned by Baxter and Grant, 11-12; and Harriet Beecher Stowe, 12; family background, 12; and Masons, 12, 208-10; owned by Adam Rankin, 12-13; married to Harriet Bell, 14; rescued, 15-18, 34; letter to former master, 36-39; leaves Canada for Detroit, 77; appears at Liberty Party convention, 87, 91-92, 94; on DW, 101; on CF, 106; speaking tours, 108, 109, 116-17, 118-19; appraised by Garrison, 108-9, 110; moves to Boston, 110; at Walden Pond with Emerson, 110-11; and Gerrit Smith, 111; and Henry Clay, 113-16; visits Vergennes, 117-18; fired by Phillips, 119-21; opens a clothing store, 121; solicits funds for CF's release, 121-22, 131; assists fugitives in Boston, 140-41, 142-32; and William and Ellen Craft, 142-43; and Shadrach, 143-45; and Thomas Sims, 145-46; and Anthony Burns, 187; and John Brown, 207-8, 211-12; and the Fifty-Fourth Massachusetts, 208; death, 220-21
Hedrick, Joan D., 34
Higginson, Thomas Wentworth, 145-46, 187

"Israel," 15, 16, 19, 25-26, 90

Johnson, Madison, C., 47, 49, 52

Kelley, Abby, 87, 88
Kentucky, education in, 2-3; slavery in, 11-12, 90-91
King, John Lyle, 192-93, 194, 199-201

Lafayette, the Marquis de, 7, 11, 13
Leavitt, Harvey, 31-32, 140. *See also* Webster, Delia: letter to Harvey Leavitt
Le Grand (Iowa) Reporter, 223-24
Lexington (Ky.) Gazette, 42, 43, 44
Lexington (Ky.) Observer and Reporter, 3, 35-36, 38, 42, 43, 44, 72, 82, 123
Liberator, 31, 45, 71, 82-83, 84, 121, 122
Liberty Party, 61, 87-88
Licking Valley (Ky.) Register, 70
Louisville Courier, 147, 149, 154, 157, 158, 160, 173, 174, 175, 176, 179
Louisville Courier-Journal, 217
Louisville Democrat, 129, 130, 138, 166, 170, 173, 174, 175, 177, 180, 181-82, 189-90, 191, 218
Louisville Journal, 50, 51, 62, 67
Lincoln, Abraham, 214-15, 220
Locke, John, 37
Lucas, Marion B., 11

Madison, Ind., 126-28, 136, *172, 191*
Madison Banner, 155, 196
Madison Courier, 168, 171, 180, 185-86, 189, 193, 196, 200, 215
Madison Star, 129, 130, 180, 216
Marshall, Joseph Glass, 191-93, 196, 199

Marx, Karl, 199
"Mr. Mason," 29, 31-32, 89, 133, 229 n 20
Masons. *See* Hayden, Lewis: and Masons
Maysville, Ky., 14, *17*, 18, 76, 90
Megowan Hotel, 5, 20, 21, 22-24, *23*, 47, 52, 53. *See also* Dix, Dorothea
Mentelle, Waldemar and Charlotte, 114, 116
Moore, Richard, 26-27, 132, 229 n 15
Moore, Thomas, 105, 164-65, 235 n 48
Muraskin, Willliam A., 209
Musick, H.G., 17, 18-19, 49-50, 51, 67-68
McCalla, John, 40, 41-42, 43, 44, 47, 49, 230 n 2
McFeeley, William, 109, 236 n 23

National Anti-Slavery Standard, 82, 93, 94, 113, 118, 120, 130, 131
New York Independent, 201
New York Tribune, 93, 94, 216, 217
Northampton Herald, 81
Norwich Courier, 82

Oberlin, Ohio, 29, 33
Oberlin College, 1, 2, 8, 33-34, 98, 131, 202, 223
Oberlin Evangelist, 98
Oberlin Theological Seminary, 4, 5
Ohio Statesman, 31, 32
Owsley, Governor William, 51, 53, 54, 61, 64-66, 98, 107, 129

Parker, Theodore, 143
Phelps, Amos, 72, 92-93, 94-101; *see also National Anti-Slavery Standard*
Philadelphia Register, 166
Phillips, Wendell, 119-21, 132, 142
Pierpont, John, 91-92
Poe, Edgar Allan. *See Broadway Journal*
Polk, James, 38, 41
Porter, Kenneth Wiggins, 187, 208

Quarles, Benjamin, 208

Ranck, George, 45
Randall, William, 195-96
Rankin, Adam, 12-13
Rankin, John, 9-10, 13, 18, 49, 68, 228 n 60
Rea, Right, 124, 127-28, 134, 169, 190-91
Remini, Robert V., 40, 41, 114
Renehan, Edward J., Jr., 207, 246 n 41
Richardson, Lewis, 114
Ripley, Ohio, 9-10, 18, 68
Robinson, Rowland E., 8
Robinson, Rowland T., 8, 46
Runyon, R., 122

Sears, Richard, 202
Shadrach rescue. *See* Hayden, Lewis: and Shadrach
Shakespeare, William, 71
Shotwell, Alfred Lawrence, 138, 153
Shy, Samuel, 44, 47, 49, 52, 53, 58-59, 62, 132
Sims, Thomas. *See* Hayden, Lewis: and Thomas Sims
Smiley, David, 122, 227 n 49
Smith, Gerrit, 87-88, 90, 111, 132
Sneed, William C., 57, 129
Southwestern Christian Advocate, 220
Spencer, Rev. and Mrs., 2, 4, 206, 217, 225 n 4
Spirit of Liberty, 46
Stapp, Milton, 126-27, 136, 147-48, 179, 196
Stendhal, 211
Stowe, Harriet Beecher, 10, 12, 33, 141, 201

Tappan, Lewis, 87, 201, 203
Thoreau, Henry David, 110
Tubman, Harriet, 208
Turner, Caroline, 26, 132, 229 n 15

Vergennes Vermonter, 3, 70
Vermont, antislavery sentiment in, 7-8
Voice of Freedom, 100

Walker, Jonathan, 91, 242 n 35
Warren, Robert Penn, 207
Watchman of the Valley, 79, 81
Webster, Benajah (father of DW), 46,
  47, 52, 67, 70, 71-72, 78-79, *80,*
  88, 95, 97, 135, 147, 218, 240 n
  41
Webster, Daniel, 31, 45, 88, 132
Webster, Delia, *222;* family
  background, 7; physical
  description, 128; early schooling,
  3, 73; and religion, 7, 148-49,
  221, 223; as educator, 2-4, 8, 73;
  and Oberlin College, 2, 8, 73-74;
  in Kentucky before 1844, 2, 4, 74,
  217, 225 n 4; and Lexington
  Female Academy, 2-3; and
  Hayden rescue, 1, 9, 11, 14-21;
  imprisoned in Lexington, 22-26,
  29-32; letter to "Mr. Mason," 28-
  33, 89, 133; prepares for trial, 40,
  41, 43, 44-46, 47; defended in the
  abolitionist press, 46, 59, 61, 79,
  81, 82, 93-94, 100-101; criticized
  in the abolitionist press, 46, 66,
  72, 79, 81, 82-83, 92-93, 95-96,
  98-99; letter to Harvey Leavitt,
  45, 46, 81, 82, 88, 133; defended
  by citizens of Ferrisburgh, Vt., 46-
  47; trial in Hayden case, 47-52,
  218; conviction, 52; motion for
  new trial, 53-54; jury petitions for
  pardon, 53; requests pardon, 54;
  in the state penitentiary, 54-55;
  meets Newton Craig, 55; and
  Kentucky Jurisprudence, 51, 52,
  66-67, 68, 70-78; treatment by
  NC, 55, 58-59, 64, 95-100, 102,
  103, 104; pardoned, 64-67; leaves
  for Vermont via Cincinnati, 67-
  68, 70; arrives in Vergennes, 70;
  and Norris Day, 78; reply to
  William Lloyd Garrison, 83-86;
  at Boston Liberty Convention,
  87-89, 91, 92-93; reply to Amos
  Phelps, 94-97, 99-100; in 1845-
  46, 111, 129, 130; renews Ky.
  ties, 118; teaches in New York
  City, 125, 180; moves to
  Madison, Ind., 126; visits Newton
  and Lucy Craig, 129, 130;
  governess to Craig children, 124,
  128, 134-36, 138-40, 240 n 41;
  letter to her mother (Mar. 18,
  1851), 147-49; denounces CF,
  159; purchases farm in Trimble
  Co., Ky., 164-66; arouses
  neighbors' suspicions, 166-68;
  ordered to leave the state, 170;
  releases NC's letters to the press,
  175-76; threatened by Trimble
  Co. citizens, 184; arrested and
  jailed in Bedford, Ky., 184-86;
  acquitted, 186; escapes from NC's
  agents and flees to Indiana, 189-
  90; captured by Right Rea, 199-
  91; habeas corpus hearing,
  191-94; appears in *Pitcher v.
  Craig,* 199; consults John Lyle
  King, 199-201; offers farm to
  John G. Fee, 201; proposes
  "South Western Seminary," 202;
  forms Webster Kentucky Farm
  Association, 203-4; in Cincinnati
  in 1861, 204-5; burnt out in
  Trimble Co., 215; alleged death,
  216; in Iowa, 221, 223-24; in
  Wisconsin, 223, 224; death, 224.
  See also Craig, Newton: sues DW;
  object of controversy involving DW
Webster, Noah, 85, 102
Webster, Warren (brother of DW),
  118, 125, 159-60, 237 n 46
Western Law Journal, 50, 51, 52
Whittier, John Greenleaf, 59, 87
Wickliffe, Robert, 7, 34, 41
Wickliffe, Robert, Jr., 34-35
Wolfe, Moses, 175-76, 177, 178
Wood, Ben, 27-31, 33, 34, 35, 50
Woolen, William Wesley, 127, 128